Virginia Bruce

Under My Skin

To Bob Grimes
Good Wishes and Cheer)

Scott O'Brien

Virginia Bruce

Under My Skin

by Scott O'Brien

Foreword by
James Robert Parish

For Joel ...

Published in the USA by:
BearManor Media
P O Box 71426
Albany, Georgia 31708
www.bearmanormedia.com

ISBN 1-59393-314-2

Printed in the United States of America.

Book & cover design by Darlene and Dan Swanson of Van-garde Imagery, Inc.

Contents

MGM publicity shot c 1937

Virginia Bruce

by James Robert Parish

It seemed Hollywood took movie actress Virginia Bruce largely for granted during her heyday in the 1930s as a contract leading lady at Metro-Goldwyn-Mayer. However, this very blonde trouper was a great favorite with moviegoers of the era. In more recent decades—thanks to television showings and DVD editions of some of her films—Bruce has gained new generations of enthusiasts who have quickly come to appreciate both the talents and quiet charisma of this fine-looking performer who boasted such captivating pale-blue eyes.

My first awareness of Virginia Bruce dates back to my childhood. It was then I saw a TV showing of *State Department—File 649*, a 1949 B movie dealing with a U.S. Foreign Service vice consul (William Lundigan) stationed in northern China and pitted against a marauding warlord (Richard Loo). Although Virginia Bruce was the film's "name" star, she had a relatively minor part in this slight Cold War action drama which focused on the villainy of sadistic Loo and his chief henchman (played by Philip Ahn). What most stuck in my memory about the still quite attractive Bruce (then nearly 40 years old) in this programmer was the haunted, distracted look of her eyes.

In subsequent years, I saw many of Bruce's old films on TV and watched her occasional new performances: such as playing the title assignment in a 1956 *Lux Video Theatre* presentation of *Mildred Pierce* and her relatively subordinate part in 1960's *Strangers When We Meet* (cast as Kim Novak's mother). Again, I was drawn to the barely concealed troubled look that seemed a permanent fixture of Bruce's performances.

As the years passed and I grew increasingly intrigued with cinema history and chose to make my career writing about Hollywood, I began acquiring more information about the professional and off-camera life of Miss Bruce. I read of her relatively short union—it was her first marriage and his fourth—to legendary screen lover John Gilbert, with whom she costarred in 1932's *Downstairs*, a minor but lively MGM melodrama. As time went by, I heard how Bruce's role as songbird Jenny Lind while on loan to United Artists for 1934's *The Mighty Barnum* had led to her being cast in MGM's 1936 extravaganza *The Great Ziegfeld*. In that Metro blockbuster, she appeared as a temperamental stage luminary whose drinking problem triggered her career demise. Myth had it among film buffs that her memorable portrayal of alcoholic Audrey Dane in *The Great Ziegfeld* led some of the public and several industry executives to believe that the real-life Bruce was much like her screen alter ego, which, supposedly, helped to trigger the actress's own career decline.

During Bruce's MGM tenure (1932 to 1939) she made scores of pictures and proved her ability of being a highly attractive cinema workhorse most noted for her porcelain-like beauty and her vibrant voice. By the early 1940s, Bruce was toiling at less elegant Universal Pictures, playing in support to the likes of boisterous Abbott and Costello in 1942's *Pardon My Sarong*. After World War II the veteran actress married a Turkish writer/producer (Ali Ipar) and endured difficult times when he returned to his homeland to visit family and then was denied reentry to the United States. Later, he was conscripted into the Turkish army and Bruce had to divorce him because an officer in the Turkish army could not be wed to a foreigner. Thereafter, they re-wed and she starred in 1953's *Istanbul*, a Turkish-made feature film that her husband wrote/produced/directed. Later on they settled in Hollywood, only to have him return to Turkey in 1960 where he was arrested during a political upheaval and jailed for many months.

Obviously, Bruce's off-screen life was far more exciting and exotic than any role she experienced on camera, and it is one of the reasons why so much allure has been attached to this leading lady of Hollywood's Golden Age. This is not to downplay Virginia's screen work, from being a chorine/ingénue at Paramount Pictures to her noteworthy berth at MGM, to her stay at Universal, and, thereafter, several freelance assignments on film and in TV. Personally, I liked the post-MGM Virginia Bruce best of all. Away from that Tiffany of studios, her film performances seemed gutsier, with Bruce playing no-nonsense, self-reliant women who had far more to offer than merely pretty looks.

And, now, in this full-length chronicle of Virginia Bruce, we have a full opportunity to learn much more about this complicated, beautiful, and charming woman who is very worthy of the professional reassessment this volume sets out to accomplish.

As Audrey Dane in *The Great Ziegfeld (1936)* (MGM)

Introduction and Acknowledgements

When I began writing her biography, I was under the assumption that Virginia Bruce was one of the top stars of her era (1932-1949). Her unique screen persona, and her skill as an actress, easily held its own among the great screen icons. Her distinctive look in the glamour department casts a deep shadow over most of her contemporaries -- she was stunning. I was surprised to learn that Virginia herself admitted that she never really reached the top. She blamed the absence of any real "push" on her behalf by the powers at MGM. Top stardom, for her, would remain an elusive dream. She left Metro in 1939 to freelance, but with the birth of her son Christopher in 1941, Virginia put her acting career on the back burner. She admitted she didn't have the driving ambition to hold out for major roles that would have put her career in the same league, as say, an Ingrid Bergman or Barbara Stanwyck.

So why Virginia Bruce? I first saw her in *The Great Ziegfeld* in the 1960s. It took awhile for me to warm up to her – she was such a bitch on screen. She was so *convincing* in her role that I assumed she must have been just like that in person. Virginia's own comment on her role as Audrey Dane, the archetypal Ziegfeld star, is that she loved playing those "so-and-sos." Virginia liked the idea of audiences thinking she "had the devil in her." The real truth? Virginia *wasn't* a fighter. She was intimidated by people like Louis B. Mayer. According to her nephew Vincent Briggs, however, Virginia could be head-strong. Vincent said that was the very thing he liked about her. During my research, I discovered that after her arrival in Hollywood in 1928, Virginia gradually acquired just enough spunk to achieve a significant level of stardom in an extremely competitive industry. In the 1980s I saw Virginia in the RKO film, *Dangerous Corner* (1934). I loved the film's premise, its unique meta-physical bent, and I was truly drawn into Virginia's character. I had to admit to myself that Virginia Bruce, the actress, was really special. I liked the understatement of her screen portrayals, which allowed her gentle essence to shine through. She was always emotionally on cue in drama, could toss off a clever *bon mot* in sophisticated material like *Arsene Lupin Returns* and the *Garden Murder Case*. As author James Robert Parish put it, "She had a sharp, tart way of handling dialogue." And, I agree with Cole Porter that Hollywood never took full advantage of Virginia's talent as a vocalist. Her light soprano was distinctive and colored each lyric to perfection. I felt that recognition for her fine work was long overdue.

Upon completing the biography of the BearManor publication, *Kay Francis – I Can't Wait to be Forgotten* (2006), I was intrigued to write about Virginia. BearManor has a great tradition of championing the stories of stars that have been overlooked. Publisher Ben Ohmart's philosophy is, "Who needs another book on Marilyn Monroe, or Bette Davis?" Ohmart asks the question, "Who's been overlooked, that should not have been?" My answer the second time around was: Virginia Bruce. Ben responded, "I'm interested." Another enthusiastic response came from Howard Mandelbaum, writer and founder of PhotoFest (a wonderful resource of classic film photos). "I'm always trying to find out more about Virginia Bruce," said Mandelbaum, "and, of course, TCM has introduced me to many of her rarer films. I'm especially fond of *Woman Against Woman* with Mary Astor. Just watching Virginia Bruce do simple things like rise from a table at a country club into the arms of her dancing partner is pure grace. She can do hard things, too, like the drunk scene in *The Great Ziegfeld*."

My own interest in film stars was influenced by my mother, Bette Morgan O'Brien. Although she was an academic English teacher and James Joyce aficionado, my mother was also a devotee of movies and big-band music. She loved telling her story about seeing Doris Day perform with bandleader Les Brown at Salt Lake City's "Rainbow Rendezvous" in the 1940s. Mother and her schoolmates would crowd around the stage when Doris approached the mike to sing hits like "Paper Doll" and "Sentimental Journey." "We just couldn't dance while she was singing," mother would say. "You couldn't take your eyes off of her. There was something about Doris Day that made the song so intimate and personal that you had to stop what you were doing and just listen." A decade later, when we lived in Stockton, California, mother went with a few ladies in the neighborhood to see Tyrone Power during his 1953 tour of *John Brown's Body*. After the performance, she walked outside the theater while her friends went backstage to catch another glimpse of Tyrone. She stood on the sidewalk near the tour bus and noticed one of the bus windows winding down. A voice said, "Hello. Did you get to see the play?" It was Tyrone Power speaking. After getting over the initial shock, mother said they had a lengthy conversation. She complimented him on his performance, and he wanted to know about her life, her work, her family. Mother was surprised at his genuine interest in *her* as a fellow individual on life's journey. Her lady friends, after waiting in line for nothing, weren't exactly thrilled with Mother's good fortune. In 1938, Virginia had teamed with Tyrone Power for a broadcast of *Lloyds of London*. Other than Cary Grant and Errol Flynn, it is difficult to come up with a major star of her era that Virginia did not work with: William Powell, Nelson Eddy, Gable, Cooper, Bogart, Taylor, Stewart, Cagney, Colman, Tracy, Boyer, Crosby, Hope, Ameche, Montgomery, Robinson, Fairbanks Jr., and numerous others all starred with Virginia.

In the 1960s, as a teenager following my mother's footsteps, I was determined to have a few first-hand experiences of meeting-the-stars. My first encounter was with Myrna Loy (Virginia's co-star in *The Great Ziegfeld*). Loy had a warm, friendly presence and readily answered my questions. She was especially inquisitive, upon our second meeting in 1970, regarding my impressions of the play *Dear Love*. She wondered what the "Love Generation" thought of the great love between Elizabeth Barrett and Robert Browning (the subject matter of her two-act play). We talked about politics, Vietnam, and philosophy. I couldn't have asked for a more genuine and thrilling experience with a film star.

In 1967, I made a point to reward my mother by taking her to see the San Francisco International Film Festival's tribute to William Holden (her favorite actor). During the question-and-answer period, I asked Holden about his work in Kenya, Africa, and told him of my request for a Peace Corps assignment there. Holden absolutely lit up, offered me encouragement, and briefly explained for the audience his interest on behalf of wildlife conservation in Kenya. His passion for the subject easily eclipsed his response to questions asked about his film career. My encounters with Loy and Holden simply proved that the real identity of "movie stars" goes far beyond the confines of Hollywood. I found this to be true of Virginia Bruce as well. Being a mother certainly took precedence over stardom for Virginia. For over a decade, politics and "helping the little guy" held her interest. As Honorary Mayor of her community, Pacific Palisades, from 1944-1953, Virginia took time during her career to listen to and be available for those in need. But Virginia's greatest passion, I discovered, was for love. On a very personal level, love emerges to be the crux of her unusual and compelling story.

Those who have given major support on piecing together Virginia's story deserve acknowledgement. First and foremost, I must thank her nephew, Vincent Briggs, who was Virginia's executor at the time of her death. Vincent's interest in the project, his spontaneous sharing of memories of his aunt, and his generous supply of photos, has made all the difference giving Virginia's story a sense of completion. Other family members, her grandson David Smith and her son-in-law Steve Marquez, offered revealing information on Virginia's retirement years.

No one was more genuinely enthused about my project than director Stanley Kramer's wife, Karen Sharpe Kramer. As a 1950s starlet, Karen had worked with Virginia on television's *Lux Video Theatre* in 1953. She treasures the experience and holds Virginia in high esteem for being what she refers to as an "actress who carried weight." The prolific author on classic Hollywood, James

Virginia, who mentioned going to psychics on several occasions, would naturally gravitate towards someone like the mystic Meher Baba. Baba took Hollywood by storm in 1932 during his promotion for "a world-wide transformation of consciousness." Having taken a vow of silence, he 'spoke' to a host of stars at Pickfair using an alphabet board. Here he shows his message for Virginia, while his younger brother Adi K. Irani looks on. Baba's devotees included such diverse personalities as Boris Karloff, Gary Cooper, Charles Laughton and Tallulah Bankhead. Baba's often repeated advice, "Don't Worry, Be Happy" was the inspiration of the 1988 Grammy-winning song by Bobby McFerrin

Robert Parish, readily agreed to write a foreword for the Virginia Bruce biography. It was a real honor to have Parish's support and interest in both the Kay Francis and Virginia Bruce books. Parish is generous with his time for new authors. I also received a great boost early on from author and *Classic Images* book reviewer Laura Wagner. Her initial response was, "You're doing Virginia Bruce? WOW! I like her very much!" This remark was followed by photos of Virginia from Laura's collection, which are included in this book. Laura was a real catalyst in getting the job done. Both Laura and Parish know their "stuff," and their keen interest in this project is further proof that Virginia deserves accolades for her contribution to the screen.

On the home front, I must thank my partner Joel Bellagio, for listening to each chapter (more than once), scanning photos, and watching lots of Virginia Bruce films. For a proofreader, I could ask for no one better than my longtime friend Martha Hunt. Martha's honest, frank appraisals and suggestions were extremely helpful. Friends and fellow film-buffs, Tim Buehl, John Drennon and John Triglia, are also due for mention.

Not to be overlooked are Diane Briggs of the Fargo North Dakota Library, who sent me material on Virginia Bruce from the NDSU Institute of Regional Studies; Sheryl Stinchcum, President of the John Gilbert Appreciation Society; Eleanor Knowles (author of the excellent *Films and Jeanette MacDonald and Nelson Eddy*); Gary Schmidt, for cueing me in on the world of horseracing (a passion Virginia shared with husband J. Walter Ruben and director John Huston). To research objectively, one must read several sources for any particular news event. As a resource, the publications of news archivist G.D. Hamann are invaluable. Hamann provided me access to his amazing library of various Los Angeles newspapers. In the process of assisting me, Hamann published *Virginia Bruce in the 1930's* (2007) for his Filming Today Press.

Lastly, I must thank Leatrice Gilbert Fountain, the daughter of screen idol John Gilbert. Leatrice was generous with her impressions of meeting Virginia Bruce in 1940, and again in 1973, when Leatrice was researching her father's life. John Gilbert was Virginia's first husband, and although they divorced after a year-and-a-half, their relationship, according to Virginia, set the tone for how she related to future husbands. She admittedly found herself spoiling the men she loved, but at what cost? Which brings me to her last husband -- the enigmatic Ali Ipar. My several conversations with Ipar were most congenial. He has a definite charm. At the same time, I could sense that Ipar was designed for being spoiled by women like Virginia Bruce. It is understandable that a "headstrong" individual like Virginia would also have a very human, vulnerable emotional side that fueled the *very thing* that audiences liked, could identify with, and respond to. Let's go back to 1936, find an aisle seat in the mid-orchestra section, and catch Virginia Bruce in one of her most memorable screen moments.

Scott O'Brien
Sonoma County, California
January 13, 2008

1936 - MGM head Louis B. Mayer and rising star
Virginia Bruce attend premier (courtesy of Vincent Briggs)

CHAPTER ONE:

"I've Got You Under My Skin"

Just below Virginia's languid, dreamy eyes -- her lips part, moist from sipping champagne. She gazes longingly and directly across from her, at a young, good-looking James Stewart . . . and sings:

"I've got you under my skin . . . I've got you deep in the heart of me . . . " The timbre of her light-soprano voice caresses the wistful elegance of each lyric. At the song's emotional pique, she stands and turns away from him, singing to herself. "Don't you know little fool, you never can win? Use your mentality. Wake up to reality." Relenting, she again faces the intrigued, yet diffident Stewart and repeats, "I've got you under my skin." Her smooth rendition of this particular song, coupled with the sweeping allegretto of Cole Porter's music, would prove to be one of Virginia Bruce's screen legacies. The film was *Born to Dance* (1936). Originally, Virginia Bruce was not part of the movie's all-star line up. The fact was, Cole Porter, in his first movie assignment, had written "I've Got You Under My Skin" for someone else. Was luck, finally, turning Virginia's way? Heaven knows her career thus far had plenty of jump-starts and setbacks.

Scene from *Born to Dance(1936)* in which Virginia introduced the Cole Porter standard to Jimmy Stewart (Courtesy of MGM/Photoquest)

Part of the reason for the recasting in *Born to Dance*, was Virginia's star-turn as a temperamental Ziegfeld girl in the recently released *The Great Ziegfeld* (1936). MGM studio heads were turned and focused more than ever in her direction. She held her own against top-ranked stars like William Powell, Myrna Loy and Luise Rainer. In retrospect, Powell's unrevealing performance had no resemblance to the great Florenz Ziegfeld. Loy's sincere portrayal lacked Billie Burke's peculiar effervescence. And, by today's standards, Luise Rainer's Anna Held (for which she won an Oscar) comes across as a trifle mannered. When the film won an Oscar for Best Picture, many protested. *The Hollywood Citizen News* railed that *The Great Ziegfeld* was, "an atrocious production . . . a picture false in biography, a glittering avalanche of legs and tinsel." [i]

The Great Ziegfeld has maintained a reputation of being elephantine, and what film historian James Robert Parish calls, "a gaudy entertainment package." [ii] Virginia Bruce, however, was able to capture what *Variety* referred to as "a composite of several Ziegfeld beauties." And, her looks *were* dazzling. As the ambitious, temperamental Audrey Dane, Bruce was able to simmer in jealousy, throw tantrums, and plunge into an alcoholic stupor. In the film's most impressive musical number, "A Pretty Girl is Like a Melody," she graced the top of a gigantic 60-foot, winding, staircase confection (a spectacle that cost more to film than Ziegfeld put into an entire show). Her charms as a singer and dancer during "You Never Looked So Beautiful" were pleasantly diverting. But, then, Virginia knew *exactly* what she was doing. She had been a Ziegfeld girl herself. She had witnessed firsthand the pampered prima-donnas corralled by Ziegfeld, Broadway's master showman. They had put the gray in his philandering follicles. Virginia knew about women like Audrey Dane, even though she herself was the antithesis of such a character. The fact is, when Virginia makes her glass-shattering exit, the overly-sanitized story loses much of its steam. Hers was one performance that would not go unnoticed.

Virginia with co-star William Powell in the 1936 Oscar-winning *The Great Ziegfeld* (MGM)

Before the cameras rolled for *Born to Dance* in July 1936, Frances Langford, a brunette, for whom Cole Porter had specifically written "I've Got You Under My Skin," was replaced with a blonde, who possessed more appeal and box-office potential. Virginia had been studying voice with Roger Edens (MGM's vocal coach) for over a year. "It all came about very accidentally," said Virginia when asked how she landed the part. "Dorothy Di Frasso had a party and everyone was clowning around, singing and dancing. More for laughs than anything else, I sang 'Annie Laurie.'"[iii] A studio executive happened to be present and the next day Virginia was told to start "cultivating" her voice. Edens was convinced Virginia had a real torch voice. Porter, who kept voluminous notes during the filming, documented Virginia's audition of the song. "She sang ... very well indeed," commented Porter, "and after she had left, they definitely decided to use Bruce."[vv] Once again, MGM "rediscovered" Virginia Bruce.[v] Frances Langford, a superb vocalist, was kept in the film, but placated with a lesser part. She needn't have felt slighted. James Stewart took over the lead from tenor Allan Jones who, along with poor little Judy Garland, was left completely out of the picture. The film also featured dancer Buddy Ebsen (Virginia's future in-law) and Una Merkle. But the film's main focus was tap-dancer Eleanor Powell, whose talent and technique far outshone any screen hoofing of her predecessors. Here, she seems to be tapping on everything in sight.

Born to Dance featured Virginia as Broadway star Lucy James who falls head-over-heels for a young sailor (Stewart) during a publicity stunt. She gets to sing another Porter number on the ship's deck titled "Love Me, Love My Pekingese," which apparently had an anatomical innuendo. (In 1929's *Gentlemen of the Press*, Kay Francis had seduced Walter Huston with the double entendre, "I'm sure you'll just love my Pekingese." Huston enthused, "Yes. I'm sure I will!"). In *Born to Dance*, however, Stewart has already fallen for the charm and terpsichorean talents of Eleanor Powell. Bruce was simply a fascinating, albeit tempting intrusion. When Bruce storms out of her dressing room to witness her *understudy* and competition for Stewart's affections (Powell) taking over one of her dance numbers, she goes ballistic. "Stop it!" she demands. "Just what do you think you're doing? Making a fool out of me!" Bruce snarls at the producer, "Fire her this minute! Get *rid* of her. Either she goes, or I go!" It's the film's only dramatically interesting moment.

Alas, with or without her Pekingese, Virginia Bruce is left in the lurch and out of the film's finale. Still, she establishes a far more interesting and complex character than the rest of the cast combined. *Born to Dance* was a huge hit at the box-office. *The New York Times* noted, "Virginia Bruce is the very archetype of all the arch if volatile leading ladies."[ii] "Menace and glamour are furnished by beautiful Virginia Bruce," raved Louella Parsons.[iii] "I've Got You Under My Skin" was nominated for an Academy Award for Best Song that year, and jumped to second place in the list of songs played most often on the radio. The Brunswick label had Virginia record her "hit," complementing it with a splendid version of Porter's "Easy to Love" for the "B" side. Her vocals had staying power. Cole Porter was more than pleased with her performance in *Born to Dance*. In 1941, columnist Sidney Skolsky overheard Porter talking to Fred Astaire on the set of *You'll Never Get Rich*. Porter was telling Astaire that he never heard any singer do "I've Got You Under My Skin" as well Virginia, and he wished that she would sing more of his songs.[iiii] ("This critical opinion of Miss Bruce by Cole Porter did startle me," confessed Skolsky.) In the 1990s, biographer Charles Higham commented on *Born to Dance* and Virginia's rendition of the Porter song, saying, "Beautiful, stylish, and sophisticated, Miss Bruce epitomized, in that song, the essence of the thirties as few others ever did."[xx]

During filming, Virginia and James Stewart developed an attraction for one another. They dated frequently, leaving plenty

Born to Dance (1936) – with James Stewart (Courtesy of MGM/Photoquest)

of room for gossip columnists. On occasion, Jimmy's roommate, Henry Fonda, would join the duo for a night on the town. In August, before *Born to Dance* was completed, Stewart asked Virginia to accompany him to the premier of his latest MGM release, the mid-nineteenth-century saga, *The Gorgeous Hussy*. In it, a miscast Joan Crawford, wearing crinolines and disgracing every man she meets, played the supposed mistress of President Andrew Jackson. An uncomfortable-looking Stewart was one of Crawford's suitors named Rowdy Dow — a role he later tried to forget. He felt the same about watching himself sing and dance in *Born to Dance*. A few years later, he reminisced to a *New York Times* reporter, "I knew I had to toughen up!" Stewart said, then added, "I just couldn't go on hemming and hawing, which I realized I'd over done . . . I looked at some of my old pictures and couldn't believe what I was watching. One of them, *Born to Dance*, made me want to vomit."ˣ

However, Stewart did enjoy himself on the set of *Born to Dance*. A camera-fanatic, Stewart was caught 'in action" focusing on his co-stars. Popular syndicated columnist Robbin Coons got Stewart to confess that his favorite photo was of Virginia. It was a reflection of her in her dressing room mirror. Coons mentioned in his column that Hollywood was speculating on wedding bells for the screen duo. He asked Stewart if Bruce was his favorite subject. "Welll," Stewart replied in his familiar drawl, "I wouldn't say that. But, I will say she's easy to photograph — you can't get a bad angle on her, no matter how her face is turned."ⁱⁱ When *Born to Dance* had its gala premier in November, Bruce and Stewart's mutual interest hadn't wavered. He escorted her to Grauman's Chinese Theatre where they were both cheered for their performances. But Stewart, who was also seeing Ginger Rogers, wanted free of romantic entanglements. By the end of December,

1936 - James Stewart captures Virginia with his camera. The two
dated frequently, sometimes joined by his pal Henry Fonda

he would begin a highly publicized affair with the Queen of the
MGM lot, Norma Shearer.

Though younger than Stewart and a romantic at heart, Virginia had been married and divorced, and she had a three-year-old daughter to attend to. Her priorities were now keenly focused on her career. Virginia envisioned stardom and considered her recent success at MGM a turn for the best. She trusted her studio and worked hard. After all, bigger parts kept coming her way. "I took them all," Virginia admitted to one reporter, "knowing that no matter what I played would give me experience. If I was the sweet heroine, that was alright; if I was the wicked other woman, I didn't object. Recently I finished *Born to Dance* and I got a chance to sing and dance. At MGM they like my voice and say that there will be future singing roles. And it has all been worthwhile."[iii]

Virginia held her breath wondering if MGM would finally allow her a lead that was *not* on loan out. She longed to display the full range of her ability. So, she waited, surrounded by "All the Stars in Heaven" (MGM's "modest" self-promotion). But, MGM wasn't one-hundred-percent convinced that Virginia could pull off the lead in an "A" picture. In early December, the studio announced she would be on loan to star in a "B" picture at Universal costarring Kent Taylor. Once again, Virginia acquiesced. After all, it was a lead part and she felt it might make MGM "see the light."

"Whatever comes to me I will be happy," said Virginia optimistically, "as long as I know that I am no longer 'decorative atmosphere.'"[iiii] It was soon after the announcement of her assignment at Universal, that Virginia sat in her MGM dressing room explaining to columnist Linda Lane the struggle of convincing directors she was not "beautiful and dumb." She was certainly capable of expressing intelligence. "If you are noted for your ability, cleverness and other qualities in the entertainment world," opted Virginia, "the way is comparatively easy for you . . . Hollywood knows that in the majority of cases, a plain girl with talent and personality can be made to look beautiful. But the beautiful girl seems to live under that terribly unfair curse of 'beautiful but dumb.'" It was a sore subject and Virginia elaborated. "Please don't think me vain, but I wouldn't be admitting that I have always been considered a beauty if I didn't think I would be helping *others*. Beauty, after all, is something we can't very well help. We are born with it, fortunately or unfortunately, which ever you choose. When I arrived in Hollywood, 'beautiful

Rather than promoting her promising talent at MGM, the studio
loaned Virginia out for "B" films such as *When Love Is Young (1937)*
with Kent Taylor (Courtesy of Laura Wagner)

but dumb' was the cry. Getting into pictures was fairly easy, but
they gave me little to do save stand around as atmosphere . . . I
became little more than a statue." Reporter Lane concurred that,
"Whereas thousands of people diligently seek beauty the world
over, an actress in the film city often finds she must run away
from it." [vvv] Would producers, directors and studio heads ever see
Virginia Bruce as more than just a decoration?

It would be a few more years before Virginia Bruce allowed
herself to see the proverbial "writing on the wall" and, to para-
phrase Cole Porter's song, "use her mentality . . . wake up to reality." Superstardom for Virginia Bruce? It simply wasn't meant
to be. "I tried, I really tried," she would reflect later. "I got a little

excited, felt I was getting a little bit of somewhere when I played in *The Great Ziegfeld*, in *Born to Dance* . . . then things just went along for a couple years. The last two pictures I did at MGM, they were my downfall. They washed over me like the waters of oblivion. I found I didn't take kindly to oblivion . . . I'd get letters from fans, asking *'Are you dead?'* . . . Maybe I should have gone in and talked to Mr. Mayer . . . But I can't do that sort of thing. I stumble over my own feet, get twisted up in my own tongue. I had such an *unwanted* feeling. I felt they were fed up with me, bored with me. There were all the new girls coming along, Lana Turner, Greer Garson, Vivien Leigh, they increased my feeling of inferiority . . . I asked to be released from my MGM contract. And that alone should have proven to me how much I want a career. Because that was the hardest thing I ever had to do in my whole life!"^{vv}

Well . . . not quite. Virginia's most difficult times would lie just ahead. And if heartache, disappointment, tragedy and strange twists of fate qualify, Virginia Bruce would indeed have ample opportunity for "meaty" drama — in her own private life.

Endnotes

i   Mason Wiley and Damien Bona, *Inside Oscar*, Ballantine Books, NY, 1996

ii   James Robert Parish, *Hollywood's Great Love Teams*, Arlington House, NY, 1974, pps. 219-222

iii   Dorothy Manners, "How Virginia Bruce Found Her Voice," *Los Angeles Examiner*, 11/22/36

vv   George Eells, *Cole Porter: The Life that Late He Led*," G.P. Putnam's Sons, 1967, pg 147

v   Tom Vallance, *"Frances Langford,"* The Independent, (London), 7/14/2005

ii   J.T.M. *Born to Dance*, The New York Times, 12/5/36

iii   review for *Born to Dance*, *Los Angeles Examiner*, 11/26/36

iiii   Sidney Skolsky, "Watching Them Make Pictures," *Hollywood Citizen News*, 6/20/41

xx   Charles Higham, *Merchant of Dreams: Louis B. Mayer, M.G.M., and the Secret Hollywood*, Donald I. Fine, NY, 1993 pg 248

x   Donald Dewey, *James Stewart - A Biography*, Turner Pub. Inc., Atlanta, 1996, pps. 273-274

ii   Robbins Coons, "Man Takes His Life - With A Camera," *The Gleaner*, Kingston, 9/7/36

iii Linda Lane, "Virginia Bruce Resents Phrase 'Beauty Is Dumb," *Oakland Tribune*, 12/6/36

iiii Ibid.

vvv Ibid.

vv   Gladys Hall, "Marriage Is Not Enough!" *Silver Screen*, 10/40

CHAPTER TWO:

Letters From Fargo

c 1938 – Posed for top stardom by MGM's portrait photographer Lazlo Willinger

It was winter, 1938. Movie star Virginia Bruce had just received a letter from her former high school chum giving her the latest scoop on the "old gang" in Fargo. It was full of small-town news and gossip: the latest from the swank Bachelors and Benedicts social club; updates on classmates; and concluded with an intimate P.S. It left Virginia in a reflective mood for her appointment with Los Angeles columnist Kay Proctor. Proctor needled her until Virginia confessed that she was "a little homesick." She talked fondly about Fargo, the town where she grew up; the old square-cut red brick house; the town ice-skating rink, which was a flat field flooded by the fire department and frozen by the winter cold. Fargo, the place she had been passed over for a part in a play at Central High School. Someone else got the only role she ever tried out for.

Proctor scoffed, "I suppose that bucolic picture of contentment seems vastly amusing to you now!" It was the *wrong* thing to say to the outspoken Miss Bruce. "I don't know why it should be!" Virginia snapped. "After all, if chance circumstances hadn't taken me away from Fargo eight years ago, that's exactly the life I'd be leading . . . As it is, I'm more than a little homesick for it. You said something about Fargo being *amusing*? It would have been, but not in the patronizing way you implied."[1] Virginia went on to explain her loyalty to Fargo. Her nostalgia for what "might have been" had been a constant in her life. But, then, not *all* "letters from Fargo" were of the pleasant, chummy variety. Not all of them made "Ginny" Briggs, as her friends back home called her, homesick. After the announcement of her 1932 marriage, Virginia received a tongue-lashing from one hometown busy-body. "Last week, when the engagement broke in the newspapers," she told a reporter at the time, "I got a letter from Fargo cussing me out and ending up with, 'The *idea* of you being the *fourth* wife of *any* man!' Divorces are still frowned upon in Fargo, you know." Virginia bristled, "I *know* what I'm *doing*."[2]

Virginia's nostalgia for Fargo had "staying power" some thirty-odd years later on NBC's *Today Show*. In 1965 she corrected the host of the popular morning news show who claimed Virginia's hometown as being Minneapolis, Minnesota. "*No*," Virginia interrupted. "I was *born* in Minneapolis and reared in Fargo. We left Fargo because my father *went broke*."[3]

Yes, Virginia's father, Earll Briggs, went broke. He had financial reversals. Oddly enough, he had every reason to succeed. Fargo, North Dakota, was situated near agriculturally rich wheat land. The city itself was founded (on still legally Native American "Sioux" territory) in 1872 by the Northern Pacific Railway and named after William G. Fargo, the founder of the Wells-Fargo Express Company. By the time Virginia was born, Fargo spelled prosperity. With the influx of immigrants from Scandinavia,

Germany, and a mix of Scotch-Irish-English, the city became "an important agricultural center as well as a regional distribution and transportation hub."[4]

Earll Frederick Briggs was born in Minnesota in 1884 and became an independent insurance broker with many social connections. His father, Frederick Earl Briggs, had been a lawyer. His mother, Helen Magill from Iowa, was the daughter of a coal dealer. The husband of Earll's aunt, H. E. Magill, was the founder of a successful seed distributing business in Fargo and was also in the insurance business. The Briggs family were neighbors and close friends with well-known attorney A.G. Divet. (Divet would later be prominently identified with the legal profession in Los Angeles and represent Virginia in a highly publicized divorce case).[5] Earll's marriage to Margaret Morris was a promising one. Some sources link the Briggs and Morris lines to Presidents William McKinley and James Garfield. Somehow the weight of all these connections failed to tip the scale in Earll's favor. (Considering the fates of McKinley and Garfield, perhaps it makes sense after all.) It was in the aftermath of World War I that prosperity took a nosedive and Earll Briggs wasn't the only one whose livelihood was in trouble.

Helen Virginia Briggs was born, in her father's home state of Minnesota, on September 29, 1910. Her parents, having located to Minneapolis from Fargo, were now eager to move back. After Virginia's birth, it was only a matter of months before the couple returned to their family roots in Fargo. The comfortable, red-bricked house at 14th and 5th Avenue South, where Virginia grew up, was the childhood home of her mother, Margaret Morris Briggs. In 1936, Margaret Briggs reminisced about those early years:

> Before Virginia was born, I remember having only one wish concerning her. It was a very silly, very feminine little wish. . . . I never prayed that she might be beautiful or talented or unusual in any way but she *must* have curls! However, after she arrived and I carefully studied her dreamy eyes and delicate features, I decided that God knew best when he gave her straight hair. Right from the very first, Virginia was a good baby, always smiling and cooing, never crying or ill. I do not recall her ever being seriously ill in all her life.
>
> We had returned to my home town of Fargo, North Dakota, where my husband engaged in the insurance business. The winters were cold and stormy . . . Virginia was an outdoor girl. She had her little sled and made good use of it. She loved to build snowmen and roll snowballs. Often I felt that the cold was too much for such a tiny child but she would only laugh and insist that she was "warm as toast." When the evenings were long, she was content with her pencils and scratch pads. It wasn't long before a few childish scratches on the paper began to take form and before she was school age, she was well on the way toward being a good little artist.[6]

Within a couple years of their return to Fargo, Margaret gave birth to a son, Stanley Morris Briggs (February 9, 1913). Their family was complete. Mrs. Briggs elaborated on the "new addition." "Like all parents," she said, "we wondered if Virginia would be jealous and took extra pains to see that she wasn't neglected or her feelings injured. We might have saved ourselves the trouble. Virginia was bursting with joy and pride. She called him her 'butter baby' — it was the nearest she could come to saying 'baby brother.' Somehow she thought that the baby belonged to her right along with her dolls and other toys. She began mothering him and looking after him in every possible way. . . . He was never

c. 1917 – Fargo, North Dakota. Helen Virginia Briggs and her brother Stanley Morris Briggs (courtesy of Vincent Briggs)

a nuisance or a bother to her as so many little brothers are to so many little girls."[7] Brother Stanley would prove a constant and supportive influence in Virginia's life.

"As soon as Virginia could stretch her little fingers enough to cover a few keys on the piano," Margaret remembered, "we started giving her lessons. She enjoyed the study and was a good pupil, never having to be coaxed into practicing. She particularly liked sewing of any kind. When there was nothing to mend, she would embroider and she did lovely work."[8] Virginia considered her childhood to be a happy one. She also enjoyed swimming and took horseback riding lessons. Admitting that she was something of a tomboy, Virginia confessed to learning boxing from her father, and had an occasional boxing bout with brother Stanley.

> When I was a growing girl in Fargo, I played
> boy's games as ardently as they did. Why, I can
> remember how I even used to lick my younger
> brother at boxing. Of course, I was two years
> older and quite a lot bigger. Dad used to get out his
> watch and referee our boxing matches in the front
> room. He'd put up 20 cents for the winner. I usually
> won by the simple expedient of landing the first
> sock.[9]

But, it would be music that would dominate her early life.[10] By the time Virginia was thirteen she gave a solo recital at the city's Stone Hall, playing an entire program of difficult classical pieces.[11]

"Virginia was . . . always easy to discipline," recalled her mother. "She had but one spanking in her life and I didn't want to give her that but I felt that I had to in order to protect her." Margaret Briggs then detailed the incident.

> One day when she was four years old she asked
> me about church and if good people went there. I
> answered absently as mothers will when they are
> busy with house work, saying, 'Yes, all good people
> go to church.' A little while later, I missed her. I
> looked all over the house for her, all over the yard,

> all up and down the block. I was frantic and called
> her father. It was before we owned a car but he took
> his bicycle and rode all over the neighborhood.
> After a dreadful, nerve-straining two hours we
> found her down by the Methodist church. She
> hadn't meant to be bad—in fact, she thought she
> was proving that she was good by going to church.
> I wanted to take her in my arms and weep over
> her safety but my better judgment told me that she
> must be whipped so that she would never, never
> leave the yard again.

Apparently, Virginia's "whipping" made an impression. When this author asked Virginia's nephew if she attended church, he replied, "Virginia wasn't religious at all."[12]

Growing up, Virginia observed her mother asserting her ambitions and fulfilling her dreams both inside and outside the home. Margaret Morris Briggs, born in Fargo in 1883, was the daughter of immigrant Thomas Reese Morris of Carmarthen, Wales. Her mother, Sophia Crane, was from Wisconsin. Margaret Briggs was an outgoing woman and three-time North Dakota State Women's Golf Champion. One such championship took place at the Fargo Country Club links on July 26, 1922, a time when men's championship golf got all the press headlines.[13] However, the 1910s and '20s were progressive eras for women, as they began to enter the professional world. Clothing reflected their new attitude. Hemlines inched up with lighter fabrics and looser styles. The suffrage movement, which first gained momentum in 1910, culminated with the 19th Amendment being ratified in 1919. The verdict was in: women were now considered to have enough intelligence to cast a vote. Margaret Briggs reflected the "new woman." While on occasion Margaret may have kept one foot in the traditions of the past, the other was firmly planted in new territory.

Virginia witnessed these changes while enjoying the latest dance crazes, listening to new jazz sounds, and eating her favorite peanut brittle on Saturday afternoons while watching film heroes like Valentino and John Gilbert on the silent screen. She was maturing into a "modern" woman in every sense of the word. And, it held. A 1940 interview with Gladys Hall (founding member of the Hollywood Women's Press Club in 1928) typified Virginia's outlook. "Marriage is not enough!" declared Virginia. "I haven't *any* of the stock reasons for saying it is not enough. I can smash to *atoms* every one of the old tried-and-true reasons women give when they say *I want a career*." "For instance," she continued, "I am content. I do not feel incomplete. I do not feel unfulfilled. And still *it isn't enough*. . . . It's not that I'd be bored at home that I want a career. It's not that I have nothing to do with my time. There's never enough of the stuff. It "fugue-its" like a frightening phantom. I'm not even the career-type, the vital, go-getting sort of woman. I've never gone out after things. I've never fought for things. I don't know how. I haven't the weapons. . . . things have always happened to me and I've simply done the best I could with them when they came my way.

Virginia zeroed to the point she was trying to make: "The modern woman lives in a different world from the world of her mother . . . the pattern has changed. Something *in* me that has no name made me stubborn . . . I could evade the issue by saying that I can't stop now because I have too many responsibilities, too much to pay out. I like to do things for my family. I can say I like to have my own money. I do. That's part of being a modern woman. . . . none of these reasons answers the question honestly." Reporter Hall listened with interest. Hall had begun her own career as a professional writer in 1912 and stuck to it. She understood Virginia, and, in fact, was a constant influence and friend. In 1936, when Bruce's 2-year-old daughter was threatened with kidnapping, Gladys Hall was her representative. Virginia respected Gladys and women like her: professional writers with *integrity* (the Hollywood Women's Press Club would suspend members for doing paid publicity.) Although Hall was only a few years younger than Virginia's mother, she was more in tune with the attitudes of Virginia's generation. On this particular afternoon she was focused on a very relaxed, yet assertive Virginia Bruce. "We live in a different world," Virginia finally surmised. "For that's the real answer: *the pattern has changed. The loom is bigger. Our capacity for living has so enlarged that nothing is enough, short of everything. . . .* We've got to use every thread in the new pattern. . . . The individual is just one thread in the pattern and as the pattern goes, the thread goes. *That's* why marriage, whether it's made in Heaven or in Hollywood, is not

c.1936 – Virginia on the set with her mother, Margaret Briggs enough."[14] One aspect of the "new pattern" was not learning to cook. "My mother told me never to learn how to cook and then I'd never have to," Virginia stated. "It has always worked."[15] (At least it worked until 1959 when Virginia fired her cook.)

The reference to "the world of her mother" did not fully apply to Margaret Briggs, for Virginia realized that she had been encouraged by her mother to follow the "new pattern." Upon arriving in Hollywood, however, Margaret would give up golf and agreeably fulfill the role of grandmother, a concession necessitated by the considerable demands of her movie-star daughter's life.

At an early age, Virginia decided to drop the use of her first name, Helen. At school she was referred to as "Gin," "Ginny," or "Briggs." At fourteen, she attended Fargo Central High School and excelled in music. She was also a member of the chorus, glee club, orchestra, debate team, and the girls tennis team (an enthusiasm she shared with brother Stanley).[16] Her favorite subjects were English and History. She preferred reading the classics. She liked to draw. Virginia was pleased with her creative output as an artist and during her career in Hollywood was always "aching" to get back to it. "Virginia was so excited when she entered high school," recalled Margaret Briggs. "She could go from room to room for her classes and have different pupils in almost every class . . . however, she couldn't, or didn't, study as well as she did in the grades. Her marks weren't just what they used to be and we were a bit worried. Then one day she got a hundred on one of her papers. The teacher was very pleased because he liked Virginia and longed for her to do better work. 'Well, Virginia,' he asked with a kindly smile, 'how did you happen to get such a good mark?' Very calmly and very truthfully, Virginia replied, 'I copied Hamilton Simon's paper.' The poor teacher was shocked and yet he liked Virginia for being so truthful. He explained to her that the mark was undeserved and that instead of the hundred he would have to give her nothing at all. That was all right with Virginia. 'Oh, I know that,' she said. 'I didn't expect to get credit for it. I just wanted to see what a hundred on my paper would look like.'"[17] Although her marks may not have been high, the popular "Gin Briggs" with her "puddle jumper" (she was the only kid at school who had her own car) *was* a hit with the football team — after practice. She felt sorry for the worn-out players and gave them all rides home.

Virginia Briggs was a romantic. As an adult she claimed it had started when she was a little girl and had seen the stalwart Royal Canadian Mounted Police in their crimson uniforms and boot spurs coming through Fargo on their way in and out of Canada. The Mounties trained in Toronto, then took the railroad to Fargo via Chicago, before heading up to Manitoba. They were often seen out to "get their man" along the Dakota boarders and would be summoned for an occasional trial in Fargo. "Her storybook hero," observed editor Jack Smalley in 1935, "took the form of one of these handsome riders of the last frontier."[18] (Virginia came to realize this fantasy in the 1930s while dating the silver screen's most famous Mountie, Nelson Eddy.) As she matured, Virginia admitted that she preferred a man of the middle class. She told a Fargo Central High School classmate, "I will never marry before I'm at least 23 years old [she held out until she was 21]. I want to go to some university or college [she got as far as being 'rushed' for a sorority] and then I want to work for at least a year [*that* she did, and for a few decades]. Money would never enter into a marriage of mine. If the man I loved didn't have very much, I would marry him anyway."[19] True to her word, Virginia's first kiss was from a poor Irish lad named Patrick. (She rushed into the house afterwards and dreamed she was going to have a baby!) Virginia was sympathetic to this boy, who, along with his widowed mother, faced financial difficulties. She loved listening to Patrick's dream of becoming a singer. When another boy asked Virginia to see the Italian tenor Tito Schipa in concert, she refused. Instead, Virginia coaxed her father to buy two tickets and to ask Patrick, as a favor, to take her. Virginia satisfied her own wish to hear Schipa, while, at the same time, saved Patrick's young pride.

While in school, Virginia avoided serious relationships. "I saw to it that I always had a few competitors around," she recalled. "I saw definite disadvantages in having a steady. The folks could never understand how I kept the boys in line. You might call this flirting, but of course it wasn't. Long ago I made up my mind to be interested in other people and what they were thinking and doing. It's more fun to talk with men than women … at least their talk is more substantial and vital. I've always liked men as friends, anyway."[20]

Romance aside; it was her talent as a pianist that really mattered to young Virginia. It actually saved her from being permanently "expelled" from school. Her golden hair, rosy skin, big blue eyes and being one of the prettiest girls in town, wasn't enough to get her out of every jam she got into. Virginia had the unfortunate habit of speaking without first considering. During her senior year, Virginia's fellow classmates watched in disbelief one afternoon as she told off the history teacher. She was requested to leave school. This was just before graduation in 1928, and Virginia had been selected as accompanist for the North Dakota State High School music competition. Author Colin Briggs, who

interviewed Virginia several
times during her final years,
told of her "rebellious" incident:

> After being expelled
> from high school
> [Virginia] felt no
> shame, only relief,
> but to her surprise
> was asked to return
> three days later
> by the principal.
> Fargo High School
> Choral Society
> was to compete
> the following week
> at the University
> of North Dakota
> State contest and
> they couldn't find
> another piano

1928 – Virginia Briggs, UCLA hopeful

accompanist as accomplished as Virginia. Fargo
won the contest and the president of the university
asked Virginia to present the silver cup to the
school. He also said he wished there could have
been a second cup for Virginia as she was the best
accompanist. Later back in Fargo, to her surprise,
Virginia received her high school diploma.[21]

While Virginia lucked out, her father didn't. Earll Briggs' career as an insurance broker began to falter during the 1920s. An

economic depression, starting with the 1920 collapse of wartime grain prices, affected the insurance business as well. Banks began closing in 1921 and that resulted in farm foreclosures. The decline in farms directly impacted the insurance business. It was tough going. By 1928, Briggs had witnessed friends and many others in his profession leave the area. He was inclined to do the same. When Virginia mentioned her desire to study music at the University of California at Los Angeles, Earll listened. He promised her that she could attend UCLA instead of Northwestern University where her friends were headed. Her dream was the catalyst that made the decision to move to Los Angeles a reality.[22]

However, Virginia's dream of an education would not be realized. Virginia, who recognized that she wasn't a "fighter," would, soon enough, have to come to terms with her father's new career and most marketable asset: his attractive daughter.

Endnotes

1   Kay Proctor, "Virginia Tells What Her Life Might Have Been - IN FARGO," *Fargo Forum*, 4/16/38

2   Fargo Library Archive, news article from 8/4/32

3   Fargo Library Archive (dated: March 5, 1965)

4   Fargo: History, Thomson Gale, Thomson Corp., 2006

5   Fargo Library Archive, news article, Marie Canel, "Determined Not to Let Divorce Embitter Life," 6/2/34

6   Margaret Briggs, "My Daughter Virginia Bruce," *Hollywood*. 3/36

7   ibid

8   ibid

9   Terry Kelly, "How to Get Along With 50 Men," *Hollywood*, 2/38

10 Colin Briggs, "Virginia Bruce - Incandescent Beauty," *Films of the Golden Age*, Summer, 2003

11 Briggs, "My Daughter . . . "

12 Conversation with nephew Vincent Briggs, 5/29/2007

13 "Jack Hintgen is Defeated in Golf Play," *Bismarck Tribune*, 7/27/22

14 Gladys Hall, "Marriage Is Not Enough!" *Silver Screen*, 10/40

15 Bob Thomas, "Virginia Bruce Makes Comeback," *Corpus Christi Times*, 12/4/59

Chapter Two

16 "1930's Hollywood Actress Called Fargo Home," *In Forum News*, 7/09/2006

17 Briggs, "My Daughter . . . "

18 Jack Smalley, "Nothing Can Hurt Her Now!" *Screen Book*, 3/35

19 Fargo Library Archive, Henry J. Hurley, "John's Ardor Revises Plans For Virginia," 8/11/32

20 Kelly, "How to Get . . . "

21 Briggs, "Virginia Bruce . . . "

22 Muriel Babcock, "The Girl From Fargo," *Silver Screen*, 4/35

CHAPTER THREE:

Hollywood's Ziegfeld Girl

"Virginia Briggs, Fargo, Given $50,000 Contract; Captivates Hollywood," read the headline for North Dakota's *Bismarck Tribune*. It was December 4, and Virginia had already christened herself with a new last name: Bruce. It all happened so unexpectedly. Having arrived in the film capital in September 1928, the Briggs family was settling in when their world suddenly took a dizzy spin. Virginia Briggs had never given films any serious thought. She wasn't "movie crazy." One fall afternoon, she accompanied her aunt, Harriet Miller, on business to the home of Mrs. William Beaudine. Mrs. Beaudine was taken with Virginia's blonde, demure, good looks and wasted no time telling her husband. As luck would have it, Mr. Beaudine was an established and rather prolific Hollywood director. After meeting with Virginia, Beaudine was impressed. He wanted to schedule a screen test for her.

In spite of Beaudine's offer, Virginia was intent on enrolling at the University of California at Los Angeles, where she hoped to prepare for a musical career. Several accounts claim that she was also being "rushed" by a sorority.[1] But things were not going as planned. Mrs. Briggs later explained, "After we arrived in Hollywood, we had serious financial reverses, and it began to look as if we wouldn't have much money . . . Virginia was having a bit of trouble getting into the University since the credits required here were somewhat different than those required in Dakota."[2] It was on a dare by the other girls on campus, after they got wind of Beaudine's interest, that Virginia decided to follow through and give the screen test a try. It turned out that what Beaudine had in mind for Virginia was the female lead in a George O'Brien western. Upon viewing her test, Beaudine decided a lead would prove too much for the 18-year-old. Virginia was devastated. "I had been scheduled for a part with George O'Brien and it didn't work out," she remembered. "I was so disappointed I was almost ill . . . I promised myself that I would never let anything hurt me deeply again. Not *anything*. You can train yourself that way, you know, just as you can get in the habit of taking every trifle to heart."[3]

There was no doubt in Beaudine's mind that the camera liked Virginia. He generously offered her a five-year contract "in hopes to develop her for stardom in the not too distant future."[4] A few days later, Earll Briggs accompanied his daughter to court and oversaw all contract approvals that would be signed.[5] Beaudine was prepared to pay her $50,000 over a five-year period, "providing she lives up to expectations."[6] This turn of events was a godsend. The Briggs family was confined to a two-room Lockwood Avenue apartment. Earll and Stanley were taking turns sleeping on a mattress on the floor.[7] In her first press interview Virginia stated, "I never had given motion pictures a thought, but it is a chance of a lifetime. I had planned to continue my vocal and piano lessons. I plan to carry on as much as possible in this direction, but I think I shall like the screen."[8]

Several cities around the country responded to the news of Virginia's "discovery" with apprehension. The *Kansas City Star* had frequently discouraged movie-struck girls from venturing to Hollywood. "We have written of the pitfalls until we almost have frightened ourselves," said the paper. "We have described the long months of waiting and hardship, until we have used up all our best adjectives. . . . We congratulate Virginia. But, we repeat the warning. It won't happen again in a blue moon."[9] Beaudine later recapped his association with Bruce:

> Well, it was a strange thing in view of the fact
> that up to the evening I first saw Virginia I know
> she had never entertained any ideas of a screen
> career. I came home from the studio one night
> and as I walked into the house I noticed an
> amazingly beautiful girl visiting with my family.
> Beauty is quite common here in Hollywood, but
> even so, Virginia Bruce was really a vision. I felt
> immediately that she had screen possibilities. I
> asked my wife about her and was told that she
> was the niece of the lady who was designing some
> clothes for her and that the girl had come along
> with her aunt. Right away I asked Virginia if
> she had ever thought of going into pictures. She
> answered in the negative, but said she could play
> the piano and sing. And she walked right over to
> the piano and began playing and singing for us.[10]

In Beaudine's version of the story, the next time he saw Virginia she was on the Fox lot (probably after being egged on by the aforementioned sorority sisters). He noticed an agent was with her. Virginia admitted that she had given some thought to picture work, but imagined the industry was indifferent to newcomers such as herself. Beaudine invited her over to his home that night and they again discussed the possibility of a screen test. He also promised to have his press representative begin to "build her up" in the public eye. (Hence, the blazing headline in the *Bismarck Tribune*.)

By the mid-twenties William Beaudine had become respected as a speedy, yet artful director. He knew the ropes of the film industry in a career that began as a prop boy/extra in 1909. Beaudine had a propensity for efficiency, and determinedly shot only one take of any particular scene, thus garnering the nickname "One Shot Beaudine." He displayed his light touch in two of Mary Pickford's biggest hits: *Little Annie Rooney* (1925) and *Sparrows* (1926). When the "talkies" arrived in Hollywood, Beaudine remained a top director who commanded a large salary. It appeared that Virginia was in good hands. Beaudine offered her a bit part in one of his last Fox silent films, a Madge Bellamy crime-drama titled *Fugitives* (1929). Her actual contract salary was $25 a week.[11] Over the next few years Virginia would be known as "William Beaudine's discovery." Oddly, "One Shot Beaudine" only gave Virginia one more shot in one of his

1929: Virginia offers her "not movie crazy" look for the camera (Paramount)

films, *Hard to Get* (1929). She played a model in a modiste's shop. Beaudine and Virginia's professional paths never crossed again. After doing an uncredited "walk-on" in a Helen Twelvetrees silent Fox feature, *Blue Skies* (1929), Virginia was encouraged by Beaudine to venture over to the Paramount lot. At this point, Virginia had distanced herself from UCLA and thoughts of a college education. She had already been advised by school officials to postpone enrollment and wait for the start of the spring semester. This delay allowed her interest in films to be piqued. She decided to learn the ropes of screen acting. Virginia never forgot Beaudine and still considered him one of her closest friends in the industry when she later signed on to MGM.

At Beaudine's suggestion, Paramount took note of Virginia's possibilities, and soon "exercised an option they held on her agreement with Beaudine. [March 1929]"[12] The studio used Virginia briefly in several films, grooming her for stardom. She did a "bit" in Victor Schertzinger's *Fashions in Love* (1929), and was also present in two Buddy Rogers features: *River of Romance* (1929), and as a party guest in *Illusion* (1929). Amazingly, she was noticed even in these non-roles. Dan Thomas interviewed Virginia in June 1929, before any of her Paramount work had been released. "Until my family moved here from Fargo last fall, I had no thought of ever working in pictures," said Virginia. "In fact," she stressed, "I had very little desire to do so. I wasn't interested."[13] Thomas mentioned her extra work (a café scene) in *Why Bring That Up?* (1929) and, her first *real* part, as a nurse, in William Wellman's grim, tough-on-crime talker, *Woman Trap* (1929). Her work in that film (in which she got her first screen credit) brought her a Paramount contract of $75 a week. This was indeed an improvement over the $7.50 she received for *Why Bring That Up?*[14] "Of course, I am more *interested* now," Virginia admitted, "but the idea of being an actress doesn't excite me a great deal."[15]

When asked about her past, Virginia claimed it to be very uninteresting. Thomas was amused at her candid replies and emphasized that she was, after all, just a kid. He said Hollywood "doesn't seem to mean a thing in her young life. This 18-year-old girl is far more interested in that thing called love."[16] Thomas was bemused by her declaration, "My chief purpose in life is still to fall in love. I don't know why I want to, but I do." She readily gave a description of her "Dream Man." He was athletic, a good dancer, was fond of music, intelligent and had a sense of humor. Virginia mentioned that co-star Buddy Rogers came pretty close to measuring up. "But, he isn't quite it," she emphasized. Dark, good looks where also important to her, "But, not enough so that he will have a foreign appearance." Money? "Money doesn't count for whole lot," she said wistfully. Her father had won and lost as an insurance broker. Wealth to Virginia seemed to be an unstable thing on which to build happiness. (However, at a future date, she would wholeheartedly embrace a "foreign appearance" for love's sake.)

Virginia repeated similar feelings to long-time Hollywood reporter Robbin Coons, who described Virginia as a willowy, blonde, soft-spoken young lady. "I don't know that I have enough ambition, or 'artistic zeal,' to achieve stardom," sighed Virginia. "The main advantage, as I see it, would be money enough to buy all the clothes — and books — I want. But then, on the other hand, to have to walk in a perpetual spotlight, in public, as the stars do — I wouldn't like that."[17] Even without "artistic zeal" things were looking up. She was assigned the part of lady-in-waiting to Jeanette MacDonald's Queen Louise in Ernst Lubitsch's musical-comedy *The Love Parade* (1929). The "advantages" of money, however, were sorely lacking. While reporting to the Lubitsch set, agents of the financially naive Virginia, devoured two-thirds of her new income.[18]

The Love Parade was the screen debut of Broadway star Jeanette MacDonald. The pairing of MacDonald's Queen with Frenchman Maurice Chevalier's Prince Consort delighted audiences. Victor Schertzinger's romantic score suited both MacDonald's

Love Parade (1929) Composer/director Victor Schertzinger lends an
ear while gazing at Virginia. Lending their harmonies were (l-r)
Helene Friend, Josephine Hall, and Rosalind Charles

timbre and Chevalier's zest. Lubitsch's deft touch as director (in
his first sound venture), coupled with his trademark of provoca-
tive sexual innuendo, turned the film into an unqualified success. Virginia's role in *The Love Parade* is considered by many to
be the first time movie fans took notice of her.

Virginia and four other ladies-in-waiting are first seen in
Queen Louise's boudoir greeting her "good morning." The Queen
isn't at all pleased. "Why am I always awaked from my dreams?"
she frowns. "I'm sure it was a *nice* dream, your Majesty," Virginia
says hopefully. It turns out that it was. MacDonald goes into rev-
erie, singing ecstatically about her "Dream Lover." When asked to
divulge more, MacDonald smiles naughtily, "I'm afraid I can't. It's

not just exactly the sort of dream for a Queen." Virginia asks excitedly, "Was it the sort of dream for a lady-in-waiting?" MacDonald snaps, "I hope not!" A matronly attendant announces that *she* had a lovely dream in which the Queen got married. MacDonald pulls a sour face. "You call *that* a lovely dream?" she demands. The film romps merrily along as MacDonald meets playboy Chevalier. Their adjustment to royal matrimony was just the kind of thing Lubitsch liked to toy with. Virginia sweeps in and out of the film always catching the viewer's eye. Another screen hopeful, Jean Harlow, is easily recognizable in a scene at the opera. *The Love Parade* garnered six Oscar nominations. During filming, Virginia struggled with her first line, and received a thorough ribbing from cast and crew. Lubitsch coached her, while she nervously parroted his thick German accent, saying, "Vas eet a nice dream, your Majesty?" Over the years whenever the two met, Lubitsch greeted her with, "Vas eet a nice dream, your Majesty?" A few months after the film's release, Virginia was posing coyly between *real* royalty for the press. Prince Leopolde of Prussia (monocled cousin of Kaiser Wilhelm) and his life-long friend and traveling companion Baron Frederic Cerrini of Berlin requested a photo with Virginia while on tour of the Paramount lot.[19]

Virginia stayed exclusively at Paramount except for a bit at First National in Corinne Griffith's unsuccessful talkie debut, *Lilies of the Field* (1930). Fifth-billed in director Louis Gasnier's *Slightly Scarlet* (1930), it was obvious that Virginia was unsure of herself as an actress, except while vocalizing at the piano. She plays the daughter of a wealthy American businessman (Eugene Palette) and his wife (Helen Ware), who occupy themselves trying to impress a phony countess (Evelyn Brent). While her parents discuss Virginia's singing lessons, Ware's fabulously expensive pearl necklace catches the eye of Countess Brent, who attempts to purloin the real pearls for fake ones. *The New York Times* thought the mediocre little film "far and away the best motion picture with which Mr. Gasnier has been connected."[20] On the set, columnist Julie Lang Hunt made a ten-dollar bet with Clive Book (Evelyn Brent's partner-in-crime in *Slightly Scarlet*) that Virginia "would never make the grade in pictures." Hunt quoted Brook as being the only person to protest loudly that Virginia "had something." "You could discover it for yourselves," Brook argued, "if you'd only take the time someday to really look at her and talk with her." Hunt countered,

> But to the rest of the studio gang, Virginia was simply a duplicate of the usual inexperienced, unskilled stock player who, usually … stayed with the studio six months or a year and then vanished pitifully into the town's back streets. . . . My feeling for her then was a strange mixture of pity and anger. Why, I raged silently the day she sat in my publicity office offering me her meager little life story . . . do studio executives taunt a kid like this with illusions of stardom? Why do her parents permit her to enter the world's most competitive, difficult and sophisticated game without a single weapon, without poise or training or even a slight knowledge of life? Why, I wondered, should this sweet, giggling, talent-less seventeen-year-old [sic] be sentenced to Hollywood's rack to be tortured and broken by future humiliations, snubs and despairs?[21]

It wasn't long before Clive Brook dropped by Hunt's office and paid off their bet. Virginia would look back on this time referring to herself in the third person. "That other Virginia Bruce fresh from Fargo," she mused, "never did make the grade. She was a failure, and yet, I'm quite fond of her." Virginia said her friendship with Brook made her frustration and inexperience more bearable. "I was working in a very small part with Evelyn Brent in *Slightly Scarlet*," she recalled,

Clive, who was playing the lead in the picture and an utter stranger to me, took me aside one day and helped me conquer a few pesky lines. The director was, as usual, bawling me out. Besides some priceless coaching, Clive gave me some wonderful advice, and he tried to force some self-confidence into me. I remember how he used to repeat his belief in my ability to be a good actress. He told me that I had talent, but that study and hard work were the only course ahead of me if I really wanted to make good. And then one day, just before I was 'let out,' he warned me not to let any of the cruelty of the Hollywood system grind me to pieces. He said, 'Never let yourself get hard or bitter. Some people can give in to such emotions but not you. You must never, never lose your gift of gentleness.'"[22]

Buddy Rogers surrounded by (l-r) Josephine Dunn, Virginia Bruce, Carole Lombard, and Kathryn Crawford in *Safety in Numbers (1930)* (Paramount)

Virginia gave a more focused performance as the purring coquette and fiancée of Gary Cooper in the Civil War romance *Only the Brave* (1930). She effectively establishes her wily character (Elizabeth) before Union army officer Cooper shows up to discover her in the arms of a new lover (Freeman Wood). Cooper offers a stormy look instead of the fresh bouquet of flowers he intended to give her. Her effete lover huffs, "You may take advantage of me if you wish, sir. I'm physically unfit!" As the embittered Cooper leaves Virginia's residence, he encounters her little sister at the gate. He gives her the flowers. "Didn't Elizabeth like 'em?" the girl asks. "No!" replies Cooper. "She prefers pansies!"

Virginia was then cast in two features with Buddy Rogers, William Wellman's aviation flick *Young Eagles* (1930), a companion piece to the Oscar-winning *Wings*, and *Safety in Numbers* (1930). Wellman was encouraging to Virginia during her downfall at Paramount. "Gosh, every actress goes through this," he said. "If you haven't a few scars to show, how the dickens are you going to become a convincing dramatic actress? Lead with your chin kid." In *Safety in Numbers* gold-digger Carole Lombard sizes Virginia up saying, "It isn't *natural* for a girl to be so nice!" They were among a comely quintet of girls that rich heir Rogers falls for (hence, the title). Apparently, Buddy was the prettiest of the bunch. *Time Magazine* noted that Rogers once again "manipulates his long-eyelashes successfully."[24] Virginia was in awe of her male co-stars, stating, "I used to giggle whenever Gary Cooper or Buddy Rogers so much as looked in my direction. If they said a civil 'good morning' I was practically pulverized with nervous joy. … I used to dream about their asking me for dates, but they never did. That snicker of mine, no doubt, scared them away."[25]

Before the studio's all-star *Paramount on Parade* (1930) began filming, William Beaudine came to Virginia's rescue once more and urged Paramount to give her a singing test.[26] It paid off. Virginia was featured in two of the film's Technicolor sequences and not without distinction. The opening number, "We're the Showgirls," was sung by Virginia backed by a chorus of beauties. In the second sequence,

Ronald Colman is tempted for a few seconds between Kay
Francis and Virginia Bruce in *Raffles (1930)* (United Artists)

Virginia joined other cast members in the song "Let's Drink to the
Girl of My Dreams." Harrison Carroll, for the *LA Evening Herald*,
wrote, "Offering no startling departures, but consistently amusing
and pleasing to the eye is *Paramount on Parade*. To this writer, the
most beautiful thing in . . . *Parade* is the 'Dream Girl' sequence, in
which appear Richard Arlen, Mary Brian, Gary Cooper, Fay Wray,
Virginia Bruce . . . the scene is one of fluid artistry . . . exquisite."[27]
Virginia's next film assignment was a big letdown. She was seen
only briefly as an attractive snob in Jack Oakie's *The Social Lion*
(1930). Were things looking up yet? Apparently, not.

During the summer of 1930 Virginia was fading into film
oblivion. *Safety in Numbers* (released after *Parade*) had been her
last credited part. Her next four features would amount simply
to what she would refer later to as being "an adornment" with
no name. Going onto the set of Samuel Goldwyn's *Raffles* (1930)
was typical. Virginia is seen interrupting a nightclub rendezvous
between Kay Francis and Ronald Colman. Looking svelte in dark
satin, elegantly scalloped with sequin accents, Bruce asks Fran-

cis, "Have dinner next week?" "Love to!" reports Francis cheerily. Virginia focuses directly on Colman and demands boldly, "Bring *him*. I'm mad about him!" A very confident Francis smiles, "So am I!" (Indeed, Francis herself had to hold back from heartthrob Colman *after* the cameras stopped turning. "God! Ronnie excites me!" she noted in her infamous personal diaries.)

Back at Paramount in Leo McCarey's musical anomaly *Let's Go Native* (1930), Virginia played secretary to old curmudgeon actor Charles Sellon. After handing Sellon an important wire, she completely disappears from the film. Virginia later reflected on her time at Paramount. "I didn't push myself . . . I went to their coaching school and learned very little. I was absolutely unprepared for progress . . . You couldn't call me stupid, but I'm the type who has grown up mentally very slowly. So, I was let go at Paramount, and . . . I began to be sorry I hadn't tried to learn more on the lot.[28] Fortunately, Samuel Goldwyn offered Virginia "new hope" by assigning her, along with Paulette Goddard, Betty Grable and Ann Sothern, to be a "Goldwyn Girl" in *Whoopee!* (1930). The film, shot in May and June of 1930, was a two-strip Technicolor version of Ziegfeld's Broadway hit starring Eddie Cantor.

Florenz Ziegfeld had a huge hit on his hands with the Broadway production of *Whoopee!* and it played to packed houses. However, his losses in the stock market crash of 1929 made it necessary to close the show and sell the movie rights to producer Sam Goldwyn. It was the only way Ziegfeld could bail himself out of debt. *Whoopee!* included the classic Walter Donaldson/ Gus Kahn songs "Makin' Whoopee" and "My Baby Just Cares

For Me." The film's director was another transplant from North Dakota, Thornton Freeland. The fetching costumes were designed by John Harkrider. *Whoopee!* was Harkrider's fifth show for Ziegfeld. Luckily for Virginia, Harkrider would prove to be an important connection, as he later took her under his wing. On location in Palm Springs, Harkrider designed costumes to adorn Virginia and a host of other "Goldwyn Girls." Virginia is easily recognizable in the film's finale, "Song of the Setting Sun" (sung by the first Native American to sing at the Met, baritone Chief Caupolican). Wearing a massive black-feathered headdress and cape that must have cost the lives of hundreds of eagles, we see her make a graceful descent toward the camera. She gradually opens her cape and displays a dazzling smile in close-up. The film's musical numbers were created from the imagination of legendary choreographer Busby Berkeley. The end result was a $2,300,000 box-office bonanza.

Had it not been for John Harkrider, Virginia's film career might have proved as uneventful as her next fleeting bit, in a ladies locker room for Paramount's *Follow Thru* (1930). The film's only claim to fame was the hit song "Button Up Your Overcoat." Before filming began, she was demoted without warning to the rank of an extra. Her option with Paramount was not to be renewed. However, Broadway beckoned. Virginia explained how this happened:

> I hadn't then learned to work for my roles so, after a few casual parts, I was no longer under contract. Then I met Jack Harkrider, designer for Ziegfeld who was picking gals for the picture *Whoopee*. I landed a job in this picture and although during the final weeks I was suffering from appendicitis,

September 17, 1930 – Arriving in New York with two other Hollywood
Ziegfeld Girls, Claire Dodd and Christine Maple. The press release stated,
"Ziegfeld picked them out of all the many beauties in cinema land."

> I stuck it out and then underwent an operation
> When I got back on my feet, I really needed money.
> I wrote to Harkrider who was in New York for
> the show *Smiles*. The group was exploited as gals
> Ziegfeld had selected from Hollywood and we were
> treated royally.[29]

So, Virginia headed to New York. "I wasn't afraid, just over-whelmed," said Virginia. "If I had come straight from Fargo I'd probably have dropped in my tracks. But Hollywood had broken the journey. . . . A theatrical agent who went along on the train with me said that all I had to do was be reasonably innocent. . . . Ziggy was awfully nice to his girls, treating them even better than the principals. He'd give them lingerie left by a salesman, and was always saying, 'don't work the kids too hard.' Sometimes at rehearsal we'd dance till we were ready to drop."[30] The Ziegfeld gals may have been treated "royally" by producer Ziegfeld, but the show's star, Marilyn Miller, was another story. During the 1920s audiences discovered Miss Miller's dancing to be akin to a "thistledown angel." One hit followed another. Ziegfeld spared no expense to showcase her. Miller was also his part-time mistress, and consequently got away with a lot. When Ziegfeld brought his five-year-old daughter, Patricia, backstage during a matinee performance of *Sally*, the little girl got an earful. Miller was seated at her dressing table wearing her heavily bugle-beaded costume. "Hello, Marilyn," Ziegfeld said. "Hello, you lousy son-of-a-bitch. Hello, you no-good bastard!" she fired back. Ziegfeld calmly inquired, "What seems to be the trouble, Marilyn dear? Is something bothering you?" Miss Miller sneered, "You goddamn well know what's bothering me! It's this piece of crap you call a costume. I've told you a thousand times it weights a ton, and as far as I'm concerned you can take it and shove it up your ass!"[31] By the time *Smiles* opened at the Ziegfeld Theatre on November 18, 1930, Virginia (who was in the chorus) had assimilated plenty of "atmosphere." And, it would pay off a few years later when she played the temperamental star in *The Great Ziegfeld*.

Ann Sothern (also from North Dakota and billed as Harriette Lake) originally had a featured role in *Smiles*. Cast member Larry Adler recalled, "Miss Lake didn't last long; her song 'Blue Bowery' was too well-received in Boston. Marilyn Miller told Ziegfeld that she wanted Miss Lake out and out she was."[32] Miller's antics aside, *Smiles*, a musical-comedy set during WWI, was blasted by the critics and only lasted 63 performances. The thin storyline had Miller (as a universally acclaimed star) falling in love with a soldier who had rescued her from deprivation. In the mix were Fred Astaire and his sister Adele playing high-society snobs. *Time Magazine* thought the Astaires to be the show's highlight, saying, "The most risible part of the program is supplied by the Astaires when they cavort in front of a small-town band."[33] All that truly lingered from the show was Vincent Youmans' hit "Time On My Hands."

Ironically, Virginia's first night out after her arrival in the Big Apple was with, as she recalled, "a boy from my home town, Glen Oslman, of Fargo. We went to the Stork Club for dinner. . . . All the parties I went to were interesting, with men like William Rhinelander Stewart, Jock Whitney [both socially prominent multi-millionaires], and Louis Bromfield, who autographed one of his books for me [Bromfield's most popular book would be *The Rains Came*]. They all treated me as a human being, not just a Ziegfeld girl."[34] New York wasn't all a party for Virginia. Sharing a cramped apartment, she sent half of her weekly $90 salary home to California. Her budget, after living expenses, did not allow for a winter coat she badly needed. She kept her chin up, though, and was rewarded when a friend gave her a new coat for Christmas. It wasn't that Virginia didn't have "opportunities" for more luxurious surroundings. "Once I had to be on my guard," said Virginia. "A man who lived at a fashionable hotel suggested I would be more comfortable there and that he would be happy to make arrangements for a pleasant suite of rooms which I would have all to myself. I thanked him for his unselfish generosity, but explained I preferred my humble quarters because they were near the theatre. He never mentioned the matter again and continued to be very nice and sweet to me. This simply went to prove that a girl could take care of herself by being sensible."[35]

"All the time I was in New York I couldn't afford an evening dress," said Virginia. "So when I was asked anywhere I'd find out if people were going to dress, and if they were I wouldn't go."[36] She threw her stubborn pride aside, however, and borrowed an evening frock when William Rhinelander Stewart asked her to accompany him to a brilliant ball. After an unsuccessful all-day search for formal foot gear, Virginia bit her lip and called to cancel their date. Stewart sputtered a reply, but Virginia hung up. "An hour later a box containing a beautiful pair of golden sandals from New York's smartest shop arrived with a note from Stewart begging her to accept them in place of a corsage and to meet him promptly in the lobby at nine."[37] She did. The story circulated among the smart set with which Virginia was mingling, and strangely enough they liked it. Virginia managed to stave off despair and remained positive and enthused about Broadway. Her candid friendship with Adele Astaire provided an opportunity to expand her cultural horizons and strengthen her self-confidence. Virginia recalled:

> Through Adele I met such people as Neysa
> McMein, the artist, Clifton Webb, the actor
> and Conde Nast, the publisher. And this group
> suddenly swept me off to such things as art
> exhibits, museums, lectures and concerts. Before
> the winter was over I had discovered a whole new
> world populated with such people as Gauguin, Van
> Gogh, Revel and DeBussy. And I also made the
> discovery that conversation can be an art, that it
> can be a brilliant, exciting adventure. My giggle, I

found was a very inadequate weapon with which to meet the darts of words and wit that swirled around me at those New York gatherings. I still wonder why people put up with me at first. But for some strange reason, these new friends regarded me as an adult, one with grown-up intelligence, and they asked for and actually listened to my opinions on any subject that happened to be under the fire of discussion. Not once did anyone smile at one of my observations, no matter how immature its import. I was accepted cordially and in time I felt the warmth of self-confidence in my veins for the first time in my life. It helped me learn how to enter a room without the usual recoil of shyness, how to accept introductions and compliments and how to execute them. That winter in New York was one of the most important periods in my life. It did more for me than a dozen finishing schools and a university degree. It taught me how to grow up graciously.[38]

Adele Astaire's admiration of Virginia was evidenced by her gift of a gold bracelet made of Chinese coins — a memento of their friendship. Adele presented it to Virginia with the hope that she "would always retain her naïve, straight-forward honesty and open frankness."[39] Virginia posed for portrait artist Neysa Mc-Mein, who created the original image for culinary icon Betty Crocker, and virtually every cover of *McCall's* magazine from 1923-37. Her portrait of Virginia graced a popular magazine cover. (McMein's portraiture included Presidents Harding and Hoover, Anne Morrow Lindbergh, Edna St Vincent Millay, et al.)

McMein, a "member" of the Algonquin club, invited Virginia to her Long Island home, introducing her to more of the bohemian crowd.

After *Smiles* closed, Virginia was cast in her second Broadway venture. Both she and Ann Sothern signed for the Rodgers and Hart production of *America's Sweetheart*.[40] "I went into *America's Sweetheart* as a showgirl and understudy to the star [Inez Courtney]," recalled Virginia.[41] Producer Lawrence Schwab cast her in a minor role as Miss Mulligan. He remembered Ann Sothern's success during the Boston run of *Smiles*, and gave her the lead of a young hopeful who goes to Hollywood. This ironic casting, of two ex-Hollywood "hopefuls," must have pleased the play's songwriters, Rodgers and Hart, who had just returned from their first film assignment on the West Coast. *America's Sweetheart* was a well-fueled spoof of their Tinseltown experience, in which Sothern's character becomes a silent film star, only to have her career tailspin when talkies arrive. She is cursed with a lisp and a nasal twang. (Echoes of Lina Lamont, in the 1952 film classic *Singin' in the Rain*.)

After tryouts in Pittsburgh and Washington, D.C., *America's Sweetheart* (directed by Monty Woolley) opened at New York's Broadhurst Theatre on February 10, 1931 and proved a modest success. It ran for 17 weeks. Reviews were mixed. *The New York World* reported it as being "Rough, tough and very funny." *The New York Times* found the wit clumsy and the humor foul, but enjoyed the Rodgers and Hart score. At one point, Virginia got a lot of attention, but *not* because of her role. "America's Boy Friend," Buddy Rogers, who would eventually marry *the* "America's Sweetheart," Mary Pickford, attended one of the matinees. Although Virginia appeared in several films with him, she doubted that Buddy would give her a second glance. Given her cue, Virginia came out dancing before the spotlight. Looking down into the front row — there sat Buddy. He caught her eye, making faces and "gesticulating with his hands." Virginia laughed afterwards, "For days after that I was the 'big shot.' Those kids in the company couldn't get over my knowing Buddy Rogers, and I had a full time job attempting to prove to them that I was really thrilled to think that he had remembered me."[42] Quite unexpectedly, Virginia's role was "expanded" . . . for one performance. Two chorus girls, each assigned one line, started slugging each other in the dressing room. Virginia cowered in a corner, while the two fought tooth and nail. "[The fight] was over a fake Count for whose dubious affections they were rivals," recalled Virginia. "Chairs and tables were knocked over as the two of them screamed and clawed and tore each other's hair."[43] Virginia admitted, "I get terrified when women fight. It's different when men sock each other—seems more natural—but the sight of women doing it?"[44] A frantic stage manager appeared to separate

May 12, 1936: Virginia was elected as President of the "Glorified Ziegfeld Girls Club" in Hollywood. (l-r) Christine Maple '31; Ethel Shutta '29; Virginia Bruce '31; Hazel Forbes '31; Helen Callghan '32; Frances DuBarry '09; May Lang '32

the two, and offered both of their lines to Virginia. Summing up her New York experience a few years later, Virginia mused:

> In New York everyone was wonderful to me. I was probably the dumbest girl who ever had hit Broadway.[45]. . . I wasn't regretful about pictures, because it was the first time I'd ever been away from home. Homesick? Why, I enjoyed the freedom from my family, I'm afraid. Though, understand, I get along swell with my family! Anyway, New York was fun; it was the big city. John Harkrider, who was Mr. Ziegfeld's set designer, promised dad to watch out for me. He and Mr. Ziegfeld and I had dinner together often, and they valiantly saw that no harm came to Little Nellie, who was terribly naïve and thrilled silly when she rated her first trip through Chinatown. I was in two Broadway shows, I was in the chorus of the first one and had only a small bit in the second, and then it closed and it seemed best to return home . . . I cried when I left New York. No, Mr. Ziegfeld didn't offer to make me a star. He wasn't interested enough—yet later I was cast as one of his typical temperamental ladies, in the movie version of Ziegfeld.[46]

When *America's Sweetheart* closed, Virginia headed back to Hollywood. But this time it was only for a visit. She had signed to do another Broadway show that fall. While in Hollywood, however, agent Nat Goldstone saw Virginia in the anteroom at Columbia studios waiting for an interview. Goldstone immediately lined up a screen test (opposite newcomer Robert Young) for her at

Metro.[47] MGM producer Irving Thalberg saw the test and took interest in her potential. Reporter Jack Smalley noted that Thalberg felt "sure that there was something deep inside this girl worth bringing out."[48] Virginia was given a scene in MGM's *Hell Divers* starring Wallace Beery and Clark Gable.

Robert Young supposedly took a liking to Virginia. He squired her around town until she left for New York via Fargo. Young's attentions, tinged with studio publicity, came to nothing. Virginia found the studio environment lacking and was eager to leave. En route to the east coast she visited Fargo. Virginia happily told *Forum* reporter Henry J. Hurley that she liked New York's Broadway better than she did Hollywood's movie colony. Why did she prefer the stage? "Your paycheck is more certain," she explained. "You meet more people," she added. "Friendships are more lasting. One gets more time for laughter, more time for chatting with friends. The screen keeps one so busy. There's little time for conversation and the constantly changing cast means that the person on the lot today may never be seen again. And then there's the long hours. Maybe one is ordered to report for work at 6:30 in the morning and will have to remain until late in the afternoon. Evening comes and one's too tired to go out."[49] Hurley asked if she had been in love yet, which brought out a real laugh from Virginia. "No," she smiled. "It seems funny too. All my friends here are married. I feel like the old maid of the bunch."[50]

After a two-day outing "at the lakes" in nearby Shoreham, Minnesota with her aunt and uncle (H.E. Magill), Virginia's manager called and beckoned her *back* to Hollywood telling her to "come at once." MGM was interested. Her screen test with Robert Young had won her a contract. Virginia had already signed for a part on Broadway for the Schwab and Mandel production, *East*

Wind. She was looking forward to rehearsals. "I didn't want to go back at all," Virginia recalled. "In fact, I cried all day at the prospect! I said I wouldn't go back, I was going to New York, and to New York I went. But at the end of a week I was on my way west."[51] She quipped, "If you can make hard-crusted New Yorkers take you seriously why not hard-crusted Hollywoodians?"[52] By the end of August, Virginia had signed a long-term contract with MGM.[53] Thalberg had decided to use Virginia for the brazen female lead in one of Hollywood's most notorious pre-Code shockers.

Endnotes

1 "Star Gazing at Virginia Bruce," *Charleston Daily Mail*, 6/29/30

2 Margaret Briggs, "My Daughter . . ."

3 Margaret Dixe, "Hollywood's Heart Problems — *and Yours*," *Movie Classic* ?/35

4 "North Dakota Girl Signs to Enter Movies," *Bismarck Tribune*, 12/4/1928

5 Fargo Library Archive, news article, "Fargoan Gets Movie Chance," 12/2/28

6 "North Dakota Girl . . ."

7 Erskine Johnson, "In Hollywood," *Dunkirk Evening Observer*, 10/30/44

8 "Call Wins Chance in Filmland," *LA Times*, 11/27/28

9 "The Tattler" *Kansas City Star*, 6/16/29

10 Fargo Library Archive, Marie Canel, "Determined Not to Let Divorce Embitter Life," news article, 6/3/34

11 James Robert Parish and Ronald L. Bowers, *The MGM Stock Company*, Arlington House (New York), 1973, pp. 94-97

12 Fargo Library Archive, news article, "Paramount Signs Fargoan," 6/16/29

13 Dan Thomas, "Pretty Fargo Girl Shining in Movies Prefers Love to Fame," *Bismarck Tribune*, 6/25/29

14 Dan Thomas, "North Dakota Girl Got Ahead in Movies Despite Adversity," *Bismarck Tribune*, 11/29/30

15 Thomas, "Pretty Fargo Girl . . ."

16 ibid

17 Robbin Coons, "Realizes Sweet Revenge," *Olean Herald* (New York), 10/29/29

18 "Virginia Bruce Learned To Take It On Hazardous Climb to Film Fame," *Vidette-Messenger*, 5/22/37

19 "Royalty Visits film Studio," *LA Times*, 2/28/30

20 Mordaunt Hall, review for *Slightly Scarlet*, 3/1/30

21 Julie Lang Hunt, "How a Sleeping Beauty Awoke to Glamour," *Photoplay*, 10/36

22 ibid

23 ibid

24 review for *Young Eagles, Time* 4/7/30

25 Hunt, "How a Sleeping ..."

26 Kay Proctor, "Virginia Tells What Her Life Might Have Been -- IN FARGO," *The Fargo Forum*, 4/16/38

27 review for *Paramount on Parade, LA Evening Herald*, 4/25/30

28 Ben Maddox, "Girls Don't Be Too Clever," *Screenland*, 4/39

29 Linda Lane, "Virginia Bruce Resents Phrase 'Beauty Is Dumb,'" *Oakland Tribune*, 12/6/36

30 Charles Darnton, "Follies Girl's Days and Nights," *Screenland*, 6/36

31 Patricia Ziegfeld, *The Ziegfeld's Girl*, Boston: Little Brown & Co., 1964, pp. 183-184

32 Tom Vallance, *Obituary: Ann Sothern, The Independent* (London), 3/19/2001

33 review of *Smiles, Time Magazine*, 12/1/30

34 Darnton, "Follies . . . "

35 ibid

36 ibid.

37 Hunt, "How a Sleeping . . . "

38 ibid

39 ibid

40 Fargo Library Virginia Bruce Archive, "Has Comedy Role," 1/25/31

41 Lane, "Virginia Bruce Resents . . . "

42 Fargo Library Virginia Bruce Archive, news article (date unknown)

43 Charles Darnton, "Follies . . . ."

44 Katharine Roberts, "Who? . . . Me?" *Modern Screen*, 5/41

45 "Everybody Helps This Blond," *Oakland Tribune*, 12/1/40

46 Maddox, "'Girls Don't Be . . . "

47 Elizabeth Wilson, "Projections of Virginia Bruce," *Silver Screen*, 11/38

48 Jack Smalley, "Nothing Can Hurt Her Now!" *Screen Book*, March 1935

49 Fargo Library Archive, Henry J. Hurley, "'It's Great to be Back,' Says Virginia (Briggs) Bruce, 8/9/31

50 Fargo Library Archive, news article (date unknown)

51 Ibid.

52 Hunt, "How a Sleeping . . . "

53 "Screen Siftings," *Lincoln Star* (Nebraska), 9/6/31

CHAPTER FOUR:

The Virgin & "The Great Lover"

1932 (MGM)

Soon after Virginia returned from New York, MGM's top producer, Irving Thalberg, put her to the test -- seven of them. He envisioned her as an ambitious girl named Lil, who climbs a ladder of beds to wealth and happiness, in an adaptation of Katharine Bush's outrageous novel, *Red-Headed Woman*. A clever script had been prepared by Anita Loos. The timing was right. In two more years the film industry's new Production Code would never have allowed such a "scandalous" script to see the light of day. Would Virginia's arduous screen testing pay off? Audiences of 1932 that were allowed to witness the completed film (it was banned in Britain), saw the handsome, virile Chester Morris vigorously slap Lil's face. She gasps ecstatically and announces, "I *like* it — do it again!" But the face in question turned out not to be that of Virginia Bruce, but Jean Harlow. Harlow's brassy edge was the quality the studio was looking for. Virginia later admitted, "Jean Harlow won the part and great fame. That jolt woke me up. I began to study. . . . Everything I did was toward learning how to act."[1]

When the MGM "hit" *Hell Divers* was released in late 1931, Virginia's vivid love scene with Clark Gable ended up on the cutting room floor. Years later, columnist Jimmy Fidler recalled Virginia's difficultly with the scene, and Marjorie Rambeau coming to her aid with several suggestions that resulted in a "perfect take." "After Virginia had thanked her profusely," said Fidler, "Marjorie turned to me with a half smile. 'Unfortunately,' she said, 'by the time an actress acquires perfect technique in scenes like these, she's too old to use her knowledge.'"[2] During Virginia's test marathon for *Red-Headed Woman,* she was supposedly allotted an uncredited bit in the controversial, anti-Prohibition film *The Wet Parade* (1932). Virginia's bit was a precursor to her role in *The Invisible Woman.* If you look hard enough, you can't find her. Some sources credit Bruce with another unbilled appearance, in Williams Haines' *Are You Listening?* (1932*).* Oddly enough, after these non-roles, Paramount came to her rescue.

In February 1932, reporter Jimmy Starr announced, "Apparently, the public, like gentlemen, prefer blondes. Virginia Bruce, once described by none other than Mr. Florenz Ziegfeld as 'the most beautiful blonde,' is fast climbing that elusive ladder of film fame and fortune." Starr continued the publicity hype saying, "Once again Paramount . . . has borrowed her from MGM, the firm which now boasts her long term signature, for a featured role in *Sky Bride* . . . replacing Frances Dee. Some months ago Paramount permitted the option of Miss Bruce's services to lapse due to a sort of over-supply of blondes. Carole Lombard and Lilyan Tashman . . . being in the featured class, got all the breaks, but it appears now that Miss Bruce is going to get hers after all."[3]

Gossip columns added to Virginia's visibility saying she had been "out places" with the handsome young actor William Bakewell, and had resumed her tête-à-têtes with Robert Young.

Columnist Harrison Carroll wagged, "Saw Virginia Bruce, that tall, good-looking blonde, lunching with four 17-year-old boys at MGM. Rushed over to hiss 'Cradle snatcher,' but it turns out they were her brother and his friends."[4] Stanley Briggs, who was turning nineteen and about to attend UCLA, was building a steady reputa-

Hockey anyone? Anita Page joins Virginia in a publicity shot 1932 (MGM)

tion as an ace tennis player. He acquitted himself well on the courts throughout the 1930s. (In 1939, the Motion Picture Tennis Tourney Championship finals put Stanley up against screen hero Errol Flynn. Bets were on Errol. When Errol dropped out of the final round, making excuses, the press declared, "Errol Flynn dropped the final round ... for no other reason except that Stanley Briggs beat him.")[5]

Back on the Paramount lot, Virginia tackled a small, but effective role in *The Miracle Man*, a definite improvement over what she had been handed at her new "prestige" studio, MGM. In *Miracle Man*, adapted from a George M. Cohan play, conman Chester Morris and his gang retreat to a small town to outsmart a faith healer. *The Los Angeles Times* thought Virginia was "effective" as a young crippled woman who is truly cured by the healer. She is featured in several scenes, and convincingly enacts arising from a wheelchair to regain the use of her legs. It is her "miracle" that turns Morris' gang into believers. The film holds attention throughout, in spite of the uninspired performance of film pioneer Hobart Bosworth in the title role.

Sky Bride was an adaptation of a story by Bogart Rogers (brother of writer Adela Rogers St. Johns). Bogart, a WWI lieutenant in the Royal Flying Corps., wrote with skill and intelligence about flying. Although Virginia's face was prominently featured in the ads, the title referred not to *her*, but aviation ace Richard Arlen's plane. Arlen is part of a barnstorming troupe, and we witness some amazing daredevil flying sequences. (Tragically, stunt flier Leo Nomis was killed doing a spin-around during filming at the Metropolitan Airport in Los Angeles.) After Arlen's best friend is killed in a mock aviation dogfight, Arlen disappears, determined never to fly again. He roams the countryside, trying to resolve his remorse and guilt. Virginia, as Ruth (billed fourth), comes into the story when Arlen wanders into her father's aviation business looking for work. Surprisingly, the only real romance in *Sky Bride* is between Arlen and his devoted buddy, Jack Oakie. The lovelorn Oakie searches until he tracks Arlen down and manages to coax him out of his depression. Their reunion is consummated with a touchy-feely romp in Arlen's boarding house bedroom. When their affectionate horseplay gets out-of-hand, the camera modestly pans to the dining room ceiling below. We see the dinner guests glancing toward the swaying chandelier and trying to decide whether the two pals are in the heat of passion, or merely engaged in a friendly tussle. The next scene shows a tearful Oakie "explaining" Arlen to Virginia. "If he don't fly," says Oakie, "he just can't live!" Virginia studies Oakie curiously and replies, "You kind of like him, don't you?" "Like my right arm!" swears Oakie. Virginia nods her approval and Oakie gushes, "Gee, Ruth, you're a swell guy!"

The New York Times decided, "*Sky Bride* falls short of being

Sky Bride (1932) (l-r) Jack Oakie, Richard Arlen, Virginia,
Charles Starrett (Paramount)

good entertainment . . . several of the flying scenes are unnec-
essarily lengthy."[6] Louella Parsons' review commented, "Miss
Bruce manages to be a presence despite the limitations of the
role."[7] The *Los Angeles Times* pointed out, "Virginia Bruce gives
a very restrained performance – too restrained, it would seem. A
little more expression would do wonders for her."[8] Before either
of her Paramount films were released (April 1932), Virginia had
her best offer yet from Warner Brothers.

In late February 1932, production began on the new James
Cagney feature *Winner Take All*, in which he played a cocky prize-
fighter who prefers blondes. Cagney's bouts in the ring are performed convincingly and justify the ads which read, "Tarzan was
a sissy compared to him!" After a successful Cagney fight, thrill-
seeker Virginia Bruce requests to meet him in his locker room.

He is immediately smit-
ten. When they smooch,
Virginia almost knocks
Cagney "out." "You could
stand a cold drink after
that one, couldn't you?"
she purrs. In truth, Vir-
ginia is only mildly
amused and toys with
Cagney's affections.
She's the type that's
never satisfied. This

Winner Take All (1932) with
James Cagney (Warners)

makes her even more interesting to him (and the audience). At
her suggestion, Cagney enlists a plastic surgeon to repair his lopsided nose. After the surgery, he is obsessed with protecting his
face. He becomes a "powder puff" in the ring and he *loses* face
with Virginia and the public. In the end, two-timing Virginia gets
her comeuppance when Cagney boots her soundly in the rump
and into the arms of her next victim. Although Cagney returns to
brunette Marion Nixon in the finale, it's in his scenes with Virginia
that he is allowed to run the full gamut of his trademark punch
and power. In its review of *Winner Take All*, Hollywood Citizen
News compared fifth-billed Virginia to the sugary-sweet lead
Marion Nixon saying, "Virginia Bruce is equally good as the cold,
thrill-seeking society-girl."[9] In truth, Virginia was a welcome relief
from Nixon's cloying personality, and she registers her character's
emotional conflicts with admirable skill. The *Zanesville Times Recorder* (Ohio) called Bruce, "a beautiful newcomer to the screen
who acquits herself nobly."[10]

On her home lot, Virginia had done nothing more than test
for a crime short with a young hopeful named Arlington Brugh.

(Brugh would eventually give Clark Gable competition at MGM, under the name of Robert Taylor.)[11] Pleased with Virginia's work, Warners asked her to co-star with Douglas Fairbanks, Jr. in a WWI drama titled *Revolt*. Virginia would portray a scheming Russian courtesan whose infatuation with Fairbanks results in tragedy for all concerned. William Dieterle was set to direct. MGM got wind of her good work in *Winner Take All* and refused another loan out. (The Russian "tragedy" was soon retitled *Scarlet Dawn*, and Virginia was replaced by Lilyan Tashman.) Not to worry. MGM found a role that would begin to establish Virginia's abilities as a dramatic actress. It would also bring her face-to-face with her first real taste of romantic love.

Virginia had been on the MGM lot for several months before she saw legendary screen idol John Gilbert. She had been on the lookout for him. "I had never seen John until one day I sat across from him in the commissary," she recalled. "When he looked at me I felt all funny inside. I've never seen eyes so intense and penetrating. I couldn't imagine anyone feeling easy and natural with Mr. Gilbert, and I was sure I wouldn't like him. But later on that same day his car passed me on the lot and he threw

Photographer George Hurrell captures Virginia's new look at the glamour factory MGM – 1932

me a kiss, and then I was sure that I would like him." Virginia was well aware of Gilbert's career problems at MGM, and their initial contact served to fuel emotions that she already held for him. "It's a funny thing," she recalled, "every time I saw him I had just one thought. I thought: 'Oh, I want him to come back again! I want him to be as great as he used to be. . . . I know that 'way back in the days when I was a child in Fargo I used to see him on the screen. In *The Merry Widow* and *The Big Parade* . . . I was always crazy about him."[12] From then on Virginia made a point of sitting in the far corner of the studio commissary with anticipation. As she explained it, "I could look through the window and watch them all as they came out of the sound stages and headed for the lunchroom. In reality, I was on the lookout for only one person. . . ."[13] Virginia's initial "uneasy" reaction to John Gilbert in the commissary should have forewarned her of trouble.

In 1924, John Gilbert (his friends called him Jack) had been one of the first stars to sign an MGM contract. While he developed a close, supportive friendship with the studio's producer Irving Thalberg (some refute this), Gilbert always locked horns with his boss, Louis B. Mayer. Mayer's unrelenting hatred for Gilbert was hardly assuaged by the fact that Gilbert became huge at the box-office. After Valentino died in 1926, Gilbert became *the* "Great Lover" of the silent screen. His teaming with Greta Garbo in *Flesh and the Devil* (1926) was nothing short of sensational. Their director, Clarence Brown, was quoted as saying,

> It was the damnedest thing you ever saw . . .
> When they got into that first love scene . . . well,
> nobody else was even there. Those two were
> alone in a world of   their own. It seemed like
> an intrusion to yell 'cut!' I used to just motion the

crew over to another part of the set and let them
finish what they were doing. It was embarrassing.[14]

Such "embarrassment" brought profits for MGM. Gilbert and
Garbo became a team on and off screen. Garbo moved into Gilbert's house. "Jack helped her enormously," said director Brown.
"He watched everything she did and corrected it. Garbo was so
grateful. She recognized his long experience in the movies and
she hung on his every word."[15] After several proposals of marriage, Garbo agreed to tie the knot on September 9, 1926. It was
rumored to be a double wedding with the officially announced
marriage between director King Vidor and actress Eleanor
Boardman. When the day arrived, Garbo was a no-show. Mayer
was present for the ceremony. During the long wait for the capri-
cious Garbo, he took Gilbert aside and said, "What's the matter with you, Gilbert? What do you have to marry her for? Why
don't you just fuck her and forget about it?"[16] Gilbert went ballistic. He seized Mayer's neck and proceeded to bang his employer's
head against the wall. After the initial shock, other guests pulled
Gilbert off Mayer, who screamed, "You're finished, Gilbert! I'll
destroy you if it costs me a million dollars."[17] It was the beginning
of the end for John Gilbert's screen career.

Things had never gone easily for Gilbert. He was born John
Cecil Pringle on July 10, 1897 in Logan, Utah. His father was a
comic with the Pringle Stock Company. John's mother, Ida, virtually abandoned her son for the stage. John's early years were spent
on the road, or with his devout Mormon grandfather in Logan.
Ida died of tuberculosis when he was thirteen. The last time he
saw her he traveled from a San Rafael military academy to surprise her. It had been months since they had seen each other.
Although he resented things she had done to him, he hoped for

John Gilbert at his home on Tower Road (Courtesy of Vincent Briggs)

reconciliation and a chance to catch her performance in San Francisco. Backstage, he found her drunk and disagreeable. She barely recognized him and snarled, "What the hell are you doing here?"[18] In her clouded mind, for an actress to acknowledge having a teenage son meant death to her career. He left her, unable to contain his tears and disappointment. The stability that Virginia had known growing up had never been available to John Pringle.

At age 16, practically broke, Gilbert (who acquired his new last name from his stepfather) entered the film business. In 1919, he abandoned his job as an apprentice writer (he enjoyed screenwriting) to work in front of the camera. He was on fire with ambition. By 1925, his glowing reviews in von Stroheim's *The Merry Widow* and Vidor's *The Big Parade* established him as a major star. By this time he had been married and divorced, twice. His second marriage was to DeMille star Leatrice Joy. A year later, soon after Leatrice gave birth to their daughter, she divorced Gilbert charging that he was a compulsive philanderer. Off screen, Gilbert seemed starved for the love that had been denied him as a child. Oscar-winning screenwriter Frances Marion "had little patience with his incredibly needy ego."[19]

When Virginia signed on at MGM, Gilbert was married to Broadway actress Ina Claire, and dating Mexican spitfire Lupe Velez. Of course, by this time, an interlocutory decree had been filed by Mrs. Gilbert III, whom he had married on the rebound from Garbo. The marriage was doomed from the start. Ina Claire, like many stage performers, looked down on Hollywood. Gilbert's and Claire's egos collided. When Claire was asked by a reporter how it felt to be married to a great star, she answered haughtily, "I don't know. Why don't you ask Mr. Gilbert?" On their return from a honeymoon in Europe in 1929, the couple battled across the Atlantic, only to be greeted with the news that Gilbert's first sound feature, *His Glorious Night,* was an "unmitigated disaster." Audiences laughed at his ardent love-making and "thin" throaty voice coupled with florid lines like, "I love you. I've told you that a hundred times a week. I love you!" The reviews were scathing. Gilbert was upset and depressed. To her credit, Claire assisted him in using his diaphragm for a more reso-nant sound. "I was the *last* person he wanted to tell him anything about acting," said Claire. The only person that was happy with these turn of events and bad reviews was Louis B. Mayer. "*That* should be the end of Mr. Gilbert," he declared.[20]

Writer Adela Rogers St. Johns was on the set of Gilbert's next picture, *Resurrection* (1930), and recalled, "He was as nervous and unsure of himself as a man could well be . . . he was fighting to keep his self confidence, or to get it back . . . He was afraid of his lines, afraid his voice would break — it was pretty ghastly."[21] The studio did nothing to help the situation and before long, Gilbert "was worth less at the box office than a bag of popcorn."[22] By the time he met Virginia Bruce, Gilbert's contract was about to expire, and he had been unable to retrieve the career that he had lost.

In the spring of 1932, Virginia was asked to make a test for a film based on story that John Gilbert had sold to MGM, *Downstairs.* When asked, Gilbert flatly refused to do a test with a newcomer like Virginia. For him the project required only the best. He had already lost out on having Erich von Stroheim (whom Mayer also disliked) for director. Gilbert had sold *Downstairs* to the studio for only a dollar — that's how badly he wanted the film to be made. The story was then shelved and collected dust for four years. Gil-bert had almost given up on the idea. Virginia recalled,

After the test, Monte Bell, the director, phoned me
to come to his house to discuss the picture, as I had
been decided upon for the part. And there I was
officially introduced to John Gilbert for the first
time. He said some very kind and complimentary
things about my test, and naturally I was very
grateful . . . After the conference he invited me to
play tennis with him that afternoon but I had a date.

But the afternoon before the opening of *Grand
Hotel*, I did go to his home for a game of tennis
with him and several of his friends. I had been
invited to the opening that night but had decided
not to go as I didn't have a dazzling new evening
gown like everyone else. John said he wasn't going
either. So Cedric Gibbons, Barney Glaezer, and
John and I all had dinner together and went to the
'Vanities' instead. I can't remember ever having
so much fun before. Every time John would make
a gallant speech, Cedric and Barney would say,
'Don't believe him, Virginia, that's the way he gets
all his women.' So naturally, I didn't think anything
he said was serious.[23]

The studio considered the part Gilbert wrote for himself to be
too dark, and unsympathetic, but the fact that it was finally to become a reality made Gilbert ecstatic. "I am happier than I have been
in years," he told a reporter, then went on to describe the plot and his
role as Karl, the chauffeur. "It's a psychological study, a cross-section
view of two strata of life . . . the chauffeur is a swaggering Don Juan
who makes up in audacity, what he lacks in conscience. He is an out-
right villain, but nevertheless, a fascinating chap. He will be hated

for his villainy, but he's bound to be interesting."[24] Karl is employed by a Viennese Baron and Baroness on the very day their head butler (Paul Lukas) and their impressionable young maid (Bruce) are to be wed. Almost immediately, Karl shows his true colors by flirting with Bruce. It isn't long before he's blackmailing the Baroness (who is cheating on her husband) and extorting the life-savings from a middle-aged, love-starved cook. Director Monte Bell tackled the assignment with a von Stroheim-like touch (a man he also admired). Upon the film's release *Time* magazine gave a rave review and noted the "audiences' mounting pleasure as the busy chauffeur piles outrage on dirty trick." The review praised Gilbert's career turn, saying, "When John Gilbert found that he had ceased to be a hero, he resolved to turn villain. The brilliance of his strategy is plain in this picture, which he wrote himself, sold for $1."[25] *The New York Times* praised the Gilbert-Bruce team. "The chief points of interest in it," noted critic Mordaunt Hall, "are Mr. Gilbert's somewhat ingenuous attempt to impersonate a rascally automobile driver and Virginia Bruce's charming presence."[26] *Downstairs* was, without a doubt, the best sound feature of Gilbert's career and his performance should have put a permanent halt to the encroaching rumor that his voice was high-pitched or feminine.

There are two instances in *Downstairs* that struck a resounding chord for Virginia, and Gilbert. In a riveting scene that should have impressed both Thalberg and Mayer, Virginia took a giant dramatic leap, and landed on her feet. When anti-hero Karl (Gilbert) manages to seduce Anna (Virginia), she is hesitant, yet willing. She is tired of husband Lukas' control and iron-will. Lukas finds out about the affair, and Anna readily confesses to her actions. He does not want to listen. "Now you just wait a minute!" she demands. "I don't deserve to have you and me go all a-smash!" She then tells him everything he does not want to hear.

I found out for the first time in my life . . . for the
first *time* . . . that there are more than two kinds
of feelings in the world. Is that my fault? There's a
way of making love that drives you mad and crazy;
so that you don't know what you're doing. Are you
going to throw me out on the street because I never
knew this before?

Downstairs (1932) with John Gilbert – MGM (Courtesy of Vincent Briggs)

Lukas resists. "Anna. Stop this kind of talk," he cautions. "You've learned something vile from a rat!" With eyes filled with hurt and frustration, she persists,

> Whatever's happened, some of it's *your* fault . . . some of it. You think you can make love in the same frozen way you do everything else. You think that's all *I* should ever have any wish for . . . I meant no harm . . . I don't want anything but you and my home. But, if you're going to be so good and so perfect and so unforgiving . . . I thank heaven that there is something else . . . something that makes you so dizzy you don't know what's happened and you don't care! Now you go ahead and believe anything you like!

Lukas is stunned. It takes the Baroness to remind him that Anna is young and no match for a man like Gilbert. (A truth, as it turned out, that mirrored life.) Virginia is emotionally on cue throughout her confrontation with Lukas, and her heart-wrenching confession was something for her to be proud of as an actress. The film critic for New York's *Syracuse Herald* found her "devastating." "The picture is fine," stated the review, "but Mrs. Gilbert IV, is better."[27] Los Angeles critic Jimmy Starr raved, "Seldom have I witnessed a wild burst of applause for individual scenes by a performer during a showing, except at a premier. However, Virginia Bruce, in a very dramatic and difficult role, received several beautiful tributes at the recent preview. Virginia proves her right to fine roles with a display of histrionic ability that would be worthy only of a cinematic veteran."[28]

In the scene that leads up to Anna's confrontation with Lukas, Gilbert has done a good job of getting her tipsy. He attempts to garner her sympathy in a manner that is uncannily autobiographical for Gilbert. He admits to his lies – and, that he is deserving of her distrust. He tellingly confesses, "Listen, Anna. I never had much of a chance. I never had anyone tell me the right thing to do. I've had to fight my way through life alone. Bad men, bad women. I've never been in love with anyone *good* like you before. I don't know how to treat you."

Lenore Coffee (who adapted the screenplay for *Downstairs* from Gilbert's story) observed on the set that Gilbert stayed "immersed" in the scene and in his part even after the cameras stopped. "All the good ones did that," Coffee recalled. "Jack was by no means an exception. Neither was Virginia. That girl just opened those big blue eyes, and Jack was ready to fall in. It was inevitable. She was so fresh and young and so astonishingly beautiful. She was not by any means a Hollywood regular. She was innocent. She was nothing from the past. And Jack fell madly in love. They both did."[29] The engagement for Gilbert and Bruce was announced during filming on May 25, 1932. The wedding itself would have to wait until August, when Gilbert's divorce from Ina Claire was final.

Virginia noted that it was the ninth day after meeting Gilbert at Monte Bell's home that Gilbert proposed. "It happened on a Saturday afternoon, right in broad daylight," she recalled soon afterwards. "We were sitting near the pool, at his house. And we were sitting quite far apart. Jack was talking to me. Suddenly he said, 'I want you to marry me, Virginia. I want you to be my wife.'"[30] "You could have knocked me over with a ping-pong ball," Virginia laughed. "Here I was, totally unknown, and the greatest man in

Hollywood was asking me to marry him. I became so confused, I stammered, 'Ye-es, Mr. Gilbert'— I was still calling him that."[31] She admitted to being reluctant afterwards, saying, "John is so intelligent and cultured and twice as old as I am. I was afraid he might become bored with me in time. He has been every place and done every thing and is remarkably well read. I led a very sequestered childhood in Fargo and have been working hard to make a living ever since, so I haven't had much time for travel and culture. But I do want to learn, and John is eager to teach me."[32]

It wasn't long before Virginia got a firsthand look at MGM's machinations behind her fiancé's foundering career. After *Downstairs* completed production, Gilbert was given a plum role in *Red Dust* opposite the new screen sensation from *Red-Headed Woman*, Jean Harlow. Gilbert saw it as another golden opportunity to reestablish his career. Soon after production started on *Red Dust*, producer Hunt Stromberg decided that Clark Gable was a better choice for the lead. When informed of the switch, Gilbert was crushed. Bruce later recalled,

> I was working on another picture when Irving
> Thalberg took Jack out of *Red Dust* and put Clark
> Gable in. It nearly killed him. Of course Jack had
> been driven half crazy by the time I married him
> but I didn't know that. I loved him madly. I was very
> young, only twenty-one, and he was thirty-three.
> Jack sent me a telegram at the studio on August
> tenth asking me to come to his dressing room at six
> p.m. for the wedding. I had no more notice than that.
> We were married right on the lot. Irving Thalberg
> and Norma Shearer were our witnesses.

But before that there was all the business about a

Gilbert gave his bride-to-be this luxury
car as an engagement present

marriage contract. My father arranged it, not Jack.
Jack agreed to write a new will leaving everything to
me and my family. In the contract, I was guaranteed
to be a virgin — my father's idea. Jack thought it
was hilarious but I think he was also excited about
it. I don't think he'd known many virgins in his life.
I know this sounds crazy, but my father allowed me
to spend one night with Jack before we were married
so that he could see for himself that I was a virgin.
But he had to promise to return me to my father in
the same pristine condition.

All the time I knew Jack, I never saw him so happy as
when we were shooting *Downstairs*. He had such high
hopes. We were so happy working together. Life was
so full and worth living. All he needed was work. But
then he lost *Red Dust* and the studio had nothing else
for him right away. He owed them one more picture
. . . but they weren't in any hurry to do it.[33]

In Hollywood, reactions to the upcoming nuptials for Gilbert and Bruce were mixed. Years later, director Lewis Milestone (who directed Gilbert in his final film in 1934, *The Captain Hates the Sea*) recalled, "What was so terribly frustrating about Jack was that everything was still there. He was marvelous-looking, he was a splendid actor, with a keen, interesting mind. He was a courteous man, a good friend, but inside was this dark destructive force at work. You couldn't get your hands on it. You couldn't stop it. Then along came Virginia and we all held our breath."[34]

Endnotes

1   Linda Lane, "Virginia Bruce Resents Phrase 'Beauty Is Dumb," *Centralia Chronicle*, 11/27/36

2   Jimmy Fidler, "Fidler in Hollywood," *Nevada State Journal*, 9/11/45

3   Jimmy Starr, column, *LA Evening Herald Express*, 2/12/32

4   Harrison Carroll, "Behind the Screen," *San Mateo Times*, 4/8/32

5   *Oakland Tribune*, 7/16/39

6   Mordaunt Hall, review for *Sky Bride*, *The New York Times*, 4/23/32

7   Louella Parsons review of *Sky Bride*, *LA Examiner*, 5/20/32

8   Review of *Sky Bride*, *LA Times*, 5/21/32

9   Elizabeth Yeaman, review for *Winner Take All*, *Hollywood Citizen News*, 7/8/32

10 Review for *Winner Take All*, *Zanesville Times Recorder*, 7/28/32

11 Axel Madsen, *Stanwyck*, HarperCollins, N.Y., 1994, pg 114

12 Magazine article, author's collection, "Will John Gilbert's Fourth Wife Be Virginia Bruce?" 1932

13 Jerry Asher, "Why Out Marriage Failed!" *Movie Mirror*, 4/34

14 Leatrice Gilbert Fountain, *Dark Star*, St. Martin's Press, NY, 1985, pg 125

15 ibid., pg 126

16 ibid., pg 131

17 ibid.

18 Fountain, pg 13

19 Cari Beauchamp, *Without Lying Down*, Scribner, N.Y., 1997, p194

20 Fountain, pg 186

21 Adela Rogers St. Johns, "The Tragic Truth About John Gilbert's Death," *Photoplay*, 3/36

22 John Bainbridge, *The Great Garbo*, Doubleday

23 Fargo Library Archive, news article, Wes Colman, "Wifely Duty To John Will

Come Before Her Art, Says Virginia," 8/4/32

24 Fountain, pg 225

25 Review for *Downstairs*, *Time*, 8/8/32

26 Review for *Downstairs*, *New York Times*, 10/8/32

27 B.A., review of *Downstairs*, *Syracuse Herald*, 8/13/32

28 Jimmy Starr review of *Downstairs*, *LA Evening Herald Express*, 8/13/32

29 Fountain, pg 225

30 Author's collection, "Will John Gilbert's Fourth Wife Be Virginia Bruce?" magazine article, c. 1932

31 Charles Samuels, "Can Virginia Bruce Beat Her Hoodoo?" *Screen Life*, 7/40

32 Ibid., Fargo Library Archive, Colman, "Wifely Duty ..."

33 Fountain, pp 226-227

34 Fountain, pg 225

CHAPTER FIVE:

Mrs. John Gilbert IV

August 10, 1932 –
Bride and Groom

It was 5:45 pm, August 10, 1932. Virginia was filming MGM's *Kongo*, a grotesque jungle melodrama that required her hair to be stringy, her nails uncut, and her face stained with brown grease paint. Interior shots for the film were largely in huts with dirt floors. Adorned in rags, Virginia wasn't a pretty sight. John Gilbert had been in limbo for several weeks waiting for his next film assignment. He and Virginia would frequently talk to each other on the telephone between takes. Gilbert had been restless and nervous. Cameras were still grinding away. Unexpectedly, Gilbert appeared on the set and interrupted the scene. Virginia, drenched with artificial perspiration, turned and looked at him. "We're going to be married at 6 o'clock," Gilbert calmly announced. "Oh, John," Virginia began. "Six o'clock," Gilbert cut in. "But there's so

much to be done—I . . . ." "Six o'clock. My bungalow. Be there."[1]
Director William Cowan excused her. Virginia ran to her dressing room. And, within 15 minutes, all washed and dressed in a
simple black crepe dress, Virginia walked over to John Gilbert's
dressing room and, with no fuss or feathers, became Mrs. John
Gilbert IV. Gilbert had gathered all the necessary guests. Earll
Briggs gave his "virgin-bride" daughter away in a double-ring
ceremony performed by Reverend James Lash. Within the confines of Gilbert's bungalow were Irving Thalberg as best man,
and Beatrice Stewart (wife of writer Donald Ogden Stewart, also
present) as matron of honor. Crammed together beside Mrs.
Briggs and brother Stanley, were Norma Shearer, Dolores Del
Rio, and Cedric Gibbons. After Lash pronounced them man and
wife, Gilbert "took his bride in his arms, crushed her to him and
kissed her twice."[2] A European honeymoon was postponed until fall. At 8:00 a.m. the next morning Virginia was back on the
Kongo set hard at work.

On October 11, Gilbert, Virginia, her parents, Irving Thalberg and wife Norma Shearer, headed for New York on the 20th
Century Limited. The Thalbergs tagged along to see the city's
sites and shows, and wish the "happy couple" *bon voyage*. Virginia's parents were part of the honeymoon package. Earll's daughter, after all, was his livelihood. The love-struck Virginia couldn't
have cared less. She crossed the Atlantic on a six-week honeymoon and maiden voyage to Europe with her girlhood screen
hero as a husband. No wonder her hometown paper *The Fargo
Forum* referred to Virginia Bruce as "the idol of Fargo's young
womanhood." "Gin Briggs" was now Mrs. John Gilbert IV. "Jack
invited my parents along on the honeymoon to Europe," Virginia
later explained. "We were simple people from North Dakota and
it was like coming into a dream-world. We weren't used to that

kind of luxury. Jack just loved Europe. He was so curious about everything, always asking people questions. We saw everything, I promise you. We even went to see a sex show in Paris."[3]

Gilbert's enthusiasm was nurtured by Virginia's presence. He raved,

New York: Mr. and Mrs. Gilbert return from their European honeymoon, November 8, 1932

> There's no one like Virginia in all the world! Her temperament, her strength of character — are magnificent! Above all, Virginia personifies peace and tranquility; a contentment of heart and soul that is a wholly new experience for me. I have been through all the turmoil, all the fire and fury of love and marriage, but never until I met Virginia did I know the happiness of peace! I feel like a shipwrecked man who has been clinging to a spar, and then suddenly finds himself washed ashore in a beautiful, sheltered haven. Virginia's sweetness, her sympathy and understanding, are beyond belief![4]

In many respects, Gilbert's declaration was true. And, he *certainly* put Virginia to the test. She later reflected back on their time spent in Europe, and commented, "We thought we were the two happiest people in the world. I suppose all lovers think that, but we two were sure of it."[5] The trip wasn't completely idyllic. A month prior to their honeymoon, Gilbert's close friend, producer Paul Bern, was found dead. The consensus was that Bern had put a gun to his head. In July, with Virginia by his side, Gilbert had stood in as best man at Bern's wedding to Jean Harlow. Rumors circulated that Bern left a suicide note that hinted at impotence and undersized genitals. Film historian James Robert Parish claims the "official" interpretation of the note was a cover (by MGM) to hide bigamy charges, and that Bern, "took his life to save Jean from career-wrecking headlines."[6] (In 1990, producer Samuel Marx offered compelling evidence in his book, *Deadly Illusions,* that Bern was murdered by a former wife.) Whatever the case, the tragedy put a shadow over Gilbert and Virginia's time in Europe. She later recalled, "I spent a lot of time in our hotel room trying to cheer him up. Jack would get into these deep depressions and not want to see anyone."[7] Years later, Gilbert's daughter, Leatrice, deduced that Bern's death propelled Gilbert all the more desperately to revive his career. Virginia concurred,

> Work was his god. Jack only wanted one thing
> in the world and that was to work. I thought
> at first that he needed a wife, that he needed
> companionship. He seemed to want me there, on
> the spot, all the time. I was ready to give up my
> career. I told that to Irving Thalberg and he agreed
> to put me on indefinite suspension so I could come
> back anytime. But I was wrong. What Jack needed
> all the while was to do what he knew how to do.
> He had all that energy pent up inside him, and all
> that anger at what they'd done to him. When they
> finally did put him in a movie, it was nothing. Just
> some B picture. It was no good for him, but he
> did it. He was determined to live out that damned
> contract.[8]

Witnessing Gilbert's troubled side, Virginia was resolved to remedy the situation. "All my life I've prided myself on looking at things honestly, on finding the truth," she told reporter Juliette Lane, "even if it proved a boomerang and hurt me. . . . You know, Jack's life has not been a very happy one. He's a fiery, tempestuous soul, and things have not come easily to him. He's had to fight for every atom of success he's had. He's been hindered and hurt by the very people who should have helped him. . . . They've been damnable to him! Jack is proud and sensitive. He doesn't go about telling his troubles to anyone that'll listen to him. For that reason everyone thinks he's hard, and callous and doesn't care. They don't know!"[9] Her statements most likely did not endear her to Louis B. Mayer.

Not everyone was happy at Virginia's decision to retire. Her father was certainly one of them. However, Earll was somewhat appeased when new son-in-law Gilbert built him and Mrs. Briggs a house in nearby Toluca Lake. Virginia would not waver on her decision, and stated, "Lots of people are taking great trouble to warn me that I won't be happy, but I'm not paying any attention to them."[10] Virginia (undoubtedly with the help of MGM's publicity department) gave dyed-in-the-wool reasons why she should quit, and announced to the Associated Press, "Jack has had two actress wives who kept on with their careers after marriage and I'm going to make a go of our marriage even at the cost of my career."[11] Jack's reaction? "Virginia thinks, as I do, that one career in the family is enough," he told the press. "Last week she explained her ideas to the studio and they were very nice about it. It makes me proud to think she is willing to give up a chance at stardom for my sake."[12] From the beginning he had thought Virginia had a future in pictures, and he was eager for her to continue. After viewing her test for *Downstairs*, Gilbert had told Thalberg, "Say, I like that kid. She's got something. She's — well, *definite*. Sure of herself."[13] Virginia told one interviewer, "Jack thinks I should go ahead. He believes that I may find success in the future. He wants me to try, at least, so that I'll never regret having given up a possible career for domesticity. Perhaps he's right. I don't know."[14] MGM had planned to co-star the couple in an adaptation of Siegfried Geyer's sophisticated continental farce *Candlelight*. However, before they left for their honeymoon, Virginia was sure of one thing: Gilbert's "troubles" precluded mixing career with marriage. He was a full-time job.

Virginia elaborated on the subject of their marriage when Gilbert's daughter Leatrice was researching his life during the 1970s. What she described was closer to a nightmare than a young girl's dream of a happy marriage. "There was some clause saying he could not be seen drunk in public or otherwise disgrace himself," Virginia began, "so he drank at home." She gave more details.

> Sometimes he'd be awake drinking all night; then
> in the morning he'd get me to throw him into the
> swimming pool so he could clear his head. I'm sure
> the shock must have been bad for him. He had
> bleeding ulcers. He used to throw up blood in the
> morning until he fainted. Jack's doctor was Sam
> Hirshfield, a kindly man. Hirshfield would come
> over to the house and inject sodium amytol into
> Jack's veins so he could sleep; otherwise he'd stay
> awake for days. Once when we were at Malibu,
> Jack was terribly sick. One of his veins collapsed
> and became infected. Hirshfield sent a nurse to
> look after him. She was a little red-haired girl who

> promptly fell in love with him. He was not very
> pretty to look at, he had all kinds of infections,
> and this girl stood at the foot of the bed with tears
> streaming down her face. Jack was something, the
> effect he had on people.[15]

Gilbert's "effect" on people could also prove harrowing. His friend and Tower Road neighbor, John Barrymore, told of an evening when gunshots rang out. Barrymore, who had received kidnap threats against his daughter, investigated the matter only to find out that Gilbert had fired the shots! Gilbert, brooding, and imagining plots against himself, fired a pistol at a car parked near his estate. "A bullet shattered a window of the motor car, interrupting the dreams of its occupants, a boy and girl."[16] Gilbert dished out $1,000 for damages to the car, and for traumatizing the young couple. A week prior to this incident, Gilbert had called the police to investigate someone breaking and entering into his house. A police report determined it was only a woodpecker at work adjacent to his bedroom window. These events took place in May 1932, when Gilbert was supposedly in the "throes of romance" with young Virginia. Chances of marital bliss on Tower Road were minimal at best.

On the day of her wedding to Gilbert, Virginia Bruce was playing a drug-addicted alcoholic, forced into prostitution in *Kongo*. "No other film of the pre-Code era can lay claim to being as perverse as this production," claims Missing Link, a British classic horror website, adding that the film is, "a non-stop onslaught on a viewer's sensibilities."[17] Mark A. Vieira, author of *Sin in Soft*

Kongo (1932) shown here with Conrad Nagel (MGM)

Focus, calls *Kongo* an "exercise in perversity."[18] Virginia may have missed out on *Red-Headed Woman*, but *Kongo* stands alone as one of the 1930s most depraved films. A remake of Lon Chaney's *West of Zanzibar* (1928), *Kongo* tells the lurid tale of a crippled African trader and magician illusionist (Walter Huston) who rules a superstitious native tribe. Virginia holds her own against seasoned thespian Huston. Her father (C. Henry Gordon) had crippled Huston years before, then abducted his wife. Their child is kidnapped by a vengeful Huston and sent to a convent for eighteen years. Huston then brings the young woman (Virginia) to his kingdom in order to pollute her soul. The film offers Virginia a variety of meaty scenes which she plays convincingly. While she's in captivity, Virginia and Lupe Velez (Gilbert's love interest prior to Virginia) vie for the affections of a drug-addicted narcotic agent, Conrad Nagel. Virginia tries to nurse him back to health. Velez gives him dope ("bhiang root") in exchange for kisses. At one point, the emotionally wrought Virginia confronts Huston, demanding to know what was behind all his evil. "You're going to tell me!" she screams. "I'm going to find out what's in back of this thing that's bearing down on me like a weight — crushing the very life out of me!" Her hands clasp her breast protectively as she remembers her sordid experience: her escape from a brothel in Zanzibar; the horror of her first night in the Congo — rain dripping down through the tent and "the hot hairy hands, pawing, mauling."

In the film's climax, native drums demand that Virginia be their next fire sacrifice. To Huston's horror, however, he learns that Virginia is really *his* daughter. His character redeems himself by providing the film with a surprise twist. *The New York Times* said Huston was on par with Lon Chaney, but thought the film did not show enough "restraint." Reviewer Mordaunt Hall added, "Virginia Bruce is competent as Ann." Hall found it "rather gratifying" that her character was allowed to escape to "a small place off Sicily."[19] In its review of *Kongo*, the *Syracuse Herald* said, "Honors must be given to Virginia Bruce, John Gilbert's new wife, who proves that she's a real actress in a most emotional role."[20] However, the film did little for Virginia's career. MGM historian John Douglas Eames noted that upon the film's release, "Ushers got little exercise."[21] *Kongo* was a tad too unusual for the average filmgoer.

According to one fan magazine, "Hollywood sat back and waited for the fight to begin . . . when Lupe Velez and Virginia Bruce were cast in the same picture."[22] The article stated that the first day on the set Lupe walked up to Virginia, held out her hand and smiled, "Hello. I'm Lupe." After saying she was glad to meet the girl Jack was going to marry, Velez fondly remarked, "He's a nice boy – Jack."[23] Scenarist Lenore Coffee mentions another Velez-Bruce encounter on the day of Virginia's impromptu wedding. At 2:00 pm Virginia received a telegram with Gilbert's message for a 6:00 pm ceremony. As no definite date had been set for the nuptials, Virginia demurred. None-the-less, she made the announcement to cast and crew.[24] Coffee (Godmother of Leatrice Gilbert Fountain) was wife of *Kongo* director Bill Cowan. Coffee recalled, "It was interesting to see how shocked Lupe was when Virginia announced one morning that she was going to be married to Jack Gilbert that evening. The scene Virginia had to play during the day's shooting required her to be up to her neck in mud – so she was to get cleaned up to be married, then

Margaret Briggs makes a rare visit to MGM on the set of *Kongo*
(Courtesy of MGM/Photofest)

go back into the mud again the next day. Lupe said, 'I think it is disgusting for Jack to allow this. For one of his girls, yes, but marriage, and for Virginia, the first time – the first time for anything. You know what I think? I think Jack say if you can prove you are virgin I marry you next day. You remember how pale she look this morning?' Lupe, looking very wise, made a pronouncement:

'Last night was the real wedding night – to night will be a repeat performance!'"[25]

Some sources indicate that MGM loaned Virginia to Maxim Productions during 1932, for *A Scarlet Week-End*. This "lost" film was adapted from "Exploitation King" Willis Kent's novel *A Woman in Purple Pajamas*. The story warned youngsters of the heartbreak and remorse awaiting those who indulge in "gin orgies" (which according to the film's publicity was rapidly on the rise). To avoid censorship, producer Kent thinly disguised *A Scarlet Week-End* (like he would 1935's *Cocaine Fiends*) as a warning to concerned citizens. This ploy of "underground" producers, gave them leeway to wallow in vice and depravity on screen. Virginia's new status as "Mrs. John Gilbert" was also exploited when the film was released in late 1932 - early 1933.[26] It is doubtful that Virginia's role amounted to much. She was 8th-billed after "Queen of Poverty Row" star Dorothy Revier. As far as MGM was concerned, after the release of *Kongo*, Virginia's career was simply on hold. Author Maude Lathem (*Science of Mind* editor) stated, "[Virginia] is the only player on record whose picture contract was suspended when she married. This is what the studio did in her case, judging in advance that chances were ten to one against her finding permanent happiness in a marriage with Jack Gilbert."[27]

When *Downstairs* was completed, John Gilbert had to wait several months before he was handed a "B" programmer titled *Riv-*

ets. Gilbert played a New York skyscraper construction worker who the *New York Times* referred to as an "intolerable braggart." Critics concurred that Gilbert did his best in an unfortunate role. When no other offers were forthcoming, depression set in. His neighbor and drinking partner John Barrymore tried to introduce Gilbert to hard drugs. Another neighbor, silent star Colleen Moore, said, "Jack wasn't that crazy. He said to Barrymore, 'My God, no! I can't even hold my liquor.'"[28] Besides, Virginia had enough to deal with. She spoke of Gilbert's "instinct for the dramatic" and his "cursed ambition."[29] Gilbert's reclusive, self-absorbed, behavior felt confining to her young spirit. "I began to wonder if we weren't just a trifle too staid . . . too middle-aged," she remembered. "The dullness, the monotony were getting on my nerves. I wanted to dance and go places. Jack didn't. He hated being dragged around. He'd done all the partying he'd wanted to, years ago, and it no longer held any thrill for him. On those few occasions that we did go anywhere, oh, very infrequently, he was so bored and miserable. So, feeling like a prisoner in solitary confinement, I went on, month after month, trying to make the best of it. Jack had loved me for my patience and understanding, I told myself, and I mustn't let him down. But in my heart I knew it couldn't last. I just couldn't go on like that for the rest of my days!"[30] When they did go out Virginia never knew what to expect. Frances Goodrich, screenwriter for the *Thin Man* series, recalled a dinner party shortly after Jack and Virginia's engagement announcement. "We never did see Gilbert," Frances wrote. "He came in tight, went upstairs and slept! Never did appear. I felt so sorry for poor little Virginia Bruce."[31]

In early December 1932, Jack and Virginia spent some time at a desert resort in El Mirada. Virginia had forgotten to bring her lipstick, and Jack, noted for wanting his women to be fastidiously groomed, was reported to have "hastily departed, following a heated argument."[32] Virginia later recalled the incident, saying, "He became very angry because he thought I had stopped wearing lipstick. . . . Jack flew into a rage. It was four in the morning, but he took the car and went home. I was terribly embarrassed and had to hire a taxi the next day to drive me back into town."[33] Soon after this highly-publicized spat, the Gilberts announced that Virginia was expecting. The baby was due to arrive in August. Jack's depression subsided, momentarily. In the spring Jack and Virginia voyaged to New York via the Panama Canal. Gilbert talked to reporters about his declining popularity and said, "Oh, what the hell. They liked me once. A man's an ass to squawk about life. Especially, me."[34] He proclaimed the Hollywood studio system was on the wane anyway. "The Depression has finally caught up with them," he stated, "it looks as if the days of the big studios are over."[35] (In January Paramount and RKO had gone into receivership.) Gilbert saw this as an opportunity for "individual expression" to emerge. He stated his own hopes of doing a play.

Upon their return to Hollywood, Gilbert sat by the phone for three months, waiting. Then, producer Sol Wurtzel contacted him about directing films. Wurtzel invited Gilbert to Fox studios to observe actor/director Kenneth MacKenna (husband of Kay Francis) direct *Walls of Gold*. While on the set, MacKenna confided to him that Garbo wanted Gilbert for the leading man in her next film. "I roared with enormous laughter," Gilbert later recalled. "I didn't believe a word of it."[36] On August 2, 1933, Virginia gave birth to a daughter, Susan Ann. Gilbert came out of hiding to tell the press, "I am the happiest man in the world." He was even happier on August 10, when his old flame Greta Garbo's request became official. Gilbert was to replace Laurence Olivier

Virginia and daughter Susan Ann, born August 2, 1933

as her co-star in the film *Queen Christina*. "I tell you, Garbo has recreated me," stated Gilbert. "If I should come back to where I used to be . . . there will be one person responsible and one alone – that wonderful woman! I am a new man. She has made me one . . . She has held out her hand to an exile and brought him home again."[37] It had been over two years since Gilbert and Garbo had seen each other. The studio photographer was challenged in documenting their highly-publicized reunion. "When they began to make publicity stills of us," said Gilbert, "the cameraman said, 'Stand a little closer to Mr. Gilbert, please, Miss Garbo.' And Greta said to me, very low, very shy, 'Not too much of this, you know. You have a lovely wife, a darling baby at home.'"[38]

September 12, 1933, Costume ball at Donald Ogden Stewart's – Gilbert as Rasputin, Virginia as Vilma Banky, Kay Francis as Nita Naldi, Kenneth MacKenna as Maurice Chevalier

It is almost as if the existence of Virginia and the baby helped set the "tone" of *Queen Christina* (Sweden's 17th-century monarch), and reinforce some of the most memorable scenes of Garbo's career. When asked to do a sizzling love scene with Gilbert (playing the Spanish envoy Don Antonio), Garbo refused. "Mr. Gilbert is a married man now, with a wife and baby," she cautioned director Rouben Mamoulian, "and I think it will be better that we tone that scene down."[39] In lieu of the "heat of passion," we see Garbo memorizing the bedroom in which she and Gilbert have spent an idyllic night together. There is but a single kiss upon their meeting again in her private castle chambers. These scenes indicate a deeper, more spiritual union, expertly executed by all concerned. Surprisingly, Joseph Breen, who supervised the industry's Production Code, was outraged by the bedroom scene. "Miss Garbo should be kept away from the bed entirely," Breen wrote. "The business of lying across the bed and fondling the pillow is, in my considered judgment, very offensive."[40] (The real Christina, rumored to be lovers with both men and women, abandoned the throne to study art and religion in Italy, where she assumed a masculine persona.) Fortunately, the review board disregarded Breen's objections. The now classic scene was left in tact.

In her biography of Gilbert, daughter Leatrice wrote, "Jack's marriage to Virginia Bruce seemed to be crumbling at its foundations. . . . Once the filming of *Queen Christina* began, Jack was totally absorbed in it. It was *his* film, *his* opportunity. He had little time for his wife or for his new daughter."[41] In late September, Virginia and her brother Stanley attempted to visit the set of *Queen Christina*. The guard at the MGM lot turned them away — a foreshadowing of events to come.[42] Virginia felt no threat from Garbo. "Never in any way or at any time has Greta Garbo, or the name of Greta Garbo, entered into the thing that eventually caused Jack Gilbert and myself to come to the parting of the ways," stated Virginia in 1934. "I have never met Miss Garbo. I have often wanted to. I have all the admiration for her in the world. When Jack worked with her in *Queen Christina*, she asked if she might come and see the baby. I begged him to bring her."[43]

Queen Christina was released in December 1933, and in spite of Garbo and Gilbert's excellent performances, the reviews and box office proved a disappointment. Depression audiences had tired of costume dramas, lining up for the more visually-inventive and snappy Busby Berkeley musicals. Gilbert had to acknowledge that his "comeback" in *Queen Christina* had failed. Resolved to gain more clarity in his life, Gilbert told Virginia he needed time out, alone. He needed to sort things out. He asked her to return to her parents. Virginia felt both defeat and relief. She needed "time out" herself. Looking back, forty years later, she poignantly remembered:

When Jack was feeling himself, he was the most

charming, exciting, intelligent man I've ever
known. He had a beautiful body and he was
a tender and considerate lover. Very patient. I
think that's why his love scenes came off so
well on the screen. They were real, or at least they
rang true. And he'd take his time until the woman
in the picture and all the women in the audience
were ready. I never understood how that kind
of lovemaking could go out of style, because it
certainly didn't in real life. What came into style
was the treat-'em-rough type of lover like Gable
or the cool type like Robert Montgomery. I think
it was because they appealed to more men. Men
could be like Gable, or think they could. But they
knew they couldn't be like Gilbert.

And he was so much more than a lover. Jack had a
brilliant, educated mind and he attracted friends
who were just as bright as he was. He adored the
English, Ronnie Colman and Herbert Marshall,
and they loved him. To the end he had friends who
adored him. Not the MGM crowd. They left him
flat. I suppose they were afraid of Mayer. Except
for Cedric Gibbons, who wasn't afraid of anybody.
There was no one like Jack when his spirits were
up. But when he was down, he was . . . Oh, you
can't describe it. It was like death.[44]

Before they separated, there were occasions when Virginia simply had to "escape." One such evening, Gilbert's manager Noll
Gurney imposed upon neighbor John Barrymore to come immediately to the Gilbert residence, as Jack was threatening sui-

cide. Barrymore told Gurney there was no need to hurry. "An actor," declared Barrymore, "will do nothing so operatic as self-immolation without an audience!" While on their way to "rescue" Gilbert, Gurney informed Barrymore that Gilbert was drinking, while brooding about his career and the slurs against his voice. He became so violent that Virginia "absented herself from the premises." "Haven't the Gilberts a new baby?" inquired Barrymore. "About three months old," answered Gurney. "Did he mention his baby at all when talking about killing himself?" Barrymore asked. "No," Gurney replied.

When they arrived at the house, Gilbert, looking hollow, but cordial, answered the door. He called to his Filipino houseboy for drinks. "There will be no more drinks tonight for anybody," said Barrymore quietly. "Understand?" Before Gilbert could answer, Barrymore spoke up. "I hear that you've been making a God-damned fool of yourself. Over what?" Gilbert said nothing. Barrymore answered for him. "All because someone says this or that. . . . Christ! Do you think the world turns on the importance or the unimportance of a ham? Well, it doesn't! Why should you give a damn about your voice, good or bad? You can dig ditches, can't you? Or get a job with Western Union? How old are you? . . . thirty-three or thirty-four?" Gilbert remained silent. "You've got a baby," said Barrymore. "Never entered your head, did it, that you owe the *child* something? No. The ham always thinks only of himself. Get up! We're going to look at the baby." Gilbert led the way to the nursery where Barrymore directed him to hold Susan Ann in his arms. Placing his hand on Gilbert's shoulder, Barrymore spoke as a friend. "Doesn't that make you feel something? Isn't *she* more important than a bit of newspaper gossip?"[45] Gilbert was crying. It was three in the morning. Barrymore stayed with Gilbert until seven. Barrymore was a mirror image of Gil-

c. 1934 – dining out with (l-r) Gertrude Olmsted Leonard, director Robert Z. Leonard, Margaret Briggs, Stanley Briggs, art director/costume designer Ralph Jester, Virginia (courtesy of Vincent Briggs)

bert — hence his understanding and compassion for a friend. In another ten years Barrymore's own drinking would prove fatal. His success as a parent was on par with Gilbert's, practically non-existent. At least Gilbert was honest about himself. When asked about his daughter Leatrice in 1927, he had told a reporter from the *Los Angeles Times*, "I go see my little girl every so often and she calls me 'daddy.' However, I don't feel a bit paternal."[46]

In early January the Gilberts finally separated. Virginia returned to her parents' home for a permanent family reunion. Since their marriage, Gilbert had barred Mr. and Mrs. Briggs from visiting Virginia at their home on Tower Road. In the aftermath of their marital troubles, Virginia's attorney (Mr. Divet of Fargo) put a humorous slant on the situation of Gilbert, his in-laws, and the reasons behind Gilbert giving the Briggs' a new house. "Maybe he gave them the house so that they'd stay away from *his* house," Divet suggested. "Or, maybe he felt that since he had given Mr. and Mrs. Briggs a home they ought to be content to *stay* there all the time. Virginia herself could never figure it out."[47] Reporters were soon inquiring at the Briggs' doorstep as to the status of Virginia's marriage. On January 30, after reporters got wind that Virginia had visited Jack on Tower Road, Mrs. Briggs told the *Los Angeles Times*, "[Jack] said he wasn't feeling well, and asked Virginia to come. So Virginia went. But it is certain there will never be a reconciliation."[48] On February 12, while Virginia revealed their divorce plans to the press, she learned that Gilbert had arrived in Honolulu on the steamer *Monterey*. She had no idea he had left.

Without Gilbert's dominating influence, Virginia began to realize all that she had given up. She told one interviewer at the time, "I find one can't destroy ambition. I had loved acting and I wanted more than anything to go back to it."[49] She admitted that her mother had something to do with her return to the screen, saying, "Mother had to practically shove me back into pictures, after my first marriage failed."[50] So, in May 1934, MGM made arrangements for Virginia to work at Monogram studios in the title role of *Jane Eyre*. "I started to pay some attention to acting," she said. "Robert Young and I rehearsed with Oliver Hinsdale in the studio's school room and learned considerably. Then I studied diction and expression under Samuel Kayser, who's coached so many players."[51]

Virginia also resuscitated her social life. After stating to the press in February that divorce was the "only solution," Virginia attended Minna Wallis' party for David Manners, who had just returned from Europe. The *Los Angeles Examiner* reported, "Virginia Bruce Gilbert, in a black crepe gown with white lingerie frills at the neck and an off-the-face hat of black straw, looked so lovely that one wondered how Jack ever let her get away. But Virginia averred there'd be no reconciliation, though she would always remain Jack's best friend. But Jack's wives always leave him like that, friendly but definitely."[52] The *Los Angeles Times*, pointed out, "This affair marked the social re-appearance of Virginia Bruce, who

Jane Eyre (1934) (Monogram)

sat at the table with Kay Francis, discussing this and that (perhaps ex-husbands)."[53] At Ted Fio Rito's opening at the Cocoanut Grove, Virginia was seen with Paul Felix Warburg Jr., a wealthy New Yorker whose father was the inspiration for *Annie's* "Daddy Warbucks." The recently-married Gary Coopers joined Virginia and Paul at the table. (Only a few months earlier, Virginia and Jack had accompanied Cooper and his fiancée, Sandra Shaw, on a trip to Arizona.) Not missing her confinement on Tower Road, Virginia enjoyed frequenting the Clover Club, the Beverly Wilshire and other popular nightspots. Virginia filed for divorce on May 2, describing Gilbert as "arrogant, violent, and abusive." "On three occasions," noted the Associated Press, "Gilbert ordered her to leave his home and suggested she obtain a divorce in Reno."[54] Virginia's more honest appraisal of Gilbert was put simply to reporter Jerry Asher. "I do not think he can be blamed or be condemned—no more than one can condemn the sky for being blue," she remarked. "He is perhaps the most colorful, the most interesting, the most exciting person I shall ever meet in my life. If I had it to do all over again, it would be worth it just to know him."[55]

In retrospect, it seems odd that a prestige studio like MGM would loan a star they were trying to "build up" to a grindhouse like Monogram. Nonetheless, Virginia was excited about her new assignment, *Jane Eyre*. It was Monogram's biggest production to date and the first sound version of the novel. Virginia Bruce, as governess Eyre, makes an appealing and sympathetic vis-à-vis for Colin Clive's brooding Edward Rochester (her employer). The film highlights Virginia's good looks, pleasant contralto vocals (Schubert's "Serenade"), and her capable understatement and honesty as an actress. Her character, as written, does not exactly mirror the Jane Eyre of the novel. Virginia is anything but plain. However, she does show Jane's spirit and strength. As a young teacher at Lowood Institution she confronts the Headmaster who is hell-bent on turning the children into Christian martyrs. To his face Bruce calls him a "cruel, stingy child-beater," and an "ugly old crocodile!" Later, as governess at Thornfield, she confronts employer Clive. His fiancée (Aileen Pringle) comments, "So! That's the new governess. Impertinent and pretty!" The film creaks with age, and occasionally slips into hackneyed comic scenes, as when Virginia's charge (Edith Fellows) falls headfirst into an urn while dusting. Slapstick doesn't exactly mesh with Charlotte Bronte's original story. Overall, the film lacks the intensity and suspense of the novel.

The reviews for *Jane Eyre*, which was in production for only eight days, were mostly positive regarding Bruce and Clive. Film

with Colin Clive in *Jane Eyre* (Courtesy of Monogram/Photofest)

Critic Maurice Kann said, "Virginia Bruce gives an unusually sympathetic portrayal of Jane and reveals genuine histrionic ability ... she is as pathetic and likeable as the novel would have her."[56] *Photoplay* thought the film was "handled with taste, but slow in the telling. Virginia Bruce, breath-taking beautiful ... reveals a lovely rich voice in the Schubert 'Serenade.'"[57] Bruce Eder's edition of the *All Movie Guide* looked back 70-odd years later to note, "Virginia Bruce does a surprising job, given the limitations of the production." Christy Cabanne, whom film historian Kevin Brownlow referred to as one of the "dullest" directors of the silent era, was hardly the person to have at the helm of *Jane Eyre*. He oversimplifies Bronte's work. Yet, the film remains a moodily atmospheric timepiece. Of course, 1934's Production Code precluded questioning religious cant, or permitting any mention of the illegitimacy, bigamy, and sexual equality that fueled the real story. Those expecting a faithful, comprehensive adaptation of the Bronte classic were in for a disappointment. Cinemagoers would have to wait until 1944 for a more faithful version teaming Joan Fontaine and Orson Welles.

Mr. and Mrs. Briggs welcomed home Virginia and five-month-old granddaughter Susan Ann. One reporter said of Susan, "She looks like Virginia, not Jack -- a regular *Ladies Home Journal* cover baby -- all rosy cheeks, blond hair, blue eyes and a big smile."[58] Closer to the truth was Virginia's own opinion: "It pleases me that my baby looks so much like Jack."[59] The house Gilbert built for the Briggs' had two additional rooms added on for the baby and Virginia. Homes in the Toluca Lake (neighbors included Dick Powell, Richard Arlen and Jack Oakie) tended to be smaller than the mansions in Beverly Hills (the Pickfords, the Swansons.) Some roads were not paved. The Briggs' house on Ponca Street was set far back on the lot, surrounded by a white picket fence halfway in from the sidewalk. Trees and flowers abounded, and a large patio gave space for outdoor living where baby Susan could roam. Her toys decorated the yard. The living room was accented with maple furnishings and a white brick fireplace, with a painting of Susan Ann above the mantel. Virginia bought a white cottage piano, upon which she placed a portrait of John Gilbert. Earll drove Virginia to many of her social functions.

Although Virginia was on her own, she preferred being known as "Mrs. John Gilbert" rather than Virginia Bruce. She told the press she felt she "had earned it." "I wish Jack and I might have remained friends," Virginia remarked, "but he would not have it so. It would be difficult to find another man like Jack. You don't often find such a combination of good looks and irresistible charm. . . . I know some of his friends have called him *mad*, but his absolute irresponsibility, his complete abandon, is the very thing that makes people love him—even people who don't always admire him. They look at him and wish they could do the same things."[60] But, realistically, Virginia admitted, "I don't believe any woman can ever really and truly make Jack happy."[61]

Not surprisingly, while Virginia ventured into single motherhood and attempted to rescue her career, John Gilbert began to contemplate Marlene Dietrich, who had decided to rescue Gilbert from *himself.*

Endnotes

1   Associated Press article, "Gilbert Gives Bride But 15 Minutes to Dress for Wedding," *La Cross Tribune (WI),* 8/11/32

2   Ronald W. Wagoner, UP Correspondent, "John Gilbert of Film Fame Weds Virginia Bruce," *Nevada State Journal,* 8/11/32

3   Fountain, p 227

4   Juliette Laine, "Remedy for Heartbreak," *Modern Screen,* 1/35

5   ibid

6   James Robert Parish, *Hollywood Beauties,* Arlington House, N.Y., c 1978, pg 210

7   Fountain, p 227

8   Fountain, p 228

9   Juliette Laine, "Remedy . . ."

10   Colman, "Wifely Duty . . ."

11   "Star Cuts Off Screen Career," *Oakland Tribune,* 9/13/32

12   Harrison Carroll, "Behind the Scenes in Hollywood," *San Mateo Times,* 9/23/32

13   Jack Smalley, "Nothing Can Hurt Her Now!" *Screen Book,* 3/35

14   Eleanor Packer, "The Fourth Mrs. Gilbert," *New Movie,* 12/32

15   Fountain, p 228

16   Gene Fowler, *Goodnight, Sweet Prince,* Blackiston Co, Philadelphia, c. 1944, pp 341-342

17   www.missinglinkclassichorror.co.uk

18   Mark A. Vieira, *Sin in Soft Focus,* Harry N. Abrams, Inc., N.Y., 1999, pg.85

19   Mordaunt Hall, review of *Kongo, New York Times,* 11/17/32

20   review of *Kongo,* "Walter Houston Villain Extraordinary in *Kongo," Syracuse Herald,* 10/8/32

21   John Douglas Eames, *The MGM Story,* Crown Pub., N.Y., 1979, pg 85

22 Magazine article, authors collection, c. 1932

23 ibid

24 "Gilbert Takes Fourth Bride," *Portsmouth Times*, 8/11/32

25 Lenore Coffee, *Storyline*, Cassell, London, c1973

26 "Virginia Bruce in Ritz Murder Mystery," *Syracuse Herald*, 1/1/33

27 Maude Lathem, "My Marriage with John Gilbert Was Not a Failure," *Movie Classic*, 10/34

28 Fountain, p 232

29 Jerry Asher, "Why Our Marriage Failed!" *Screenland*, 4/34

30 Laine, "Remedy . . ."

31 David L. Goodrich, *The Real Nick and Nora – Frances Goodrich and Albert Hackett*, Southern Illinois University Press, 2004 pg 63

32 news article "Gilbert Walks Out," *Nevada State Journal*, 12/9/32

33 Jerry Asher, "Why Our Marriage Failed!" *Movie Mirror*, c. 1934

34 Fountain, p233

35 ibid

36 Gladys Hall, "John Gilbert's Confession," *Modern Screen*, 11/33

37 ibid

38 Gladys Hall, "John Gilbert's Confession," *Modern Screen*, 11/33

39 Grace Kingsley, "Hobnobbing in Hollywood," *LA Times*, 9/13/33

40 LaSalle, "Complicated . . . ," pg 196-197

41 Fountain, p 236

42 Harrison Carroll, *LA Evening Herald Express*, 9/21/33

43 Jerry Asher, "Why Our Marriage Failed!" *Movie Mirror*, 4/34

44 Fountain, p 228-229

45 Gene Fowler, *Goodnight, Sweet Prince*, Blackiston Co. Philadelphia, c. 1944, pp 347-349

46 Alma Whitaker, "Best-Laid Plans of Screen Stars Most Often Go Awry," *LA Times*, 4/15/34

47 Fargo Library Archive, Marie Canel, "Determined Not . . . "

48 Grace Kingsley, "Hobnobbing in Hollywood," *LA Times*, 1/31/34

49 Laine, "Remedy . . . "

50 Ben Maddox, "Girls! Don't Be Too Clever," *Screenland*, 4/39

51 ibid

52 "Minna Wallis Party Gay Affair," *Los Angeles Examiner*, 2/25/34

53 Tip Off, "That Certain Party," *Los Angeles Times*, 2/25/34

54 Associated Press release, "Gilbert's Fourth Wife Asks Divorce," 5/3/34

55 Asher, "Why Our Marriage . . . "

56 review of *Jane Eyre*, Maurice Kann, *Syracuse Herald (NY)*, 7/8/34 & 9/10/34

57 review of *Jane Eyre*, *Photoplay*, 9/34

58 Fargo Library Archive, Muriel Babcock, "Former Fargo Girl, Returning to Work at Studios," 8/5/34

59 Lathem, "My Marriage with . . . "

60 Ibid.

61 Ibid.

CHAPTER 6:

Dangerous Corner

"Love tricks you into a false sense of security," Virginia stated to a British journalist. "Maybe the fairy tales are to blame. The old idea that people got married and lived happily ever after. So we take love for granted, till the gray morning when some of us wake up to find it has vanished."
Picture Play (MGM publicity photo c. 1935)

Virginia frequently expressed her gratitude for the time she had spent as Mrs. John Gilbert. Certainly, the emotional demands placed upon her as Gilbert's wife helped instill the "dramatic force" necessary to become a convincing actress. In the summer of 1934 she revealed to Fargo resident-turned-Hollywood reporter Muriel Babcock, "I don't think I knew what real feeling meant — as far as anything emotional . . . I wasn't awake and alive to what was going on. Suffering — and you always suffer when you love — does something to your insides. I *couldn't* have acted before. Now, I know I can act."[1]

As a matter of course, Virginia

aired her grievances to Judge Marshall F. McComb at the divorce trial on May 25, 1934. She alleged that Gilbert "belittled her intelligence and ability, insisted that she stay at home, told her she was extravagant, used profanity in her presence and objected to her parents."[2] With the legal assistance of former Fargo resident and neighbor, A.G. Divet, a complaint was prepared by Attorney W. I. Gilbert which stated that John Gilbert countermanded her requests to servants and "would not allow her to have any voice in what should be done."[3] Virginia's secretary, Jean Bray, provided the corroborating testimony, attesting that Gilbert "frequently called his wife vile names . . . humiliated her in public . . . and on three occasions [she] heard the actor order his wife out of the house."[4] Bray asserted that Gilbert "was intoxicated most of the time during a trip to New York via the Panama Canal, just before their baby was born, and . . . was abusive to Mrs. Gilbert on the voyage."[5] Divet said of Virginia, "She's a strong character . . . Virginia Bruce has taken her experiences seriously and is looking at life squarely, without being disillusioned in any way."[6] Virginia wanted monetary compensation for three years, feeling confident that by then her career would be soundly reestablished. Gilbert would be free to visit Susan Ann at any time. Virginia got her final decree from Gilbert on June 3, 1934. She received $92.31 a week in alimony for a period of three years. Susan received $150 a month for child support. Gilbert paid these obligations in one lump sum of $42,500.

Gilbert expressed regret at the loss of Virginia, but he did nothing to try and keep her. "I am sorrier about Virginia than I am about anything that has ever happened to me in my life," he said apologetically. "It was my own fault . . . I was sick over the way I was playing my part in *Christina*. I was afraid of giving a bad performance. I felt the conditions around me were unfriendly. The whole thing kept twisting in me like a knife. Perhaps I thought that she would understand. I forgot how young she is. . . . But it's over now and I shall not see Virginia again. I don't believe in Hollywood's super-friendly divorces. I love Virginia and I wanted her for my wife or not at all."[7] Gilbert's excuses did not hold any credibility. He failed to take into consideration that his drunkenness on the trip to Panama was well before he had any inkling *Queen Christina* was going to be filmed. The months of "understanding" she had offered him up until the time of *Christina* he brushed aside. Gilbert blamed her "youth" for not being able to "hang in there" with the wreckage that had become his life. No, Virginia was not tagging along. She was moving on. Virginia took responsibility for her relationship with Gilbert, admitting, "I did understand, I did sympathize, and because I loved him so desperately, I thought I would feel and think like that always. But I didn't. I changed. I didn't live up to my own specifications!"[8]

Virginia's next film assignment was at RKO. *Dangerous Corner* (1934) was a clever and unusual type of screen fiction. It was a rare instance of Hollywood exploring the metaphysics of "time." The film gave Virginia first billing in an important lead part (opposite Melvyn Douglas). An adaptation of J. B. Priestley's 1932 play, *Dangerous Corner* also explores the perilous consequences of total candor. A discussion about telling the "truth" leads to a series of confessions, revelations, and hidden secrets amongst a group of friends and co-workers in a publishing firm. The players take this "dangerous corner" only after a radio tube burns out. With no music to dance to, they opt to discuss the meaning behind a new book titled, *Let Sleeping Dogs Lie*. Someone suggests the phrase implies that truth is best left undisturbed. Bruce, who had contracted the deal for the book, best expresses the author's viewpoint. She carefully considers, "Well, the real truth, that is every single little thing with nothing missing at all, wouldn't be dangerous. I suppose that's God's truth. But, what most people mean by truth is only half the real truth. It doesn't tell you all that went on inside everybody; everything they thought and felt. It simply gives you a lot of facts that were hidden away. And, perhaps a lot better hidden away." Senior partner Conrad Nagel disagrees. He believes that truth, no matter how disturbing, is healthy. "I'm all for it coming out," he announces. When Nagel's wife (Erin O'Brien-Moore) offers Virginia a smoke from a musical cigarette holder, Virginia comments that she's seen the holder before. His wife says, "That's impossible." Virginia looks surprised and claims she is sure she has seen it, then quickly drops the subject. Both women look uncomfortable. Nagel jumps in and insists on them "telling the truth" about their disagreement. It seems inconsequential at first, but their revelations lead to a flurry of confessions that spiral dramatically. Feelings are hurt, voices are raised, relationships are shattered. During the evening's "festivity" Nagel's wife confesses that she is really in love with his brother! Truth, apparently, is dangerous stuff. Conversation turns to deep silence.

Melvyn Douglas and Virginia retreat to the patio for some fresh air. She makes a solemn observation. "It doesn't seem quite real does it? Rather frightening — like being in a car when the brakes are gone." When they return, Douglas tells a distraught Conrad Nagel that his insistence on finding the "truth" has built up a "fool's hell for him to live in." Nagel, acknowledging his mistake, feels he's lost his capacity to create "beautiful illusions." He disappears to his office and shoots himself. The film comes to a screeching halt. At this point the script uses the clever ploy of reverting back in time for an alternate scenario. After the radio tube fails, a new tube is located. The music continues and the guests opt to dance rather than "discuss." Love, in this alternate ending, takes precedence over unspoken half-truths.

Dangerous Corner (1934) tense moment with Conrad Nagel
(Courtesy of RKO/Photofest)

Dangerous Corner is a wonderful ensemble piece and the cast works well together. Max Steiner is credited for a soundtrack that doesn't emerge until the last 60 seconds! Steiner's talent is sorely missed and would have added dimension to the highly emotional and well-conceived screenplay. Film critic Chester B. Bahn found *Dangerous Corner* "distinctive," saying, "unusual plot construction, variations in technique and sparkling dialogue – are the very things that are likely to cost the picture popularity . . . certainly, experimental cinema . . . expertly directed by Phil Rosen . . . splendidly played by Conrad Nagel, Virginia Bruce, Melvyn Douglas, Erin O'Brien-Moore, Ian Keith and Betty Furness."[9]

Out of work and feeling desperate, John Gilbert turned his own "dangerous corner." After telling the press that he was through with marriage, he incredulously proposed to his neighbor, actress Colleen Moore. She refused him. In February 1934, he ventured to Hawaii in pursuit of another relationship. Myrna Loy was on board during Gilbert's return trip home, and recalled, "That voyage . . . turned out to be a very sad coming back, because John Gilbert was on board. He would appear occasionally on an upper deck somewhere, thin and ghostly, with a male nurse in anxious attendance. He seemed so far gone. He'd gone off to Hawaii in pursuit of Princess Liliuokalani, but she had spurned him."[10] Gilbert waited months more before being offered a role at Columbia by his old friend and director Lewis Milestone. He tested successfully for the part in *The Captain Hates the Sea*. Studio head Harry Cohn told Gilbert, "If you behave yourself, stay sober, and do your work, you'll be a star again. I'll bet my shirt on you. It's up to you."[11] Virginia kept close track on Gilbert during his new screen assignment. She knew how important it was to him. The day after *The Captain Hates the Sea* was released, she got up early and anxiously awaited for the New York reviews. She tore out the column and ordered her driver to head up to Tower Road. Gilbert's butler answered. Virginia thrust the clipping into his hands. "See that he reads that as soon as he wakes up," she said.[12] The consensus was that Gilbert had done well. Milestone later recalled, "Jack did a good job, despite being drunk most of the time . . . He had bleeding ulcers and sometimes fever and hallucinations—raving out of his mind. When it was over, Jack knew Cohn would never hire him again. He was too much trouble."[13] In the film's last scene Gilbert's wife asks him if he had stopped drinking. He answers, "No." This was the last word John Gilbert would utter on screen.

After his picture at Columbia, Gilbert found himself stuck once again, mulling over the half-truths conjured up by his mind. He was like the phantom car that Virginia's character mentioned in *Dangerous Corner* — out of control, and with no brakes. Then, for reasons only known to her, Marlene Dietrich suddenly appeared. She became his *deus ex machina*. Her job? To rescue the "great lover" from his downward spiral. She insisted he stop drinking, see a psychiatrist, and get out of the house. They were soon seen together socially, at restaurants, and movie premiers. In a letter to her 10-year-old daughter Maria Sieber, Dietrich wrote, "Gilbert has emerged out of his 'trunk' and enjoys life again like a child." On a more personal note, Dietrich would confess to Maria, "Everything was really easy until he fell in love with me — then it got difficult . . . he has a force that one always secretly yearns for and when one finds it—one gets frightened."[14] Dietrich elaborated to her child, saying "the passion was too hot" and Gilbert was "out of his mind" when she held back and didn't reciprocate. She felt an entanglement with Gilbert might be difficult to get out of.[15] When Maria first met Gilbert, she was warned by her mother, "He is beautiful . . . his eyes are like coals—burning! Look at his eyes when he comes. You will see what I mean."[16] Maria noticed how Dietrich mothered Gilbert and "enjoyed her new cause tremendously."[17] Aside from hiding his alcohol, Dietrich prepared her elixir of beef-tea as a cure-all. The smitten Gilbert referred to her as "Pie Face." At one point, when Gilbert was out of Marlene's protective influence, he began drinking again. They "had words." She later wrote him a letter of apology (and made a carbon copy to send to her husband). Upon receiving it, Gilbert telephoned her at the "break of dawn." She rushed to his bedside. They were together again.

Virginia retained her love for her ex-husband, albeit from a distance. She appeared to ignore Dietrich's doting attentions. The engagement ring Gilbert had given Virginia still adorned her hand. "I always wear that and my wedding ring," said Virginia, "and I always intend to."[18] In September 1934, Virginia requested to be part of a private MGM screening of Gilbert's 1925 mega-hit *The Merry Widow.* She had seen the film in Fargo when she was fifteen. Reporter Robbin Coons sat next to her in the screening room, and when Gilbert first appeared in his eloquent portrayal as the dashing Prince Danilo, Virginia literally beamed with joy. She commented, "Isn't he cute?" When Gilbert donned a uniform, Virginia said, "Hasn't he the longest waist? I think he and Ronald Colman are the handsomest men on the screen." After the last reel Virginia's deep sentiment was evident. "I never hope to see another smile like that!" she remarked. Virginia then answered reporter Coon's query, saying she was *not* sorry she had married John Gilbert.[19]

The private screening of *The Merry Widow* was the closest Virginia got to doing anything at her home studio in 1934. They had promised her that after Monogram's *Jane Eyre*, she would be assigned to an MGM picture. Instead, she had gone to RKO. Now they offered her to 20th Century for Darryl Zanuck's *The Mighty Barnum*. At this point, Virginia wasn't really concerned where the studio sent her as long as she was working. "I'm working because I want to," she told reporter Juliette Laine. "Work is the only cure for heartache, the only intelligent, civilized thing to do. Life nowadays is too big, too wonderful, for any normal woman to collapse in the midst of the debris and confusion of a shattered romance or a broken marriage. In our grandmother's day a woman dramatized her broken heart. In fact, it was expected of her. She either pined away and died, or else she lived on and be-

As Jenny Lind in *The Mighty Barnum (1934)* (United Artists)

came a nuisance to everyone around her. It wasn't lady-like to do anything else!"[20] Virginia, refusing to dramatize anywhere but on screen, was excited about portraying Jenny Lind in the film *The Mighty Barnum*.

"The Swedish Nightingale," as Lind was nicknamed while on tour in the United States, had received tremendous acclaim in Europe since 1838. In 1850, through P.T. Barnum's relentless publicity, over 40,000 people heralded her arrival at the New York harbor. The profitable association of Barnum and Lind lasted two years. Virginia prepared diligently for the vocals of "(Believe Me If All) Those Endearing Young Charms" and Bellini's aria "Casta Diva" from *Norma*. On screen, she was so thoroughly convincing that few knew she was dubbed (by soprano Francia White.) One may wonder why Zanuck didn't have Virginia use her own voice. Virginia explained, "I have a little voice and I *can* carry a tune, but I never could sing opera as Jenny Lind was supposed to have sung it. It would have been ridiculous for me to have tried. They took records of Miss White's singing. I took these home and played them over and over again, singing right along with her and timing each note and each breath to the record. I practiced for days until I was letter perfect. Then they shot the picture and I actually did sing only they didn't use my voice."[21] Opera diva Grace Moore had played Lind in 1930's *A Lady's Morals*. In Moore's version Wallace Beery made a brief appearance as P.T. Barnum, handing out Jenny Lind cigars, and promoting her as the "ideal virtuous woman." *A Lady's Morals* has Jenny taking a lover instead of opting for marriage. Virginia's Jenny takes no such bold step. Her presence, midway into *The Mighty Barnum*, is virtually a cameo appearance. Aside from her aria, Virginia utters but a few lines with a Swedish accent. Film critic Harrison Carroll summed her performance up by saying, "Seen all too briefly, Virginia Bruce is gorgeous to look upon as the Swedish nightingale, Jenny Lind."[22] *The Mighty Barnum* focused on Wallace Beery in the title role, and Adolphe Menjou as James Bailey (here referred to as Bailey Walsh). The film spans the years they exploited "freak shows" for public consumption. Jenny Lind enters Barnum's life at the inevitable point where, puffed-up with self-importance, he goes "highbrow." The screenplay is filled with hokum and half-truths. When screenwriter Gene Fowler was asked by reporters if he had tried to follow history, Fowler said, "We *tried* to throw it out the window!"[23]

New York Times critic Andre Sennwald found *Barnum* entertaining and declared, "Mr. Beery, a fetching though slightly monotonous comedian, gives his usual entertaining show . . . Virginia Bruce's Jenny Lind is a considerable pictorial improvement on the original . . . and the dubbing process by which Miss Bruce appears to be singing a lyric soprano is the most convincing that this reporter has ever seen."[24] Across the board Virginia received praises for her sparkling presence as Jenny

Society Doctor (1935) Chester Morris, Virginia, and her frequent dating pal, Robert Taylor (MGM)

Lind. Los Angeles critic Jimmy Starr rated the film "excellent" saying, "Virginia Bruce is indeed a revelation as the lovely Jenny Lind."[25] The *Los Angeles Times* raved, "Virginia Bruce . . . reveals breath-taking loveliness and a gracious womanliness which point the way to a high place among Hollywood's bona fide artists."[26] *Silver Screen* compared Virginia to her previous work and raved, "You catch the first glimpse of the beauty that is hers and her potentialities. She quite takes you off your feet in some of those scenes as Jenny Lind."[27] Virginia herself admitted, "This is the first time I have played with all the glamour of an expensive production, and it was quite thrilling."[28]

Praises for Jenny Lind, however, were unable to assuage the disappointment Virginia felt when John Gilbert refused to see her at Christmas. He showed no interest in seeing Susan Ann. He returned all presents unopened, including the photo of his baby daughter.[29] Louella Parsons was outraged and railed, "What's on Jack Gilbert's mind? Why is he so perverse about pretty Virginia Bruce, who is heartbroken over his attitude toward her? He sent back unopened her Christmas present, a picture of their little daughter . . . and refused to acknowledge the messages of affection and sympathy she has sent him. Jack is in a sanitarium and very few of his friends have seen him."[30] Gilbert was determined to let go and Virginia understood. "I knew I would always love him," she said. "Nothing has ever changed that conviction; nothing he has done or could do could ever change that."[31]

MGM finally brought Virginia to her home lot for a trio of pictures. The *New York Times* called the first, "a comic-dramatic description of the kaleidoscopic life in a metropolitan hospital."[32] This aptly describes *Society Doctor*, which takes a stab at hospital management catering to the whims and demands of the elite. Director George B. Seitz made sure the laughs outweighed the dramatics. Chester Morris gives an impressive turn as Dr. Morgan, a strong-headed intern, who calls the snobbish head physician a "perfumed quack." This remark gets him sacked immediately. Fortunately, Dr. Morgan's perpetual patient, a wealthy socialite (Billie Burke), has a crush on him and demands he be reinstated. Burke visualizes setting up Morris in a private practice where he can don colored smocks and operate on her in rooms with green and pink tile. Virginia plays a nurse who is also smitten with Morris. When asked if she is jealous of Burke's attentions, Virginia replies, "Jealous of what? A checkbook and a double chin?" Prior to an intense session in the operating room, Virginia delivers another good line as she and intern Robert Taylor are about to "light up" in the staff lounge. She glibly offers, "There's nothing like a cigarette before a tonsillectomy." Soon after this remark Taylor is inspired to ask Bruce to marry him. In the film's climax, Taylor, with nurse Virginia at his side, operates on Morris' bullet-ridden body in a risky procedure which Morris directs *himself* — with the use of mirrors! Critic Sennwald thought the trio of stars played "with an appropriate sense of glamour [in] an ecstatically foolish fable."[33] Surprisingly, it was Taylor who got the response from fans. MGM raised his salary to a "whopping" $50 a week! Reporter Jack Smalley made a number of visits to the set of *Society Doctor*. He was impressed with Virginia's "dramatic force." Chester Morris noticed Smalley observing her and nodded wisely, "Watch that girl, she's going places."[34] MGM next paired Virginia and heartthrob Taylor for *Times Square Lady*. It wasn't long before the screen duo became an off-screen item. But this was nothing unusual, as Virginia was often seen out-on-the-town with her co-stars. Taylor would escort her to the 1935 Academy Awards ceremony.

The legacy of *Times Square Lady* was the phenomenal hit song, "The Object of My Affection." Virginia sang it along with its composer, Pinky Tomlin, as he milked a cow during a "car-breaks-down-in-the-country" interlude. (When the film was released, Tomlin received close to $100,000 from the infectious ditty.)

Shadow of Doubt (1935) with Ricardo Cortez (MGM)

The storyline for *Times Square Lady* involved big city crooks trying to milk a country gal (Virginia) out of her inheritance. She arrives in New York to be greeted by her deceased father's business managers, who are confident that Virginia will sell out immediately and drop a fortune into their laps. She's one step ahead of them, however. "I'm a little dumb," she declares. "My mind doesn't work that fast . . . I'm going to run these properties myself!" Virginia's charm and intelligence eventually win over the manager of her nightclub (Robert Taylor). He falls for her and, in an about turn, helps her outsmart everyone else. The *LA Evening Herald Express* praised the teaming of Taylor and Bruce in *Times Square Lady*, saying, "Clever dialogue and excellent acting make Taylor and Miss Bruce an ideal screen pair. Natural and vibrant, the couple play their roles with finesse, combining romance with a great many wise-cracks."[35] *Photoplay* was definite: "Virginia Bruce moves up another notch toward stardom."[36] Critics concurred *Times Square Lady* was better than the usual.

Two weeks before *Times Square Lady* opened, Virginia had another MGM film release. Her co-star, Ricardo Cortez, was also her sometime dating/dancing partner. Cortez's black panther grace combined with the golden presence of Virginia Bruce was a striking merger. They were, in fact, dancing at Hollywood's Trocadero in early December 1934, when they heard the buzz that Cortez would be borrowed from Warners to be Virginia's co-star in *The Shadow of Doubt*. The clever whodunit began filming on December 22. Noted Shakespearean actress Constance Collier (in her "talkie debut") stole every scene she was in. As dowager Aunt Melissa, Collier comes out of a twenty-year seclusion to snoop around when her nephew (Ricardo Cortez) gets mixed up in murder. Virginia plays his movie-star fiancée. The suspects are many, Virginia being the most obvious as she owns the murder weapon: a Lugar pistol. Filled with the usual implausibility, *The Shadow of Doubt* gets interesting once Collier becomes determined to save Cortez and Bruce from the electric chair. Collier, wearing Victorian finery and a gigantic plumed hat, barges into Virginia's hotel apartment demanding to see her alone. Having never met the peculiar-looking recluse, Virginia declares, "I don't want to see you alone or in groups of five!" and calls for the manager. Collier appreciates Virginia's spunk. She softens while they talk, realizing Virginia truly loves her nephew. Collier then gives Cortez her approval of Virginia, saying, "She insulted me savagely — I adore her!" Cortez and Bruce shine as a team, but it's Collier who sets the trap for the murderer and walks away with the picture.

Two film assignments announced in 1935 for Virginia never materialized. *House of Trujillo* (from *The Saturday Evening Post*), a South American revolutionary epic, was to co-star Bruce Cabot; *Gold Eagle Guy*, which had been a play on Broadway, would have reteamed Virginia with Wallace Beery, and cast her as the notorious actress/poet Adah Menken. (In the 1850s, "The Frenzy of Frisco" Menken was touted as "the most undressed actress" of her time.)

Virginia had a total of eight films released in 1935. She needed the work. Her family needed money. Things had gone no better for Mr. Briggs in Los Angeles than they had back in Fargo. Approaching twenty-five, Virginia had the responsibility of her daughter, her parents and her brother. For several months she supported Mrs. Briggs' brother and four children who had also moved into the Briggs' Toluca Lake residence. Virginia located her uncle a job as a night watchman at one of the studios. "He's so happy now and they are doing nicely," she told *LA Times* reporter Alma Whitaker. "He had been having a dreadful time of it." Virginia proudly added, "My young brother, Stanley Briggs, goes to UCLA and is captain of the tennis team. He's doing so well. It's sweet when I go home and have them all so thoughtful for me. They all adore the baby, who is 17 months old now, I don't think they could bear to be parted from her. My parents were always sweet and did their best to give me all the breaks, so I am happy to be able to help them now."[37]

Virginia was financing Stanley's education. She accepted this responsibility and found it satisfying. She was definitely in charge of even the smallest details, including her brother's "allowance" of $5 a week. "Naturally, if something very special turns up," Virginia said, "I give him a little more, but he's supposed to get along on $5, and I want him to keep inside his allowance." Virginia pointed out the economic challenges for a young college man in Hollywood. "I'm sure the girl he takes out never goes 'Dutch.' They usually eat at home and then go to the Biltmore Bowl or the Cocoanut Grove to dance. There's a cover charge and all they need to order is something light – it's food that costs so much at those places. When he's low in funds they go to a picture show. But he'd be terribly annoyed if the girl suggested that she pay her way at those times. It would hurt his pride."[38] However budget-minded, Virginia was far from being stingy, and liked entertaining her friends at popular restaurants. She also expressed her dislike for men who

Let 'Em Have It (1935) with Richard Arlen (United Artists)

were tightwads. "I loathe the type of man who evades the check," she complained. "Sometimes, when three or four couples go out together, nobody the host, just all deciding to participate in the party, there's nothing worse than being with a man who doesn't notice when the waiter brings the check, who isn't listening at the time and is carefully looking at something else. I always nudge him and say: 'See what's going on. Don't you want to be in on this?'"[39]

On screen, audiences were definitely paying attention to Virginia Bruce. She stood out in whatever scene she was in, and brought a realistic fervor to her characters. Her first release in the summer of 1935 was a treatise on the Bureau of Investigation ("B.O.I.," which officially became the "F.B.I." in January 1936). For this assignment Virginia headed over to Reliance Pictures, the successful brainchild of producer Edward Small. Unlike Sam Goldwyn, Small kept a low profile in a prolific career that lasted decades. His films were distributed by United Artists. Titled *Let 'Em Have It*, the film was part of a recent cycle on "G Men" (a term reputedly coined by gangster "Machine Gun Kelly" in 1933). Three-time Oscar-nominated director Sam Wood put the master's touch to a story that *The New York Times* thought, "a trifle on the Boy Scout side."[40] An earlier release, "*G*" *Men*, with a signature Jimmy Cagney performance, put an indelible mark on just how tough these guys operated. In *Let 'Em Have It*, agent Richard Arlen's dapper group come across as dilettantes. However, we are privy to an insider's look into the "B.O.I." where experts examine a well-worn glove taken from the scene of a crime. From this evidence they are able to determine (convincingly) a complete description of the culprit, his occupation and his general whereabouts. The glove in question belongs to parolee Joe Keefer (Bruce Cabot), a former chauffeur of Virginia's family, who once

had failed in an attempt
to help kidnap her. Cabot,
out to get a million bucks
for himself, decides to rob
banks instead. He meets
his end, not so much from
J. Edgar Hoover's boys, but
from an elderly plastic surgeon. Cabot, with his face
recognized throughout
the country, wants a "new
look." The surgeon gives
him one — he carves Keef-
er's initials into Cabot's
face. The horror expressed
by his buddies when Cabot
unwraps his surgical tape, is

Escapade (1935) with William
Powell (MGM)

worth the price of admission. Smashing a mirror, Cabot growls,
"If I knew where that doctor was buried, I'd dig him outta that
grave and cut him to pieces!"

Cabot's tough, embittered Joe Keefer is the film's most
memorable performance, but some critics thought Virginia
stole the show. As a strong-willed society girl she received high
praise from *Time* magazine. "The heroine of *Let 'Em Have It*
. . . is the sister of one agent; the sweetheart of another. In this
role handsome Virginia Bruce gives the best performance in the
picture."[41] This was Virginia's third film with Richard Arlen and
they socialized regularly. After the film's release, Virginia frequently took Susan Ann over to the Richard Arlen home to play
with Richard Arlen, Jr. (who was born the same year as Susan). On
two separate occasions the adventuresome Susan Ann fell into the

Arlen fish pond. After her second plunge, Arlen filled in the pond for a flower bed.

Back at MGM, Virginia was given a supporting role in an "A" production, *Escapade* (a remake of the German film *Masquerade*). William Powell and Myrna Loy starred. Powell played a debonair Viennese artist and ladies man, with charm so penetrating, husbands shake in their boots. Loy was cast as a naive young woman whisked from obscurity into headlines. Loy felt the part was all wrong for her, and the script "terrible." "Don't put me in this thing," Loy told MGM. "I'm not that wistful little girl selling flowers on the streets of Vienna."[42] A week into shooting, Loy was replaced with Viennese actress Luise Rainer. On screen, socialite Virginia creates a scandal when Powell unveils a semi-nude portrait of her (for modesty sake, she is wearing a mask). He convinces her husband (Frank Morgan) that the portrait is of someone else! When questioned, Powell creates a fictitious name for his model, "Miss Major." Lo and behold, a "Miss Major" (enter Rainer) really exits. She's a companion to an aging Duchess. According to the *New York Times* Rainer's abilities were akin to a damn burst. So copious was her sobbing, that the film had trouble keeping its head above water. "Its story thread is so tortuous," said the *Times* critic, "and Miss Rainer's tears and hysterics so abundant that interest is bound to droop."[43] The *Times* described Rainer's turn as "Alternately shy, demure, vivacious, petulant, happy, miserable, tragic and broodingly maternal ... a broad sweep for any picture. . . . We should have been happier had the story chosen to limit its emotional range a bit."[44] *Variety* referred to Virginia's character as "a willing-to-philander married lady" and said of her performance, "the pert minx of Virginia Bruce is a standout on the performance end."[45]

1934 – Back at MGM – publicity shot
(by Ball) showing her long tresses

Between scenes, Virginia retreated to a chaise lounge in her studio dressing room, a small affair, right in the midst of MGM's
"Dressing Room Row." She had her room decorated in blue and
white (blue, being her favorite color). A framed photograph of

Virginia and baby Susan graced one wall. Another photo, a smiling portrait of John Gilbert, sat on her dressing table. Virginia received visitors wearing something casual, yet striking; such as deep garnet, Charvet lounging pajamas, which accentuated her camellia complexion and deep blue-grey eyes. Writer Juliette Lane observed that Virginia's hair, "long and uncurled, hung down her back in a quaint Alice-In-Wonderland fashion."[46] Like RKO star Ann Harding, Virginia had resisted cutting her long blonde tresses, which reached to the knee. After one of his visits, reporter Jack Smalley gave further details. "By her dressing table," noted Smalley, "were beige linen towels exquisitely embroidered in cerise with a monogram composed of the letters 'VBG' — Virginia Bruce Gilbert. She is proud of the man whose name she bears, and those initials are to her a badge of loyalty . . . She is served by Hazel, the pretty colored maid long in the employ of Greta Garbo. Virginia greatly admires Garbo. There should be a sense of affinity between them, for that matter."[47] The "affinity" Smalley referred to, of course, was the man behind the embroidered monogram. It's doubtful Smalley would have broached the subject of Garbo and Gilbert. But, one certainly wonders what stories *Hazel* could have told.

Spencer Tracy made his MGM contract debut with Virginia in an absorbing "B" picture, *Murder Man*. He played a top-notch crime reporter who continually "stops the press" with groundbreaking coverage. The film focuses on the murder of a wealthy financier/womanizer, and Tracy's ploy to condemn an innocent man for the crime. James Stewart (in his film debut) plays a cub reporter and Virginia does double duty as advice columnist and love interest for Tracy. No doubt newsman Tracy is good at what he does, but what's behind his moodiness and drinking? What is he hiding? Tracy's own excuses are vague. Virginia and the viewer remain clueless until the last reel when Tracy admits to the murder. The reason? He had been swindled of his life savings *and* his wife. *The New York Times* thought Tracy "interesting" and commented that "so little is required of the other performers that their work does not merit comment."[48] From Los An-

Murder Man (1935) **with Robert Barrett and Spencer Tracy (MGM)**

geles, critic Elizabeth Yeaman concurred with the east coast, saying, "Miss Bruce, as a sob sister, has little acting to do and is present chiefly for ornamental purposes. Tracy turns in his usual workmanlike performance."[49] In truth, Virginia registers strongly in her scenes with Tracy. Her deep concern for his emotional snarls and drinking binges give credence to, and underscore his almost insular performance. In the final scene, trying to explain himself, Tracy asks Virginia to always remember something he had once told her. "You're caught in the rapids and you go exactly where they take you." His remark hits home. She understands his torment. As if she were looking into the eyes of John Gilbert instead of Spencer Tracy, Virginia replies, "I'll remember a whole lot more than that."

By the summer of 1935, through Marlene Dietrich's insistence, John Gilbert was doing a color screen test for her new Paramount film, *Desire.* Dietrich was intent to succeed with Technicolor, where Garbo had failed with *Queen Christina.* Gilbert was cast in the role of Carlos Margoli, Dietrich's sophisticated accomplice in jewel thievery. The Lubitsch film would also co-star Gary Cooper. Dietrich's plan came to an unexpected halt right before New Year's, 1936, when she witnessed Gilbert suffer a mild heart attack in his swimming pool. Paramount backed out of the picture deal. Gilbert was now an insurance risk. His recovery looked promising, but on the morning of January 9, 1936, he experienced a massive coronary. He awakened Marlene, who was spending the night with him. According to her daughter Maria, Dietrich dialed "one of her string of unsavory doctors, who could be counted on to keep their mouths shut."[50] Dietrich scurried about removing all traces of her ever being there. Maria emphasized that, "the proclaimed epitome of pure motherhood could not be discovered in her lover's bed!"[51] Marlene left Gilbert, his face grayed, his eyes glazed, his back arched with agony, and escaped before the police arrived and newshounds devoured the scene.

After hearing a radio broadcast announcing that Gilbert had died *alone*, young Maria, who had grown fond of him, rushed to her mother's bedroom. "I found her," Maria recalled, dressed in a monk's robe of black velvet, arranging dozens of tuberoses into vases placed on every available surface . . . Small flames flickered in red-glass votive candles; they stood before John Gilbert's picture, throwing a soft blush onto that gentle face. In a voice of woe and abject misery, my mother sent me from her room. . . . I was ordered not to disturb her . . . she locked the door behind me. For days, she remained entombed . . . my mother's gramophone playing Rachmaninoff permeated the house. . . . This was the first time I witnessed my mother mourning as a widow. In the years to come, she did this so often that by the time her real husband died, her grieving widowhood had become a *deja vu*."[52]

Dietrich's mourning was entwined with guilt. The abandonment of her lover at such a crucial and final moment left her with an agonizing remorse. To relieve herself from responsibility, she needed someone else to blame for her actions. She selected an obvious target: Virginia Bruce.

Endnotes

1   Muriel Babcock, "The Girl From Fargo," *Silver Screen,* 4/35
2   "Divorce Suit on John Gilbert Up For Trial," *LA Evening Herald Express*, 5/25/34
3   Ibid.
4   "Gilbert's Wife Given Divorce," *Los Angeles Times*, 5/26/34
5   "Virginia Bruce Becomes Fourth Ex-Mate of John Gilbert, Actor," *Florence Morning News (S.C.)*, 5/26/34
6   Marie Canel, "Determined Not to Let Divorce Embitter Life," *Fargo Forum*, 6/3/34
7   Fountain, pg 239
8   Laine, "Remedy for Heartbreak . . . "
9   Chester B. Bahn, review for *Dangerous Corner, Syracuse Herald*, 11/5/34
10   Myrna Loy, *"Being and Becoming,"* pg 87
11   Fountain, pg 243
12   Smalley, "Nothing Can . . . "
13   Fountain, pg 244
14   Maria Riva, *Marlene Dietrich*, pg 354
15   ibid
16   Riva, pg 355
17   Riva, pg 356
18   Tip Off, "That Certain Party," *Los Angeles Times*, 9/2/34
19   Robbin Coons, "Hollywood Sights and Sounds," *Evening Tribune (Albert Lea, Minn.)*, 9/12/34
20   Laine, "Remedy for Heartbreak . . ."
21   Muriel Babcock, "The Girl From Fargo," *Silver Screen*, 4/35
22   Harrison Carroll, review of *The Mighty Barnum, The LA Evening Herald Express*, 1/18/35
23   review of *The Mighty Barnum, Time*, 12/31/34
24   Andre Sennwald review of *The Mighty Barnum, New York Times*, 12/24/34
25   Jimmy Starr, review of *The Mighty Barnum, LA Evening Herald*, 12/21/34
26   Norbet Lusk, review of *The Mighty Barnum, Los Angeles Times*, 12/30/34
27   Babcock, "The Girl From . . ."

28   Alma Whitaker, "Emotional Days, These, in Life of Virginia Bruce," *Los Angeles Times*, 1/16/35

29   Babcock, "The Girl From . . . "

30   Louella Parsons, "Movie-Go-Round," *LA Examiner*, 2/2/35

31   Smalley, "Nothing Can . . . "

32   review of *Society Doctor, New York Times*, 2/4/35

33   ibid

34   Smalley, "Nothing Can . . . "

35   Rialtn, review of *Times Square Lady, LA Evening Herald Express*, 4/5/35

36   review of *Times Square Lady, Photoplay*, 5/35

37   Alma Whitaker, "Emotional . . . "

38   Alice L. Tildesley, "Are Women Making "Saps" of Men?" *Lincoln Star (Neb.)*, 11/11/34

39   ibid

40   Andrew Sennwald, review of *Let 'Em Have It, New York Times*, 5/3/35

41   review of *Let 'Em Have It, Time Magazine*, 6/10/35

42   Myrna Loy, *Being and Becoming*, Knopf, N.Y. (1987) pg 98

43   F.S.N. review of *Escapade, The New York Times*, 7/6/35

44   ibid

45   review of *Escapade, Variety*, 6/35

46   Laine, "Remedy for Heartbreak . . . "

47   Smalley, "Nothing Can . . . "

48   F.S.N. review of *Murder Man, New York Times*, 7/27/35

49   Elizabeth Yeaman, review of *Murder Man, Hollywood Citizen News*, 8/8/35

50   Riva, pg 372

51   ibid

52   Riva, pg 373

CHAPTER 7:

Virginia Bruce vs. "Widow" Dietrich

January 11, 1936. It was gray and drizzling the day of John Gilbert's funeral. The service was held at the Beverly Hills Episcopalian Church of St. Mary of the Angels. In striking contrast to the passages of other film greats, Gilbert's body did not lie in state for hordes of fans to stare upon. A select forty friends and family members attended the ceremony. Guests were seated in a dimly lit chapel where Gilbert's closed cedar casket was covered with a gray broadcloth. Three glowing six-foot candles were on either side of the coffin. Among the intimates attending were Gary Cooper and wife Sandra Shaw, producer Arthur Hornblow and Myrna Loy, Gilbert's co-star Raquel Torres, John Barrymore, director King Vidor, and Jetta Goudal. Gilbert's stepfather, Walter Gilbert of San Francisco, was present. Virginia was accompanied by her father and brother Stanley. They sat not too far from Gilbert's second wife Leatrice Joy, and his daughter little Leatrice, whose "tender pink roses, pale gardenias, and lilies of the valley . . . covered [her] father's resting place."[1] Two-year-old Susan Ann was not taken to the services. During the Reverend Neal Dodd's recitation of the twenty-third Psalm, both ex-wives wept softly. There was no eulogy. Gilbert had often requested that his funeral would be, "quiet, simple and unostentatious."[2] He did not get his wish.

As the last limousine arrived outside the church, a large crowd of onlookers pressed against police lines. Out stepped Marlene Dietrich. Wearing black silk, she entered the tiny chapel and stumbled down the aisle toward her own spectacular floral piece, a star of gardenias, which lay at the head of Gilbert's coffin (some reports say it was a sheaf of white gladiolas).[3] Approaching the casket, she suddenly clutched her heart and collapsed. Her "display of grief [was] so theatrical that it almost stopped the show."[4] From out of the surprised onlookers came Gary Cooper. He rushed to her side and helped her up. She clung to his arm as he escorted her to her seat. Dietrich's audible sobs eclipsed the gentle sound of organ music and the Reverend's recitation. She sobbed throughout the service. Fortunately, it was short. The newspapers had a field day reporting Dietrich's "dramatics." Upon leaving the church, she stayed 'in character.' A typical report stated that, hands trembling, "Miss Dietrich was so near collapse that she was led to her car by Dolores Del Rio ... and Cedric Gibbons."[5] Pallbearer Irving Thalberg, who felt remorse for not supporting Gilbert during his decline at MGM, thought Dietrich's exhibition was overdone. He commented that there was, "No need for it." Norma Shearer's biographer, Gavin Lambert, states that Thalberg was so appalled by Dietrich's display he later asked Norma to tone down her balcony scene farewell to Romeo during the production of MGM's *Romeo and Juliet*.

Virginia, who was also visibly upset upon leaving the service, was unfazed by Dietrich's theatrics. If anything, it prepared her for more of the same. Not long after Gilbert's service, Virginia and Marlene both received invitations to a party given by Countess Dorothy di Frasso. Virginia dressed in white and made no display. She knew she was no longer Gilbert's wife. Marlene, who had announced she would be wearing mourning for a year, made it clear that *she* was the grieving "widow."[6] Looking back on the event, columnist Kirtley Baskette succinctly remembered: "It was characteristic of Virginia to make no pretense. She hadn't been John Gilbert's wife at the time of his death. But the memory of that incident lingers, accented, because another woman who had *never* been his wife, Marlene Dietrich, showed up at the same party in deepest black — and all evening she didn't smile once."[7] In early February 1936, either out of love or morbid curiosity, Dietrich made a point of witnessing the cremation of Gilbert's remains.[8]

In 1932, Irving Thalberg had encouraged Virginia not to drop her career. In 1934, after the divorce, he was influential in getting her contract reinstated. That's as far as his help extended. He was busy at the helm of MGM's prestige pictures, especially those starring his wife Norma Shearer. Virginia had no guiding hand, other than her own. Her last MGM release for 1935, director Paul Sloane's *Here Comes the Band*, has to be among the studio's worst musicals. Sloane's previous film, *Down to Their Last Yacht* (1934), was RKO's biggest money-*losing* musical. Twenty-five percent of the scenes had to be reshot using a different director. *Here Comes the Band* (also written by Sloane) was a hopeless hodgepodge. The story opens, amusingly enough, with a radio talent contest. For a lark, wealthy socialite Virginia decides to sing an aria from *Lucia di Lammermoor*. The contestant before her selects the same aria, only she clucks it, impersonating a chicken. Virginia's more serious attempt is laughed off stage. Next up, is crooner Harry

Here Comes the Band (1935) Radio Master Gene Morgan listens to Virginia sing "Chi mi frena in tal momento" from Donizetti's *Lucia di Lammermoor.* (MGM)

Stockwell (father of actor Dean Stockwell), who wins the competition with his cowpoke hymn, "Hell-Bent for Heaven" (the Hays Office insisted the song be retitled "I'm Going to Heaven" before the film's release). In a bizarre scene shift, we are transported to the trenches of WWI for some nonsense with Ted Healy (original straight man to the 3 Stooges) and entertainer Ted Lewis (who appears from nowhere with his band blaring "The Stars and Stripes Forever"). Another shift finds us at Virginia's posh mansion for a pleasant interlude in which she and Stockwell woo one another with a melodic tune, "Tender is the Night." Virginia's vocals show off her uniquely pleasant mezzo soprano. She looks breathtakingly elegant, as if she stepped out of . . . another movie.

Not knowing where else to go, the film ends with a scene in court after a publisher steals one of Stockwell's folksongs. To his rescue come contingents of yodeling hillbillies and chanting Native Americans to bear witness. After this dumbfounding exhibition, judge and jury rule in Stockwell's favor. Case dismissed. The film fades out with a frightening close-up of Ted Lewis' smiling face as he marches down the street cheering, "Is Everybody Happy?" "Everybody," hopefully, has already left the theatre.

Pirate Party on Catalina Isle (1935) was an on-location MGM short, which featured Virginia as herself along with screen heroes Errol Flynn, Chester Morris, Cary Grant, and Randolph Scott. The highlight of this musical romp was the ebullient musical talent of Buddy Rogers who played every available instrument in his orchestra. An amused Virginia sat at a table, smartly dressed for her first Technicolor close-up.

Virginia's plans for a vacation in Hawaii were delayed when she was offered the opportunity to play opposite baritone Lawrence Tibbett in Darryl F. Zanuck's *Metropolitan* (1935). The film was 20th Century-Fox's first production. It had a good director, Richard Boleslawski (*Les Miserable)*, the inventive camerawork of Rudolph Mate (*The Passion of Joan of Arc)*, and included excerpts from *Faust, I Pagliacci, Carmen,* and *Barber of Seville.* Virginia, having honed her lip-syncing

Metropolitan (1935) with Luis Alberni, Cesar Romero, and opera baritone Lawrence Tibbett (20th-Century Fox)

skills in *The Mighty Barnum*, was ready to offer a similar splendid job with "Michaela's Aria" from *Carmen*. All these pluses, lent themselves for an impressive photoplay.

In *Metropolitan* we first encounter Virginia in the countryside attempting to fix her stalled car. The car radio is blaring symphonic music that passerby Tibbett, on foot, sings along to. After learning he performs at the Met, Virginia is smitten. She attends one of his performances only to find him lost somewhere in the chorus, *behind* the company's fading prima donna (Alice Brady). Bruce comments to escort Cesar Romero, "With a voice like *that*! We have to go around a fat woman to find him!" Virginia's operatic ambitions soon place her in the Met's chorus where she observes Tibbett playing "yes man" to Brady. Virginia overlooks his predicament. "With a voice like yours," Virginia tells Tibbett, "a woman must forgive you everything!" Upon hearing Virginia's rendition of "Michaela's Aria," and getting drift of her interest in Tibbett, a jealous Brady surprises no one with her temperamental theatrics by calling the opera off! Virginia however, has her own surprise in store. She's rich! She writes a big, fat check and saves the show. Throughout the film, Tibbett's voice is nothing short of sensational. And, "with a voice like his," we can forgive the film its rather trite and perfunctory ending.

Not surprisingly, Virginia received high approval for her lip-syncing in *Metropolitan*. "Though she cannot sing," noted *Newsweek*, "her arias are dubbed in so perfectly that it is impossible to notice the voice does not belong to her."[9] The review commended the production, saying, "*Metropolitan* succeeds in lifting the taboos from opera once more making it good box-office — an achievement many put beyond Hollywood's capabilities." *The New York Times* raved, "Alice Brady gives a gloriously demented performance . . . Virginia Bruce, whose timing in *The Mighty*

Barnum was so perfect that spectators refused to believe someone was singing for her, is equally effective this time as an ambitious soprano . . . *Metropolitan* is very likely the best musical film of the season."[10] It is interesting to note that Madge Bellamy, who was the star of *Fugitives* (Virginia's first film), had one close up and one line in *Metropolitan*. In *Fugitives* Virginia had one close-up and one line. Fate played strange tricks in Hollywood.

Edmund Lowe, who was twenty years Virginia's senior, frequently escorted her about the Hollywood social scene, to the opera, and football games during 1934-36. He had firmly established his reputation as a film actor in 1926's *What Price Glory?*, playing the tough-talking Sergeant Quirt and popularizing the catch phrase "Sez you!" Lowe was an established "safe" date. He often sported purple ties and wore yellow gloves. The gay actor's wife, Lilyan Tashman, an unapologetic lesbian, had passed away in early 1934. The couple had one of tinsel town's "lavender marriages," and part of Hollywood's sophisticated clique. Lowe was well-read and articulate, which accommodated Virginia's penchant for improving herself. No doubt she was pleased when MGM cast her opposite him in a new Philo Vance detec-

Garden Murder Case (1936) with
Edmund Lowe (MGM)

tive piece, *The Garden Murder Case*. Lowe was the fifth actor to play the poised detective Vance (a role associated with William Powell). *The Garden Murder Case* featured Lowe solving a series of murders committed under hypnosis. Author S. S. Van Dine created Vance as cynical and impersonal. "An irrational human weakness like romance would be alien to his nature," said Van Dine.[11] In *The Garden Murder Case*, however, Van Dine created a softer side to Vance. MGM accented the romantic element, allowing Lowe to appear more personable and giving ample screen time for Virginia's character. As a consequence, not much of the original plot was retained. Still, *The New York Times* thought the film "a stimulating and ingenious murder mystery . . . an experienced cast does an excellent job with it."[12] The brisk, 61-minute feature's most suspenseful moment occurs in the last five minutes, as Lowe, hypnotized by the perpetrator, stands precariously on a balcony edge overlooking the city below.

The preliminaries which get Vance to this predicament involve a number of interesting characters — the attractive, strong-willed Virginia being the standout among them. Philo meets her at the racetrack after her rich uncle (Gene Lockhart) chastises her for betting on a losing horse with his money. Incensed, she answers back, "Yes, uncle *dear*. Wearing *your* clothes. Drinking *your* wine, and breathing *your* air!" Virginia's opportunistic boyfriend shushes her, saying, "Shut up, will you?" "All shut up for the day, darling!" she smugly answers back. Enter Philo Vance. As an alternate suitor for Virginia, Vance provides the added advantage of solving any family murders that pop up. And pop up they do. Almost immediately he must rescue Virginia from her own family after Lockhart is found dead. Her grandmother (Jessie Ralph) is convinced Virginia pulled the trigger and calls her a "smirking Jezebel." She orders Vance to take Virginia out of the house. "Take her out and hang her!" she bellows. (The slightly incestuous love-hugs between Jessie Ralph and son Lockhart in an earlier scene might explain her wrath.) Instead of a hanging, Virginia and Lowe find themselves in an unexpected romantic clinch from which Lowe backs off. "Getting forward, aren't we?" he says. "*Getting* forward?" she answers back, "We're *there!*" It's exactly this aggressive self-assured energy of Virginia's character that makes her so appealing. She easily steals the picture.

While columnists gossiped about Virginia's "captivating rumbas" with Cesar Romero, and "romances" with Edmund Lowe, Robert Taylor, William Bakewell, Dick Powell, and Nelson Eddy, Virginia herself was only interested in going out and having a good time. Responsibilities at work and home were time-consuming challenges. Going out, meant relaxing. She wanted to marry again, but decided to wait, "because I must have time in which to grow up mentally and emotionally," she told her friend Gladys Hall. "I need five years to make of myself what I want to be. You see, I've reversed the customary tables. I am beginning my career . . . living at home with my parents, going out with boys, having my growing-up time *after* marriage instead of before. And my work is what I want now. I gave it up once. I shall not give it up again. As a matter of fact my chief claim to fame still lies in the fact that I once married John Gilbert. I want five years to *stake a claim for myself.*"[13] As part of her self-improvement campaign Virginia attended a summer philosophy class at U.S.C. in 1935. "It's interesting, refreshing and quite a change from Hollywood," she told one reporter.[14] Virginia's reasons for attending class were part of a larger vision. "I want to be an intelligent, poised woman

Nelson Eddy doting on Virginia at 1934 costume party (Courtesy of Photofest)

of the world, not merely another pretty girl," she told writer Eleanor Packer. "I want to be able to change my personality, adapt my conversation to fit all types of people and situations. I want to learn to be at ease with everyone, wherever I may go. Of all the people I meet, particularly the women, the ones I admire most are the ones who are constantly changing. ... You've often heard people say, 'Be sure to invite so-and-so. She fits in everywhere.' That's the kind of a person I hope to be some day. ... The ones who are elastic, who can be depended upon to fit any picture, are never tiresome. It's a real art, that ability to adapt."[15]

Virginia often caught herself prattling on and on about "nothing" to Stanley's college friends, as well as co-workers at the studio. During her time in New York, and as Gilbert's wife, she observed a caliber of intelligence, an appreciation of art and literature, which made her determined to let go of her "gushing ingénue." Virginia was peeved when she was acknowledged simply for being beautiful. Being *looked* at was not enough. "I discovered that you have to develop a versatility of charm and intelligence as carefully as you train and foster a singing voice or any other artistic ability," she stated. Virginia's motivations for improvement where given a definite nudge by having a young daughter. "I've made up my mind to go forward, in my work and in my own life," she said. "I hope that Susan will be proud of me,

April 22, 1935: Countess di Frasso party. Virginia sang "Annie Laurie" at the affair, which paved the way to her role in *Born to Dance*. Virginia is seated next to Dolores Del Rio, di Frasso, and Clark Gable

that she will think that I am the most charming, most fascinating woman she knows. . . . Do you know the one thing in this world which terrifies me? A person who knows a great deal more than I do. People like that make me tongue-tied and self-conscious . . . some day, I'm going to know enough to hold my own with everyone." Virginia had to smile to herself when her session with Packer concluded. "At least, I've learned how little I know," she laughed. Nothing, however, not a University course at U.S.C. or an intense study of arachnids could have prepared Virginia for the further antics of Marlene Dietrich.

Four years before his death, John Gilbert's net worth was close to $800,000. Upon his death, attorney Peyton H. Moore explained that divorce settlements figured heavily into Gilbert's estate. For example, he had paid Ina Claire $46,000 plus "incidentals" for a combined total of $75,000. Although Gilbert's salary was $500,000 yearly for 1929, 1930, and 1931, $200,000 went to annual taxes. In addition to his residence on Tower Road, Gilbert had invested in a Los Angeles business block. His investments, however, in real estate, stocks, and bonds, had definitely taken a hit during the Depression.[16]

On January 13, 1936, John Gilbert's will was filed in the probate court. The will was dated October 7, 1932, two months after his marriage to Virginia. The first bequest of $10,000 was left for his daughter, Leatrice Joy Gilbert. Newspapers announced that his worth was estimated at $250,000, with Virginia Bruce slated to receive the bulk of his estate. Gilbert provided her six annuities totaling $150,000. Depending on various reports, somewhere between $53,000 -$60,000 was bequeathed to various friends.

$25,000 was put in a trust fund for Dick Hyland, Jr., son of writer Adela Rogers St. John. Attorney Peyton H. Moore, Sr., (who received $10,000) declared the will was the last one made by Gilbert.[17] But, someone wasn't happy.

A few days after the news of Gilbert's estate was made public, Marlene Dietrich called his second wife, Leatrice Joy Hook. She told her that Gilbert had written *another* will that favored his daughter Leatrice. She also claimed his Filipino houseboy had witnessed it. Dietrich encouraged Leatrice to contest the 1932 will. On January 18, following the instructions of Gilbert's bereaved lover Dietrich, Leatrice Joy Hook went to court to seek a larger share of Gilbert's $250,000 estate for her daughter. Leatrice contended that "Gilbert promised half of the estate to his first daughter."[18] A few days later little Leatrice received a bouquet of flowers tied with pink ribbons. A card was attached, saying, "I adored your father. Let me adore you." It was from Marlene Dietrich.

Dietrich's daughter Maria recalled her mother's conversation with her father, in which Dietrich launched into a tirade saying,

> That gold-digger Virginia Bruce, she has stolen his
> last will! . . . Yes! she *has*! She gave them the will
> he made *before* the heart attack, the one where
> he leaves *her* everything. . . . I told him he could
> not leave everything to that awful woman, that
> he had to give everything to his child! But now,
> nobody can find that will. So I said 'I *saw* him write
> it' — so now, of course, everybody is searching and
> that Bruce woman is shaking in her shoes! I got his
> Filipino servant a job at the Studio . . . in the Art
> Department. He deserves something. He is so loyal
> and doesn't *talk*. I also gave him money."[19]

Providing Gilbert's houseboy with a job at Paramount and a little hush money in his pocket indicates Dietrich had something to hide, or something she was trying to hide *from*. Was the "phantom will" something that Dietrich instructed Gilbert to undertake . . . "*I told him* he could not leave everything to that awful woman." Dietrich's conversation with her husband indicates that the new will (which no one would ever find) was written *after* Gilbert's heart attack, when he was most vulnerable — a month prior to his death. The whole episode has the markings of something spiteful and contrived. Dietrich's daughter surmised, "There are so many versions of my mother's role in the death of John Gilbert that it is a hopeless task to attempt to unravel the maze of lies and suppositions."[20]

One thing remained clear. Dietrich's machinations were delayed until October 16, 1937, the start of proceedings in superior court to distribute Gilbert's $407,453 estate (a re-estimate from July 15, 1936). Leatrice Joy had abandoned, or wised up to, Dietrich's scheme. She had been told that if the will was contested and the case lost, little Leatrice might end up with nothing. So, Leatrice simply asked to be appointed legal guardian of her daughter's $10,000 legacy from the estate.[21] Looking back years later, daughter Leatrice felt that the relationship that developed between her and Dietrich filled the void her father had left. She called Dietrich her "fairy godmother." For some time Dietrich's "adoration" of Leatrice included invitations to theatre openings, long walks, and to her home to bake cookies. Leatrice was certainly aware of Dietrich's dislike for Virginia. Understandably, she believed Dietrich's "missing will" story, telling an interviewer as late as 1999, "Virginia Bruce hired [Gilbert's] last crooked attorney, and the two of them destroyed or repressed it or whatever. Marlene kept up the good fight and encouraged my mother to fight Miss Bruce and the crooked attorneys. She dropped it, and Marlene was furious."[22] When Leatrice was researching Gilbert's life in the 1970s, Virginia was cooperative and divulged many personal stories about her marriage to Gilbert. She was upfront about what Gilbert and Mr. Briggs had arranged, telling Leatrice, "Jack agreed to write a new will leaving everything to me and my family."[23] When "fairy godmother" Dietrich was contacted in the 1970s, she refused to talk to Leatrice.

The flames of Dietrich's indignation were fanned anew by the news that Gilbert's estate would be sold. "Marlene was even more incensed," said Leatrice, "when she learned that Virginia Bruce was putting all Jack's property up for public auction. Virginia was selling *everything*."[24] Leatrice's mother, however, maintained a sense of humor amid the drama when she heard about the auction proceedings. A United Press release from August 26, 1936, titled "Star's Toilet Soap Worth 15 Cents," is black comedy at its best. The article describes a portly, perspiring man banging his mallet and announcing in his train-caller's voice, "Sold for $11.50 — John Gilbert's sharkskin pants." The crowd, predominantly women, sweltered in a barn-like building and "sighed romantically" as each item to be auctioned passed by. The report stated that "clothing which presumably had personal contact with the Gilbert torso aroused the most spirited bidding among women." Each time his intimate apparel went on the block, ladies leaned forward in their chairs, lips set grimly, and bids were made "until they reached the bottom of their pocketbooks."[25] It was mentioned that "several wrangles" occurred between women. But, apparently, Gilbert had also stirred the hearts of a few men. A thin white-haired lady in her sixties "groaned audibly" when Gilbert's BVD's went to a "prosy little man with white spats." The real capper involved Gilbert's eight-foot bed which was purchased for $1,250 to be installed in the Summit Hotel near Uniontown, Pennsylvania. Lucky couples would be able to enter a drawing for a chance to win twenty-four-hour romp in the "John Gilbert Honeymoon Room." At this, ex-wife Leatrice commented, "Jack would have laughed himself sick."[26]

Virginia was not present for the auction, but had a representative acquire a volume of Shakespeare's sonnets. Eleven-year-old Leatrice got her father's make-up box (it was actually his mother's), put up a spirited battle for his chess board (he had taught her to play), and outbid a calf-bound copy of Shelley's poems. Clarence Brown, who had directed Gilbert in films, bid for expensive Italian antiques and a leaf of the Guttenberg Bible. Marlene Dietrich was in England, but sent an agent who was instructed to buy Gilbert's bed sheets at any price. Thirty plain cotton sheets valued at a dollar apiece went for $300. The newspapers said she made no effort to obtain anything else, but paid ten times the intrinsic value of the sheets "because the late John Gilbert slept between them in his Hollywood mansion."[27] Dietrich's purchase certainly raised a few eyebrows. It was an odd move for someone who had once made such a frantic effort to escape not only the very same sheets, but John Gilbert *himself* on his deathbed.

After the auction, Gladys Hall was surprised by Virginia's attitude regarding Dietrich. Hall wrote, "Virginia said, with such sincerity, that she is glad John Gilbert had Marlene Dietrich to spoil him in those last months of his life. It was so good for him. Virginia said Marlene bolstered up his ego, which so badly needed bolstering. He could, she explained, still feel that he hadn't lost the compelling fire of the 'great lover' when he could attract one of the most glamorous women in the world."[28] "I wasn't with him," said Virginia. "I couldn't be. So I am glad that

Marlene was."[29] Virginia's true feelings regarding Dietrich were most likely mixed. In writer/producer Samuel Marx's *Mayer and Thalberg – The Make-Believe Saints*, Marx mentions Virginia bitterly referring to Dietrich, and remarking, "She behaves like *she's* his widow!"[30]

Perhaps the saddest part of Gilbert's passing was the burial of his ashes at Forest Lawn. In an October 10, 1936 column by the United Press it was stated, "Although the screen's romantic star had been worshiped by millions when he was at the crest of his fame, only a former employee was present yesterday when Gilbert's ashes were buried under the tree in a sealed urn."[31]

Endnotes

1   "Noted Beauties Week At Bier of Gilbert, Once Filmland Idol," *Charleston Gazette (W.V.)*, 1/12/36

2   "Gilbert Funeral Saturday is to be Quiet, Simple," *Modesto Bee*, 1/11/36

3   Relamn Morin, "Marlene Dietrich and 'A Fan' Weep at Gilbert's Funeral," *Portsmouth Times (OH)*. 1/12/36

4   Gavin Lambert, *Norma Shearer*, Knopf, N.Y., 1990 pg 228

5   "Simple Ceremony," *San Mateo Times*, 1/11/36

6   Samuel Marx, *Mayer and Thalberg – The Make-Believe Saints*, Random House, NY, 1975, pg 246

7   Kirtley Baskette, *Second Chance at Love*, *Photoplay*, 2/38

8   News article, *Syracuse Herald (N.Y.)*, 2/15/36

9   Review for *Metropolitan*, 10/26/35

10   Andre Sennwald, review for *Metropolitan*, *New York Times*, 10/18/35

11   Jon Tusken, *The Detective in Hollywood*, Doubleday, N.Y., 1978, pg 45

12   B.R.C. review of *The Garden Murder Case*, *New York Times*, 3/2/36

13   Gladys Hall, "Why Virginia Bruce Won't Marry for Five Years," *Photoplay*, 11/35

14   article, author's collection, c. 1935

15   Eleanor Packer, "Love Opened My Eyes!" *Screen Book*, 11/35

16   "Virginia Bruce is Major Heir In Gilbert's Will," *Fargo Forum*, 1/14/36

17   "Many Named in Gilbert Will," *San Mateo Times*, 1/13/36

18   "Wives Battle Over Estate," *Ogden Standard Examiner*, 1/19/36

19   Riva, *Marlene Dietrich*, pp 373-374

20   Riva pg 372

21   "Wives Scrap Over John Gilbert Will," *Yuma Daily Sun*, 10/16/37

22   Jimmy Bangley, "An Interview with Leatrice Gilbert Fountain," *Classic Images*, 1999

23   Fountain, pg 227

24   Fountain, pg 258

25   "Star's Toilet Soap Worth 15 Cents," *Nevada State Journal*, 8/26/36

26   Fountain, pg 259

27   "Marlene Buys sheets Used by John Gilbert," *Fresno Bee*, 8/25/36

28   Gladys Hall, "Do Women Spoil Men?" c. 1936

29   ibid.

30   Samuel Marx, *Mayer and Thalberg-The Make-Believe Saints*, Random House, NY, 1975, pg 246

31   "Hollywood Roundup," *Oshkosh North Western (Wisc.),*, 10/10/36

CHAPTER 8:

ℳℊℳ - All The Stars In Heaven

Virginia and Susan Ann c. 1936

"Virginia Bruce's Baby Is Target of Kidnappers," read the headlines on February 25, 1936. Suddenly, amid the legalities involved with John Gilbert's will, Virginia had her priorities set straight. There was imminent danger to Susan Ann. The incident began when a stranger approached Virginia's friend, Gladys Hall, at Hall's home. Hall, a popular writer in the film community, often represented Virginia whenever the press was involved. The unidentified woman told Hall that she wanted Virginia's phone number and street address. Hall informed the woman that she should contact Virginia through MGM. The woman panicked and exclaimed, "No. No, they are watching the studio. If I should see her there, I would have to leave town to escape them."[1] The woman mentioned there was a plot to kidnap Susan Ann, and specifically stated that both Virginia and her daughter were in "great danger and must be notified."[2] When

Hall attempted to question her further, the woman left hurriedly. Virginia immediately put her parent's Toluca Lake home under police protection.

The panic caused by aviation hero Charles Lindberg's baby being kidnapped and murdered was still fresh in everyone's mind. The 1932 incident, its bungled investigation, and 1934 trial of suspect Bruno Hauptmann, was turned into a media circus. Congress rushed through legislation making kidnapping a federal crime. At the time of the threat to Susan Ann, the Lindberg case was again in the news, as Hauptmann was scheduled for execution that April.

The day following the threat, it was announced that Mr. and Mrs. Earll F. Briggs had taken two-and-a-half-year-old Susan Ann "to a safe place."[3] Search was underway for what Hall described as a "well-to-do Scandinavian woman." Virginia had exercised caution, but she suspected the threat was the work of a crank. She also took into consideration that the press was saturated with news that the bulk of Gilbert's estate had been bequeathed to her. The Lindberg case had been riddled with fortune hunters, opportunists and imposters who took advantage of a dire situation. Virginia told the press, "I wouldn't be surprised but what this scare is the result of some crank's idea, but I'm taking no chances-- my baby means the whole world to me and I'll do anything to keep her from being endangered."[4] Armed guards continued to patrol the Briggs' residence for several days. Fortunately, Virginia was correct in her assumption that the threats were bogus. Although the FBI was not brought into Virginia's case, the incident brought home the ever-present liability of being a celebrity. By mid-March, the Briggs household, Virginia, her daughter, Mr. and Mrs. Briggs, and Stanley, had assumed some semblance of their normal routine.

From the beginning, motherhood had fit Virginia like a glove. Soon after Susan Ann's birth, writer Eleanor Packer visited Virginia and her baby in the hospital. Packer quietly observed the two of them. Virginia gazed into Susan's eyes and reflected that they were "just like John's." Beautiful and frightened. "Sometimes I feel like the mother of the whole world," said Virginia. "I'd like to take care of and mother everyone. There's nothing I enjoy more than listening to other people's problems, trying to help them forget their worries and troubles. That probably sounds silly, but it's true."[5] Over the next couple of years, Virginia doted on Susan. There were plenty of hand-crocheted jackets and embroidered dresses of Virginia's making to prove it. "I really believe that being a mother . . . was the turning point for me," said Virginia. "It made me serious, less self-centered, more confident of myself and taught me a great love and understanding. Being a mother is the greatest thrill I've had in my entire life."[6] A few months before the kidnapping threat, Virginia told Gladys Hall, "I would be *really* unhappy now if I had not had Susan Ann." Her daughter also allowed Virginia to maintain a connection with what she referred to as the most important relationship in her life: John Gilbert. She liked to recall Gilbert's first visit to the hospital when she asked him to name their baby. He responded by throwing out both hands and happily declaring, "Susan Ann!" Virginia, however, had known his mind was preoccupied with his troubled career. "I thought the advent of our baby would be the one thing that would save us," she said. "A week after the baby was born, he was given his role in *Queen Christina* and he came rushing down to the hospital. He was so jubilant he could hardly contain himself."[7] The contrast between Gilbert "the new father"

and Gilbert "the new Garbo co-star" stuck in Virginia's mind. She could see the inevitable. After the divorce, Virginia was left with the stinging observation that Gilbert showed little interest in seeing his daughter. Nonetheless, just before Gilbert's death, Virginia observed, "The baby has my sort of quietness and calm, and she has, also, Jack's fire and artistic temperament and drama. I think she is going to be a remarkable person . . . Jack is there, in her gestures, in her quick likes and dislikes, in the fire that animates that darling baby face. And I am glad."[8]

As for another marriage, Virginia stated that she wanted to be free for her baby and not entangled in another serious relationship. "When I am through here at the studio," Virginia explained, "I go home and have time with Susan Ann before she goes to bed. I undress her and play with her. I read nursery rhymes to her. I teach her her prayers. I can be with her all I want. There is no other demand upon me. . . . Mother does all the housekeeping and managing. I live exactly as a girl lives at home before marriage. . . . My career and my baby — it is to them that I dedicate the next five years of my life."

Regardless of Virginia's new 'dedication', her close friends kept an eye out for her. One of Bruce's few female confidents was Maureen O'Sullivan. "I always wanted friends," admitted Virginia, "but being reserved and shy, I never invited confidences, and Maureen's friendship is like the answer to prayer. She's meant so much to me." After the Gilbert-Bruce divorce, Maureen stuck close by. "With my own happiness established," said O'Sullivan, "my chief desire was to see Virginia happy. Slowly she became conscious of the world about her, tossed aside crushed illusions, and came back to the screen, lovelier and more poised than before. John [Farrow] and I insisted that she go about with us and we included her in all our fun. She used to go with us on our sail-

1937 – Virginia on the court at Westside Tennis Club (courtesy of Vincent Briggs)

boat, even though she's too tender-hearted to fish." O'Sullivan detailed one successful excursion in which they discovered a shoal of fish which filled an entire container. Towards sundown, their 'catch' had somehow disappeared. "When we cornered Virginia," O'Sullivan recalled, "she confessed she thought it was cruel to keep the pretty little fish in a can, so she dumped them back into the ocean! Virginia is a blend of the sophisticate and a very little girl." [9]

Virginia recognized that her social life also brought her much joy. She kept up the friendships she established as Gilbert's wife, especially the Cedric Gibbons (Dolores del Rio), and the Gary Coopers. She was frequently a dinner guest at the home of producer Gene Markey and wife Joan Bennett. Joining the tradition of Hollywood's "theme parties," Virginia rented an entire roller dome in the fall of 1936 for a skating party that rivaled in

Icing on the cake? Virginia's most famous pose in MGM's *The Great Ziegfeld*
– note: her stand-in actually posed for this photo

popularity a Kay Francis' event that turned the Vendome Café into an ocean liner. Aside from an occasional party or evening out, Virginia might find herself enjoying a tennis luncheon at Dolores del Rio's, shopping with her mother (who rarely came to the studio), or taking Susan Ann over to play with other "Toluca Lakers" such as Ricky Arlen, Jr., or Bing Crosby's boys. Summertime was good for getting out the 10x10 rubber swimming pool (a new novelty) that Virginia had purchased for her and Susan to splash around in, and enjoy the sun. High temperatures in the 80's and clear skies graced the Toluca Lake area from May through October. The forecast for Virginia's personal and professional life appeared just as sunny and promising.

MGM, the studio that was the recipient of Virginia's "dedication," had profits of $11 million for 1935-36. This was a reflection of their product, their star power, and a shift in the overall economy. Paramount had emerged from bankruptcy, and Depression movie attendance had risen by 15%. Feature production was on the upswing. At the helm of this promising future was Louis B. Mayer, MGM's domineering studio boss. Mayer had begun his career in 1907 by investing profits from his father's junk dealer business into what became New England's largest theatre chain. He then moved into film distribution. In 1924, Mayer merged with Metro and Goldwyn to form MGM. Glossy, star-studded fam-

The Great Ziegfeld (1936)
a 'devilish' Virginia vs.
an emoting Luise Rainer
(MGM)

ily entertainment became MGM's trademark. In most cases, it was Mayer who could make or break a star's career.

Virginia's star was on the rise. Of the dozen films she had made since reemerging from her divorce, half of them were loanouts in which she had acquitted herself nicely. She was featured significantly in two of Metro's biggest grossing films for 1936, the Oscar-winning *The Great Ziegfeld* and Cole Porter's *Born to Dance*. She gave up the lead in Samuel Goldwyn's film *Come and Get It* in order to meet her obligation for the Porter musical. The question for Virginia was whether or not MGM and Mayer were going to reciprocate for all her cooperation and hard work. She had put in her time and was ready for the star build up that would place her in the stellar ranks of Garbo, Shearer, Loy, MacDonald, Harlow and Crawford. Virginia had the "look" and "feel" for the MGM product. Female stars at other studios often expressed their envy at the treatment the women at MGM received. Warner's top box-office draw, Kay Francis, put it bluntly, "The only fly in the ointment is that Warners is primarily a man's studio. MGM is first of all a woman's studio . . . Our executives and writers understand men thoroughly, but they have no grasp whatever of woman's psychology."[10] Myrna Loy gave her honest appraisal of Metro saying, "Once you were an MGM star, that's the way it was. It helped to have talent, of course, but that constant saturation [publicity] created this legendary kind of thing. We couldn't help becoming legends."[11]

Virginia's role as the quintessential "follies" girl in *The Great Ziegfeld* got people talking about her status at MGM, her talent, and her performance as Audrey Dane. She grabbed hold of the unsympathetic role and relished it. Virginia later confessed, "I liked playing those so-and-sos. When you're not a so-and-so in real life it's sort of fun to be that way on the screen. People whisper, 'Ah-ha, she's got the devil in her!'"[12] One rumor had it that during production Virginia had plenty of "devil" in her. While shooting the "Pretty Girl . . . " number, cast and crew took vengeance and deserted her at lunchtime. Virginia, unable to move in her huge hoop skirt, sat propped atop the mammoth wedding cake for over an hour. She sat there "under hot lights, until at last they relented and rescued her."[13] Critics kept busy wondering exactly *who* Virginia's character was based upon. A few mentioned Marilyn Miller, but the consensus targeted another of Ziegfeld's "greatest passions," Lillian Lorraine. Jack Welch, who was a longtime aide to Ziegfeld, complimented Virginia's performance, and stated that she reminded him of Lorraine.[14] Lorraine was still alive when *The Great Ziegfeld* was released. MGM didn't dare use her name. The raven-haired beauty would have sued, and *how*. The mercurial Lorraine was mixed up in everything from bigamy and blackmail to murder. Metro had no choice but to disguise Lorraine as a volatile blonde, and using the alias Audrey Dane.

Ironically, Lillian Lorraine had skyrocketed to fame in the Ziegfeld production *Miss Innocence* (1909). As with Audrey Dane in *The Great Ziegfeld*, it was well known that Lorraine was the reason the great showman split from his common-law wife, Anna Held. Lorraine was Ziggy's mistress for many years, but drinking and a fiery temper destroyed her career. She made headlines in 1941 after she was rescued from the apartment she had set on fire. The furniture was ablaze, the place littered with empty liquor bottles. While being dragged from her apartment to a psychopathic ward, she thirstily pleaded with the fire department for "just one more drink."[15] Actress Ruth Gordon related the time a reporter found Lorraine living in shambles on

Broadway and 96th. When asked what went wrong, Lillian put her cards on the table. "[Ziegfeld] had me in a tower suite at the Hotel Ansonia," she said, "and he and his wife lived in the tower suite above. And I cheated on him . . . I had a whirl. I blew a lot of everybody's money. I got loaded. I was on the stuff . . . if I wanted to do it I did it and didn't give a damn. I got knocked up. I had abortions. I broke up homes. I gave fellers the clap. So, that's what happened." Asked if she could have done anything differently to change the outcome, Lorraine thoughtfully raised an eyebrow and stated, "Yeh. I never shoulda' cut my hair."[16]

Virginia finally relented and had her own hair cut for the 1936 release *The Garden Murder Case*. According to reporter Harrison Carroll, she was swamped with requests for locks of her hair. Unlike Lillian Lorraine, the change for Virginia was a necessary and definite improvement from the braids and buns piled atop her head. It gave her a contemporary look more conducive to superstardom. Of course, superstardom depended on more than a new hairstyle. Various criteria, perseverance, and clout — especially with Louis B. Mayer, were a prerequisite. One simply has to look at Virginia's competition at MGM.

Aside from her own well-deserved star status, Norma Shearer had the advantage of being producer Thalberg's wife. When he passed away in September 1936, she became a major MGM stockholder (which did not please Mayer). After Mayer tried to nullify Thalberg's estate, Shearer did not hesitate to claim what was rightfully hers. She told him, "If you don't agree to the original terms, my lawyers will fight you year after year until your legal fees put you back in that junkyard you came from!"[17] Mayer quailed before her wrath. Jean Harlow was a brassy, marketable talent — not the MGM "image" Mayer usually held out for, but he tolerated her and recognized she was strong at the box office, especially when paired with Gable. Harlow held her own at the studio until her untimely death in 1937. Joan Crawford's *raison d'etre* was to be a star. A self-promoter, she had a huge, loyal, fan base. In author Gary Carey's study of MGM, he states that Crawford was in awe of Mayer. After registering a complaint with Mayer, she would leave feeling "guilty and disloyal." "Which, of course," notes Carey, "was precisely the way Mayer wanted her to feel."[18] Carey states that supporting players such as Virginia, on their way to becoming stars, were in an even more vulnerable position. Someone like Jeanette MacDonald, Queen of the Musicals at Metro, had no need to worry about Mayer. She was a smart businesswoman and had the advantage of a phenomenal pairing with baritone Nelson Eddy. More importantly, Mayer was infatuated with the redheaded soprano and she enjoyed "toying" with his affections in order to get what she wanted. Greta Garbo, the studio's import, had a reputation for being moody, "difficult," and walking off the set. Mayer often referred to her as "that damned Swede." Nonetheless, Garbo created a mystique which the camera amplified. Mayer recognized that the remote star, more than any other on the lot, gave the studio the prestige upon which it measured its self-proclaimed superiority. Myrna Loy had intelligence and fought MGM (successfully) for better roles and higher pay. She was not afraid of Mayer. Her teaming with William Powell in the *Thin Man* series secured her position at the studio. She also had the guidance of a top producer, Arthur Hornblow (the two lived together until their 1936 marriage). Years later, Loy, who had more innate wisdom than all the studio's females put together, commented that she was able to hold her own with Louis B. Mayer. "Mayer was a character, devious and manipulative," said Loy, "but how could you dislike him? Judy Garland and I used to discuss the 'MGM syndrome,' as she called it, all the

Women of Glamour (1937) with Melvyn Douglas (Columbia)

people who ended up on the psychiatrist's couch or worse after the coddling ended. 'You should have run away as I did,' I told her, 'instead of staying and taking more pills.'"[19]

Metro kept promising Virginia they were working on "something" especially for her — a role that would elevate her status at the studio. The film they selected was a Sidney Howard adaptation of Sinclair Lewis' *It Can't Happen Here*. Irving Thalberg began preliminaries to film the nation's best-selling novel in early January 1936. The dramatic story told what would happen if the United States fell into the hands of a dictator, and included an episode in which Virginia (playing the daughter of Lionel Barrymore) shot the Fascist president (Walter Connolly). Barrymore was cast a liberal small-town editor. J. Walter Ruben was to direct. It came as a shock to everyone when Will Hays (of the Production Code Office) ordered cessation of the film. The major reason the Hays Office gave was that the film "might offend Adolf Hitler or Benito Mussolini."[20] When MGM backed out of the venture (Mayer worried about losing revenues in Europe), Jack Warner told the press it was "difficult to understand . . . that the company owning it lacked the courage to make it."[21] Warner pointed out his own company's success with controversial subjects (i.e., *I Am a Fugitive from a Chain Gang*). A week after the film was "banned," the Authors League of America called for a resolution to remove Will Hays from office. When Mayer refused to appeal the Hays Office ruling, Thalberg was irate. "We've lost our guts!" he snapped, "and, when that happens to a studio, you can kiss it goodbye!"[22]

After producer Thalberg's death (September 1936), it was announced that Virginia would be reteamed with Robert Taylor in a remake of the William Haines' hit *The Duke Steps Out*, but nothing came of it. In the meantime, they loaned her to Columbia and Universal for two "B" films in which she received top billing: *Women of Glamour* (1937) and *When Love is Young* (1937). Director Gordon Wiles, who won an Oscar for Art Direction in 1932's *Transatlantic*, did a standout job with his cast in *Women of Glamour* (a remake of Frank Capra's 1930 effort *Ladies of Leisure*). Virginia inherited the Barbara Stanwyck role as a gold-digger who falls for a wealthy artist (Melvyn Douglas). After escaping an orgiastic free-for-all aboard a yacht, Virginia believably establishes her character's "rough edges" when she first bumps into Douglas. "I'm a wildflower," she explains. "I toil not and I haven't spun in years!" Douglas has also made an "escape" from the "beautiful, expensive, people" that fill his meaningless life. He's engaged to a socialite (sensitively played by Broadway actress Leona Maricle). The gist of *Women of Glamour* is a mix of *Pygmalion* and *La Traviata*. Virginia agrees to pose for one of Douglas' paintings and he decides to give her "culture." In doing so, they *both* learn, and they fall in love. After giving Douglas back his ring, Maricle requests a private moment with Bruce to tell her she must *also* give Douglas up. Because of Bruce's "shady past" it would mean "social ruin, etc., etc.," for Douglas. Predictably, love conquers all in the end, but not without some highly amusing, and sensitively played dramatic moments. Pert Kelton, as Virginia's wisecracking roommate, is wonderful throughout, especially in a fancy restaurant where the ladies are having tea. Kelton lets Maricle know what she thinks about Douglas' "art." "I've got no patience with an atheist!" Kelton blurts out. "An atheist?" Miracle queries. "Some people can't leave well enough alone!" Kelton fires back. "They always got to be improving on the works of the Creator." Before Virginia can pull Kelton away, she's accusing Maricle of being an atheist.

Attending the opera is part of Virginia's metamorphosis in *Women of Glamour*. After she and Douglas return from a performance of *Traviata*, Virginia gives one of the best emotional scenes of her film career. While dining on Douglas' veranda, she offers a touching retelling of the opera she has just seen. Virginia empathizes with Violetta's sacrifice for love. "But, she paid for it with her life!" counters Douglas. "Why not?" says Virginia. She then reveals to Douglas the details of her own mother's death and her drunken father who was never a provider and her mother's undying love for him. In the telling, she realizes, for the first time, the reason behind her mother's composed departure. "She died smiling, because she knew he was waiting for her," says Virginia. Her voice softens. "Can you believe it? She *died* smiling."

Virginia gets up from the table and walks away. "What is it?" asks Douglas. Her eyes moisten as she explains, "It's that ... all of a sudden I know she was right. She never had anything. No money, no nothing. And, she loved somebody. All these years I've been feeling sorry for her, but she didn't need anybody to be sorry for her!" Virginia states her realization simply, "If you've got nerve enough to

When Love is Young (1937) with Christian Rub and Greta Meyer (Universal)

give yourself up to something like that . . . You're a cinch to die smiling!" Her dramatic intensity works and allows the film to shift gears at exactly the right moment.

In author Clive Hirschhorn's studio tome *The Columbia Story*, he calls *Women of Glamour* "a weak remake of *Ladies of Leisure.*" It is anything but. Aside from its weak title, *Women of Glamour* is an improvement over the early Frank Capra original. *Women of Glamour's* editing (Oscar-nominated Otto Meyer), photography (Oscar-nominated J. Peverell Marley), and director Wiles' brisk take on the original gels and entertains throughout. *Ladies of Leisure*, despite some trademark Capra touches, is plodding and melodramatic. To her credit, Barbara Stanwyck does her usual standout job, but she has the misfortune of playing opposite a clueless leading man, Ralph Graves. One is ready for the film to end long before Stanwyck's attempted suicide. The Douglas-Bruce combination has spark. *Women of Glamour* deserves to be rediscovered.

*When Love is Young (1937)*After a complete make-over, Virginia returns home for class reunion. Seen here with Jean Rogers, Nydia Westman, Sterling Holloway, Kent Taylor, and Walter Brennan (Universal)

The New York Times had nothing but compliments for Universal's *When Love is Young*. "Under Hal Mohr's direction," said the reviewer, "the picture is fresh and crisply paced . . . Virginia Bruce as Wanda displays an unexpected talent for comedy . . . The change does her—and us—good. . . . the others in the cast are first rate. It just shows that pictures really do not have to be colossal."[23] Indeed, it is the film's simplicity that plays best. Surrounded by her Scandinavian plain folk family, and looking like she just stepped off the boat at Ellis Island, Virginia is genuinely effective. She's the inside joke at high school, but doesn't realize it until graduation when her classmates vote her "most likely to grow the largest pumpkin in the State of Pennsylvania." She is deeply hurt, but courageously heads to New York to study voice. Up to this point the film registers well. Character actors Chris-

When Love is Young (1937) with Kent Taylor (Universal)

tian Rub, Greta Meyer, and Walter Brennan do an impressive job creating the "old country" warmth and love that surround Virginia at home.

After a few months in New York, Virginia runs into a livewire press agent (Kent Taylor) who takes charge of her career. As a publicity stunt, we see Virginia driving a flock of geese through Times Square. Taylor, eyelashes a-flutter and striking poses, gamely offers her lessons on how to be alluring on stage. Such publicity and coaching, we are led to believe, catapult her to Broadway stardom. The production number from her "hit" show (staged by Virginia's "follies" pal, Jack Harkrider) is pretty forgettable. But, her rendition of Jimmy McHugh's songs, "Did Anyone Ever Tell You?" and "When

Love is Young," are infectious. (Both numbers were recorded soon afterwards by jazz greats Duke Ellington and Fats Waller.)

When Love is Young gets back on track when Virginia returns home for a class reunion. As a celebrity, she is greeted royally by classmates. Amid all the brouhaha Virginia sees through their pretense, and discovers that her feelings for Taylor go deeper than she thought. She returns to New York for a delightfully whimsical and romantic reunion with Taylor. *When Love is Young* was a definite notch above the usual "B" feature fare. *Time Magazine* said the film "follows established lines of Cinderella fables, but manages to keep out of the dullard class. Designed for neighborhood houses rather than Academy Awards, *When Love is Young*, is a neatly streamlined little double-biller." Film critic Wood Soanes for the *Oakland Tribune* said, "Virginia Bruce . . . gives good account of herself as a timid maiden from the hinterland who crashes Broadway. . . . Miss Bruce is able to retain that poignant quality that has given her charm in the past, to wear gowns with the grace of a model and to engage in fiery patter with Kent Taylor. . . . Miss Bruce and Taylor make an agreeable team and are given first rate direction by Hal Mohr."[24] Los Angeles film critic Philip K. Scheuer agreed. "The mere featuring of Virginia Bruce in the chief role," said Scheuer, "does not long conceal her eligibility for stardom. She's simply swell."[25] Virginia was given the *Los Angeles Times*' "Best Performance in a Current Picture" mention on March 21. The column praised, "Virginia Bruce in *When Love is Young* runs away with the show, because of varied and capable efforts."[26] On March 17, 1937, Virginia received "an award of merit" at the Pantages Hollywood Theater. The honor was presented by orchestra leader Ted Fio Rito on behalf of the Modern Musicians Society. According to the *Los Angeles Times*, "Miss Bruce was singled out for the award because of her individual style of singing in the rendition of two songs, "When Love Is Young," and "Did Anyone Ever Tell You." [27]

With two good "double-billers" under her belt, Virginia returned home to the kingdom of Louis B. Mayer. At Metro, the top female players were given vehicles that were purchased, written, or developed with them in mind. Myrna Loy had signed on as a supporting player in 1932, and by 1934 was carrying features like *Stamboul Quest* on her own. Producers and writers were creating "Loy" parts for "Loy pictures." Virginia had technically been with the studio since 1932 and as of the spring of 1937, she still had not been given a real opportunity in a star vehicle. Nothing had been specifically tailored for her. Granted, Virginia was not a star 24/7 like Crawford. She had no Garbo "mystique." Mayer's penchant for redheads did not extend to blondes. Virginia was not a fighter like Loy or Shearer, and readily admitted she wasn't. She did not have a producer-husband as a source in whom to confide. Her dilemma seemed tied up with Mayer himself. Virginia was intimidated by him; in spite of the "paternal atmosphere" he claimed permeated his studio. Virginia's fears were understandable. She had married the man whom Mayer hated the most: John Gilbert. With the demise of Irving Thalberg, Virginia was left to fend for herself.

After acquitting herself so nicely in lead parts on loan, at her home studio Virginia inherited third billing, below Franchot Tone and Maureen O'Sullivan (both supporting contract players). The film was a soap opera titled *Between Two Women* (1937). The story was similar to Sidney Kingsley's *Men in White*, which Spencer Tracy and Virginia had played on *Lux Radio Theatre* (Gable and

Loy had done the film version). *Between Two Women* was written by director Erich von Stroheim during his wife's arduous stay at a hospital. Von Stroheim had titled his story *General Hospital,* and suggested Clark Gable and Virginia Bruce for the leads. He also completed a shooting script. Von Stroheim envisioned Virginia playing the part of a nurse and Gable a doctor. The story was collecting dust by the time filming started, and von Stroheim was in Paris. He would later smugly comment, "Evidently they thought it was good enough to make into a 'C' picture and they handed it to George B. Seitz . . . When the film was finished, MGM found that they had made an 'A' picture by mistake. . . . I did not see the film, but was informed by my attorney that not one word had been changed in my screenplay and dialogue, although other writers received screen credits — what *for* I shall never know!"[28]

In *Between Two Women,* Virginia inherited the part of the wife, which is actually more interesting and complex. She does extremely well as a society playgirl who marries Tone, only to tire of his dedication as a physician. Maureen O'Sullivan, as the nurse, is also in an unhappy marriage. Empathy between doctor and nurse inevitably led to what *New York Times* critic Bosley Crowther saw as "a final, clinical clinch." Crowther did not concur with von Stroheim's high opinion of his own screenplay, and thought the lead roles were a punishment inflicted by Metro on the trio of stars. Crowther stated, "Dr. Tone and his colleagues amputate nearly everything in sight except the long arm of coincidence, which provides a climactic train wreck from which Dr. Tone's restless wife and her lover are delivered simultaneously to the operating tables."[29] The "climactic" coincidence Crowther mentions is indeed farfetched, as is the miraculous healing of Virginia's disfigured face. When O'Sullivan's husband also rolls in on a gurney, it's impossible to take the story seriously. Von

Stroheim's screenplay constantly leans toward the preposterous. It's especially laughable when Dr. Tone slugs another physician during surgery! In spite of everything, Virginia's scenes play strongly. Her character grows substantially, while her role establishes the plot's conflict. By the finis, she knows more about herself, the trouble she's created, and what she's losing. Her final close-up, replete with tears and emotion, speaks volumes for her character. It also documents, rather breathtakingly, that Virginia Bruce was truly one of the great screen beauties.

While on the set, Virginia explained to UP correspondent John Dunlap how screen acting had changed since she first came to Hollywood. "Take for instance [*Between Two Women*]," said Virginia. "In it I am a rich siren who wages an aggressive suit to win the love of my doctor, Franchot Tone. I am a patient in his hospital. Just imagine how the vamp of 1929 would have handled such a romantic setup. I can see her now, bewitchingly shifting her lovely shoulders and heaving throaty sighs every time her hero came close to her convalescent bed. She would stretch her arms toward him, undulating and flashing claw-like finger nails. . . . Now, thanks to sound photography, and a change in audience reaction, one must be able to reveal their charm with the gleam of an eye, the curve of their mouth or the tilt of the head."[30] Critics were applauding Virginia's "technique." Philip K. Scheuer, for the *Los Angeles Times,* commented, "The picture falters several times before ending, but the players carry it safely through. Miss Bruce could carry any movie for me."[31]

When Jean Harlow died in June 1937, MGM considered recasting Virginia opposite Clark Gable in Harlow's almost completed film, *Saratoga.* Now, as the studio's major blonde star, Virginia was the logical choice. But, when MGM was bombarded with fan mail insisting that the "Blonde Bombshell's" last film be released with *her* in it, Harlow's few remaining scenes were shot with body and voice doubles. A Gable-Bruce pairing was not to be. Instead, Virginia's career moved sideways once more, albeit in an "A" picture. She was cast at 20th Century-Fox (as a replacement for Barbara Stanwyck) for third billing below Loretta Young and Warner Baxter in *Wife, Doctor, and Nurse* (1937). *Photoplay* raved, "With a simplicity and lack of melodramatics that make an outstandingly convincing portrait of hospital life, Director Walter Lang has created a superb picture." In truth, the film is hardly a "convincing portrait" of its subject matter, and miles away from any kind of probable reality. For instance, the opening scene which establishes the "necessity" of nurse Virginia in Dr. Lewis' (Baxter) professional life, has her command Baxter to take off his pants. "Get them off, or we'll take them off!" she barks. A pouf-tailor enters the office and immediately begins to measure Baxter's rear-end. "Oh! Isn't that lovely across the seat?" he gasps. "Terrific!" Bruce agrees. Between routine consultations, an X-ray analysis, and prescribing brandy to injured socialite (and future wife) Young, Baxter is fitted for a new suit. But, even amid such whimsy, *Wife, Doctor, and Nurse* is a fresh take on the "old triangle."

Virginia's character doesn't realize that she's 'in love' with her Park Avenue employer until his wife (Young) takes her to lunch in order to find out the "truth" of their professional relationship. Following their tête-à-tête the plot thickens. In rapid succession, Virginia decides to quit, Dr. Lewis becomes ornery, and wife Loretta, admitting the necessity of Virginia in her husband's life, heads for Reno. In a new spin on an old tale, the two women eventually join forces — but, only after Young admits to Virginia the dilemma of their sex. "If we were men," she says in jest, "I could just shoot you!" Both wife and nurse decide that the *real* "patient" here is the Doctor.

After completion, *Wife, Doctor and Nurse* ran into trouble

with the Production Code. Joseph Breen claimed it unacceptable, saying it made "comedy out of the postponement of a consummation of the marriage vows."[32] Darryl Zanuck fired back to Breen he would "not cut a G—D— inch out of the picture."[33] Zanuck finally relented, but the film maintains its spice. Author Roger Dooley later said of *Wife, Doctor, and Nurse*'s novel solution, "The wife and the nurse decide the doctor needs both of them — a decidedly unusual *ménage a trois* under the Production Code."[34]

Virginia and Clark Gable rehearse for a 1937 Lux Radio broadcast of Edna Ferber's *Cimarron*

The New York Times agreed, saying, "Although *Wife, Doctor and Nurse* is indubitably old hat, the . . . haberdashers have brushed it to a fine gloss and have put it on at a jaunty angle . . . Count that to the credit of Walter Lang, who has directed it glibly; to the trio of writers who have laced their script with humor, and to Loretta Young, Warner Baxter and Virginia Bruce — as the titular triumvirate. . . ."[35] Film critic Norbert Lusk, for *The Los Angeles Times*, gave Virginia one of her best reviews: "Baxter wins no new laurels, nor does Miss Young . . . Miss Bruce does more for herself. She plays with singular poise and effortlessness, making her role by far the most interesting because she contrives to suggest subtleties of character overlooked by scenarist and director."[36] According to author Colin Briggs, who interviewed Virginia during her retirement, "Virginia did not enjoy working with Loretta."[37]

By the fall of 1937, with a new contract, Virginia still had no real champion at the studio to promote her. She had yet to make a strong team effort with one of Metro's male stars, although she was finally paired with Clark Gable in *Lux Radio's* presentation of Edna Ferber's classic *Cimarron*, on September 27. A screen teaming with Gable could have indeed made a difference. The two "looked" as if they belonged together.

And, as far as "looks" were concerned, Virginia was definitely the blonde crowning glory of the MGM multi-tiered cake. Dorothy Manners began one of her columns saying, "Joan Crawford once told me Virginia Bruce was so beautiful that she made her (Joan) feel all hands and feet when she was around her. Now, that's what I call praise from an expert."[38] Virginia would politely dismiss such appraisals, especially regarding her screen work. "I hate to think," Virginia opted, "that the most important thing people remember about me is the way I happen to be photographed by some marvelous cameraman."[39] Ultimately, Virginia found herself in a situation similar to that described by another MGM contract player, Rosalind Russell. "I was never a top star at Metro," Russell admitted. "I was in the second echelon. That was the way they ran the lot. I once said I never got a part at Metro unless Myrna Loy turned it down."[40] Even with her strong performance in Columbia's *Craig's Wife* (1936), Metro didn't seem to know what to do with Russell. It was becoming apparent that the studio was still undecided about Virginia. The "second-echelon" at Metro is exactly where they kept Virginia Bruce perched, waiting, and forever gazing upward toward Garbo, Shearer, Loy and "all the stars in heaven."

Endnotes

1   "Virginia Bruce's Baby Is Target of Kidnappers," *Bismark Tribune*, 2/25/36
2   Associated Press news article, "Virginia Bruce Home Guarded After Threats Against Child," 2/25/36
3   "Guard Daughter of Virginia Bruce," *Hammond Times*, 2/26/36
4   "Bruce Home Under Guard," *Los Angeles Times*, 2/26/36
5   Eleanor Packer, "Love Opened My Eyes!" *Screen Book*, 11/35

6   Linda Lane, "Virginia Bruce Resents Phrase 'Beauty Is Dumb," *Centralia Chronicle*, 11/27/36

7   Jerry Asher, "Why Our Marriage Failed," c.1934

8   Gladys Hall, "Why Virginia Bruce Won't Marry for Five Years," *Photoplay*, 11/35

9   Maud Cheatham, "A Friendship that's Real!" *Screenland*, December 1939.

10   Dick Mook, "Kay Francis On the Real Tragedy of Hollywood," *Film Pictorial*, 11/3/34

11   Myrna Loy, *Being and Becoming,* Alfred A. Knopf, N.Y., 1987, pg. 118

12   Ben Maddox, "Girls, Don't Be Too Clever!" *Screenland*, 4/39

13   Charles Higham, *Merchant of Dreams: Louis B. Mayer, M.G. M., and the Secret Hollywood*, Donald I. Fine, NY, 1993 pg 248

14   Philip K. Scheuer, "Ziegfeld Aide Compares Film to Stage," *Los Angeles Times*, 11/1/36

15   "Ex-Ziegfeld Beauty Lands in Hospital Ward--a Broken Woman," *Oakland Tribune*, 2/19/41

16   Ruth Gordon, *My Side, Ruth Gordon*, Harper & Row, N.Y. c. 1976, pp 383-418

17   Lawrence J. Quirk, *Norma: The Story of Norma Shearer*, St. Martin's Pr. N.Y., 1988, pg 179-180

18   Gary Carey, *All the Stars in Heaven*, E.P. Dutton, N.Y., 1981, pg 174-175

19   Loy, *Being and Becoming*, pg. 117

20   "Lewis Tells Of Dictatorship Film Ban," *Los Angeles Times*, 2/16/36

21   Read Kendall, "Around and About Hollywood," *Los Angeles Times*, 2/25/36

22   Samuel Marx, *Mayer and Thalberg - The Make-Believe Saints*, Random House, NY, 1975, pps 245-246

23   Frank S. Nugent, review for *When Love is Young*, NYT, 4/17/37

24   Wood Soanes, review for *When Love is Young*, "Virginia Bruce Makes Debut as Comedienne," *Oakland Tribune*, 5/7/37

25   Philip K. Scheuer review for *When Love is Young*, *Los Angeles Times*, 3/18/37

26   "Best Performance in Current Pictures," *Los Angeles Times*, 3/21/37

27   "Musicians to Honor Screen Star," *Los Angeles Times*, 3/17/37

28   Peter Noble, *Hollywood Scapegoat*, Arno Pr., N.Y., 1972 pp 109-110

29   Bosley R. Crowther, review for *Between Two Women*, NYT, 8/6/37

30   John Dunlap, "Hollywood Film Shop," *Hammond Times (PA)*, 7/2/37

31   Philip K. Scheuer, review for *Between Two Women*, *Los Angeles Times*, 8/12/37

32   Turner Classic Movies website, notes on *Wife, Doctor and Nurse*

33   ibid

34   Roger Dooley, *From Scarlett to Scarface*, Harcourt, Brace and Jovanovich, N.Y., 1979, pg 268

35   Frank S. Nugent, review for *Wife, Doctor, and Nurse*, *New York Times*, 10/11/37

36   Norbert Luck, review of *Wife, Doctor, and Nurse*, *Los Angeles Times*, 10/17/37

37   Colin Briggs, "Virginia Bruce - Incandescent Beauty," *Films of the Golden Age,*

Summer 2003

38   Dorothy Manners, "How Virginia Bruce Found Her Voice," *Los Angeles Examiner*, 11/22/36

39   Dorothy Manners, "How Virginia Bruce Found Her Voice," *Los Angeles Examiner*, 11/22/36

40   Loy, *Being and Becoming*, pg. 111

West Side Tennis Club c. 1937 – with Henry Fonda, George Murphy, Betty Furness, and James Stewart

CHAPTER 9:

Love - On Location

Even after his death, no other man meant as much to Virginia Bruce as John Gilbert. She lacked the capacity within herself to venture into a second marriage. Something was in the way. "Sorry about my marriage to John Gilbert?" she would say. "You can't be sorry for the most wonderful thing in your life!"[1] Gladys Hall claimed that friends thought Virginia was clinging "fearfully" to a dream of which she would not let go. Hall noted that after Gilbert's death, Virginia had a reluctance to move on emotionally in her private life — a "reservation." Virginia's preference to continue being called by her married name was mentioned by several columnists. "She had fairly worshipped John Gilbert," wrote Margaret Dixe. "Unquestionably, she still does. Even yet, Virginia would infinitely prefer being called 'Mrs. Gilbert,' rather than 'Miss Bruce.'"[2] Virginia always wore a long gold chain and locket containing Gilbert's photo around her neck. "It's pretty hard to find a man to follow Jack," Virginia admitted. "He was like no one else could be."[3] She claimed that his death did not automatically free her to love again. Besides, Virginia was getting recognition for her screen work. It was the progress of her career upon which she was focused. While alcohol had consumed what was left of Gilbert and his career, he was certainly aware of Virginia's rise as a Hollywood star. After their separation, and before his death, she made close to a dozen films to his one. Whether Gilbert was ever truly happy for her success was a question left unanswered.

Virginia's preoccupation with Gilbert induced some interesting fantasies. In the summer of 1937, she told columnist Jimmie Fidler, "Someday, I've simply got to meet Greta Garbo. I'm going to walk into her dressing room and say, 'Look, you used to be in love with John Gilbert. I married him. I think we have a lot in common. So, let's get acquainted.'"[4] It is highly unlikely *that* exchange ever took place. Garbo was unavailable to all her co-workers. Myrna Loy, whose dressing room was right next to Garbo's, made several friendly gestures, but gave up. "One day we ran into each other in the hall," Loy remembered. "I looked at her and smiled. She lowered her head, and in that low, lingering voice said, 'Hallooo . . .' and hurried on by. That was my only exchange with Greta Garbo. I never knew what to do with her after that. . . . She never encouraged anybody. In her dressing room . . . she had a secret door put in for quick getaways. She [was] a very scared lady. . . . "[5]

In the fall of 1937, Virginia's association with John Gilbert took an unexpected turn. Hollywood released its own "variation on a theme" about Virginia and Gilbert's life together. The film hit very close to home and was titled *A Star is Born*. Immediately after Gilbert's demise, producer David O. Selznick began the project which resembled his 1932 RKO production, *What Price Hollywood?* The original film told the story of a young waitress, living in Hollywood, who wants a film career. She is "star struck" and has savvy, if not about acting, about life. She befriends a director who helps jump-start her career, while his own is on the skids from drinking. Her career takes off and his winds up in the gutter. She marries a wealthy, blue-blooded polo player, and the director, in spite of the young star's attempts to help him, commits suicide. Adela St Rogers John wrote the screenplay (for which she got an Oscar nomination).

By the time *A Star is Born* began filming at United Artists in October 1936, RKO's lawyers had prepared a plagiarism suit claiming that the new film copied *What Price Hollywood?* Although a suit was never filed, it is obvious what producer Selznick was doing. He simply blended the two male characters into one: an alcoholic screen idol named Norman Maine whose career is on the way out. And, instead of a young waitress, Selznick turns the girl (Esther Blodgett) into a still star-struck, but naive young thing from North Dakota (who happens to have a younger brother). Arriving in Hollywood, Esther ends up catering at a party and bumps into Maine. He falls for her immediately, helps her get started at Paramount, and arranges for her to co-star in his latest film. She changes her name to Vicki Lester and gets great notices. The two marry. Lester has one success after another, while Maine fades into oblivion. Like John Gilbert, when no studio wants to hire him, Maine talks of filming in England. Adolphe Menjou (similar to Thalberg's relationship with Gilbert and Bruce) plays a producer trying to deal honestly with two stars he cares about: Norman Maine and Vicki Lester. But it isn't long before Maine drowns himself, not only in alcohol, but in the Pacific Ocean. After his death, Esther, still very much in love with him, resumes her career. At the premier of her latest film, she introduces herself for the radio hookup outside Grauman's

Chinese Theatre. She doesn't refer to herself as "Vicki Lester," however. Looking gallant, courageous and with tears welling-up in her eyes, she says, "Hello, everybody. This is *Mrs.* Norman Maine."

In J.E. Smyth's study *Reconstructing American Historical Cinema: From Cimarron to Citizen Kane*, it is pointed out: "The connections between Norman Maine and Gilbert were evidently obvious ... the romantic actor with a short temper, deep thirst, and cynical sense of humor loses his box-office appeal. . . . There were many similarities between Gilbert and Maine, as well as be-tween Virginia Bruce and Esther Blodgett."[6] Aside from the suit being prepared by RKO's lawyers, there was also a writer from France who began legal proceedings against Selznick for plagia-rizing a short story about a silent French screen star whose life played out a similar scenario. Smyth notes, "Selznick could have saved himself and his lawyers time by claiming that the film was a screen biography of John Gilbert, but he might have incurred a libel suit from Virginia Bruce."[7] Ronald Haver's *A Star is Born: The Making of the 1954 Movie and Its 1983 Restoration* claims the metamorphosis of the two male characters in *What Price Hol-lywood?* had shadings of both John Gilbert and John Barrymore. "Gilbert later married the young actress Virginia Bruce," writes Haver, "and her career forged ahead while his ended in a para-noid, alcoholic daze. Gilbert's death of heart failure at the age of 38 came in January 1936, just as work began on the screenplay of *A Star is Born*."[8] Indeed, the story of John Gilbert and North Dakota's Virginia Briggs, who still referred to herself as "Mrs. John Gilbert" (down to the monogrammed towels in her dress-ing room), was fresh in everyone's mind.

Copyright jurisdiction precluded historical events. In order to protect Selznick, lawyers prepared a brief that claimed *A Star is*

Born was inspired by *real* events in Hollywood. Mentioned were: Garbo's tie with director Mauritz Stiller (who was gay and died of pleurisy), Barbara Stanwyck's failed marriage to actor Frank Fay, and the John Gilbert-Virginia Bruce relationship.[9] Stiller was a mentor to Garbo, not a husband. He wasn't alcoholic and did not commit suicide. Frank Fay, a severe alcoholic, was never a film star of *any* magnitude. No one would accuse Stanwyck of being as naïve as Esther Blodgett, ditto for Garbo. This underscores the significance of the Gilbert-Bruce relationship as inspiration for *A Star is Born*. Gilbert's being instrumental in facilitating Virginia's "big break" when she played opposite him in *Downstairs* — a role that redefined her career, is yet another significant similarity to the film. There is also a familiar ring to Norman Maine's real name, "Hinkle," sounding much like "Pringle" (Gilbert's surname). Smyth's study notates the absence of any reference to Maine's heyday as a silent star, but emphasizes, "Still the trace of Gilbert and the specter of sound remain with the images of *A Star is Born*."[10]

Some credit silent actor John Bowers as Selznick's inspiration for Maine's character (among them, Adela St. Rogers John, who also claims she suggested that Maine take his final walk into the ocean). However, Bowers was not mentioned as source material by Selznick's lawyers. It is a fact that Bowers did drown in the ocean several weeks after filming started for *A Star is Born*. He sailed into the Pacific and jumped overboard after begging Henry Hathaway for a part in a film. Not to be overlooked, and along the same line, is an incident recorded by Marion Davies in her autobiography *The Times We Had*. After Gilbert had one of his break-ups with Garbo, he attended a party at Marion's beach house. In the early evening about 30 or 40 guests headed out to the shoreline, and it wasn't long before Gilbert was in a heated ar-

1937 Virginia and director/artist Jean Negulesco, who
greatly admired Virginia and did her portrait. At this
point in his career Negulesco was a screenwriter (courtesy
of Vincent Briggs)

gument with some writers in the group. Davies heard Gilbert say,
"I'm going to commit suicide!" They dared him, saying, "Prove
it. You've talked about suicide so much, prove it to us. If you've
got the guts to do it, show us." Davies noted, "He went out and
walked into the waves. And, he kept walking until I thought,
'This is not funny.' I said, 'Somebody stop him.'"[11] Davies describes the pitiful sight of Gilbert attempting to drown himself,
only to come wading back and fall onto the shoreline, bursting
into sobs, beating the sand and crying his heart out. With so
many witnesses to this spectacle, the story could have easily fueled Selznick's imagination for *A Star is Born*. Davies' mention of

Gilbert's frequent threats of suicide certainly adds an edge to her story. (The Internet Movie Database states that the film's director, William Wellman, and Robert Carson wrote *A Star is Born*, along with six uncredited contributing writers.) Whatever the case, Gilbert's threats were finally fulfilled on screen, when Norman Maine's body washes ashore. On April 20, 1937, Virginia was in attendance at the premier of *A Star is Born* at Grauman's Chinese Theatre. The parallels to her own life unfolding on film must have made for a sobering experience. After the preview she made no comment to the press, nor did anyone ask for her reaction to what she had just witnessed.

Just before her twenty-seventh birthday, the fates intervened in Virginia's life and romantic love found its way into her heart once more. She was on location for an MGM film titled *The Bad Man of Brimstone*. The town of Kanab, known as "Utah's Little Hollywood," was a-bustle with its latest tinsel town connection. In 1924, the Parry brothers established the tie between Kanab and Hollywood by promoting the area's scenic vistas to producers. In 1931, they opened Parry Lodge to accommodate cast and crews. Aside from the lodge, which had its own hitching post, Kanab consisted of a general store, a movie house, and a church. The closest railroad was 135 miles away. The surrounding community profited $50,000 during the three-week stay of *Brimstone's* cast and crew, due mostly to filming delays caused by rain. On film, the Utah location would be rechristened as somewhere in Arizona. An on-location report on September 3, from Zion National Park (40 miles from Kanab), gives an insider's view of what it was like when Hollywood came to cow-town.

A drizzling rain is falling as cars head for Zion
Lodge, a whole stream of them. . . . For ten days
Bad Man of Brimstone has been on location in
southern Utah . . . Mothers with children and
young movie-career-minded girls have sought out
Director J. Walter Ruben, asking for screen tests.
The lodge veranda is crowded with people. . . .
Wallace Beery, star of the picture, drives up just in
time to be besieged by forty autograph fans. . . .
Virginia Bruce, blonde and dainty in riding pants
and white wool sweater, emerges from the curio
shop door. She states that her illness [ptomaine
poisoning] was mostly an exaggeration . . . Guy
Kibbee, hatless, scurries up the walk in the rain . .
. Bruce Cabot whittles on a long willow, seated on
the steps. . . . Hotel guests stand around, looking
at the film stars. . . . Director Ruben moans the
weather, and several locations await the sun to
shine. Studio cars await call. The rain still drizzles
and thousands of dollars are lost on the delay.
Members of the company play cards and checkers
to pass away the time. All hope for a bright day
tomorrow to start "shooting."[12]

Columnist May Mann noticed one shy youth "standing away
a respectful distance of ten feet" from Virginia. He held a Kodak
camera, and a hopeful expression. "Would you mind if I took
your picture?" he asked. "You see you're one of the first picture
stars I ever saw in my life. I took one of Wallace Beery – and I
was surprised to death, that he'd let me . . . . " Virginia chimed
in, "Why, go right ahead. I know just how you feel. When I first

September 4, 1937 – Virginia and J. Walter Ruben on the set of
Bad Man of Brimstone (Zion National Park, Utah)

arrived in California I was just as anxious as you are to see movie
stars."[13] Virginia told Mann that she had been on location for
two weeks and had only worked one hour. She felt relaxed and
enjoyed herself anyway. Wallace Beery, star of *Brimstone*, was
perfectly at home in the Utah surroundings. He had been fishing
and hunting in the state for years. Big brother Noah Beery played

a bartender in the film. Director Ruben, who had written the story for *Bad Man of Brimstone*, had specifically asked for Virginia as the female lead. He was thrilled to have her on board. He had read her the storyline at MGM and she had liked what she heard. She later recalled, "Just before the picture started I went to his office quite often to talk over my part with him. His advice was wonderful. He'd help me with lines, tell me how to read them to get the most out of them . . . I don't remember labeling him in my mind as definitely attractive or the reverse, I think now I just had the sense that he was *there* and that I didn't need to go beyond that."[14] As they became better acquainted, Virginia especially enjoyed the fact that Ruben could make her laugh.

J. Walter Ruben (his friends called him "Jack") didn't cross Virginia's mind when it was predicted a man would soon enter her life. While getting a shampoo at a Sunset Blvd. salon that featured "psychic readings," Virginia was told, "You are going to have a romance. I see a whirlwind courtship and you will be married — immediately." Virginia balked. "It can't be," she said, unconvinced. "I'm starting a new picture and we go to the desert on location tomorrow. We'll be away *weeks*, and the only men in the picture are Wallace Beery and Dennis O'Keefe. You know Wally's married and Dennis has a girl. You must be wrong."[15] Before leaving for Utah, Virginia and Ruben's acquaintance was strictly professional. Those that had seen them together at MGM, thought nothing of it. Ruben held an attraction for most of the female stars with whom he had worked — among them, Jean Harlow and Luise Rainer. Something began to change, however, the day Ruben left with the location company. He told Virginia, "I'll see you up there." She spontaneously declared, "Not unless you promise to give me a big kiss when I get there!" Stopped dead in his tracks, Ruben smiled, and nodded, "It's a deal!"[16] First thing upon arriving in Kanab, Virginia tracked down Ruben, who was taking a shower. He speedily dressed and presented himself. "Pay off," she said. He didn't hesitate for a second. Something had started and it was helped on its way by the breathtaking scenery and intoxicating air of Southern Utah and Zion National Park.

"The little village of Kanab, in Utah," Virginia recalled, was "a sleepy, remote little hamlet with live oaks brooding over it, and everyone simple and folksy. Everything was real and heartening as bread and work, and all the hills a sort of dark tangerine color, and life so peaceful. It was my first location trip, the first time I've been out of California in over four years."[17] How did she manage in a company that was primarily male? "Don't tell Wally Beery," she told one reporter, "but you've got to treat men like they are little boys. They may appear to resent it, but down in their hearts, bless them, they love it. That's what I did on the set every day. I never missed being solicitous about a person on the set, prop boys and all. And I soon found all of them responding. . . . I don't believe it is an injustice to them to say they would have just as soon been totally without feminine representation. They could cuss better, and more often, for instance. . . . But they were good sports."[18]

Without the distractions of the big city, Virginia and Ruben were able to talk about themselves and share personal feelings. In the intimate setting of mountains bathed in moonlight, and stars just beyond reach, what they saw and felt about their lives became more fluid and easily expressed. There was time to be alone together. "Well, practically alone," Virginia would recall, laughing, "except for eight or ten of the boys who always went walking with us."[19] Ruben reminded Virginia that he had made a couple attempts to get to know her after her divorce in 1934. He had called twice and asked her out to dinner. She had declined, saying that her family didn't think it would look right. Under

J. Walter Ruben and the ex-Mrs. Gilbert find romance on location

Utah skies, she had to admit that she simply didn't want to go out. But, she did wonder why he never tried to call her again. "I never ring up more than twice," Ruben replied. "What's the use?"[20] In hindsight, Virginia was glad they had waited. Before signing on to *Brimstone*, she was in no way ready for the "real thing" to come along. Playing poker every night at the Parry Lodge, Virginia quietly observed her director. O'Keefe, Joseph Calleia, and Lewis Stone joined them at the table. Virginia saw all the qualities she liked in a man — a jovial spirit, honesty, friendliness, and a touch of daring. "A game of poker it was to the onlookers. A game of hearts to Ruben and Virginia."[21] She began calling Ruben "Sonny," and he loved it.

Ruben was straightforward and frank about himself with Virginia. Eleven years older than her, Ruben had graduated from Columbia University, where he played basketball and football.

He developed an athletic heart, which now and again acted up on him. Tan complexion and of medium height, Ruben kept active in polo, his hobby, and excelled as an expert player and rider. He had been married and had no children. He told her that he didn't believe in waiting for life to happen, one must live while he has the chance. He was a great conversationalist and had an engaging sense of humor. Virginia listened to him. Her resolve to wait five years after her divorce began to melt away. While in Kanab one night she had to acknowledge her feelings. "As I was leaving the others to go to bed," Virginia remembered, "Sonny asked me, half-laughingly, to kiss him goodnight. And suddenly I felt that I couldn't, not then, not in front of the others. Suddenly I felt self-conscious and didn't know what to say or to do and stood there, awkwardly, like an adolescent girl with her first beau. And then I gave him a sort of peck on the check and ran off. I think I must have known then, in my heart, though my mind didn't put into words what my heart knew."[22]

Jack Ruben campaigned for Virginia with thoughtful attentions she could not ignore. He had reserved the only suite in the town's lodge for her. He told his assistant, "Don't call Virginia early. We'll make some other scenes first."[23] Virginia welcomed Ruben's advances, but used some caution. She wanted to be certain he hadn't been fooled by her glamorous screen image. "When we first went out together, Sonny and I," said Virginia, "I made it a point to have him see me without lipstick or make-up of any kind. It occurred to me that he might have got his first impressions of me from seeing me around the studio, in make-up, all doozied up in glamour and glad-rags — not me, at all. I wanted to be sure that he would see me at my plainest. . . . Better make sure, before marriage, that the boy friend loves you as God, not Glamour, made you."[24] Regardless of God or Glamour, Ruben's interest never wavered.

After location shooting in Utah was completed, Virginia and Ruben boarded a train for Los Angeles. As nothing definite was established between them, nothing written in stone, Virginia grappled once again with her feelings. "I remember so well sitting with him on the train," said Virginia, "feeling a sort of ache all over me because the trip was over, because when we got into Los Angeles we would be going our separate ways alone, because I would always be alone without him. And then he asked me to marry him. I can't tell you how beautifully he asked me, how reverently. It was the way I had dreamed, long ago, that a man should ask a woman to marry him. It made marriage seem so real and warm and lasting . . . he said many lovely things and I knew he meant them. . . . And I said, 'Yes,' because there was no other answer in my heart that I could have given. I said, 'Yes,' with all of me, for all my life."[25]

Ruben was a rare combination of intelligence and heart. It reflected not only in his proposal to Virginia, but in his work. His screen heroes and heroines were not altogether perfect. "Pictures are constantly being attacked for lacking dramatic strength and verity," he pointed out. "Film audiences have been raised on a diet of fairy stories, because they consistently refuse to let the hero they admire be defeated, or see the heroine they love die." Ruben emphasized, "Films need be neither grim nor unbelievably happy when they deal with people who really live. They will grip the emotions and come closer to the heart because they are about the things familiar to us."[26] Ruben and Virginia announced their engagement in early October, and planned a Christmas season wedding. Columnist May Mann felt she had lost her "nose for news." She had been on location at Kanab. "Every day we were in the company of Virginia Bruce and J. Walter Ruben — yet we never suspected a romance was brewing between them," said Mann. "The day after we left for home they returned to Hollywood and announced their engagement. . . . it burst into bud and blossomed right under our nose, and we couldn't see it."[27] Weeks after the announcement, many inquired as to why Virginia wasn't wearing an engagement ring. Virginia frankly admitted, "Sonny wanted to get me a big-square-cut diamond. For some women this would be the perfect gift. But the truth is, I don't care anything about diamonds, and I'm Scotch enough to think of the money involved. It could be used to so much better advantage in other ways."[28]

If ever there was proof of a director being in love with his leading lady, *Bad Man of Brimstone* is prime evidence. Whenever Virginia appears on screen, the camera is documenting Ruben's heart. From the moment she first shows up to get a bucket of beer at the Brimstone saloon for lawyer-dad Lewis Stone, Virginia's gentle energy lends a realistic and sincere touch to the proceedings. Midway through the picture, as Virginia's love interest, played by Dennis O'Keefe, heads east on horseback to study law, the camera moves in gently toward Virginia's face as she waves an emotional farewell. At that moment, one simply forgets the story and absorbs her amazingly lovely presence.

Beery's character, "Trigger Bill," is apt to "blast the innards out" of anyone he dislikes and brings enough humor into the bloodshed that one can't take the tale too seriously. This "Bad Man" is strictly there to entertain. He softens his tough-guy reputation while his son, O'Keefe, establishes law and order in a frontier community. *Brimstone* was Dennis O'Keefe's first lead part. He had been playing uncredited bits since 1930. Clark Gable, who noticed him from the extra ranks, encouraged MGM to give him an opportunity. When May Mann visited Kanab during filming, the tall, 6' 2" O'Keefe had to confess, "I've had good luck in playing opposite so glamorous a star as Virginia Bruce in my first picture."[29] O'Keefe (a replacement for James Stewart) photographed well and had an unaffected sincerity that was appealing. He seemed comfortable in his role.

According to Wells Root, Ruben's friend and occasional co-writer, Ruben had a steadfast rule that the phrase "I love you" would never be heard in any of his films. Ruben felt the "oldest cliché" could never be given a fresh reading.[30] Ruben broke his own rule for *Brimstone* when O'Keefe goes into court with the possible outcome of exposing the fraudulent law practices of Virginia's dad. Before entering the courtroom he tells her, "Regardless of what happens in this trial . . . I love you." Although she didn't understand the full import of what he was saying, the words communicated and the reading was fresh.

The *New York Times* thought *Bad Man of Brimstone* a "lively and engaging show," admitting, "Beery has an undeniable gift for such matters. His corrugated scowls, blubbery mouth, tousled hair . . . build him into the perfect image of a clumsy St. Bernard with a latent streak of viciousness . . . other Brimstonites have been served rather well, with emphasis on Dennis O'Keefe a screen newcomer . . . Lewis Stone as the back-sliding frontier judge . . . Virginia Bruce as Mr. O'Keefe's reward and Noah Beery as Brimstone's bartender. As the 'Madame X' of the horse operas, *Bad Man of Brimstone* is a pretty neat job all around -- in performance, script and production."[31] *Brimstone* included a *Stella Dallas*-type ending with Beery, peering lovingly through a window while O'Keefe and Bruce take their wedding vows. Out west, *The Los Angeles Times* agreed with the east coast's assessment of the film, adding, "Virginia Bruce looks beautiful and gives a fine performance. Interesting to remember that it was during the making of this picture the friendship of director Ruben and Miss Bruce ripened into love and marriage. The direction of J. Walter Ruben can not be praised too highly"[32] Theatres also screened a four-minute promotional short on *Brimstone, Behind the Movie Lens* (1938). It featured Virginia and cast members on location in Utah.

Virginia and Ruben celebrated their engagement by giving a party at the West Side Tennis Club. Among the entertainments was an impromptu rumba given by Cesar Romero. Phil Baker and George Murphy alternated as masters of ceremonies. Those present included Countess di Frasso, Kay Francis, Betty Furness, Claire Trevor, Margaret Sullavan, Gloria Stuart, Cary Grant, Jimmy Ritz, David Niven, William Haines and Nigel Bruce. On November 23, there was another pre-nuptial celebration at film writers Hope Loring and Louis Lighton's Mediterranean Bel-Air estate. Rolling lawns and sylvan landscapes surrounded what *LA Examiner's* Reine Davies' called "the unanimous approval of the Bruce-Rubin match." The party's "blithesome gayety" included such "felicitating cocktailers" as Mary Pickford and Buddy Rogers, Kay Francis and her almost-ex-lover, scenarist Delmar Daves, Countess di Frasso, the Robert Montgomerys, the David Selznicks, the Gary Coopers, and Cesar Romero.[33]

Virginia and Ruben leased a home in Beverly Hills and readied it for the December 18th wedding. They opted for a quiet wedding without swank and formality. For the ceremony, Virginia wore a street-length powder-blue jersey suit, with an orchid corsage. Congregational minister Dr. J.W. Fifield Jr. presided. Sur-

Wedding quintet: Ruben, Virginia, Fay Wray,
Sandi and Gary Cooper

rounding them were Virginia's parents, her brother Stanley, an aunt, cousin, grandmother, and, sitting very quietly, their little flower girl Susan Ann. The ceremony went smoothly until Earll stepped forward to give his daughter away. The evening before the wedding Virginia had to work late at MGM and cancelled the rehearsal. So, after Earll answered the conventional question "who giveth this woman in marriage?" he remained standing at the altar with the bride and groom. "So close to us," Virginia said afterwards, "that Sonny could hardly put the ring on my finger. We whispered to him to get back but he didn't hear us and just kept standing there, knowing something was wrong, but not knowing exactly what to do about it. Of course, it didn't matter, but it was hard on him and it all happened because I couldn't find time to rehearse."[34]

After receiving a round of congratulations from those present, Ruben broke tradition and carried Virginia *out* of the house instead of over the threshold. The wedding party then moved to the home of Countess Dorothy di Frasso in nearby Bel Air. Kay Francis and Mrs. Jack Warner gave a reception for the newlyweds.

Those in attendance were: Doug Fairbanks, Jr., Marlene Dietrich (!) and Fritz Lang, Maureen O'Sullivan and husband John Farrow, Claire Windsor, Raquel Torres, Mr. and Mrs. Bert Taylor, Fay Wray, singer Gertrude Neisen and Jon Hall. The day after the ceremony the newlyweds took a jaunt over to a popular tennis club for the afternoon. A honeymoon would have to wait until January. On December 21, Virginia was back on the set of the mystery film *Arsene Lupin Returns*. Ruben visited MGM daily to bring her a "healthy" lunch. He truly looked out for her and sat with her while she ate. They both decided to spend Christmas at home and make it something special for Susan Ann.

Work at MGM created havoc once more when Virginia was called by surprise on her day off to report to the studio immediately. She was in the middle of writing "thank you" notes for the wedding gifts and had each gift with the donor's card next to it spread across tables and beds. She left hurriedly only to return several hours later and find "the well-organized mess" all tidied up by her new housekeeper. The cards had been carefully stacked together tied with a ribbon. "Of course Sonny and I sorted things out as best we could before I wrote any more notes," said Virginia, "but we didn't do too well. I thanked Norma Shearer for salad plates when it should have been dessert plates. ... And worse than that, I thanked a business acquaintance of Sonny's for some prints only to find out later he never gave us anything."[35] Virginia emphasized that her career never intruded on the harmony in her relationship with Ruben. "Sonny being right in the middle of the business and knowing exactly how things are helps a lot," Virginia explained. "And that makes all the difference in the world."[36] In January 1938, the Rubens' honeymoon was spent on Jock Whitney's estate in Virginia. Whitney, a Yale graduate who was part of Virginia's social circle while he was in New York

Arsene Lupin Returns (1938) with Warren William (MGM)

"When we returned from our honeymoon to Washington, D.C. and Virginia," recalled Virginia, "Mr. Louis B. Mayer called Jack into his office. There had been quite a little speculation among our friends as to whether I would continue in films. Mr. Mayer wanted to know the truth of it. 'Why, yes,' said Jack. 'Virginia wants to continue and I want her to. She would never be happy otherwise.' Mr. Mayer was kind enough to reply that that was as he had hoped, as the studio had great things planned for me."[37] Before the honeymoon, it was announced that Robert Taylor had requested Virginia to play opposite him in the Technicolor *Northwest Passage.* On January 14, it was reported she would play opposite Robert Montgomery in a version of Thorne Smith's role-reversal comedy, *Turnabout.* Censorship requirements most likely postponed that idea (it was filmed two years later with Carole Landis and John Hubbard). MGM also planned on a version of William Faulkner's Civil War drama, *The Unvanquished*, to star Virginia and Spencer Tracy. In February and March 1938, the studio did heavy negotiations with Paramount to loan Virginia for the lead opposite Randolph Scott in *The Texans*. Instead, Virginia was given a career-wife role opposite Montgomery in director Richard Thorpe's *The First Hundred Years*. While the film was in production, *Arsene Lupin Returns* was released.

Metro had successfully filmed *Arsene Lupin* in 1932. John Barrymore was the gentleman jewel-thief Lupin, showcased along with brother Lionel as prefect of police. When Melvyn Douglas signed with Metro in 1937, they immediately placed him in the role of Lupin. The world thought Lupin was deceased, based on the conclusion of the original film. He is cinematically resurrected for the light-hearted sequel, and found retired in France, raising show dogs and schooling prize pigs. Warren William is aligned with an insurance company and searching for a stolen emerald necklace that belongs to Virginia's family. Virginia provides romantic interest for *both* male leads. *The New York Times* summed the film up by saying, "As a combination who-dun-it and who-got-the-jools enterprise, it is fairer than most in its presentation of clues . . . and more fortunate than most in its cast. . . . Virginia Bruce seems to enjoy having [Douglas] as a leading man."[38] Even though the focus was on the male characters, Virginia had achieved "the look" of an MGM leading lady, and could toss off a rebuff with polish. "If you're counting on me to make your stay in France more enjoyable," she tells an amorous Warren William, "prepare yourself for a lot of solitude." Virginia favors Douglas from the get-go. The film does a clever job of making sure no one will guess the real culprit. Director George Fitzmaurice can be commended for a smoothly done caper.

The chemistry between Melvyn Douglas and Virginia made

for an excellent cinematic brew. Her pairing with Robert Montgomery, however, wasn't the heaven-made match that Metro had hoped for. During filming of director Richard Thorpe's *The First Hundred Years*, *LA Times*' Erskine Johnson reported, "Robert Montgomery and Virginia Bruce, portraying honeymooners in a new film, are far from the best of friends off the set."[39] Maybe Virginia's sizeable and meaty role was a problem for Montgomery. After his successful, dark dramatic turn in Thorpe's *Night Must Fall* perhaps he wanted more of the same? Or, perhaps Montgomery really *did* goose her in the opening scene. Whatever the case, they were a striking-looking duo. Norman Krasna created a career-versus-career tale in which Virginia's salary as a New York theatrical agent exceeds that of husband/yacht-builder Montgomery. "Has it been fun keeping me?" he teases, after announcing his new promotion. Montgomery assumes she'll drop everything and relocate to New Bedford, Connecticut. Virginia's

The First Hundred Years (1938) with Binnie Barnes
and Robert Montgomery (MGM)

five-year contract precludes a move; besides, she argues, "My work means as much to me as yours does to you!" Understandably, Virginia grapples with her inner conflict. Their five-year marriage has a lovable grip on her. An inevitable separation is finalized by a judge who chastises Virginia, saying she should be "ashamed." She digs in her heels and counters that he has "a man's point of view," but balks when he demands she pay $400-a-month support to Montgomery. Up to this point Krasna's story is strong, interesting, and entertaining. It loses steam, however, when Montgomery's college pal, Lee Bowman, and man-hungry Binnie Barnes show up with prolonged, predictable consequences. As *The New York Times* pointed out, "The trouble is that it is so inexorably feature-length. After living through *The First Hundred Years*, the wandering mind is apt to find itself meditating on the title, playing with such periphrastic fancies as 'the first 100 minutes' and so on."[40] The strength of Virginia's character remains intact until she discovers she's pregnant. The *Times* felt it shouldn't have made any difference. "We think that Miss Bruce should have held out . . . right now there doesn't seem to be much future in yachts." Virginia had commented on the film's conclusion to *Los Angeles Times* reporter Alma Whitaker. "I'll wager that after a year or so," said Virginia of her character, "that she arranges to return to her career. Luckily my husband approves of my career."[41] Film critic Wood Soanes also zeroed in on the film's ending, saying, "It isn't until the very final scenes that [Krasna] finds himself in a cul-de-sac and has to rely on a shop-worn device to extricate himself and his principals. . . . Montgomery and Miss Bruce, fashionable in attire and smooth in manner, slide along gracefully through their roles."[42]

The confidence which allowed Virginia to "slide gracefully" through her performance, she credited to Ruben's influence.

"Jack is giving up all his spare time to coaching me," she acknowledged. "Every night I rehearse my lines for the next day with him. He doesn't try to tell me just how I should play the scene for Mr. Thorpe, who himself takes infinite pains with me, but it is a tremendous help to have someone at home who understands the problem and can discuss the psychology of the character. You have so little time on the set for real study."[43]

MGM saw something in the Montgomery-Bruce combination and immediately paired them for a more serious assignment. *Yellow Jack*, based on Sidney Howard's 1934 play, takes place at the turn of the century in Cuba (1900-1901), and features Stegomyia, a mosquito whose bite induces yellow fever. The film is an absorbing retelling of the experiments done to resolve the problem. These experiments required the cooperation of enlisted men residing in Cuba after the Spanish-American War. In his first dramatic turn since *Night Must Fall*, Robert Montgomery, as Sgt. John O'Hara (a role essayed on Broadway by James Stewart), plays the prime guinea pig. Focusing on Major Walter Reed's discoveries, MGM fleshed out the scenario with threads of comedy and romance. In the shoes of Major Reed, Lewis Stone was a perfect choice and provided the gravity of the situation by his mere presence. To underscore the courage of those involved in a tense and deadly situation, the camera needed a "sympathetic face," and the narrative, a woman's point of view. Virginia was that face and presence. She played the nurse-assistant to Major Reed.

The attraction between Virginia and Montgomery was not allowed to tamper with the story's innate realism. Virginia put in her two-cents worth letting the love-struck Montgomery know exactly where she stood. She was both amused and annoyed by his flirtations, which she thought conflicted with the real work going on around them — the need for volunteers. "I'm talking to

Sergeant O'Hara," she reminds him. He listens. "Now maybe for the first time since armies began," she says pointedly, "soldiers are given a chance to do good, not harm. To make the world better, not worse, as a place to live in. I can't understand why with all these men, no one has come forward for Major Reed." Montgomery, convinced she's shaming him, storms off. Although Virginia sees his point and later apologizes, she recognizes the necessity for the army to have a new kind of "hero." The dedication of Major Reed and the volunteers helped wipe out a scourge that had plagued Cuba for 150 years. It also cleared way to make possible the building of the Panama Canal.

The New York Times noted that Montgomery's "Sergeant O'Hara, with a Galway brogue and his eye on Nurse Virginia Bruce, is . . . shrewd and practical . . . There is a welcome lack of false heroics. *Yellow Jack* is a superior job of picture-making."[44] Some critics noted that the 83-minute film tended to drag. This is noticeable in scenes in which Montgomery's tent mates mouth dialogue that goes nowhere. The clowning of Andy Devine and Buddy Ebsen's droning hillbilly also dilutes the film's impact. Ads for *Yellow Jack* promoted the Montgomery-Bruce flirtation. "To hold her in his arms," read one ad, "he would face any danger . . . even the unknown . . . the dreaded 'Yellow Jack!'" Unfortunately, the film just missed its mark and real potential.

One can't mention *Yellow Jack* without acknowledging the basis for Virginia's character — the very real, young, and attractive nurse, Clara Louise Maass. How playwright Sidney Howard could ignore the only American and the only *woman* to die during the US Army's Yellow Fever Commission studies is difficult to comprehend. Maass had been in Cuba during the Spanish-American War and seen the gruesome, hemorrhaging disease wipe out more men than died in battle. She returned in 1900 as part of the first recorded consent in human experimentation. One of the nation's most courageous nurses, twenty-five-year-old Maass volunteered along with the men, being bitten several times over a period of five months. In August 1901, she tested again for immunity, was bitten for the seventh time, and died six days later. Virginia's role as Frances Blake was an extension of a minor character from the original play. MGM scenarist Edward Chodorov (who would later be blacklisted) did a good job of developing a woman's presence in an important screenplay. It's a pity Chodorov didn't lean more in the direction of Clara Maas. A death scene for Virginia would have given her equal footing with Montgomery's role, and helped the meandering scenario keep a stronghold on the audience.

Director Richard Thorpe observed a "difference" in Virginia's screen work. "Marriage gives a new bloom, a new beauty, a greater sincerity," said Thorpe, "all of which is registered on celluloid. The camera inevitably picks it up."[45] Virginia confirmed Thorpe's suggestion, saying, "For the first time in my life I have found someone who not only has confidence in me but who can persuade me to believe in myself. My hardest task has always been heretofore, to make myself think that I must have some talent, or I wouldn't have progressed this far. Also, I must confess it's a delight to have a husband who can assume some of the home responsibilities and who isn't beyond babying me once in a while. I am tremendously happy, and whether the happiness itself reflects on the screen or not, it is making me work harder and more enthusiastically than ever before. If that results in stardom, then I owe it to my marriage."[46]

One thing that enabled Virginia and Jack Ruben's relationship to sail, and maintain its course, was the fact that Ruben had known John Gilbert. He was not threatened by Virginia's mention, or memory, of her first marriage. "I call Jack 'Sonny,'" Virginia explained, "because — well, I naturally didn't want to call him Jack. . . . Sonny understands about Jack and me," she said. "He knew Jack, was his good friend, was fond of him. So that I can talk to him about Jack without embarrassment or constraint. Other men I have gone out with in the past few years have been so different; they have seemed to resent it when I've spoken of Jack; their attitude has been: 'Oh, can't you forget him . . . ' But Sonny knows that every experience becomes a very part of the person who has experienced it and should not be 'forgotten.'"[47] A level of maturity that was not available to Virginia in her relationship with Gilbert was easily accessible with Ruben.

Two months before Virginia's marriage to Ruben, she decided to visit another psychic in the Los Angeles area. After her reading, she returned to the MGM set for some final work on *Bad Man of Brimstone*. Director Ruben called, "Action!" and Virginia came running out of a false-front western home that she resided in on celluloid. As she gazed toward the painted "Arizona" backdrop, something stuck in her mind. Fate had revealed this time that she was to be married . . . *three* times.[48] She raised her hand and waved farewell as the camera came in for a close-up. Her eyes filled with tears of joy, and the bitter sweetness of never *really* knowing what would lie ahead.

Endnotes

1 Margaret Dixe, "Hollywood's Heart Problems - and Yours," film magazine, date unknown
2 Ibid
3 Babcock, "The Girl from Fargo."
4 Jimmie Fidler, "Hollywood," *Chronicle Telegram*, 6/26/37
5 Myrna Loy, *Being and Becoming*, Alfred A. Knopf, N.Y., 1987, pg 121
6 J.E. Smyth, "Reconstructing American Historical Cinema: From Cimarron to Citizen Kane," University of Kentucky Pr., Lexington, page 270
7 J.E. Smith, "Reconstructing ..." pg 272
8 Ronald Haver, "A Star is Born: The Making of the 1954 Movie and it's 1983 Restoration," Applause Books, New York, pg 58
9 J.E. Smyth, "Reconstructing . . . " pg 272
10 Ibid
11 Marion Davies, *The Times We Had*, Ballantine Books, 1985, pp 143-144
12 May Mann and *Standard Examiner Staff*, "Going Hollywood," *Ogden Standard Examiner*, 9/9/37
13 May Mann, "Going Hollywood," *Ogden Standard Examiner*, 9/6/37
14 Gladys Hall, "I Didn't Think it Could Happen Again," *Motion Picture*, 2/38
15 Franc Dillon, "Virginia Bruce Speaks Out!" *Screen Book*, 8/38
16 Kirtley Baskette, "Second Chance at Love," *Photoplay*, 2/38
17 Gladys Hall, "I Didn't Think . . . "
18 Terry Kelly, "How to Get Along With 50 Men," *Hollywood*, 2/38
19 Franc Dillon, "Virginia Bruce . . . "
20 Kirtley Baskette, Second Chance . . . "
21 Kelly, "How to Get . . . "
22 ibid
23 Franc Dillon, "Virginia Bruce . . . "
24 Gladys Hall, "Does Your Boy Friend Love You?" *Modern Screen*, 6/39
25 ibid
26 Alanson Edwards, "Bits of Gossip About Hollywood's Film Folk," *Vidette Messenger (IN)*, 1/24/34
27 May Mann, "In Hollywood," *Ogden Standard Examiner*, 12/11/38
28 Kelly, "How to Get . . . "
29 May Mann, "Going Hollywood," *Ogden Standard Examiner*, 7/10/38
30 Wells Root, *Writing the Script*, Owl Books, 1980, pp 112-113
31 Frank S. Nugent, review for *Bad Man of Brimstone*, New York Times, 2/4/38
32 Sara Hamilton, review of *Bad Man of Brimstone*, Los Angeles Examiner, 1/20/38
33 Reine Davies, "Hollywood Parade," *LA Examiner*, 11/24/37
34 Marian Rhea, "A Hollywood Bride Has Problems," *Hollywood*, 11/38

35 ibid

36 ibid

37 Virginia Bruce, "Careers versus Marriage," Picturegoer Weekly, 8/19/39

38 Frank S. Nugent, review of *Arsene Lupin Returns, New York Times*, 3/9/38

39 Erskine Johnson column, *Los Angeles Examiner*, 3/2/38

40 Bosley R. Crowther, review of *The First Hundred Years, New York Times*, 5/13/38

41 Alma Whitaker, "Virginia Bruce Combines domestic, Film Careers," *Los Angeles Times*, 4/4/38

42 Wood Soanes, review for *The First Hundred Years, Oakland Tribune*, 5/15/38

43 Fargo Library Archive, news item, "Virginia Claims Marriage Has Made New Star of Her, 3/20/38

44 Frank S. Nugent, review of *Yellow Jack, New York Times*, 5/20/38

45 Fargo Library Archive, news item, "Virginia Claims . . . "

46 ibid

47 Gladys Hall, "I Didn't Think . . . "

48 film magazine column, author's collection, c. 1937

CHAPTER 10:

Happy Interlude -
Sonny & Sweetie Pie

Before Susan Ann woke up each morning, Virginia confessed that peeking in on her was like discovering a rare and beautiful blossom. That is, if Susan hadn't already made a beeline to her mother's bedroom. After being overly pampered by adoring grandparents and Uncle Stanley, Susan, in her new surroundings, had become more demonstrative. She no longer hesitated to give affection, and sought out opportunities to do so. The change of environment was also a godsend for Virginia. She loved the home she and Ruben were leasing, and the role of running a household. Before, she had simply let her mother take charge.

By the time Susan had her fifth birthday, both Virginia and Ruben recognized their propensity for extravagance. They made efforts to economize household expenses. Virginia enjoyed the challenge, going so far as to place a new ironer by the window to cut down on the overuse of electric lights. "How much did that remarkable invention cost, Sweetie Pie?" Ruben asked the day it was delivered. "Oh, I have it all planned out Sonny," Virginia replied. "Look. Here are the figures." In the long run she assured Ruben that it would be much cheaper than sending the laundry out. "Good," Ruben laughed. "Then I can count at least four more years of this marriage until we get out of the red with the laundry situation, right?"[1] As it turned out, his remark would be an uncanny presentiment.

As the holiday season of 1938 approached, Virginia wanted it "understood" that no extravagant gift-exchange would take place between her and Ruben. Her request from Santa Claus was a tree. If extravagance was to be had, it would be channeled into the new house being built in Pacific Palisades. "What we need and want most of all," she explained to Ruben, "is dozens and dozens of great big new trees!" "Trees?" he repeated. She nodded. "And a 'spreading chestnut,'" she pointed out, "the kind *I* want is five-hundred dollars with the planting, and the guarantee, and all."[2] Ruben listened. "I'll make a note of it," he smiled. And, he did. He was equally excited about their new home. For someone who believed in living "now" Ruben listened and remembered. The contrast between Virginia's marriage to Ruben and that to Gilbert was pretty phenomenal. The natural availability of intimacy, companionship, and understanding was something new for her. She was more focused. "I've always been a poor listener," Virginia pointed out, "preoccupied, letting my mind wander while people were talking . . . since I married Walter, I don't do that anymore. I love to listen now. Oh, I've never been so happy in my life before."[3] Virginia and Ruben celebrated one another. They expressed gratitude for what they shared on a daily basis. Something so simple made a huge difference. Understandably, Ruben had had advantages that John Gilbert *never* knew.

Jacob Walter Rubin was born August 14, 1899, in New York City. He was the son of Max Rubin, a salesman and Turkish immigrant. Like John Gilbert, young Jacob had early exposure to the world of theatre. His mother, Ruth Walters Rubin, was an actress. At the age of eleven Jacob took on the assignment of 'playing' her son in a theatrical production. An article from 1931 stated that his performance was, "for both charitable and wise reasons, his first and last appearance on any stage."[4] Soon afterwards, his parents enrolled him at New York's Peekskill Military Academy for young men. He then attended the all-boys DeWitt Clinton High in Manhattan. After graduation, he stayed in the city and enrolled at Columbia University, focusing on psychology. He left college his junior year determined to become a writer. Ruben stated that when he failed to reach literary heights immediately, he resorted to becoming a press agent. His stay with the publicity game was also short lived. He cast it aside after accumulating a fortune of $50. He then focused on rewriting some of his discarded sketches for the vaudeville circuit. A few of these were produced — with success. At the peak of this new venture he was hired as a regional distributor for the newly-formed MGM in 1924. By 1926, Ruben was helping out with scenarios for Fox. He left Fox for Paramount in 1927 and began writing scripts and adaptations. His interest in the "Wild West" was triggered by being assigned to no less than five Zane Grey films. In 1929 he moved to RKO. The studio liked his work on a couple of Richard Dix films and asked Ruben to direct Dix in 1931's mystery-crime thriller *The Public Defender*. The film was a smash hit for Dix and a bond was established between director and star. Within a couple years Ruben had directed Dix in five films. Dix asked Ruben to be his best man when he was married in 1931.

Ruben's work was enriched with psychology, humor, the risqué, a social consciousness, and still maintains a contemporary feel. MGM was impressed with Ruben's success at RKO and put him under contract in 1935. He got off to a good start for the studio with *Public Hero #1* (1935). Ruben directed two of MGM's biggest stars, Jean Harlow and Spencer Tracy, in *Riffraff* (1936),

Robert Montgomery in *Trouble for Two* (1936), followed by two Wally Beery features. He had Beery in mind when writing the script for *The Bad Man of Brimstone*, which would be his last directorial job. In mid-winter 1938, Ruben was assigned to direct Mickey Rooney and Spencer Tracy in *Boys Town*. He made a trip to Nebraska to get the layout for location shooting, and came back enthusiastic. MGM suddenly "promoted" Ruben to the role of producer and gave *Boys Town* to director Norman Taurog. Ruben took on the new job, but wasn't keen on having that kind of responsibility. According to Virginia, Ruben was under the impression that Mayer's decision indicated he didn't care for Ruben's ability as a director.[5]

Virginia gained a new perspective being married to a director-producer. "I've learned so much about every phase of picture making," she admitted. "I see the thing as a whole now, whereas before I used to think of only my own part. But through [Sonny] I have a better understanding now of all the various elements and efforts which put together, make a picture. . . . I'm more able to feel each line of dialogue, each scene, because I know what birth pains are involved with the creation of each little detail. I've always liked acting but now I'm beginning to have a real affection for the industry as well."[6] On many an evening Virginia accompanied Ruben on half-pleasure, half-business appointments. She would sit back and listen to executives talk about film projects. She had little part in the dialogue, and simply reveled in her new position as a producer's wife.

In May 1938, MGM had announced a sequel to *The Great Ziegfeld* using the talents of the same scenarist, William Anthony McGuire. Virginia was to be prominently featured along with Joan Crawford, Eleanor Powell and Walter Pidgeon. McGuire's sudden death brought the idea to a halt. (By the time the pro-

Woman Against Woman (1938) with Mary Astor and Herbert Marshall (MGM)

duction was finally realized, in the fall of 1940, Virginia had left the studio.) Her summer release for 1938 was MGM's *Woman Against Woman*. In the advertisements, Herbert Marshall's name imposed itself above the two women in question, who were billed as "Virginia Bruce vs. Mary Astor." This head-on collision takes place after Herbert Marshall remarries and brings his new wife, Virginia, back to his hometown where ex-wife Astor resides. Riddled with insecurity, Astor has banned together practically everyone in town to make Virginia feel miserable as hell. Producer-scenarist Edward Chodorov adapted the story from Margaret Culkin Banning's "Enemy Territory," and the result was, according to *The New York Times*, "ponderous." Critic Bosley Crowther commented that he could "hardly hear the thud" when the two women met face-to-face. As written, he found Astor's attack too "patent" and Virginia's retaliation "uninspired." In the end, the two ladies call it a draw. "And Mr. Marshall settles back with a sigh."[7] Another review stated, "Virginia Bruce and Mary Astor, as the principals, talk their way out of the problem, which should have remained what it was — a good women's magazine story."[8] Mary Astor agreed. Her own impression of the film was dismissive. She looked back in her 1967 autobiography *A Life on Film* and stated,

> MGM had the best stable of contract players. That gives you an idea: 'stable.' As in horses, not as in permanence. They could really make "all-star" pictures and they made bad ones too. Like this little job I took: *Woman Against Woman*. Producer Edward Chodorov, director Robert B. Sinclair, cameraman Ray June were top men. And stars Herbert Marshall and that beautiful gal Virginia

Bruce. Margaret Culkin Banning's nice little short story underwent some unfortunate change on its way to the screen, however. Let's draw a veil over this "seriocomic marital drama . . . "[9]

While working on the film, Astor expressed her gratitude for the part, saying after seventeen years in film she liked being the "heavy" for a change and was looking forward to playing more "thoroughly dislikable characters." "Someone who messes up the plot," added Mary, "is always more interesting than someone who just lets the story do things to him or her."[10] Indeed, Astor had no reason to complain. It was this type of role that paved the way to an Oscar win for her in 1941's *The Great Lie*. Critics be damned, *Woman Against Woman*, in truth, holds up very well. The drama is taut and made interesting by the three principals. At first, Virginia does her best to settle into "enemy territory." But, when Marshall drives her to the picturesque, hilly, three-acre site of their proposed home, she breaks down and confesses she is having second thoughts. "I married a divorced couple," she cries. "I'm an outsider with the town, with your mother and with you!" Virginia does a splendid job of releasing her pent-up emotions with a natural and appealing performance. She finally confronts Astor at a country club function, in which Astor is about to make yet *another* dramatic exit to gain sympathy from the elegant-looking onlookers. Taking full charge, Virginia stops her. "Cynthia! Please don't go!" Bruce accuses, "You put on this act once before right here in this club. What was the idea of getting all dressed up and making a late entrance, just for the pleasure of leaving when you see me? What *was* the point?" Humiliated, Astor threatens to take her and Marshall's daughter to New York and live. Virginia calls her bluff, saying, "You wouldn't know what

There Goes My Heart (1938) (United Artists) (Courtesy of Laura Wagner)

to do without a couple hundred shoulders to cry on! But, you've overplayed your hand. All you have to do is behave yourself from now on and we'll call it quits." It works. Virginia is left with the upper hand, and Astor, we are left to believe, becomes a social being. This not "too overwrought" showdown makes for a believable ending. *The Los Angeles Times* noted, "Marshall and Miss Bruce give sincere and smooth performances."[11]

During filming of *Woman Against Woman*, Virginia stepped before the camera to do a scene with an actress named Claire McDowell, who was to play her maid. When Virginia was told that McDowell had played John Gilbert's mother in his biggest screen hit, *The Big Parade*, Virginia was very touched. Her own "mother instinct" prompted her to invite McDowell to lunch, and send her car home to bring Susan Ann to the studio. She thought it important for Susan, "to meet the actress who played in her father's greatest screen hit."[12]

Next up for Virginia was a role opposite Fredric March that was rumored for, or turned down by, Carole Lombard, Constance Bennett, Claudette Colbert, and Barbara Stanwyck. Most likely, these ladies had read the uninspired script. *There Goes My Heart*, released through United Artists, was penned by columnist Ed Sullivan. Many considered it a carbon copy of Frank Capra's Oscar-winning triumph *It Happened One Night*. Unfortunately, Bruce's transformation from a spoiled rich girl into a down-to-earth woman doesn't score as well as Claudette Colbert's in the Capra film. In Gable's newsman shoes, Fredric March is lost. The repartee between him and Bruce lacks wit, and comes across as tepid. Both stars seem uneasy in their roles. The few one-line zingers that do pop up are given to Virginia's roommate, Patsy Kelly (an old-time Hal Roach crony), who steals the show. In fact, when gag-master Kelly drops out of sight midway into the picture, so does the entertainment. At the weak finish, when Virginia finally declares, "Having so much, made me realize how little I had," it doesn't have nearly the impact intended. Far funnier was an exchange between Virginia and Stan Laurel, who was also on location at Catalina Island (where initial scenes for *There Goes My Heart* were shot). A special dressing room trailer was built for Virginia, but she only spent about five minutes inside before having to vacate it. She stated she appreciated the effort on her behalf, but couldn't stand the smell of fresh paint. Laurel happened to overhear her and advised, "Just put a sliced onion in one corner of the trailer and it will take away the paint odor." "But how are you going to get the smell of onion out of the room?" Virginia asked. "That's easy," replied Laurel. "Just repaint it."[13] Things took an unexpected dramatic turn on the set during the filming of an ice-skating sequence. An extra fell with considerable force against Virginia. According to one news report, "Her feet flew up in the air and she landed heavily, her head striking the ice, rendering her unconscious for several minutes. A doctor was at hand and applied restoratives."[14]

Frank S. Nugent summed things up for *The New York Times*, saying, "Fredric March and Virginia Bruce play it rather more soberly than Clark Gable and Claudette Colbert did, and the script — in its few moments of originality — is not half so resourceful as [*It Happened One Night*] . . . This admittedly is a prejudiced report; we can't help being prejudiced against copy-cats."[15] The *Los Angeles Times* stated, "Ingratiating as Fredric March and Virginia Bruce are, the story saddled on them is so feeble and trite that

There's That Woman Again (1938) as bad as it's title –
with Melvyn Douglas (Columbia)

the stars are overshadowed by the comedians, Patsy Kelly and
Alan Mowbray."[16] Another review blamed the director, saying,
"Norman McLeod, who directs *Topper* pictures . . . buries this
stale tale as well as he can under a mound of gags."[17] Although no
reviews targeted Virginia, it could well be that screwball comedy
simply wasn't her cup of tea. She was thrown into a similar situation for her next picture.

There's That Woman Again was a follow up to a successful husband-wife detective film at Columbia, *There's Always a Woman.*
Melvyn Douglas and Joan Blondell had teamed for the surprise
hit. When a sequel was planned, Blondell was at home becoming a mother, so the studio borrowed Virginia from MGM. It
was a mistake. Throughout the film Virginia seems off-key as the

dim-witted help-mate to Douglas. Clive Hirschhorn (author of *The Columbia Story*) noted, "Virginia Bruce . . . did her best and sometimes overdid her best trying to re-create Blondell's charming daffiness."[18] Hirschhorn added, "The screenplay . . . was sardine-packed with clichés and inconsistencies which may, in part, have accounted for the disappointing box-office."[19] Critic Robert Ford's review said of Virginia, "The story follows the *Thin Man* pattern and does it well enough, except that there should be some limit to the antics of Miss Bruce, who plays the wife . . . she overacts the part or else the part was written with little finesse. . . . Miss Bruce's deductions, as you might have suspected, do more towards solving the case than those of her husband."[20] Amid the mayhem of jewel robberies and murder, Virginia gets one good chuckle at a beauty salon. She is breathing thru a tube — her face under layers of facial wax, and suddenly she finds herself under arrest. Completely unrecognizable, she blows through the tube, sounding like a frantic canary, while trying to convince Douglas she's his wife. This was hardly Nick and Nora Charles. Virginia and Douglas were asked to do a lot of contrived, silly stuff. Virginia's antics would have been appropriate for someone like Patsy Kelly, or Joan Davis. As Ford's review pointed out, Virginia's role, as written, lacked finesse. She had been more at home in a sophisticated comedy-mystery like *Arsene Lupin Returns*.

Virginia knew she was in over her head. Reporter Ben Maddox caught her on the set between scenes as she was being groomed by no less than three attendants. She was feeling edgy. "I never had the faintest notion of becoming an actress," she told Maddox. "I thought my mother must be out of her mind when she'd say I was as attractive as most of those girls in Hollywood. . . . There are," she added thoughtfully, "a number of things I don't believe in." Suddenly, Virginia turned her head and snapped at the hairdresser, "I don't believe in having my *hair* combed to a fare-ye-well!" After everyone took a collective deep breath, she continued. "I don't believe in being too proud, for instance. When an opportunity bangs at my door . . . I don't worry over whether it banged on someone else's first. . . . Who am I to be so *wonderful*? I understand they wanted Joan Blondell for this role, Carole Lombard for the one I played before this one. All I hope is they're not sorry they got me instead."[21] When the assistant director interrupted, Virginia rose from her chair and changed the subject. "I am more domestic than you'd guess a Hollywood girl would be," she said. "Not that I can cook worth a hoot." Already in a "mood," she stepped before the camera and into the required action. During filming, her mind (unsurprisingly) was focused somewhere else. Columnist May Mann observed Virginia spending as much time planning the evening dinner menu, as she did concentrating on her role. "I think we'd better have peas," Mann overheard Virginia tell her cook. "Well, you call Jack over at Metro and ask him if we should have pie with the sauce or without. Yes, then call me back." Ten minutes later the phone rang. Ruben had settled the matter. Their dinner guests were having pie with the sauce. Mann concluded her column saying, "After the phone call she continues being Melvyn Douglas' wife in the picture — and forgets — (or does she) about the pie for dinner at home."[22] During production director Al Hall kept referring to Virginia as "Miss Blondell." Virginia found it amusing, but confessed she hadn't seen the original film. At one point she asked if they could run it for her in the projection room. Melvyn Douglas nixed the idea, telling her, "Don't run it now. Wait until you finish this picture and then see it as a sequel."[23] In hindsight, it may have helped Virginia immensely to see the original before tackling her assignment.

Surprisingly, not long after the release of Columbia's *There's*

That Woman Again, MGM decided to cast Douglas and Bruce in the third installment of their popular *Thin Man* series. Sidney Skolsky reported in September 1938 that William Powell's agent was asking too much money. Powell, with no contract, had been off screen for almost two years (he had withdrawn from the screen after Jean Harlow's death; then, he had a bout with cancer). After deciding to cast Douglas for Powell's part, Virginia was considered to take over for Myrna Loy. (In the previous *Thin Man* release Nora Charles was "expecting." The studio would not allow Douglas to be the father of William Powell's child.) Virginia did several screen tests for the part. Fortunately, MGM finally agreed to Powell's price, and he was reunited with Loy for *Another Thin Man.*

In *Hollywood Goes to Town (1938),* a promotional short for Norma Shearer's *Marie Antoinette,* thousands of worshipping spectators watched a host of celebrities entering Carthay Circle Theatre for the film's premier.

The Rubens were seen smiling for the camera while moving at a fast clip toward the lobby. Jeanette MacDonald stepped before the microphone and, as if addressing deity, implored, "Bless you, Norma!" A few months later, Virginia and Sonny teamed again for the *Screen Snapshots* series, about

*Let Freedom Ring (1939)*with
Nelson Eddy (MGM)

celebrity horse fanciers. The couple was a logical choice for the Columbia short. Ruben, an avid polo player, instigated a steeple-chase in October 1938, for the Riviera Country Club in Pacific Palisades. As chairman of the race, Ruben coordinated a committee that included singer Allan Jones and actors Jack Holt and Walter Connolly. Steeplechases are a challenging form of horse-racing that traverse obstacles such as fences and hedges. Virginia, wreath in hand, decorated the winner for the November 8 championship. Over the next few years she would frequently be asked to do the honors for such events and her photo would appear in the Sports Section of Los Angeles newspapers.

For her next MGM release, Virginia saddled up to co-star with former beau, Nelson Eddy. In *Let Freedom Ring*, she did more than just swoon as Nelson sang. Virginia put a voice to scenarist Ben Hecht's views on the exploits of railroad barons. The Eddy-Bruce teaming was understandable. They looked good together. In the fall of 1935, the two made an impression at Hollywood nightclubs. Nelson was considered "in the running" as Virginia's sweetheart. Virginia loved dancing, and admired what she referred to as Nelson's "tall kingly bearing" on the ballroom floor.[24] Heads turned whenever the striking blonde duo waltzed by — Virginia, in a white Grecian gown with coordinating white roses atop her coiffure, and Nelson, beaming. Virginia admired Eddy, thought him noble, and especially liked the way he treated his mother, Isabel. He was interested in a variety of things, had a business background, and had worked for the Fourth Estate. "He knows radio, concert work, tennis, good books, and psychology," Virginia enthused, but added, "Nelson Eddy has a remote, unap-proachable quality about him which would make most girls fear him a little, stand in both awe and admiration."[25]

This author had a similar impression of Eddy in 1966, when

I met him after one of his San Francisco nightclub performances. Eddy was a master showman and in excellent voice at age sixty-four. I waited backstage near his dressing room, and listened to the merry banter between him and singing partner Gale Sherwood. When Eddy appeared to dutifully greet, and shake hands, he seemed somehow remote and distant. Even a little sad. The United States was in such turmoil at the time (Vietnam). Students were protesting and questioning everything they had grown up with. I read an interview with Eddy, soon after our meeting wherein he expressed his curiosity about what was going on with young people. He felt he was "missing out" on something significant. His concerns, coupled with the recent loss of screen partner, Jeanette MacDonald, colored his personality and added to his complexity.

In *Let Freedom Ring*, Eddy personified American youth questioning the "powers that be" in the wild west of 1868. As a recent Harvard grad, Eddy returns west to help his pioneer dad, Lionel Barrymore, fight railroad magnate Edward Arnold. Scenarist Hecht established the crux of the matter as: "Wall Street vs. The People." Virginia, proprietor of the Clover City saloon, loathes Arnold and his doting attentions. When the opportunity presents itself, she confronts him.

"You've got lots of money, haven't you?" she asks him.

"Oh!" Arnold grins. "I keep it in barrels!"

"Then why do you go around robbing poor people, stealing their land and burning them out?" she inquires. "Why, are you a *thief*?"

Arnold defends himself, saying where he comes from he's called a "financier."

"And, just what *country* do you come from?" she says impatiently.

"It's not a country," replies Arnold. "It's a street. Wall Street."

"Well," declares Virginia, "that street isn't big enough to run this country, Mr. Knox. You own the sheriff and the court, and you've got all the money in the world. But, you haven't got enough to win, because there is something stronger than you are!"

Arnold is amused. "Really," he chuckles. "What is that?"

"Honest folks," replies Virginia. "And, all they need is someone to show them how to fight and *no one* can lick them!"

Picking up on Virginia's cue, Nelson Eddy arrives. He's the "someone" with a plan. Eddy coddles Arnold, while plotting to usurp the nefarious profiteer. It's pure corn, but scenarist Ben Hecht has some pointers to make that are timely. Considering the struggle of minorities, or the "little man," vs. corporate megapowers seventy years after *Let Freedom Ring* was released, it is easy to see the importance of what Hecht was saying. On film, Nelson empowers the landowners and railroad workers of various ethnic backgrounds, by using the "power of the press." He also knocks sense into Arnold's thick-headed foreman, Victor McLaglen. Director Jack Conway did a slick job with the fight scenes. "[McLaglen] was a real tough character in real life," said Eddy afterward. "And brother, he was really a good boxer. I had to fight Vic for three long days while they shot that fight scene. He kept knocking me down on to rocks--rubber 'rocks,' fortunately. It was rough going for me."[26] Eddy's performance didn't suffer, however; he was excellent on all scores as the hero. For a highly improbable ending, Edward Arnold throws in the towel after Virginia begins a chorus of "My Country 'Tis of Thee." This cinematic flag-waver was all about giving the audience what it wanted -- something to believe in.

Let Freedom Ring was released in 1939, a few months before World War II was declared in Europe. Some critics felt the film intended to "forestall a wave of U.S. anti-Semitism."[27] Lionel Bar-

Saloon-owner Virginia with H.B. Warner in *Let Freedom Ring (1939)* (MGM)

rymore expressed the popular view that the patriotic western was good fodder for the country's morale. "It's the one type of picture," said Barrymore, "in which audiences can be sure that the villain will get his just desserts. And, believe me, in this day and age audiences *need* to believe that some villains do get their just desserts. Youngsters eat it up. After all, they're the ones who demand that the hero shall be spotless and that the heavy, deep-dyed rat shall be punched or shot into hamburger before the final reel. So long as boys are interested in emulating the Western type of hero there's hope of the pioneer spirit prevailing. So never treat the Western too lightly. They do a lot of good."[28] If anything does prevail in *Let Freedom Ring*, it is the golden baritone of Eddy's voice. His rendition of Drigo's "Serenade" at the Clover City saloon is a stunner. Producer Harry Rapf originally planned on

Let Freedom Ring (1939) Virginia standing up for 'honest
folks' in the Wild West (MGM)

Virginia and Eddy performing "Love's Serenade" as a duet – not
wanting to "waste Virginia's rich soprano."[29] Instead, she simply
listens to him from an adjoining room, her face expressing all
the rapture of a die-hard Eddy fan. *The Los Angeles Examiner*
summed things up in their review, saying, "*Let Freedom Ring*
is sure to be analyzed as a 'flag waver' by the more critical. But
in these troubled times a little flag waving can do no harm . . .
Nelson Eddy emerges as a two-fisted hero, fighting as well as he
sings. Virginia Bruce is excellent as the owner of the town restaurant who loves Eddy."[30] *Variety* echoed this sentiment calling
the film, "Momentous. It's the first in the cycle of film offerings

to stress the American type of democracy and freedom for the classes and masses." Countering this view was the *LA Evening Herald's* remark that the film was "reliable movie hokum and should entertain you if you are not too exacting."[31]

One thing that Virginia's role did for her was release her fear of horses. After a traumatic fall from a horse back in Fargo, she hadn't the nerve to get back in the saddle. When filming *Let Freedom Ring*, she had no choice. Jack Conway opened the film with a shot of Virginia on horseback watching the "Iron Horse" creep across the plain toward Clover City. Several scenes required her to look not only comfortable on horseback, but to be "pals" with her steed. By the time filming concluded, Virginia had made a complete turn around. She and Susan Ann began regular rides on the bridal paths of Bel Air. One report noted that they were joined by Spencer Tracy and his son on a morning ride. Virginia's interest in thoroughbreds was augmented by Ruben's own passion for the animals. She turned professional upon purchasing "Big Ed" and entering him in the races. The following June, "Big Ed" raced home and paid $22.60. (Sadly, she and Ruben had only bid $10 on the nose!) By 1938, celebrity interest in horses had reached epidemic proportions. Aside from Ruben's exciting steeplechases at the Riviera County Club, 70,000 hysterical fans gathered that year for the $100,000 Santa Anita Handicap. Virginia, according to Louella Parsons, was "a vision in a Kelly green hat with a dark blue suit [cheering] for Seabiscuit all the way around the track."[32] Virginia was among those who sighed at the finish of the March 5 event. Stagehand (carrying 100 pounds) nipped Seabiscuit (burdened with 130 pounds) at the wire, by a nose. Sports editor Art Cohn fumed that Seabiscuit was like a prizefighter with an arm strapped behind his back. "I am not in the habit of calling horses bums," complained Cohn, "but I am confident that if Seabiscuit were allowed to carry only 100 pounds yesterday he would have made Stagehand look like a fugitive from a dray wagon."[33]

Society Lawyer paired Virginia with Walter Pidgeon in a remake of MGM's 1933 film *Penthouse*, which had starred Warner Baxter and Myrna Loy. Screenwriters Frances Goodrich and Albert Hackett, who did wonders with the *Thin Man* series, were responsible for *Society Lawyer's* sharp, funny, and suspenseful script which pushed forward the idea that the common classes have more ethics than the synthetic and pampered rich. The key person that figures into this idea is Virginia's heart-of-gold chanteuse. She hooks up with Walter Pidgeon after his uppity fiancée snubs him and his law firm fires him. Pidgeon had gained a reputation (and publicity) for defending public nuisances like racketeer Tony Gazotti (Leo Carrillo). After being saved from the electric chair, Gazotti calls Pidgeon "Sweetheart" and smothers him with kisses for the photographers. He also supplies Pidgeon with two bodyguards, and introduces him to the main attraction at Gazotti's nightclub: Virginia Bruce. We first see her in a spotlight, descending a staircase, singing "I'm in Love with the Honorable Mr. So and So" (Virginia trained with Judy Garland's coach Roger Edens). She joins Pidgeon at his table, and Carrillo orders her to show Pidgeon a good time. She explains to Pidgeon why she acquiesces to Gazotti's demands. "I sing for an orchestra," she says matter-of-factly. "The orchestra works for a club. The club is owned by Mr. Gazotti. Well . . . I'm not crazy!" She forgoes her next number and readily agrees to go to Pidgeon's place. Her visit turns into a permanent stay after Pidgeon intuits her life is in danger. As the plot thickens, Pidgeon jokes that the real culprit, Eduardo Ciannelli, is a "woman pretending she's a man." (In truth, Ciannelli's gripping menace instills a heavy dose of suspense.) When Virginia risks her life to protect Pidgeon, he suspects her of working against him. He discovers his mistake, and she offers him some free analysis. "You know, the trouble with you is you're not the *type* to be mixed up in gyps and racketeers. They muddle you up until you don't believe that anyone can be on the level!" Her honesty is teeming with tenderness. When he tries to kiss her, she warns him, "Don't *ever* kiss me. Not unless you *really* mean it!" He does . . . and they do.

Thanks to the scenarists Goodrich and Hackett, *Society Lawyer* has the essence of the early *Thin Man* films. The plot is filled with bumbling crooks, and scene stealers like Herbert Mundin as Pidgeon's man servant (wonderful in his film swansong). Director Edwin L. Marin liked working with Virginia. He commented on her eyes, giving them top rating for their "beautiful sensitiveness."[34] Marin's direction was on par with Woody Van Dyke's *Penthouse.* Virginia was a believable figure in the nightclub world, whereas Myrna Loy's innate sophistication had been a handicap in the original. Critic Chester Bahn thought *Society Lawyer* a "smartly turned out murder mystery . . . expertly directed and consummately acted by an ace cast . . . Miss Bruce registers strong."[35] London critic Lionel Collier stated, "Walter Pidgeon teams well with Virginia Bruce who is also well on the up-grade and has a deal of charm."[36] Cameraman George J. Folsey, who was behind the lens

Society Lawyer (1939) on the set with director Edwin L. Marin (MGM)

for *Arsene Lupin Returns,* focused rather harshly on Virginia this time round. *The New York Times* said, "Miss Bruce seems very nice, but the lights tear her to pieces. Has she been foolish enough to offend the cameraman?"[37] One of the problems in lighting Virginia was her translucent complexion. It was mentioned time and again that she had Hollywood's "most perfect" skin. Virginia acquired the moniker "Camellia Girl of the Screen." She had little need for make-up. Her problem with camera lighting was, for some reason, especially noticeable in *Society Lawyer.*

By 1939, Mayer's enthusiasm for star-making was being channeled into Greer Garson and Hedy Lamarr. He had contracted both ladies in the summer of 1937, during his European "expedition" and talent search. Garson, being a redhead, had grabbed old bull Mayer by the horns. He doted on her. Virginia's star-turn at the studio had become a back-burner item for Mayer. Ruben, naturally, was one-hundred-percent behind her. Louella Parsons made a point of saying, "Jack Ruben spends three-fourths of his time watching Virginia act -- that's how crazy he is about her."[38] Virginia expressed the hope that Ruben would direct her again, but knew it was highly unlikely. After the release of *The Bad Man of Brimstone,* MGM had announced Ruben would direct Bruce and Robert Taylor in the Technicolor *Northwest Passage.* The film was released in 1940 with Spencer Tracy in the lead, opposite Ruth Hussey. Virginia, in any case, was more focused on hearth and home. When INS reporter Milton Harker asked her about Metro's big plans to make her into a superstar, Virginia hesitated. "Most of all of what the future may bring I want another baby," she told Harker quite frankly. "I want to do fine things on the screen. I've always given the very best in me . . . and if I am to get even better roles, you know I'll keep doing my very best." She thought a moment, then brightened. "You know. I'd just love to have a son. I know Walter would like to have a boy too. . . . I think children are everything in life, more important than a career or anything. Home life is so important." At the time, Virginia, had been at her daughter's bedside for several days, nursing Susan's cold. "I look forward to the day when I retire and devote my whole time to my home," Virginia said thoughtfully, "then I'll do all the things I can't do now."[39] These were hardly the thoughts of a driven actress.

After the Rubens had their house-warming on January 15, 1939, Virginia was sued for $830 by landlord, T. H. Morgan, owner of the Brentwood home her parents had occupied during 1937-38. Mr. Morgan claimed his seven-year-old furnishings had been damaged. On hand for the trial was Virginia's cook, who was questioned if the Briggs had "wild parties." The defiant cook testified, "The Briggs' don't stand for no drinking and carousing and neither does Miss Bruce!" Taking the stand, Virginia complained that the plumbing "sounded like thunder." "It made so much noise it scared me," she told the judge, then added, "When I moved in, the bathroom curtains were in shreds. I told Mrs. Morgan I would buy new ones." Virginia mentioned that she had not been reimbursed. In a countersuit against Morgan, Virginia contended she was owed $176 for plumbing bills and repairing the washing machine. "And, as for the radio," said Virginia, "the day after I moved in I turned it on and couldn't get a sound. We tried to fix it but never succeeded."[40] Apparently, his Honor was moved by Virginia's performance. He ruled that the landlord should receive nothing. The following day, news headlines read, "Virginia Bruce Wins $50 From landlord - After He sues Her!"[41]

Louella Parsons dutifully reported that Virginia took her entire family to the Brown Derby for dinner after "her strenuous day in court."[42] Harrison Carroll echoed tinsel town's consensus on the trial, saying, "Hollywood is jubilant over Virginia Bruce winning a decision in her landlord's suit. Film celebs have been carried to court so many times over asserted damages to houses that most of them now have the condition of all furnishing notarized before they take over a place. James Stewart is going this one better and having pictures taken of all valuables in the Malibu house he rents."[43] Mr. and Mrs. Briggs had moved into a new eleven room Cape Cod style residence. "I built my mother and dad a house in Brentwood," Virginia reported, "taking advantage of the reasonable cost of lumber is why we were building two houses at once. So we haven't very much money [left] over. I really need to work for awhile anyway, to take care of my own family obligations."[44] Virginia was ecstatic about their new home on Maroney Lane. Its completion wasn't without a few headaches. A great Southern California brush fire was making front page news shortly before they moved in. Virginia stated that the fire "paid our newly-built house a very close visit. In fact it blistered the new paint! In the excitement I was all for standing there myself, with a hose turned on the roof and walls, for those flames looked as relentless as time itself."[45]

While nestling into their new home, with its soft apple-green carpet and rich reddish-brown hardwood furnishings, Virginia and Ruben's relationship reached a new plateau. Virginia wasn't so much interested in career decisions as she was in deciding whether or not Susan Ann would do best by going to public school along with other children in the neighborhood. At her "other" home, MGM, the studio's new roster listed 25 stars, now including newcomer Hedy Lamarr. Virginia was still lumped in the mix with 52 other "featured players." It wasn't long before Ruben suggested they have a heart-to-heart talk about the future of Virginia Bruce, "movie star."

Endnotes

1   Kay Frings, "Sonny, Susan and Sweetie Pie," magazine article, c. 1/39

2   Kay Frings, "Sonny, Susan . . . "

3   Alma Whitaker, "Virginia Bruce combines Domestic, Film Careers," *LA Times*, 4/4/38

4   "At the Movies," *Bismark Tribune*, 11/10/31

5   Charles Higham, *Louis B. Mayer, M.G.M. and the Secret Hollywood,"* Donald I. Fine, Inc., N.Y., 1993, pg 328

6   Kay Frings, "Sonny, Susan . . . "

7   Bosley Crowther, review for *Woman Against Woman, New York Times*, 8/23/38

8   Hayden Hickok, review for *Woman Against Woman, Syracuse Herald*, 6/18/38

9   Mary Astor, *A Life on Film*, Dell, NY, 1967, pg 141

10 movie column, *Syracuse Herald*, 6/14/38

11 Edwin Schallert review of *Woman Against Woman, LA Times*, 6/23/38

12 Louella Parson's column, *Fresno Bee*, 4/20/38

13 Erskine Johnson, "Behind the Make-Up," *San Mateo Times*, 11/15/38

14 Erskine Johnson, "Behind the Make-Up," *San Mateo Times*, 11/15/38

15 Frank S. Nugent, review for *There Goes My Heart, New York Times*, 10/14/38

16 Norbert Lusk, review of *There Goes My Heart, LA Times*, 10/24/38

17 film magazine review of *There Goes My Heart*, author's collection

18 Clive Hirschhorn, "The Columbia Story," Hamlyn, London, 1999, pg 89-90

19 Ibid

20 Robert Ford, review for *There's That Woman Again, Austin American*, 12/24/38

21 Ben Maddox, "Girls Don't Be Too Clever," *Screenland*, 4/39

22 May Mann, "Going Hollywood," *Ogden Standard Examiner*, 10/27/38

23 Sidney Skolsky, "Watching Them Make Pictures," *Hollywood Citizen News*, 10/21/38

24 news item, "Choose Modes with Style," *Fitchburg Sentinel (MA)*, 11/9/35

25 Gladys Hall, "She Knows Her Lovers," *Radio Stars*, 12/36

26 Sharon Rich, *Sweethearts*, Donald I. Fine, Inc., N.Y., 1994, pg 237

27 review of *Let Freedom Ring, Time*, 3/13/39

28 news article, "Fox Oakland Star Lauds Westerns," *Oakland Tribune*, 3/12/39

29 "Virginia Bruce Sings With Nelson Eddy," *Port Arthur News*, 1/15/39

30 Dorothy Manners, review of *Let Freedom Ring, Los Angeles Examiner*, 4/27/39

31 Harrison Carroll, review of *Let Freedom Ring, LA Evening Herald*, 4/27/39

32   Louella Parsons, "Movie Notables Add Color," *LA Examiner*, 3/6/38

33   Art Cohn, "Cohn-ing Tower," *Oakland Tribune*, 3/6/38

34   Antoinette Donnelly, "Daily Beauty Secrets From Donnelly," *Oakland Tribune*, 4/25/39

35   Chester B. Bahn, review of *Society Lawyer*, *Syracuse Herald*, 4/16/39

36   Lionel Collier, review of *Society Lawyer*, *Picturegoer Weekly*, 8/19/39

37   Bosley Crowther, review of *Society Lawyer*, *New York Times*, 3/31/39

38   Louella Parsons column, *Fresno Bee*, 1/19/38

39   Milton Harker, "In Hollywood," *Charleston Mail (Pa)*, 2/28/38

40   "Virginia Bruce Sued by Landlord," *Galveston Daily News*, 3/11/39

41   "Virginia Bruce Wins $50 From Landlord - After He sues Her!" *Syracuse Herald*, 3/11/39

42   Louella Parsons, *LA Examiner*, 3/11/39

43   Harrison Carroll, *LA Evening Herald Express*, 3/16/39

44   Gladys Hall, "Does Your Boyfriend Love You," *Modern Screen*, 6/39

45   Virginia Bruce, "My Heart was Set on Colonial," *House and Garden*, 2/40

1940 – Built in the summer of 1938, Virginia and Ruben's seventeen-room Colonial home at 1141 Maroney Lane occupied a knoll and a commanding view of the Pacific Ocean. The cost was $65,000. In 2008, the historical Palisades estate was listed for $12,000,000. (Architect – Herbert G. Riesenberg)

CHAPTER 11:

Stronger Than Desire

The Ruben's colonial home on Maroney Lane in Pacific Palisades, surrounded by dozens of new saplings and a large spreading chestnut tree, commanded a view of the Pacific Ocean. They called their estate, "Wildtree." Virginia and Sonny were settled in and taken up the simple life of evening walks and "lights out" by 10:30 pm. They might step out socially one evening a week. "And even then," said Virginia, "no matter how late we're out, I'm awake at 8:30. I can't stand being awake in bed when there might be something going on. I hear the birds and the squirrels, the sun is shining, and I've got to be up. I putter around in my garden, I read, and I work at my needlepoint, and play with Susan. I'm never idle a minute. Of course, it seems to me I never get anything done, but I'm always busy."[1] Virginia sat on the arm of her large chintz-covered sofa in the library conversing with popular syndicated columnist Robbin Coons. Of course, she could have pointed to her prize-winning dahlias and brag about her corn and watermelon patch — the results of her "never getting anything done." Virginia was defending herself from a comment that Joan Bennett made, saying next to herself, Virginia was the laziest girl in pictures. "I'm not really lazy," explained Virginia, a little puzzled. "I'm nearly always busy. Maybe Joan said it because I know how to conserve my energy and relax." Virginia reflected for a moment. "I suppose I do *look* lazy," she began. "I can't stand not having enough sleep, and I take a nap on the set whenever I can. I always have lunch alone in my dressing room — it's a strain having interviews over food, but I work hard when I'm working." Reporter Coons jotted down that Susan Ann popped in after her nap to say goodbye. She was on her way to a kid's party at Robert Montgomery's house. Coons described Susan, almost 7, as "plump, rosy, and be-curled." "She's very good about naps," said Virginia, zeroing in on the subject at hand. "She seems to know when she needs rest." Could it be that Joan Bennett's "laziest girl in pictures" remark referred to Virginia and her career?

It was spring 1940, and Virginia had been off the screen for almost a year. She was content being a freelance actress, and planned on taking career opportunities as they came. Her pleasure in being at home, her love of Ruben and Susan, and her plans to have another child, took precedence over any desire for major screen roles. Virginia stated it simply. "I know that if I *had* to make a choice between my marriage and my career, I'd take my marriage like a shot out of heaven."[2] "The truth about me," she emphasized, "is that . . . I want to be sure — about the few fundamental things that seem significant to me. I want to be sure of my husband, of my home, of children. I don't want suspense and sensationalism."[3]

Hollywood reporter Ben Maddox said of Virginia, "I think, it is notable that she has developed into a star without ever being the least ruthless, and this is all the more singular because she has done her rising at a studio where the competition is, to put it politely, slightly cut-throat."[4] Or, as Virginia herself put it, "I haven't run ragged after opportunities. But, I've taken advantage of my *best* opportunities. . . . "[5] In the fall of 1939, Virginia and Ruben had decided that the "opportunities" at MGM were getting rather slim. Virginia would refer to her last few films at Metro as the "Waters of Oblivion." She felt lost and out-of-place. As Maddox mentioned, Virginia was not the type to fight her way to the top of the MGM heap. "I never have fought for better parts," said Virginia, "and I *don't* think I'll start now. I quaked when I did that Ziegfeld girl. . . . Mother wanted me to fight for the lead in *Idiot's Delight*, but I couldn't. If some people force themselves to try to be what they aren't they lose what personality spark they have, and I'm one of those people."[6] Virginia had her own opinion on stardom. "Some campaign for it, some fight for it," she said. "In my case, I've found that anything I fought for I've failed to achieve, or if I got it, it wasn't worth while having. . . . No, I've discovered that the best way to get along is to relax, not to be tense, angry or frightened. Anger and fear poison you, so why give in to them?"[7] It wasn't that Virginia hadn't attempted to express her frustration during her eight years at Metro. "I tried to throw a tantrum once," she recalled, "but I gave it up in the middle. You might say it was because it was too much trouble to go on, but the real reason I stopped myself short was that I thought of Bruce in a tantrum, and the thought was so funny I had to laugh."[8]

Virginia realized she couldn't simply take off her make-up and be a homebody full-time. "I get on the set," said Virginia, "see the people I know, the crew, the cast and all, and I get to talking, working, all excited, and think, 'Oh, I couldn't give this up. I *couldn't*. I've worked for this. I love this, too, and this is me too.' After the preview of *Let Freedom Ring*, I remember Sonny and I drove home together and all the way home he told me that he was proud of me, very proud of me, that he liked the way I said

Virginia and Walter Pidgeon *Stronger Than Desire (1939)* (MGM)

my lines, liked a definiteness, he thought I gave the character. And there I was, thinking I want him to be proud of me like this — I want to go on making him proud of me."[9]

Before leaving Metro, Virginia finally received top-billing in an MGM production. It would be her last film for the studio. The story, based on W.E. Woodward's novel *Evelyn Prentice,* had been a moderately successful pairing for Myrna Loy and William Powell in 1934. The remake was to have co-starred Virginia and Robert Montgomery. Walter Pidgeon filled in for Montgomery, and did an excellent job as a slick, yet reputable lawyer who defends a young woman for murder. As the plot thickens, he comes to believe the crime was committed by his own wife (Virginia). *Stronger Than Desire* is intense dramatic turf, implausible, yet manages to come off a notch above the original film. Myrna Loy commented on her and William Powell's involvement with *Evelyn Prentice,* saying, "*The Thin Man* had been so perfect for us, such a ball to make, that going into this thing was kind of a bore. It sent Bill into occasional depressions. I'd never seen that side of him."[10] Indeed, a certain melancholy followed Powell's performance. Pidgeon's take on the role comes across stronger. In the film's climatic moment Loy was excellent on the witness stand, as was Virginia. Both women brought poignancy and natural understatement to the part. Virginia, however, breathed more texture into her character, and polish to her performance. *Stronger Than Desire* had the advantage in dialogue, and the direction of Leslie Fenton a more realistic edge.

The sticky situations that fuel *Stronger Than Desire* are blackmail and murder. In the process of retrieving some embarrassing "love letters" she had penned to an unscrupulous man (Lee Bowman), Virginia accidentally shoots him. In a daze, she hurriedly leaves his apartment. The next morning she reads headlines that he has been killed. The man's wife (Ann Dvorak) is accused of the crime. Virginia persuades Pidgeon to take the case and have Dvorak (wife of director Fenton) acquitted. *The Los Angeles Times* raved, "The treatment is fresh, the writing clever, and the direction . . . shrewdly applied. Besides eliciting ingratiating performances from his cast, Fenton makes full use of his sound camera to achieve effects of timing and surprise."[11] Film critic John L. Scott thought, "Miss Bruce and Pidgeon are paired most advantageously."[12] Although she never returned to the 520-acre MGM lot, Virginia's swansong for the studio was something she could be proud of.

Virginia, known for her "brilliant" *faux pas*, was guilty of yet another during filming. This time it was an innocent remark made to Ilka Chase, who played her confidant on screen. Chase had recently come to Metro to repeat her stage role from *The Women*. Due to a studio hitch, Rosalind Russell got the part. Chase, instead, was cast in *Stronger Than Desire*. Sitting next to Chase on the set one day, Virginia casually asked, "Did you happen to see the play, *The Women*, when you were in New York?" Ilka stared at her. Virginia . . . said nothing. She admitted later, "What was there to do? By the time I realized I'd said the wrong thing it was too late to do anything. If it had slipped my mind that she was a great hit in *The Women*, that's nothing to be ashamed of, is it? I mean I wouldn't do it on purpose, would I? So, I didn't say anything."[13]

Virginia's top-billed assignment opposite Spencer Tracy for MGM in William Faulkner's Civil War drama, *The Unvanquished*, never materialized. The studio had announced plans to cast her

Cast from MGM's *Stronger Than Desire (1939)* (l-r) Lee Bowman, Ann Dvorak,
Rita Johnson, Walter Pidgeon, Ann E. Todd, Virginia, Ilka Chase

in a singing role for *Broadway Melody of 1940,* and, as the chorus
girl who tugs hair with Rosalind Russell in *The Women* (Paulette
Goddard ended up with the part). Less promising were supporting
roles in Joan Crawford's *Susan and God* and newcomer Laraine
Day's *And One Was Beautiful.* Hedy Lamarr had been at MGM
for less than a year and had already played opposite Robert Taylor,
Tracy and Gable. Columnist Jimmy Fidler chastised MGM saying,
"Virginia Bruce is worth exploiting -- not just Hedy Lamarr."[14] In
the fall of 1939, Virginia bid *adieu* to her dressing room, across
the hall from Freddie Bartholomew's, in the building known as
the "women's apartment." The building also housed Rosalind Russell, Billie Burke, Jessie Ralph, Una Merkle, Maureen O'Sullivan,
and Eleanor Powell. When columnist Sheilah Graham visited the
MGM lot a few weeks later, she innocently asked, "Whatever happened to the career of Virginia Bruce?" Graham noted in her column, "Someone echoed 'Virginia Bruce?' As though he had never
heard of the lady."[15] "I didn't work at all for eight months," Virginia
said afterwards. "I got a new agent. He did for me what I, being I,
could not do for myself. He gave me a new enthusiasm and brand-

new courage. Aided and abetted by him, I asked to be released from my MGM contract."[16] Virginia never looked back.

Although she missed North Dakota's 1939 "Golden Jubilee" celebration (Governor John Moses, had extended her a personal invitation), Virginia's screen sabbatical allowed her to join the Hollywood Chapter of the Red Cross. "You could have heard a pin drop at the Westside Tennis Club as Claudette Colbert, Kay Francis, and Virginia Bruce took their first aid examination for the Red Cross," stated one report, "they certainly came through with flying colors." After war was declared in Europe on September 3rd, Virginia also offered her services as a spokesperson for the Union for Concerted Peace Efforts (UCPE). A mass meeting was held at the Los Angeles Philharmonic Auditorium. Virginia contacted the news media to reinforce the support for President Roosevelt "in his attempt to obtain revision of the neutrality law." "We must be gathered permanently together to see to it that we stay out of war," Virginia emphasized. "This meeting will help us to understand the dangers which may involve us and what we can do to prevent them."[18] The UCPE was one of many organizations that encouraged sympathetic Americans to make contributions to the allied cause, and boycott aggressor nations (Italy, Germany, and Japan). Most likely, Virginia had been prompted to participate by her political-minded co-star, Melvyn Douglas. Douglas had been involved with the UCPE for several months, along with director Herbert Biberman, actors Edward G. Robinson, Charles Bickford, Groucho Marx, and others.

For her return to the screen, Virginia agreed to sign on at

Warner Brothers for *Flight Angels* with Dennis Morgan. Other "irons in the fire" included: the lead opposite Morgan in Sigmund Romberg's *The Desert Song* (for which she did a Technicolor test); director Edward H. Griffith's *Virginia* (Madeline Carroll took the part); *Music in My Heart* (Tony Martin got to woo Rita Hayworth instead); and, *Earthbound*, a Fox fantasy with "dead man" Warner Baxter resolving his own murder (Andrea Leeds replaced Virginia, as the wife who brings murderess Lynn Bari to justice). While making career choices, Virginia recognized a newfound enthusiasm for films. "I'd go out of my mind if I couldn't be in them," she admitted. "I love the work. But, I know *why* -- because my husband loves pictures so! . . . He's so intrigued with the future of the screen, that now I am, too."[19] Ruben was intimately involved with Virginia's screen projects. "He helps me enormously with my work," she acknowledged, "my scripts, the parts I play, clothes, lines, everything. . . . When a man takes a vital interest in a woman's personal problems, that's love. [Sonny] helps me work things out. When your husband shares your problems with you, whatever they may be, that's love, the right kind."[20]

Virginia's family was also making transitions. Brother Stanley had graduated from UCLA in May 1936, where he was the school's tennis team captain. Following graduation, he served his apprenticeship in MGM's production department. He was designated as script clerk on the set of Jeanette MacDonald and Nelson Eddy's *Sweethearts* (1938). Stanley made his first trip down the aisle with Mary Lawrence, the seventeen-year-old daughter of scenarist Vincent Lawrence (*Test Pilot*). The February 1938 ceremony took place at the California Club. Virginia was ma-

Flight Angels (1940) Virginia's first free-lance film. Here with co-pilots Wayne Morris and Dennis Morgan (Warners) (Courtesy of Laura Wagner}

tron of honor. The following May, the young couple made Virginia an aunt for the first time, with the birth of her nephew Vincent Lawrence Briggs. By June 1939, Stanley was assistant director at MGM. It was at this time he defeated Errol Flynn in the men's championships at the 14th annual Motion Picture Tennis Tournament. Virginia's mother, Margaret, kept busy helping to launch the "Motion Pictures Mother's of America" in the summer of 1939. Monthly meetings were held at the Beverly Hills Hotel. Harold Lloyd's mother was chairman, Margaret Briggs, treasurer. The group focused on organizing charity events. Mrs. Briggs also made the society columns when hosting parties at her Brentwood home for out-of-town guests from Dakota.

Flight Angels dealt with the plights of airline stewardesses. Up-coming Warner star Dennis Morgan played a handsome pilot intent on perfecting the stratosphere plane. Virginia's role was originally assigned to Olivia de Havilland. Olivia refused the part in October 1939, and went off salary. She still hadn't drawn a penny when Virginia tested for the part in February 1940. Ann Sheridan, the monopolist of 'oomph,' had also turned down the role. "The front office just cast sorrowful and reproachful glances at Sheridan," wagged one report. "After all, Warners couldn't suspend *everybody* in the studio because of *Flight Angels*." Olivia's battle culminated in a landmark court decision that stated studios could not add suspension periods to an actor's contracts. Producer Hal Wallis liked Virginia's take on the role and signed her for a two picture deal. She remained 'Miss Congeniality,' and wasn't inclined to bargain for better parts. "I've never been able to see any advantage in temperament," said Virginia, but admitted, "I'm never absolutely certain I'm right."[23] Happily, her approach to her role as stewardess was completely on-target.

In the air, flight attendant Virginia keeps her 'cool' when her plane turns into a flying maternity ward. On ground, she exercises savvy and a sense of humor with the man-hungry women in the stewardess lounge. She patiently observes the girl-in-every-port flirtations of her special guy, Captain Farber (Dennis Morgan). Virginia marries him after he receives the sobering news that, due to poor eyesight, he is officially and permanently grounded. Following the honeymoon, Morgan feels cheated out of his career. He decides to leave Virginia and go somewhere where double-vision isn't considered a handicap: China. Morgan claims he's poison for her. In a strong emotional scene, Virginia tells him the *real* truth.

> Don't sell yourself on the idea that you're doing
> this for me! What you want to do is go someplace
> where you can have everything the way *you* want
> it. Where you can run roughshod over rules and
> regulations and people, if they don't happen to
> fall in step with you. Well, I'd like that too. . . . But,
> most of us soon find out that we can't have it that
> way. We try to adjust ourselves. But not you. Oh
> *no*! That isn't your way!

Flight Angels is peppered with enough whimsy, that we can predict a happy ending for the Bruce-Morgan duo. Jane Wyman's humorous machine-gun delivery targets anyone who gets in her way – especially her beau, Wayne Morris. She's intent on not becoming an old maid. "I have my heart set on being a young and innocent bride — *with teeth*!" she tells Morris, who keeps evading the subject of matrimony. The ingredient in (future producer) Jerry Wald's story that dates itself is the assumption that the only thing women care about is finding a man. Walter Winchell found, "Every cliché nicely in place," in *Flight Angels*. "You never have to wonder," he barbed. But Winchell admitted, "Virginia Bruce keeps it from a complete tailspin."[24] The *Los Angeles Times* classified the film as "light, pleasant entertainment . . . Miss Bruce and Morgan are well matched."[25] Film critic Jean Craig especially focused on Bruce, saying, "Virginia Bruce is pretty, snappy, and a good actress. Wonder why she isn't cast in more pictures?"[26]

After deciding against a role in Columbia's *Three Girls About Town* with Joan and Constance Bennett, Virginia moved right into her second feature at Warners, *The Man Who Talked Too*

Much. Although George Brent hated playing the lead, he was impressed with director Vincent Sherman. *The Man Who Talked Too Much*, based on Frank J. Collins' 1929 play, was a remake of the 1932 file *The Mouthpiece*. Loosely based on the career of gangster-lawyer William J. Fallon, *The Man Who Talked Too Much* has legal trickster Steve Forbes (Brent) putting the electric chair out of business. His reason? He's doing penance for sending an innocent man to the "hot seat." He rationalizes his unscrupulous methods by declaring, "I'd rather see 100 guilty men go free than one innocent man condemned." Brent also enjoys the steady cash flow from his association with slick underworld kingpin Richard Barthelmess. Brent's kid brother (William Lundigan) joins Brent's firm, but is disheartened by Brent's tactics. His doting secretary, Bruce (a replacement for Claire Trevor), is equally upset with Brent and confronts him. "I've always believed that you were pretty decent," she tells him. "I know you used to be. That's why I've stuck to you so long. But now, I don't know. Suddenly you seem to be plastered so thick with mud and slime that it'll take a miracle to get you clean again!" The "miracle" takes place. A frame-up by Barthelmess gets Lundigan on death row. A predictably happy ending takes the film out of the dark clutches of *film noir* where it would have fared better.

Sherman's fine direction of *The Man Who Talked Too Much* pleased the crowds, but not the critics. Sherman, who liked working with Virginia and Brent, didn't care for the script. He later recalled being baffled by studio chief Jack Warner's logic. "After the film was released," wrote Sherman, "Warner stopped me in the corridor. 'You didn't want to make that picture,' he said. 'But we're going to net over a hundred grand on it.'"[27] *Silver Screen's* review stated, "Virginia Bruce and Richard Barthelmess have important assignments and handle them expertly."[28] *The New York Times* found *The Man Who Talked Too Much* "ponderous" and "windy." The reviewer agreed that Brent "talked too much," and that Virginia simply tagged along "wistfully."[29] Virginia might have wondered if leaving Metro was such a good idea. She was scheduled next to lure Jimmy Stewart from wife Rosalind Russell in Warner's *No Time For Comedy*, but *The Man Who Talked Too Much*, did so, and went over schedule. Instead, she held out to play with Roz Russell (whom she admired as an actress) in the comedy *Hired Wife*.

Hollywood's Best Dressed (according to Margaret Lindsay) Kay Francis and Virginia c. 1940

Actress Margaret Lindsay, who had worked with Virginia at Columbia, commented to fashion columnist Antoinette Donnelly on Virginia's style and looks. In the 1940 interview, Lindsay stated that she topped her 'Best Dressed' list with Virginia and Kay Francis, "because these two women dress to their own type exactly. They never adopt styles that are new, or sensational, consequently their clothes are always interesting." This was indeed a compliment. Francis had been listed as "Best Dressed Woman in America" by New York's Fashion Academy. Warner's top designer Orry-Kelly admired Virginia's exquisite taste when it came to clothes. He made a point of mentioning her ensemble at a dinner party the Ruben's gave at their home in Pacific Palisades. "Virginia wore one of the striking new formal pajamas of white raw silk," Kelly raved, pointing out the interlacing pattern of grayed lilacs shading alternately into a deep purple and silver. Virginia placed violet tourmaline and moonstone clips on either side of the low neckline.

By now, Virginia had claimed her place among Hollywood's most beautiful actresses. At the end of his long career, celebrated cameraman Ernest Haller named Virginia among his 10 most photogenic screen beauties. Haller had been behind the camera lens since 1915. When a stunningly gorgeous Virginia Bruce appeared in Universal's 1940 release *Hired Wife*, columnist Jimmy Fidler declared, "If sheer beauty won Academy Awards, Virginia Bruce would be an annual contender."[33] In the 1950's Fidler echoed his earlier sentiment, "I never heard people talk about Hollywood's most beautiful gals without remembering Virginia Bruce."[34]

Well-coiffed, beautifully made-up, and elegantly gowned by Vera West, Virginia aptly filled the bill as a professional model in *Hired Wife*. She vied Rosalind Russell for the attentions of cement tycoon Brian Aherne. Initially, we find Russell, Aherne's secretary, on assignment to hire Bruce to pose for an ad campaign. Virginia, looking chic and fresh from an afternoon tryst with a distinguished suitor, listens to Russell's proposition. "Will it be a big campaign?" Virginia asks. Rosalind eyes her up-and-down. "Oh," she hums, "I think it will be . . . one of his *biggest!*" Virginia, noting Russell's catty attitude, relishes the challenge, and agrees to come to Aherne's office. Terrified of losing Aherne, Russell telephones Bruce at a posh restaurant the next day saying the deal's off. She also tells Bruce that Aherne called her a "fiend." What Russell *doesn't* know is that Bruce and Aherne are lunching together. Virginia hangs up the phone, smiles lusciously at Aherne, and coos, "Hello, *fiend.*" Russell has the edge, however, as she knows more about Aherne's cement business than he does.

Hired Wife (1940) with
Brian Aherne (Universal)

Overwhelmed by a series of business complications which necessitate a quick marriage, or bankruptcy, Aherne has Russell fetch Virginia for an emergency wedding. Russell uses no tact in relaying Aherne's "proposal." "Do you think I'm a *dope*?" Virginia fires back at Russell, who appears not to be on the level. "I love your *lies*," says Virginia. "They're not good, but they're very, very funny. You should be wearing brass buttons! You were born to be a cop, and the only way you'll ever get a man is to *arrest* him!" Virginia dismisses Russell, with a message. "Tell him I'd love to marry him tonight, but my trousseaus in the laundry!" Up to this point the film is charming, madcap, and funny. But Russell's psychotic machinations begin to get annoying, and a little scary. Critics, however, were impressed with her. *The New York Times* thought to film to be, "a lot of likable nonsense, all expertly performed. The picture is really Miss Russell's. Her magnificent self-possession, her ability to fling a barbed retort, her vast superiority over lesser females in matters requiring maneuver . . . clinch it without a doubt . . . we think she's perfect."[35] Virginia, who easily held her own during confrontations with Russell, was noticed by the *Los Angeles Times* critic, Phillip K. Scheuer, who stated, "Virginia Bruce creates a real character out of Phyllis, a gold-digging model. She is also much the same easy eyeful as ever."[36] Virginia enjoyed playing Phyllis, and found it a pleasure to be undignified for a change. She hated being typecast (because of her height) as the "stately type." "The stately type (I hate that word)," said Virginia, "gets stuck with stuffy parts . . . The average man would have to think twice before he kisses one. When he does, it's a dutiful peck on the forehead. If you're lucky, you get to be the other woman and have a chance to philander with the leading man."[37]

Off screen, Virginia's innate honesty irked Russell, who had purchased a new hat, one of those with various objects on it that defied description. Virginia walked onto the set one morning, and Russell asked brightly, "How do you like my hat, Virginia?" Reporter Helen Walker was on hand to observe Virginia's expression. "Your heart would have bled for Virginia at that moment," she noted. "You could see Virginia getting hold of herself. Finally she said, 'Well — err, I don't know yet. You see, I've never seen you wearing a hat before. . . . '" A disgruntled Russell replied, "That wasn't *quite* the right thing to say. But at least I know what you think . . . Never mind."[38] Virginia sat down next to Walker and continued gazing at the hat. She looked worried. "I wasn't as bad as I am sometimes," Virginia confided. "You know. I'm beginning to *like* that hat. But, I couldn't say so now, could I? I can't even say the right thing after I think of it! The trouble is I talk too fast. I can't lie — not even little lies — and I don't want to. But I wish I could keep quiet sometimes."[39] In the aftermath of the hat incident, reporter Paul Harrison showed up on the set. The studio's still photographer looked discouraged. He was camera ready for candid shots of the three very glum-looking stars. A reticent Aherne, an (understandably) low-key Virginia, and purposeful Russell weren't exactly a riotous trio. As a last resort the photographer suggested they get up on stage and dance for some informal shots. Everyone was in for a surprise. "Why, sure!" the threesome agreed. As studio musicians began to jive, "Miss Bruce dead-panned a torrid routine, forefingers and bustle waggling as she trucked on down. Miss Russell nearly fell off the stage trying a high kick in her long evening gown. Mr. Aherne, heretofore considered pretty much of a stiff-collar man, went into a tap routine and set the extras to whooping and clapping."[40] Too bad the cameras weren't rolling!

Portrait 1940 - "A friend of mine – a big producer," Virginia told reporter Franc Dillon, "took me into a corner at a party not long ago and lectured me about being so frank. He said I was just crazy to go around telling the truth all the time. He gave me some good advice, and I appreciate it, but I can't change."

Like many contract players, Virginia made herself available for numerous radio appearances. Radio became a steady venue for her in the 1940s, and offered a variety of roles and costars that she wasn't privy to on screen. Aside from appearing on *Lux Theatre's Cimarron* with Gable, Virginia was cast for *Hollywood Playhouse* opposite Tyrone Power in *Lloyds of London*, and performed in George Du Maurier's *Peter Ibbetson* with Charles Boyer. *Ibbetson*, one of Virginia's favorite films, had starred Gary Cooper and Ann Harding. The ethereal love-story told of two lovers who are tragically separated, and make a pact to meet in their dreams. Virginia and Sonny worked intimately together to bring her role to life. "My husband read the play to me and I started to cry," recalled Virginia. "You know how a man reads, sort of simply, unaffectedly, making it so real. Well, I cried so that I had to say, 'Stop it. I can't stand it!' At such times if a man didn't love you, he would say . . . 'Must you be a

Peter Ibbetson aired on *Hollywood Playhouse*. With Charles Boyer and Jay
Clark (Courtesy of NBC/Photofest)

fool?' But if he loves you he will close the book, as Sonny did, pat your hair, and say comfortingly, 'Does get to you, doesn't it?' It's that test of sharing that is the test of love."[41]

Virginia was a frequent guest on the Edgar Bergen-Charlie McCarthy Show, as well as *The Good News of . . .* (1938-40), a variety show, which was basically ballyhoo for MGM. *Good News* had funny stuff with Fanny Brice as Baby Snooks, the befuddlements of Frank Morgan, gallant hosts like Robert Taylor, and the contagious musical offerings of Meredith Willson (future composer of *The Music Man*). Virginia's appearances involved her doing romantic skits with Taylor, parodying *The First Hundred Years* with Robert Montgomery, or being appointed Chief of Police by the Honorary Mayor of Tarzana, California, Robert Young (in his first "official" capacity). Newspapers across the country jibbed, "the Tarzana jail, whenever it happens to be built, is going to be the most popular spot in the San Fernando Valley!"[42] Virginia had fun during the hijinks, and introduced herself as "good old Virginia ham."

The summer of 1940 found Virginia de-mothing rugs and drapes, picking and arranging flowers, uprooting old petunia beds and spraying geraniums with Vitamin A. "I've called up some little girls and asked them to come and play with Susan this afternoon," she told visitor Gladys Hall. Virginia was taking up piano again; improving her tennis; attending UCLA to study gardening and psychology, but she preferred the domestic. "If a woman is really domestic," offered Virginia, "there are certain things she does in her home herself, no matter how many servants she has. And neither nursery schools nor a governess take a mother's place with her child."[43] In July, Virginia took Susan and a dozen other youngsters to the beach for an old-fashioned 4th of July weenie bake. Virginia made Susan Ann's birthday on August 3rd extra special by inviting Susan's half-sister, Leatrice Gilbert. The two sisters had never met. In 2007, this author contacted Leatrice in Connecticut. She had vivid memories of that day and recalled:

> I was sixteen, and drove to their large white Colonial house to attend the party. In my new racy, black Mercury convertible, with white sidewall tires and a chrome spotlight, I felt very special. I had never seen Susan before, and being an only child for most of my life, I was delighted to make the acquaintance of a little sister. She was very shy, but I felt that she enjoyed having me there. She introduced me to all her young friends and we played games together and watched a puppet show. Virginia was exquisitely beautiful. She wore a white dotted Swiss bouffant dress, the dots were red. Her lovely blonde hair was floating around her face and she was gracious and charming. I left thinking that she was a very special lady."[45]

Susan's birthday celebration concluded with a sunset hayride through the Santa Monica hills and along the beach. Joining the fun were Susan's "boyfriend" Gary Crosby, Ricky Arlen, the Dix boys, Richard Zanuck, Melinda Markey (Joan Bennett), the Zanuck girls, Katherine Thalberg (Norma Shearer), Barbara Warner and Joan Benny.

Virginia's workload was steady from March through August 1940. After reporting that Virginia had suffered from sunstroke, Louella Parsons mentioned on September 2, "Virginia Bruce and

J. Walter Ruben's friends are sympathizing with them in the loss of their baby from pre-maturity."[46] The miscarriage was an unexpected disappointment. Virginia and Ruben had been anticipating a child for over two years. Still, they remained hopeful. Ruben assuaged Virginia's sorrow with a topaz-diamond ring and matching bracelet for her birthday. She mused that her best gift was from Susan Ann: a pair of gloves and a bottle of cleaner.

1940 – Gardening at her home
in Pacific Palisades

In October, Virginia tackled a new screen assignment at Universal: *The Invisible Woman*. The film was not without controversy. The invisible woman, theoretically, was to romp around in the nude. Virginia also found herself locking horns on the set with the formidable screen legend John Barrymore.

Virginia, now centered on home and family, readily acknowledged that Ruben's belief in her ability as an actress kept her motivated. "The team-work, the cooperation, the share-and-share alike determination that is the only basis for a happy marriage is working out so successfully for us," said Virginia, "that I am probably happier than I ever hoped to be. And I'm certain that whatever success I attain in the future is going to be due to my marriage."[47]

Endnotes

1   Robbin Coons, "Hollywood Speaks," *Mansfield News Journal*, 5/7/40

2   Gladys Hall, "Marriage Is Not Enough," *Silver Screen*, 10/40

3   Maddox, "Girls! Don't Be Too Clever," *Screenland*, 4/39

4   Ben Maddox, "Girls! . . . "

5   Ibid

6   Ibid

7   Virginia Bruce, "Getting the Most Out of Life," *Oakland Tribune*, 10/1/39

8   Coons, "Hollywood Speaks . . . "

9   Gladys Hall, "Does You Boy Friend Love You?" *Modern Screen*, 6/39

10   Myrna Loy, "Being and Becoming," Alfred A. Knopf, N.Y., 1987, pg 93

11   P.K.S. review of *Stronger Than Desire*, *Los Angeles Times*, 6/21/39

12   John L. Scott review of *Stronger Than Desire*, *Los Angeles Times*, 3/25/39

13   Helen L. Walker, "Honesty is an embarrassing Policy," *Hollywood*, 1/41

14   Jimmy Fidler column, *Los Angeles Times*, 1/1/40

15   Sheila Graham, "It's that Way in Films," *Kansas City Star*, 10/13/39

16   Gladys Hall, "Marriage Is Not Enough," *Silver Screen*, 10/40

17   Louella Parsons column, *Fresno Bee*, 12/3/39

18   "Actress Urges Peace Efforts," *Los Angeles Times*, 9/26/39

19   Ben Maddox, "Girls! Don't . . . "

20   Gladys Hall, "Does Your Boyfriend Love You," *Modern Screen*, 6/39

21   "Briggs Masters Errol Flynn in Movie Tennis Finals," *LA Times*, 6/12/39

22   Charles Samuels, "Can Virginia Bruce Beat Her Hoodoo?" *Screen Life*, 7/40

23   Virginia Bruce, "Getting the Most Out of Life," *Oakland Tribune*, 10/1/39

24   Walter Winchell on *Flight Angels*, *Charleston Daily Mirror (WV)*, 6/3/40

25   John L. Scott, review of *Flight Angels*, *LA Times*, 5/4/40

26   review of *Flight Angels*, *Hammond Times*, 6/30/40

27   Vincent Sherman, *Studio Affairs*, University of Kentucky Pr., pg 87-88

28   review of *The Man Who Talked Too Much*, *Silver Screen*, 10/40

29   review of *The Man Who Talked Too Much*, *New York Times*, 6/29/40

30   Antoinette Donnelly, *Things New and Feminine*, *Oakland Tribune*, 3/21/40

31   Orry-Kelly, "Hollywood Fashion Parade," 4/25/41

32   "Ingrid 'Most Luscious' Says Film Photographer," *The Independent (Long Beach)*, 9/25/59

33   Jimmy Fidler column, *Appleton Post-Crescent (WI)*, 12/26/40

34   Jimmy Fidler column, *Valley Morning Star (TX)*, 1/24/51

35   Bosley Crowther, review of *Hired Wife*, *New York Times*, 9/14/40

36   Phillip K. Scheuer, review of *Hired Wife*, *LA Times*, 9/4/40

37   Charles G. Sampus, "New York - Hollywood," *Lowell Sun*, 5/27/40

38   Helen Louise Walker, "Honesty Is An Embarrassing Policy," *Hollywood*, 1/41

39 Ibid

40 Paul Harrison, column *Kingsport Times*, 8/9/40

41 Gladys Hall, "Does Your Boyfriend . . . "

42 "Miss Bruce Police chief at Tarzana," *Charleston Daily Mail*, (WV), 4/23/39

43 Gladys Hall, "Marriage Is . . . "

44 Louella Parsons column, *Syracuse Herald*, 7/5/40

45 Leatrice Gilbert Fountain, e-mail sent 1/19/2007

46 Louella Parsons column, *Fresno Bee*, 9/2/40

47 Virginia Bruce, "Careers versus Marriage," *Picturegoer Weekly*, 8/19/39

CHAPTER 12:

Becoming Invisible

A very visible
Virginia 1940
(Universal)

"Lots of devices are used to get around censorship rulings, but there never has been anything like a picture Universal is making. The heretofore-demure Virginia Bruce will be seen taking off all her clothes right in front of the camera. She'll do it several times, too – and without opposition from the Hays office. Trick is Miss Bruce has the title role in a modern fantasy called *The Invisible Woman* – and when she removes her clothes she becomes invisible. Peels off a stocking, and her leg is gone; sheds her whachamaycallums and that part of her has disappeared – and so on. Technically startling, but not in the way to interest a burlesque audience."[1]

In *The Invisible Woman*, Virginia plays Kitty Carroll, a discontented and outspoken fashion model. She's tired of being ogled by customers, persecuted by a boss she can't stand, and she wants revenge. So, she volunteers for wacky scientist John Barrymore's electric-ray treatment, which allows her to completely disappear. It's imperative that she completely strip in order not to be detected. After a quick zap and some serum, Kitty's off and running to give her now ex-employer, Mr. Growley, a well-deserved swift kick in the rump. Her invisibility is a temporary fix which can be instantly reinstated, whenever she chooses, by guzzling alcohol! "When you dissipate, you disappear!" exclaims Barrymore. Which she does, frequently. Correspondent Paul Harrison felt that "audiences [would] be stimulated by the suggestion [of] a pretty girl running around stark naked and a little drunk."[2] He predicted that the film would completely confound the censorship boards across the U.S., and "do quite a bit toward adding zip and spice to the normally quiet and wholesome screen personality of Miss Bruce."[3] Hedda Hopper wagged, "Virginia Bruce . . . the Invisible Woman? Seems such a waste of what God gave her."[4]

While on the set, Virginia wasn't entirely pleased with old satyr John Barrymore's pernicious comments. Harrison watched her blush as Barrymore told her he was creating a potion which allowed him to see the very things about *her* that the ray-machine made invisible! He then mentioned he wished he could have made women invisible a long time ago. "It would have saved me a lot of trouble!" he joked. Virginia didn't laugh. Barrymore's remark put her in a "mood," which she carried into the film's next scene where Barrymore's housekeeper, Margaret Hamilton (*Oz's* Wicked Witch), is pounding frantically behind a locked door. Virginia attempted to take the latch off quickly, and release Hamilton. "After struggling with it for several seconds," reported Harrison, "[Virginia] turned to the camera and said, 'I can't get the _____ door open!'" A blue comment from Virginia was indeed something unusual. Through the grapevine Louella Parsons got drift of the incident well before Harrison got his feature published. "Not all Hollywood arguments are political," tooted Parsons, "Virginia Bruce and John Barrymore had quite a flare up about a scene in *The Invisible Woman*."[5] When columnist May Mann showed up, Virginia and John Howard (the "invisible" woman's love interest) were enacting a torrid love scene under a prop apple tree. Mann noted, "Virginia suddenly let out a yelp, 'Something *bit* me!'"[6] After an intensive search, the crew discovered she had sat on a tack. It had been strategically imbedded (perhaps by a wacky scientist) in the fake grass. The scene was deleted. Barrymore, gray-wigged, mustached, and be-speckled, looking more like brother Lionel, was a real scamp. Whenever he administered serum into Virginia, it was actually injected into a sponge in her hand. One time he "just happened" to miss the sponge, and squirted Virginia. When asked how he liked his role, a playful Barrymore told everyone he was "having a lot of fun at it."[7]

Understandably, *The Invisible Woman* set was a popular destination for Hollywood reporters. Columnist Robbin Coons noticed Virginia was miffed with the whole production, because, according to her, it was just "too easy." "John Fulton, the special effects man who hitherto has specialized in 'invisible men,'" wrote Coons, "does most of the work for her when a double in black tights *isn't* doing it. Virginia drew a line at the tights."[8] In fact, she was adamant about not wearing them. Tights were an essential element in Fulton's trick photography, and would have covered her from head to foot. "Virginia, as an invisible star," mused Coons, "can sit on the sidelines sewing, or reading, or watching 'herself' act."[9] When "invisible" Virginia smoked or had a cocktail on screen, fine wires were used to maneuver her props in a natural manner. Fulton also used mirrors and black velvet

John Barrymore taunting *The Invisible Woman (1940)* (Universal)

to create "invisibility." Virginia delivered her lines into a microphone just outside camera range. Barrymore and John Howard
appeared mentally unhinged, saying their lines to someone who
wasn't there.

When the cumbersome tights weren't required, Virginia
acquiesced to wearing a black velvet mask, black leggings and
gloves for scenes in which her "invisible self" wears clothing.
"She stands in front of a velvet backdrop," observed Coons,
"where moving one inch either way would ruin the scene. Fulton with his 'magic' removes the backdrop and restores the real
background in his laboratory."[10] (Fulton's achievements in spe-

cial effects for *The Invisible Woman* would be nominated for the 1942 Academy Award.)

The Invisible Woman was a hybrid of H.G. Wells' more serious original work, *The Invisible Man*. Director Edward Sutherland made sure the new film played strictly for laughs, as when Virginia is caught undressing outdoors. "Kinda chilly!" she shivers, "Wonder how the nudists stand it?" One of the most unforgettable scenes had invisible Virginia coyly putting on a pair of hosiery so Howard could contemplate her "lower half." Aside from Virginia wrecking havoc at Growley's Continental Dress Company, a new layer of humor interrupts things when gangster Blackie Cole (Oskar Homolka) gets drift of Professor Barrymore's dramatic breakthrough, and kidnaps him. Virginia uses her invisibility to foil the crooks. And, instead of being driven mad by the serum, as Claude Rains in *The Invisible Man*, Virginia falls in love instead! Barrymore's real triumph takes place after his rescue. Virginia (now married to Howard) has given birth to a baby who has the capability of turning . . . *invisible*. "*Hereditary!*" squeals the delighted Barrymore.

Virginia landed the role in *The Invisible Woman* by happenstance. She was slated initially for *Caribbean Holiday* opposite Allan Jones (released as *One Night in the Tropics*), but recovery from her miscarriage took longer than expected. Columbia then paired her with William Holden to co-star in *Texas*. She was replaced by Claire Trevor. When former Metro player Margaret Sullavan refused to play Kitty Carroll (Sullavan preferred suspension to invisibility), *The Invisible Woman* fell into Virginia's lap. One of the aspects that made *The Invisible Woman* work, was Virginia's engaging disembodied voice. She may have thought the job too easy, but her breezy manner and sprightly line delivery delighted audiences. *The New York Times* took the expected jabs at *The Invisible Woman*, calling it "silly, banal, and repetitious," and giving Barrymore an unrelenting blast. "Mr. Barrymore takes to this trash as if he were to the manner born," railed the reviewer, "He . . . lampoons his brother Lionel, who would be perfectly within his rights to sue John as an impostor and a plagiarist. ... There is also the glamorous, if invisible, nonentity known as Virginia Bruce, who has perhaps the most thankless assignment since Constance Bennett in *Topper*."[11] Edwin Schallert for the *Los Angeles Times* disagreed, saying the film "reveals a mastery of camera magic. The picture surpasses in that respect . . . its predecessors, besides having a plot that is well contrived at all points. Miss Bruce is decorative when she is actually seen . . . vocally, she carries out the role with good comedy accent."[12] After the release of *The Invisible Man* "Legacy Collection" in 2004, critic Glenn Erickson stated *The Invisible Woman* was "one of the more entertaining titles" in the set of five invisible-themed Universal releases. Erickson found Virginia's voice and mime "excellent," and thought *The Invisible Woman* "one of the few vehicles to make use of [Virginia's] talent. She was busy acting for fifteen [sic] years, but this appears to be her best role."[13]

In the spring of 1941, Virginia and Barrymore were paired again on *The Rudy Vallee Show*. Playing a dance hall girl in a rough-and-tumble gold-mining town, Virginia was menaced by Barrymore until hero Vallee shows up. Barrymore was a regular on Vallee's show. During the filming of *The Invisible Woman*, Barrymore, heavily in debt, battled his fourth wife in divorce court, and suffered from serious health complications. He relied heavily on cue cards to remember his lines. Still, acting provided some semblance of escape from his surmounting problems. He died of cirrhosis of the liver the year following the film's release.

From her bedroom, Virginia could gaze out the window and look upon the blue Pacific. She was content staying at home when she wasn't working, and enjoyed what she called her "dressed-up farmhouse." Playing with Susan in the small pool, or taking advantage of riding the saddle horses housed in the property stables, seemed pleasant enough distractions when not doing housework and gardening. Virginia rarely gave any thought to travel, unless Sonny brought up the subject. After the completion of *The Invisible Woman*, Ruben decided on a trip to New York City. It would be an opportunity for him to act as tour guide and show "his girls" where he grew up. Virginia would have a chance to see how the city had changed since her Ziegfeld Girl days. Along with Susan's governess, Virginia decided it would be fun if her best little girlfriend and school chum, Patricia Murray, tagged along. They all ventured off to one of New York's swankier hotels the day after New Year's.

After settling into the hotel, Virginia agreed to talk to members of the press – one being Katharine Roberts, a former foreign correspondent during World War I. Roberts, taking a break from writing a spy story, ventured to where the Rubens were staying, and approached the desk clerk. "Miss Virginia Bruce, please," requested Roberts. "Twenty-third floor," was the reply. "Apartment number?" asked Roberts. "None," the clerk said firmly, "just the twenty-third floor." "So we went up," wrote Roberts, "and, as we emerged from the elevator, there was Virginia Bruce and likewise the twenty-third floor – all of it. It was a relief to see that she was all there, too, because we had lately seen a wacky little cream puff of a picture called *The Invisible Woman* in which she was currently

... disappearing ... and there was a feeling that she might have carried the habit of atomic dissociation into private life."[14] Roberts got to talk to both Sonny and Virginia. As far as her decision to freelance, Virginia admitted that her mild protests at MGM for better parts earned her the nickname of "Squawkie" at the studio. They just laughed at her. "The trouble with me," Virginia confessed, "is that I've always lacked ambition." She also admitted that she wasn't much of a disciplinarian with Susan. "Every time I try to scold her," explained Virginia, "it seems so foolish I get to laughing. She and Jack understand each other perfectly, so now he's taken over the responsibility of training her."[15] Standing nearby, Susan agreed that she liked the idea. Sonny talked about the "old days" when he and Virginia were both on the Paramount lot. Whenever he tried to approach her, she would giggle and run away. He felt there was still a good deal of Ginny Briggs from Fargo that came out whenever Virginia spoke. He tipped his nose in the air, smoothed the back of his hair in a languorous fashion, and said, "When she does this, she thinks she's sophisticated – and heaven knows she ought to be, but as a matter of fact she's the most naïve thing alive!"[16] Virginia just smiled and said,

Ruben and Virginia arriving in New York January 1941 (courtesy of Vincent Briggs)]

"Who, me?" They all had a good laugh. Roberts' interview is a well-written piece, and appeared in the May issue of *Modern Screen.* The spy yarn she was working on, *Center of the Web,* received excellent reviews when released in 1942.

Before the Rubens'

New York stay was complete, Broadway columnist Walter Winchell had to have his say. "Virginia Bruce being beautiful at 55th and 5th," wrote Winchell, "oughtagetta' ticket for obstructing sidewalk traffic like that!"[17] With winter temperatures between 8 and 20 degrees, the climate change didn't agree with Virginia. She came down with a bad cold. Once back in California, she rested up before her next appearance: Washington, D.C. But, Virginia didn't have to go far for that. Columbia studios had built a replica of the U.S. Senate chambers for her role as a female correspondent in a project titled *Senate Page Boys*.

Vice President of the United States, John Nance Garner, received an offer to co-star with Virginia in her new film. "Cactus Jack" Garner retired on January 20, 1941, after serving two terms under Roosevelt. He was opposed to Roosevelt's running a third term, and declared the Vice Presidency wasn't "worth a bucket of warm spit." The press made quite a to-do about Garner's Hollywood invitation. However, the idea of even *playing* Vice President for one more week didn't interest him as much as returning to his Texas ranch. Garner told producer Charles R. Rogers that he would decline all such offers.

Columbia had great success with Frank Capra's Oscar-nominated *Mr. Smith Goes to Washington* (1939), and hoped for a good follow up. The new production used the same sets as *Mr. Smith* and was retitled *Adventure in Washington*. Virginia played a "man-in-the-street" radio broadcast reporter and, for her opening scene, spouted off a five-page "live" newscast with the rapidity of Walter Winchell. Her confrontations with a certain Senator Coleridge (Herbert Marshall) are understandable.

Adventure in Washington (1941) with Gene
Reynolds and Herbert Marshall (Columbia)

Coleridge doesn't allow female reporters into his private press
conferences (so much for equal rights). The film's main focus was
an unruly Senate page, played by Gene Reynolds, who, out to get
even, sells Senate secrets to a big-city political boss. Sixteen boys
were cast as Senate pages, which duplicated the actual number
employed by the government. Other familiar faces were pages
Tommy Bond (from *Our Gang* comedies) and Dickie Jones, who
had played a similar role in *Mr. Smith*. Reynolds does an admirable job of metamorphosing from hoodlum to responsible and
conscientious Senate gofer.

A key scene provides Reynolds the wherewithal to make a change
in character. After being reprimanded for using his fists to resolve a
conflict with another page, Reynolds seeks out Virginia to confide
in. She takes him bowling. She listens to him as intently as she plays

her game, seriously. Pointing out the disadvantages of "leading with your fists," she leads up to and reinforces the values of human rights. "Take away rights from anyone," she cautions Reynolds, "and you weaken your own chances!" Her warmth and perceptiveness strike a chord in Reynolds which sets the tone for what follows.

Reynolds transformation goes one step further when he puts Marshall's career at risk. (In truth, dating back to 1910, the situation is usually the reverse: *pages* needed protection from manipulative congressmen.) When the question of punishment for Reynolds' misdeed comes up, Marshall suggests that the other pages give Reynolds a mock trial. Marshall's suggestion strengthens the pages understanding of law far more effectively than answering to the orders of finger-snapping Senators. Feeling remorseful, and recognizing the power of due process by his peers, Reynolds takes the stand. He gives a rendition of "The American Creed" that is rich in feeling, and brings a well-deserved lump to the throat. The writing is top notch. Oscar winners Lewis R. Foster (*Mr. Smith Goes to Washington*) and Arthur Caesar (*Manhattan Melodrama*) created a script which deserved the indelible mark of a director like Frank Capra. Alfred Green's direction appeared routine. *The New York Times* pointed out: "When the camera is spying on the hazing ceremonies pages undergo and the boyish pranks they perpetrate in the Senate chambers . . . *Adventure in Washington* affords pleasant and chucklesome entertainment." Surprisingly, the review found the transformation of Reynolds unbelievable, saying he had "been painted so black you just can't believe in his regeneration even though . . . Reynolds plays his climactic scene with commendable restraint."[18] "Virginia Bruce," the review commented, "makes a fetching Capital Hill radio reporter, and the feud between her and [Marshall] which ultimately blossoms into romance is nicely handled."[19] Most critics agreed that Herbert Marshall (unmistakably British) was miscast as a U.S. Senator. Seen today, Reynolds' change in character is nicely paced and always believable. *Photoplay's* assessment of his performance was on target, saying, "It is Gene Reynolds who steals the show. The manner in which he redeems himself provides material for a heart-touching scene that Gene meets like a veteran. Here is a truly fine young actor."[20]

During filming, Washington commentator Dorothy Thompson visited the set of *Adventure in Washington* to give Virginia the inside dope on her profession. *Time* magazine considered the outspoken Thompson (the persona for Katharine Hepburn's *Woman of the Year*) one of the two most important women in the United States – the other being, Eleanor Roosevelt. After interviewing Hitler, Thompson announced his "messiah-like" performance was simply a take on "an old Jewish idea." She was kicked out of Nazi Germany. Whatever Thompson told Miss Bruce must have also rubbed off. Virginia's interest in politics was piqued, and a couple of years later she would consider running for a seat in the California State Legislature.

At the completion of *Adventure in Washington*, Virginia staged a party for cast and crew, and announced that she would retire until January 1942. The reason? She was expecting, and making sure she would carry full term. "To me it is tragic to see a child brought up with no brother or sister," said Virginia. She had noticed that Susan, being an only child, naturally felt everything revolved around *her*. Having a sibling would emphasize for Susan that she was a member of a family.

Producer Sol Lesser had disclosed that Virginia and Charles

1942 – Susan Ann and Virginia's niece and nephew Reary and Vincent Briggs
(children of Stanley) (Courtesy of Vincent Briggs)

Boyer would appear in an adaptation of the Rose Franken novel
Strange Victory. But, Virginia's decision for a screen sabbatical
was final. In March, she did join Fay Wray for "Buy British Week."
The duo rang sales at a popular Los Angeles department store in
conjunction with Bundles for Britain. While not having to report
to a studio, Virginia happily focused on home, and philosophized
about one of her favorite subjects: motherhood — from a celebrity's point of view. "It's too bad that you can't let your children
have the freedom of normal children," said Virginia. "But, there's
a high wire fence around our house and when Susan wants to
play with other children, they have to make dates way in advance
– just like grown-ups do."[21] "In Hollywood we have the working
mother's problems *plus*." Virginia illustrated her point,

When I was a child, my parents took my brother
and me to the circus, the zoo, on sightseeing
trips and picnics . . . but, everyone knows that
the children of film stars can't go where there are
crowds. So, if they can't go to the circus, it comes
to them. That's why we have merry-go-rounds
and pony carts and animal acts come to our
homes when we have parties for our children. . . .
Having these parties at home gives the children an
opportunity to enjoy themselves without feeling
that strangers are watching them as they would
at a public place. You know, one of our greatest
problems is to keep our children from feeling they
are any different from other children. I get tired of
hearing and reading how the Hollywood children
are pampered. These parties do cost money, but
what are we to do? When some popular motion
picture star does take his child to the circus . . .
they are surrounded by cameramen and fans, they
are pushed and shoved around and such a crowd
gathers that the child has no opportunity to see the
circus."[22]

In Virginia's mind, "spoiling" had more to do with behavior
rather than having "things." "What I call spoiling a child," she
said, "is allowing it to act in a manner that makes people dislike it. That is unfair to everyone, especially the child. Do you
know what I think should be done about spoiled children? Their
mothers should be spanked! I'd run and hide if Susan Ann acted
as some children I've seen, for a child's behavior is entirely up to
the parents." [23]

Susan Ann's governess, Helen York, was affectionately referred to as "Hiya" by the Rubens. Virginia had nothing but praises for York, saying, "She is a child psychologist, she loves children and knows what they are going to think about everything. She has been with us since Susan was two and the child adores her."[24] Susan Ann also adored her pony rides each Sunday at the Riviera Country Club stables. Decked out in her cowgirl outfit, Susan would sidesaddle with Sonny. Virginia usually opted to sit on the sidelines and knit. On one particular Sunday a friend of the Rubens showed up asking why they weren't at a certain yacht party to which they had been invited. "We would have," explained Virginia, "but we always bring Susan Ann out to ride on Sunday morning. She looks forward to it all week and we hate to disappoint her. So, here we are." "Oh, you spoil her," the friend said disapprovingly. But, Virginia considered Susan's Sunday rides "a pleasure earned."[25]

Another "big thrill" for Susan was spending an hour with her parents before going to bed. Virginia admitted in an interview with Franc Dillon, "Susan Ann isn't a perfect child by any means." She recalled one evening, when out of the blue, Susan slapped Sonny across the face! No one looked more astonished afterwards than Susan herself. "Now my mother told me I should have spanked her hard right then and there, but I don't believe in physical punishment," said Virginia. "Still, something had to be done to make her realize the seriousness of such behavior, so I sent her to bed immediately . . . and for three evenings following she was not allowed to spend that hour with us. It was explained to her that until she could be a lady she couldn't associate with us. I'm sure she was punished more effectively than if she had been spanked. . . . I'm not setting myself up as an expert, but we've learned she responds to reasoning."[26]

Writer Dillon commented, "It is the verdict of her friends among Hollywood mothers that [Virginia's] theories about training a child are not just something you read in books, but that they are workable, sensible rules. There is no question but that Susan Ann is a fine example of how a small girl should behave."[27] It was into this "sensible," "workable," family scene that Christopher Briggs Ruben was born on Tuesday, August 26, 1941. Weighing in at 6 pounds 11 ounces, Susan's little brother made his debut at the Good Samaritan Hospital. Dr. Norman Williams reported that both mother and son came through in excellent condition.

Instead of serums and ray machines, motherhood maintained Virginia's "invisibility" on screen throughout the remainder of 1941. In November, she whetted her appetite for acting by appearing on the premier presentation of radio's *Herbert Marshall Show*. On December 8th, she and Melvyn Douglas paired up for *Lux Radio's The Doctor Takes a Wife*. Virginia, as a famous author, and Douglas, a university doctor, charade as husband and wife. Despite the unconventional storyline, the comedy's most memorable moment was an unexpected, "mid-air" bulletin by broadcaster John Daly. He gave a five-minute reality check for Americans on the U.S.'s five-hour-old entry into World War II. 300 American planes had been destroyed, and the West Coast was preparing for air raids. Fifty unidentified planes were

Virginia c. 1941

sighted flying toward San Francisco, which was completely blacked out. All of the city's radio stations were ordered off the air. Recruiting offices were reported being swamped with enlistments. President Roosevelt scheduled an emergency "fireside chat" for the following night. After this sobering "update," programming resumed. But, the focus of the audience and the world had changed irrevocably. Overnight, Hollywood was obligated to redefine itself. 1942, a period of transition for everyone, would prove to be an especially devastating year for Virginia Bruce.

Endnotes

1   Paul Harrison, "Virginia Bruce Takes Off All Her Clothes and the Hays Office Doesn't Raise Even A Squawk!" *Daily Times News (NC)*, 11/14/40

2   Paul Harrison, "John Barrymore, Hard At Work On New Film Career," *Port Arthur News (TX)*, 11/15/40

3   Ibid.

4   Hedda Hopper column, *LA Times*, 10/3/40

5   Louella Parsons column, *Modesto Bee*, 11/6/40

6   May Mann, "Going Hollywood," *Ogden Standard Examiner*, 11/13/40

7   Paul Harrison, "John Barrymore, Hard At Work . . . "

8   Robbin Coons, "Hollywood," *Delta Democrat (MS)*, 11/15/40

9   Ibid

10   Ibid

11   T.S. review of *The Invisible Woman, New York Times*, 1/9/41

12   Edwin Schallert review for *The Invisible Woman, LA Times*, 12/28/40

13   Glenn Erickson, review of *The Invisible Woman, DVD Savant Review*, c. 2004

14   Katharine Roberts, "Who? . . . Me?" *Modern Screen*, 5/41

15   Ibid.

16   Ibid.

17   Walter Winchell, "On Broadway," *Zanesville Signal (OH)*, 1/10/41

18   Review of *Adventure in Washington, New York Times*, 8/1/41

19   Ibid

20   Review of *Adventure in Washington, Photoplay*, 10/41

21   Dee Lowrance, "Movie Mothers – and Proud of it!" *Port Arthur News (TX)*, 5/11/41

22   Franc Dillon, "Hers Is a Problem Child," *Modern Screen*, 12/39

23   Ibid

24 Ibid
25 Ibid.
26 Ibid
27 Ibid

CHAPTER THIRTEEN:

Her Greatest Loss — J. Walter Ruben

J. Walter Ruben's career as producer was sailing full-steam ahead during 1940-42. He was at the helm for three Wally Beery films, the breadwinning "B" *Mokey,* starring a youngster named Robert Blake (later known for TV's *Baretta*), and Norma Shearer's screen swansong *Her Cardboard Lover.* Ruben also produced a remake of his excellent *Public Hero #1* (retitled: *The Get-Away*). His greatest legacy as a producer was Ann Sothern's *Maisie* series (a role intended for Jean Harlow), which was a big money-maker for MGM, and made Sothern a household name. Ruben fought tooth and nail for Sothern to be cast in the part after he saw her play a tough-loving secretary in 1938's *Trade Winds.* "If only you had ever known," Ruben told Sothern afterwards, "what I had to do to get you for the part! . . . my neck was out there!"[1] As the flip adventuress and problem-solver with a heart-of-gold, *Maisie* lasted through no less than ten releases. Ruben produced six of the low-budget and profit-making comedies, which always placed Maisie in a new locale. After *Maisie* premiered, MGM signed Sothern to a lucrative long-term contract. Louella Parsons confirmed, "J. Walter Ruben surprised even Leo the Lion by making a hit out of the B picture."[2] Sothern was grateful to Ru-

Butch Minds the Baby (1942) with "baby" Michael Barnitz
and Broderick Crawford (Universal)

ben, telling him that after *Maisie* "she lacked nothing whatsoever
to make her happiness complete, except maybe a Jersey cow."[3]
Ruben took Ann at her word. Soon after her remark, she found
herself face-to-face with the bellowing bovine for a scene in *Gold
Rush Maisie*. In January 1941, with three films ready for release,
Ruben had definitely earned his aforementioned New York vacation. Although he and Virginia saw the sites, Ruben insisted on
making it a busman's holiday and took in all the new plays. He
took his work seriously.

Ruben, and his frequent co-writer, scenarist Wells Root,
teamed up for what turned out to be Ruben's most harrowing
assignment. A nightmare in the making, *Tennessee Johnson* was
a biographical epoch about Andrew Johnson, the first American

President to undergo impeachment. Touted as one of 1942's most distinguished productions, the film ran into unforeseen controversies. Things looked promising at the outset. Mayer hired director William Dieterle, noted for his impressive biographical films on Louis Pasteur, Florence Nightingale, and Emile Zola. Ruben himself had a reputation for allowing every production advantage, and insuring that dramatic films had authenticity. *Tennessee Johnson* was more than he bargained for.

While Ruben tackled the trials and tribulations of Andrew Johnson, Virginia contemplated a more mild form of screen entertainment for her "comeback" following Christopher's birth. Author Damon Runyon's short story *Butch Minds the Baby* surrounded Virginia with assorted unsavory characters; thieves, and mugs who, underneath their rough exteriors, are really soft-boiled. *Newsweek* paid high praise to the film classing it along "with such prize Runyoniana as *Lady for a Day* and *Little Miss Marker.*" "With Runyon lending a hand on the set," said the review, "Leonard Spigelgass' adaptation and Albert S. Rogell's direction are notably successful in capturing the special flavor and regional humors of the Runyon original. Broderick Crawford tops a good cast with his appealing impersonation of Butch."[4] Crawford is Butch Grogan, a safecracker, and fresh from a ten-year stretch in Sing-Sing. He reluctantly takes on a janitorial position in a rundown brownstone where Virginia, a penniless widow, and her 13-month-old baby reside. Butch agrees to take care of the boy while Virginia tackles her evening shift as a café cigarette girl. He develops a manly crush on the kid which surprises pals like Blinky Sweeney (3 Stooges Shemp Howard in a hilarious turn as a near-sighted thug). But, the real shocker comes when "the boys," whose IQ's are only slightly lower than the baby's, attempt one final safe-cracking job. They forget that the baby (who

Pardon My Sarong (1942) Universal

Butch is "minding") might want to play patty-cake with a bottle of nitroglycerin! *The New York Times* felt *Butch Minds the Baby* had "a haphazardly amusing flavor. . . . Broderick Crawford creates a creditable portrait of mental insolvency; Virginia Bruce looks coolly maternal as the widowed mother."[5]

Soon after Virginia completed *Butch,* Ruben adopted Susan Ann (she retained the Gilbert surname). To support the war effort, the Rubens let go of most of their household staff. "We're just finding out the blessings of people who have to live simply," Virginia told Hedda Hopper.[6] She mentioned that mealtimes, much to her liking, had become a private affair. Like most stars, Virginia put in her time at the Canteens entertaining men in uniform. In March '42 she was joined by her sister-in-law Mary Lawrence Briggs at the Ft. MacArthur Canteen, where they served donuts and coffee.

Virginia's next assignment at Universal must have appealed to Susan, who was about to turn nine years old. Why else would Virginia pair up with the antics of Abbott and Costello? "Here I wear a sarong!" Virginia exclaimed to May Mann. "Imagine, the mother of two in a sarong!"[7] Aptly titled, *Pardon My Sarong,* the quasi-spoof of Dorothy Lamour's Paramount flicks, turned into another smash hit for Abbott and Costello. Syndicated columnist Frederick C. Othman referred to the comedy duo as "America's newest $40,000,000-per-year enterprise."[8] Their partnership at Universal settled into a four-picture-a-year groove. Abbott and Costello were Hollywood's most popular money-makers when Virginia signed on for what one report aptly labeled a "thankless job." No ambitious actress would take on such an assignment. Louella Parsons gave her condolences to Virginia, saying, "I hope Virginia is well and strong for she will need to be after playing with these two, who stop at nothing to get a laugh."[9]

Pardon My Sarong (1942) with Bud Abbott and Lou Costello (Universal)

More than ever before, Virginia's acting career had become a sideline. "I don't think pictures are so important," she remarked in reference to her career. "I'd much rather stay home and mind my youngsters." Between takes on the set of *Pardon My Sarong*, someone asked her about the responsibility to her "public." Virginia gave a hearty laugh. "I've got a good public right at home in my children."[10] For the most part, she enjoyed herself on the set, while experiencing a steady diet of what she called the "whim-whams." There was no way to prepare for the raucous action that fueled the Abbott-Costello team. "Right in the middle of a scene they start adding comedy bits on the spur of the moment," Virginia told a visiting reporter. "And, I want to laugh at them. I have to play straight, and suppress the giggles." She then gave a hopeless shrug and admitted, "After a few days of it, I'm getting so that I can't concentrate on my own lines."[11] On screen, Virginia got to ask Bud Abbott, who was always beating up on Costello, the question on everyone's mind: "Why are you so mean to the little fella?"

When the cameras weren't rolling, Abbott and Costello's jollity could evaporate into temperament. Reporter Jimmy Fidler showed up on the set in late March to find the usually distant Bud Abbott screaming at associate producer Alex Gottlieb, "I'm tired. You're a producer? So produce me a chair!"[12] The outgoing, lovable Lou Costello was frantically calling home every few minutes to check on his daughter's mastoid. And, rumor had it that "the boys" had their own private feud going on at the time. Costello's daughter, Chris, concurred that a "chill" developed over billing and percentage cuts, which kept the duos relationship mostly a business proposition. When writing her father's biography years later, she stated Costello had control over the shooting schedule. At 4:00 p.m. sharp, filming came to a halt whether the director wanted "one more take" or not. "I cease to be funny at four o'clock," Costello would announce before making his exit. [13]

Director Earle Kenton, a Mack Sennett veteran, guided *Pardon My Sarong*, and as *The New York Times'* Bosley Crowther observed, "The boys are swept along by nothing more compelling than their volatile gag-writers' wits. . . . they don't make sense, but they make eighty minutes fly."[14] The "wits" included Nat Perrin who had worked with the Marx Brothers in such hits as *Duck Soup* (1933). Crowther mentioned that Lionel Atwill's menace and "the incidental presence . . . of Virginia Bruce . . . in amorous mood" both served as a "springboard for a wild chase with a Keystonic climax." "Plot is a normal convention which this picture manages to avoid," wagged the reviewer.[15] True, the boys seem to be driving a bus one minute and stranded on an island the next. Virginia Bruce, lost in the shuffle, is indeed "incidental" with nothing more to do than let out a few yelps. The most interesting thing she does is to slap the rather deserving face of her supposed love interest (Robert Paige). There are a couple of things worth preserving in *Pardon My Sarong's* relentless, routine-ridden plot: the two elegant and refreshing musical numbers performed by the talented Ink Spots.

When *Pardon My Sarong* was released, Ruben found himself in the middle of what was the worst snarl of his career. Things had gone from bad to worse on the set of MGM's *Tennessee Johnson*. The film was the brainchild of Louis B. Mayer, and based on an unpublished story, *The Man on America's Conscience*. Mayer as-

Pardon My Sarong (1942) with Samuel S. Hinds
(courtesy of Laura Wagner)

284

signed scenarist John L. Balderston (noted for horror classics such as *Dracula* and *Frankenstein*) to rework the plot and glorify President Andrew Johnson (a role assigned to Van Heflin). As a President, Johnson has the legacy of setting racial equality back for decades — a fact not mentioned in the film. Johnson, a Southerner, vetoed Reconstruction. He supported restrictions which would forestall the black vote, and establish the South's "separate, but equal" policy. Black-American author and abolitionist Frederick Douglass emphasized that he detected "a bitter contempt" for blacks in Johnson's demeanor.[16] After depicting Johnson in heroic light, Balderston proceeded to create another of his *monsters* out of pro-black Pennsylvania representative Thaddeus Stevens (played by Lionel Barrymore). Balderston gives Stevens a scathingly villainous treatment. In reality, Thaddeus Stevens had dedicated his life to end slavery and, according to his wishes, was buried in the only cemetery that accepted people regardless of race.

In *Tennessee Johnson*, amid a sea of white faces, the black population appears to have simply evaporated. Only one black performer (uncredited Louise Beavers) was given dialogue. Ruben, troubled by the script, was faced with "the knowledge of what a disaster it might cause in racial relations."[17] He wasn't the only one. During production, Walter White, secretary of the NAACP, requested a copy of the script, as did Lowell Mellett, secretary of the Office of War Information (OWI). Both men felt the nation could not afford a "political incident" during wartime. *Tennessee Johnson* was considered a "crucial test case of OWI's power."[18] The script, as written, was divisive and could disrupt national unity. White was especially outraged. Mayer hastily wrote to White reassuring him that MGM would never release a film that was anti *any* race. "I live and breathe the air of freedom and I want it for others as well as myself," declared Louis B.[19]

As stress took its toll on Ruben's health, he asked Virginia's brother, Stanley Briggs, to become his assistant. Wells Root continued offering moral support and tried to iron out problems with the script. The tension on the set escalated, when out of the blue (or anti-Red), MGM screenwriter James K. McGuinness, noted for his reactionary right-wing political beliefs, entered the scene. (McGuinness had recently made news in his publicized divorce settlement for beating his wife.)[20] He told Mayer that Communist elements were behind the black communities concern about the film. Martin Dies, creator of the House of UnAmerican Activities Committee (HUAC), had already created a stir with his initial investigation of Communism in Hollywood in 1940.[21] Mayer believed McGuinness and hired him to take over all responsibility from Ruben.[22] Ruben was out, although he did receive screen credit. Indirectly, Ruben's dismissal identifies him as an early victim of the HUAC anti-Communist crusade.

After *Tennessee Johnson's* completion (September 1942) Walter White and Lowell Mellet saw a preview of the film and were furious. They demanded retakes and substantial changes. In October, director Dieterle reshot many scenes in order to soften Barrymore's characterization of Thaddeus Stevens.[23] In 1943, McGuinness would deny that the government tampered with the film. "At no time did the government through OWI force us to re-shoot," he stated. "The original agitation was by Communists who stirred certain elements of the Negro press."[24] Upon final release, the film still ran into problems. A celebrated cast of protesters, which included scenarist Ben Hecht, Vincent Price, Lillian Gish, black actor Canada Lee, and Lee Strasberg, sent a petition to the OWI asking that the film be "scrapped."[25] Mayer refused.

The year following *Tennessee Johnson's* release, James K. McGuinness became the founding member of the Motion Picture Alliance for Preservation of American Ideals (MPA). According to blacklisted writer Allen Boretz, McGuinness was the "real guru of the right-wing movement in Hollywood."[26] An FBI investigation of the MPA came to the same conclusion. McGuinness would again bring up *Tennessee Johnson* when he testified as a "friendly witness" for the House UnAmerican Activities Committee in 1947, saying that Communists were attempting to indoctrinate scriptwriters at MGM.[27] At the hearings, McGuinness mentioned the "Communist opposition" to *Tennessee Johnson*, identifying opponents such as writers Ring Lardner, Jr., one of the "Hollywood Ten," and Donald Ogden Stewart.

By 1949, McGuinness had been whispered out of Hollywood. He left for New York, and threatened to write an exposé (fictionalized) on "Communist Hollywood" with easily identifiable characters.[28] Ultra right-wing Hearst columnist Westbrook Pegler, an ardent fan of McGuinness, claimed that Hollywood had "broken" McGuinness' heart. Consumed by disappointment, McGuinness attended a Christmas party in 1950 at which he "insisted on singing 'Nearer My God to Thee' repeatedly . . . then went to bed and died."[29] Not to worry, the following year newly-elected MPA President John Wayne handed out a $1,000 check to the first recipient of the James K. McGuinness Award for Outstanding Americanism."[30]

Tennessee Johnson remains unreliable history, and a whitewash of Andrew Johnson. Columnist Jimmy Fidler summed up the film's eulogy saying, "Added proof that brilliant acting can't save a bad story."[31] The talented Van Heflin gives a persuasive and powerful turn in the lead role, although the film's climactic moment, with Johnson giving a rousing oration in his own defense, *never* took place. In fact, Johnson made no appearance at his impeachment trial. Even with Dieterle's noteworthy direction, *Tennessee Johnson* is unable to overcome its mark as a politically dubious effort. In the wake of all the film's turmoil, J. Walter Ruben died.

Years later, Virginia told author Charles Higham for his controversial take on Louis B. Mayer, *Merchant of Dreams*, that "the problem of making [*Tennessee Johnson*] was the most crushing that had beset Ruben, following as it did Mayer's decision that he was no good as a director and could only serve as a producer."[32]

The Rubens 11/10/1941: J. Walter, Virginia, Christopher and Susan Ann

Leaving the turmoil at MGM behind, Ruben entered the Good Samaritan hospital on August 16, 1942, just two days after his 43rd birthday. Some reports indicate that he had been in ill health for several months with a streptococcus infection. Virginia was "in almost constant attendance" during his hospital stay, and was at his bedside when he died of a heart ailment on September 4, 1942.[33] His burial (cremation) was a few days later at Forest Lawn. A few friends attended his service, among them Gary Cooper and Dolores Costello. According to her biographer, Ann Sothern was "deeply saddened by [Ruben's] passing. Although they were never close friends,

Ann commiserated with Virginia." [34] It had been five years since Virginia and Ruben had discovered their love for one another in Zion National Park while filming *The Bad Man of Brimstone*. Their years together were loving and nurturing. The foundation they created for their family was solid and meaningful. Ruben would be Virginia's greatest loss. Her life came to a sudden standstill.

Careful, Soft Shoulders (1942) with James Ellison (20th Century Fox)

When she finally reemerged from the numbness of grief, Virginia faced a court decision involving Ruben's exwife, Mildred Stephenson. Stephenson had divorced Ruben in 1936. It was discovered that Ruben had left no will for Virginia after she petitioned to superior court for letters of administration in the estate.[35] Throughout October she awaited the outcome, hoping that an existing will leaving everything to his first wife (except $1,000 each to Ruben's brother and sister, both of New York) would be revoked.[36] She got her wish. Jimmy Fidler reported on October 18, "Virginia Bruce Ruben will get the entire widow's share of her late husband's estate; the first Mrs. Ruben relinquished claims."[37] Afterwards, Virginia, understandably, kept out of the limelight and picture business. Rumor had it that she was planning to retire from films.

In the fall of 1942, 20th Century-Fox released *Careful, Soft Shoulders*, a film that Virginia had completed just before Ruben entered the hospital. It turned out to be a tidy "B" concoction of counter-espionage. Virginia plays a *tres chic* fashion model and social gadabout who tries her luck as a streamlined Mata Hari. Her facetious, catty, scatterbrained character shines throughout the film. It's one of her best performances. The story begins on December 7, 1941. Virginia, daughter of a late Senator, attends a Washington, D.C. cocktail party filled with what she calls a "jungle of nobody's and second-hand celebrities." The news of the Japanese attack on Pearl Harbor fills the room creating an understandable stir. Guests wager how they will help the war effort. Half-joking, Virginia suggests that she could be a spy and quickly takes offense when everyone laughs at her idea. Before her sharp tongue cuts everyone down to size, she leaves in a huff. Little does she know that a complete stranger has been watching her. She finds him waiting inside her apartment. He turns out to be a government agent named Mr. Fortune (Aubrey Mather). He had overheard her at the party, knew of her access to the best homes in Washington and offers her a chance to "serve her country." She's intrigued and asks Fortune to join her in a cigarette. He informs her that cigarettes are bad for his capillaries. "Oh, don't be vulgar!" she razzes him. He doesn't laugh. It's doubtful he ever has. Unbeknownst to Virginia, Fortune is an imposter, a German agent. His imposing presence maneuvers Virginia exactly where he wants her – getting US Navy convoy secrets from handsome playboy James Ellison.

Ellison was also at the aforementioned D.C. cocktail party

and in "hot" pursuit of Virginia. Knowing of Ellison's reputation with women, she zeroes in to ask him, "Should I *swoon*, or bite you?" He's completely smitten. The next day, Virginia feigns further disinterest in Ellison over lunch. "They're rationing women now," he smiles. "I guess I'll have to cut down and concentrate on *you*!" Despite his technique, Virginia begins to melt. Her true feelings for Ellison emerge later on, after they are kidnapped. A whirlwind of action along the Hudson River (for which Virginia had to learn to swim) concludes with Fortune being tied up and gagged. Virginia stares at him. "Mr. Fortune!" she scoffs, "Now *that's* not good for your capillaries!" Ellison, it turns out, works for U.S. Intelligence and strategically radios *mis*-information to the Japanese. At the *finis*, Virginia's tongue-in-cheek narrative informs the audience, "And *that*, darlings, is how *I* sunk a Japanese submarine!" The film's success relies on the fact that Virginia's catty character is aware of her own antics and enjoys it. The story is condensed by her narrative, into an effective, albeit predictable, plot. *Photoplay* unjustly thought *Careful, Soft Shoulders* "a poor man's Alfred Hitchcock . . . Only this one lacks the Hitchcock charm and sophistication. It lacks pretty nearly everything else too, except the lovely Virginia Bruce."[38] The film was written and directed by Oliver H.P. Garrett, a versatile talent and screenwriter (*Manhattan Melodrama*, John Ford's *Hurricane*, and many others). Garrett's ripe, sharp wit in *Careful, Soft Shoulders*, provides a tantalizing mix of suspense and comedy that deserves to be remembered.

After the Christmas holidays of 1942, Virginia headed to New York. While reminiscing about her time there with Ruben, Vir-

At Ciro's 1943 – Earll Briggs, Virginia, future producer James Hill,
Margaret Briggs and Stanley Briggs (Courtesy of Vincent Briggs)

ginia tested herself to see if she really wanted to return to acting. She appeared on several radio shows, including the *Phillip Morris Playhouse*. For that, she starred in *Fifth Avenue Girl* (a story which takes place in the same block Virginia had lived in 1931) and *Mr. and Mrs. Smith* (with Chester Morris). She also guest-spotted with Bob Hope for Cleveland's USO *Stage Door Canteen* opening. Before heading for home, she traveled to Virginia for the *Jack Benny Show* at the Quantico Marine Base. The scenario for Virginia's appearance on Benny's popular show went as follows:

> Announcer Don Wilson began the "funny business" by introducing the orchestra's first

number, "Brown Eyes, Why Is Your Nose So Close
to My Face?" Benny's wife, Mary Livingston, was
unable to make it to Quantico, so Benny informed
singer Dennis Day they would need a female
replacement. Day panicked, "Don't look at me.
I'm just a tenor!" Benny explained that Virginia
Bruce was going to fill in. "Virginia Bruce! Virginia
Bruce!" Day repeated, confessing he was in love
with her and would have to propose marriage.
Realizing Virginia would probably refuse him,
Day wailed to Benny, "I'll have to hang myself with
that lousy necktie you gave me for Christmas!"
After the buildup, Virginia walked on stage to
thundering applause and a pack of wolf whistles.
A jealous Benny huffed, "You got more applause
than I did!" Virginia just laughed, and reasoned,
"My last pair of nylons are doing a good job." This
obligated Benny to pull up his trousers and proudly
show off his own legs. Virginia balked, "I'd hate to
get an order of mashed potatoes with that many
lumps in them!" Next up, was a sketch wherein
Benny auditions to be Virginia's new leading man.
Gregory Ratoff joined in as their director. The
scene opens on a summer night in the "Old South."
Benny, as Finchbottom, searches in the garden for
Virginia. "Oh, Magnolia!" he cries. "I'm over here
by the birdbath, sugar," Virginia swoons. "Oh!"
Benny hesitates. "If you're taking a bath . . . I'll
come back later!" When Benny attempts to kiss
her, Virginia pulls away to complain to Ratoff that
Finchbottom is drooling. The Marines hooted and

hollered when Benny calmed down to give Virginia a real Southern smooch. "Well, do I get the part?" Benny inquires. "Wow! You certainly do as far as I'm concerned!" Virginia declares. "Now kiss Gregory and see what *he* thinks." Ratoff puckers up and begs, "Kiss me, Finchbottom, Kiss me!" "Ah, cut that out!" Benny complains.

Virginia enjoyed the tomfoolery, and joined Benny for shows at Newport News, and the Navy base at Norfolk, Virginia. Radio would become a steady diet throughout the rest of the year for Virginia. And, for awhile, so was Clark Gable.

Louella Parsons got the initial Gable-Bruce "scoop," and rhapsodized,

> Two people brought together by mutual tragedies in their lives are Virginia Bruce Ruben and Clark Gable. Few people know that these two saw a great deal of each other when Clark was here a few weeks ago. In the days when Carole Lombard and J. Walter Ruben were alive, the Rubens and Clark and Carole were close friends. Then came the tragic accident that snuffed out Carole's life [a plane crash returning from a War Bond Tour], and later in the same year Jack Ruben died. Virginia and Clark did not meet again until a few weeks ago when Gable was on a brief furlough. It was an entirely accidental meeting – in a Beverly Hills store. Clark

invited Virginia to dinner and took her to the
home of director Walter Lang.[39]

Parsons claimed that the duo had seen each other a number of
times. Whatever the case, the rumors about Virginia and Gable
persisted for well over a year. In February 1944, while performing on an episode of CBS's *Suspense*, Virginia confided to cast
members that her tabloid romance with Captain Clark Gable
was exaggerated. "Of course," she smiled, "I have no objection
to the rumor; only it isn't fair to Captain Gable. We *are* friends.
As to anything further – Well!"[40] Virginia's hometown paper, *The
Fargo Forum*, went gaga over the Bruce-Gable story and provided a capsulation of all the gossip from Hollywood, such as:
90% of Captain Gable's V mail came from Virginia; Gable's letters were finding a regular spot in Virginia's own mailbox; and
Virginia was flying to Minneapolis to meet Gable, and they were
to be married there.[41] Virginia was contacted by the Hollywood
press on the evening she was to have left for Minneapolis. "How
utterly ridiculous!" she said upon hearing of her supposed nuptials. A reporter asked if the wedding would take place the day
afterwards. "Still, utterly ridiculous," came her reply. "Well, then,
some day next week, or some other future time?" he persisted.[42]
Here, she paused, failing to utter . . . anything at all.

Most likely, the Gable-Bruce friendship was based on consolation – working through the loss of the very individuals they
held dearest, Carole Lombard and J. Walter Ruben.

Virginia spent a great deal of time with her close friend Cesar
Romero before he was inducted into Uncle Sam's service in June

1943. Romero liked showering Susan and Christopher with gifts and toys. Some reporters thought it meant matrimony for the duo, especially after Romero asked Virginia to attend the wedding reception for Ann Sothern and Robert Sterling. But, as mentioned, Romero, Hollywood's "most confirmed" bachelor, was simply someone who Virginia could relax with and be herself. In late summer 1943, Louella got the second "scoop" of the year on Virginia – her return to the screen. "I am very glad Virginia Bruce is returning to pictures," reported Parsons. "The death of her husband . . . was a terrific shock and there were months when Virginia felt she would never return to the screen. But time does heal all wounds and Ginny looks prettier than ever now. She has been signed by Charles Koerner [RKO production chief] for the femme lead opposite George Sanders in *International Zone*. She is crazy about her role and says it is the one she has been waiting for all these months."[43] Before *International Zone*, Virginia had toyed with the idea of taking over Constance Bennett's controversial strip-teaser role in *Hi Diddle Diddle*. The role had been written for Lupe Velez. As it turned out, June Havoc ran away with the part. Virginia also nixed the role of a society reporter with "ice in her veins and icicles on her heart" for a film based on Whitman Chamber's novel *Once Too Often*. The film finally showed up in 1948 as *Blonde Ice*, starring low-budget queen Leslie Brooks.

News columnist Inga Arvad was one of the first reporters in over a year-and-a-half to visit Virginia at her home. She found Virginia enthusiastic. "For nearly two years I have been out of the movies," Virginia said, "and I am looking forward so much to getting a good part once more. As a matter of fact, I play a spy who shoots no less than two men in the back. Not a bit sporting, is it? But . . . ," Virginia was suddenly cut off as a door fell ajar, and a

The Rubens 1944: Virginia Christopher (3) and Susan Ann (11)

wee hand pushed it open. A sturdy little fellow appeared with loving eyes looking up at his mother. Christopher pointed vigorously at something, and tried to communicate with a long sentence . . . a sentence that Arvad admitted was "unintelligible to everyone except to the woman who bore him." They laughed as he rushed to her and buried his little face. "This is what the two years off gave me," Virginia smiled, as she gave her son a hug. "Isn't he wonderful?" Bearing a resemblance to both Virginia and Ruben, young

Christopher settled into his mother's lap. Looking out of the large window across six acres of ranch nestled in the hills of Pacific Palisades, she continued with the conversation saying, "This is rather a big place to keep up. I love it all, because I enjoy the outdoor life. And by that I mean the work that must be done. I plant the seeds, feed the hens, and, by the way, did you know that one can have eggs without having a rooster?" Virginia shook her head in amazement. "My *closest* contact with nature," she said, "was the night the gardener called me and said that the colt would be born any minute. I rushed down to the mare and we stayed with her for hours before it actually happened. That picture of the first time the mother saw her baby is so vivid in my mind. The look in her eyes was almost human. It didn't take her but a few minutes to get on her feet and take care of all the duties of a mother."[44]

Reporter Arvad felt the atmosphere enveloping the Rubens' home to be a blend of "culture and serenity, with a mixture of deep, happy laughter." Virginia guided her on a tour to peek at the children's rooms, and then up the winding staircase to Virginia's boudoir. Prominently displayed was a photograph of "Sonny" in a large silver frame. Pausing for a moment, Virginia regarded the man that meant so much to her. "All that you see in his face, he had," she said quietly, "generosity, tolerance, and intelligence. . . . He was my man."[45] Arvad commented that there was something so definite, so final in Virginia's statement, that it stopped her from asking any further questions.[46]

Endnotes

1   Colin Briggs, "Cordially Yours, Ann Sothern," BearManor Media, 2007, pg 283-284

2   Louella Parsons, "Hollywood," *Syracuse Herald*, 7/24/39

3   News article "Seen on the Set of "Gold Rush Maisie," *Dunkirk Evening Observer(NY)*, 9/14/40

4   Review of *Butch Minds the Baby*, *Newsweek*, 4/13/42

5   Review of *Butch Minds the Baby*, *New York Times*, 5/1/42

6   Hedda Hopper column, *LA Times*, 3/26/42

7   May Mann , "Going Hollywood," *Ogden Standard Examiner*, 4/17/42

8   Frederick C. Othman, "Comedy Team Film Quota St At Four Yearly," *Charleston Daily News*, 4/19/42

9   Louella O. Parsons, "Abbott, Costello Will Pursue Virginia Bruce in New Farce," *Modesto Bee*, 2/10/42

10 News article, "Virginia Bruce Appears with Abbott and Costello," *Vidette-Messenger (IND)*, 10/7/42

11 Ernest Foster, "Hollywood Film Shop," *Vidette-Messenger*, 5/19/42

12 Jimmie Fidler, "Universal's 'Pardon My Sargon' Set at a Glance," *Chronicle Telegram*, 3/25/42

13 Christ Costello, *Lou's on First*, St. Martin's Griffin, 1982, pg 68

14 Bosley Crowther review of *Pardon My Sarong*, *The New York Times*, 8/27/42

15 Ibid

16 Nathan Miller, *Star-Spangled Men: America's Ten Worst Presidents*, Scribner, c1999, pg 132

17 Charles Higham, *Merchant of Dreams*, Donald I. Fine, c. 1993, pg 328

18 Clayton R. Koppes and Gregory D. Black, *Hollywood Goes to War*, The Free Press, N.Y., 1987, pg 86

19 Higham, *Merchant . . .* pg 328

20 "Divorce Delayed by Alimony Fight," *Ogden Standard* Examiner, 10/10/39

21 Paul Harrison, "Film Colony Burns Up Over Charges of Martin Dies That Communism Pervades Industry," *Port Arthur News*, 3/1/40

22 Higham, *Merchant* ...pg 328

23 News article, "Movie Portrays 'Thad' Stevens In Better Vein After Protests," *Gettysberg Times (PA)*, 9/25/42

24 Frank Kuest, "Moving Pictures Are Not Bogged by U.S. Censors," *Kingston Daily (NY)*, 3/12/43

25 Koppes and Black, *Hollywood Goes to War*, pg 90

26 Patrick McGilligan and Paul Buhle, *Tender Comrades: A Backstory of the Hollywood Blacklist*, St. Martins, c. 1999, pg 117

27 "Committee Lists 79 as Communists In Film Capital," *Middletown Times Herald (NY)*, 10/22/47

28 Dorothy Kilgallen, "Voice of Broadway," *Olean Times Herald*, 12/24/49

29 Westbrook Pegler, "Jimmy Hoffa Paid For The Stevenson Show," *Lima News*, 8/2/60

30 Eric Bentley and Frank Rich, *Thirty Years of Treason*, Thunder's Mouth Press, c. 1971, 2002, pg 300

31 Jimmie Fidler on *Tennessee Johnson*, *Nevada State Journal*, 12/29/42

32   Charles Higham, *Merchant* . . . pg. 328

33   "Death Comes to J. Walter Ruben," *Delta Democrat*, 9/8/42)

34   Briggs, "Cordially . . . " pg 280

35   news article, *Ogden Standard Examiner*, 9/13/42

36   "Contest Looms Over Estate of Film Producer Ruben," *Los Angeles Times*, 9/16/42

37   Jimmie Fidler, "Fidler in Hollywood," *Nevada State Journal*, 10/18/42

38   Review of *Careful, Soft Shoulders, Photoplay?/42*

39   Louella Parsons' column, *Fresno Bee*, 4/4/43

40   Joe Rathbun, "Joe's Radio Parade," *Zanesville Signal(OH)*, 2/13/44

41   Ruth Fairbanks, "Chaff And Chatter," *Fargo Forum*, 2/6/44

42   Ibid

43   Louella O. Parsons' column, *Modesto Bee*, 9/3/43

44   Inga Arvad, "Virginia Bruce's Daughter Desires Swimming Pool," *Kingsport News(TN)*, 10/7/43

45   Ibid

46   Ibid

CHAPTER FOURTEEN:

Espionage, Politics, & Ali Ipar

M.V. Heberden's novel *The Fanatic of Fez* revealed the world of espionage in the Middle East during WWII. U.S. involvement in the area discouraged RKO from using Heberden's original title. The studio rechristened it *International Zone*, and hired Russian native and exile Leonide Moguy to direct. Moguy complemented his own work with desert scenes taken from Merian C. Cooper's never-completed RKO epoch on the life of Lawrence of Arabia.[1] During production, *International Zone* was retitled *Action in Arabia*. The stars, Virginia and George Sanders, made a cohesive pair for the *noir*-ish thriller. However, Virginia's return to the screen wasn't an easy task. In late November, she collapsed on the set and was taken to St. Johns Hospital in Santa Monica for observation. Her physician's diagnosis was incipient pneumonia. Newshounds reported that Dr. Clark Gable made several visits during her two-week stay.[2] As much as Virginia desired a romantic attachment, she and Gable, it would turn out, were politically estranged. After Virginia's recovery, *Action in Arabia* wrapped up in December, and was released in February 1944.

In *Action in Arabia*, audiences followed the trail of the impeccably cool Sanders, a reporter, who wears white sport jackets

Action in Arabia (1944) with George Sanders (RKO)

while hunting down Nazi sympathizers in Damascus. No one wants him there, not even the American embassy. He has a reputation for stirring up trouble. Virginia's character, however, feels differently. She's attracted by his urbane attentions. Sanders suspects her of using glamour as camouflage for something lethal. But, lethal for whom? The most atmospheric scenes in *Action in Arabia* take place at a popular and posh hotel. One evening, "refreshed" from losing at the gambling tables, Virginia agrees to dine with Sanders. They dance exceptionally well together, even in a crowd. But, before the music ends, Sanders guides her to the portico, saying, "I couldn't permit our talent to be bumped all over the floor." She agrees. They gaze upon the lights of Damascus. "The oldest city in the world," sighs Sanders, "and here I am, right in the middle of it – suffering from the oldest emotion." Before Virginia can catch her breath, Sanders is called away by the police. Virginia exudes an air of mystery and Sanders is never quite sure what to make of her. While investigating a murder, he enters the palatial home of the suspect, to find *her* there, playing the piano. "You're a very disturbing person," he tells her. Once again, she agrees. But, it only takes a passionate kiss for her to unveil her mystery. She shows him her Cross of Lorraine. She's in the desert to free France from Nazi occupation. Now she and Sanders are allies in love *and* war.

The action in *Action in Arabia* isn't nearly as interesting as the darkly atmospheric scenes that lead up to it – that is, the interior shots just described. After that, the chase is on. While Nazis solidify Arab tribes against the Allies, Virginia and Sanders become entrapped. In order to flee from the Arab world's spiritual leader (H. B. Warner, who had portrayed Christ in silent films), Virginia dutifully stabs one of the Swastika boys in the back. After pulling off the film's most gruesome moment, she and Sanders manage to escape. Virginia and Sanders end up exactly where you expect them to — aboard a plane, happily headed home to the USA. *The New York Times* cheered, "*Action in Arabia* is the sort of buncombe you get in the muscular fiction field . . . Moguy has directed it for that flair of exaggeration which distinguish the best B-grade intrigues. Mr. Sanders gives a beautiful perfor-

mance . . . Miss Bruce is particularly pallid in such hot-blooded company . . . the desert scenes smoke with honest dust. Taken as purest buncombe, this *Action in Arabia* is good fun."[3] Another review claimed the film had, "little else to offer except the suavity of George Sanders and the beauty of Virginia Bruce."[4] *Action in Arabia* was a far cry from being another *Casablanca.*

Action in Arabia (1944) Virginia and Sanders gambling with their lives in Damascus (RKO)

As a side note, the 2nd-unit director on the film was Robert Wise (*West Side Story, Sound of Music*).

The scenarist for *Action in Arabia* was Herbert Biberman, a founding member of Hollywood's Anti-Nazi League (1937). Biberman would gain notoriety in 1947 as one of the HUAC's "Hollywood Ten." He was blacklisted, spent six months in prison, and fined $1,000 for standing on the 1st Amendment of the U.S. Constitution. The careers of Biberman and his actress-wife Gale Sondergaard came to a definite halt. Prior to Biberman's conviction, a hotbed of political issues had been steadily escalating in the film colony. The political "left" had become synonymous with "Communist." After having witnessed the effect of an ultra-right campaign on husband Ruben, Virginia wasn't easily intimidated when it came to her own political beliefs. (Ruben had also belonged to the Hollywood Anti-Nazi League, considered a "leftist" organization. According FBI files, he gave a speech on behalf of the HANL at a Los Angeles First Unitarian Church, on the topic, "Documented Proof of Secret Fascist Operators Within Our Borders.") In the fall of 1942, Virginia actively campaigned in support of Democratic nominee Will Rogers, Jr., (a Stanford graduate) when he ran for California's Sixteenth Congressional District.[5] Once elected, Rogers was aggressive on Capitol Hill. Being part Native American, he was concerned for minorities and supported the Rescue Resolution (1943) for saving Jews from internment camps. The *Washington Post* had confirmed in November 1942, that at least two-million Jews in Europe had been murdered. Washington was ignoring the Holocaust. It was out of Rogers' crusade, on behalf of the Jews of Europe, that Roosevelt reluctantly created the War Refugee Board in 1944.

Virginia's campaigning for Rogers whetted her political appetite. Still, it came as a surprise to many when she tossed her hat into the political arena. The Beverly-Westwood Village democratic committee asked her to run for the state legislature. The February 28, 1944 headlines of Virginia's hometown paper read:

"Virginia Bruce Is Candidate For Legislature"

Fargo's principal contribution to the motion picture industry, Virginia Bruce, is starring in a new role and a novel one for the woman who has taken the lead in many a Hollywood production. She's a candidate for the Democratic endorsement for the legislature from her home district, Santa Monica. The California primary is August 29th.[6]

The real catalysts in Virginia's political interest (aside from J. Walter Ruben), were Melvyn Douglas and his wife Helen Gahagan-Douglas. The couple was motivated politically, and close friends with Eleanor Roosevelt (who had guest-stayed at their home). Melvyn, an eloquent public speaker and member of the Motion Picture Democratic Committee, was credited by California Governor Culbert Olsen for helping him sweep Southern California in the 1938 gubernatorial race. The Douglases were involved with the Anti-Nazi League, and dedicated to helping migrant workers. Virginia was impressed with their political astuteness. Her own involvement with their work began in December 1938, just after the completion of *There's That Woman Again*. She participated in a political broadcast "to call to the Nation's attention the serious problems of migratory families, forced out of the Middle West,

Virginia with June Allyson and Jean Peters 1944

but existing in California under sub-normal living conditions."[7] As mentioned, Douglas was influential in getting Virginia to participate, on behalf of the allies, as a speaker for the Union for Concerted Peace Efforts in the fall of 1939.

The first mention of Virginia's running for the Legislature was made by NEA Correspondent Erskine Johnson. He announced on February 8, 1944, "Hollywood glamour has finally invaded politics. Virginia Bruce is planning to run for the California state legislature . . . and Helen Gahagan, wife of Melvyn Douglas, will be a candidate for Representative Thomas Ford's seat in Congress."[8] Hedda Hopper thought the odds were in Virginia's favor, saying, "May seem funny to some, but Virginia Bruce has a good chance of getting the nomination for Congresswoman."[9] The same month as Virginia's announcement, Louella Parsons attended a birthday party for long-time MGM executive Eddie Mannix, noted for his unsavory methods of "covering up" star scandals. Captain Clark Gable, one of Mannix's best pals, was there, along with Virginia. "Virginia Bruce who has become very politically minded," snapped Parsons, "waxed into a deep discussion. She is serious about running for Congress." The columnist made a point of adding that Capt. Gable retreated, "while the discussion was at its height, to play gin rummy with Kay Williams." (Kay and Gable would eventually marry in 1955.)[10] This was probably the beginning of the end of the Gable and Bruce "romance." Gable was politically conservative along the same lines as his devout Republican boss Louis B. Mayer, who was known to solicit contributions for the Republican Party from his employees.[11]

Almost as quickly as Virginia decided to run for Congress, she decided against it, albeit reluctantly. Virginia told the press, "Maybe some time later, five years or so from now." She added that she "most certainly was interested, but it would take too much time from my work in pictures."[12] She also felt that her lack of experience would be a handicap. The International News Service pointed out that, "Miss Bruce has been actively interested in politics for some time in a Hollywood group that includes Melvyn Douglas and Helen Gahagan. She said her particular interest was legislation to 'help the little fellow.'"[13] Helen Gahagan-Douglas' campaign went full stream ahead with the support of Hollywood's more liberal supporters, Virginia included. In the *Biographical Dictionary of Congressional Women*, author Karen Foerstel states, "With the campaign help of such Hollywood luminaries as Eddie Cantor and Virginia Bruce – as well as migrant workers and organized labor – Gahagan-Douglas won the election by almost 4,000 votes."[14] The newly-elected Congresswoman abandoned her acting and opera career to make politics her life's work. In the fall of 1944, Virginia participated in two radio broadcasts for the Democratic Party. On September 18 she joined Mrs. Edward G. Robinson for a broadcast at the California Democratic Convention and on November 6 joined a host of other stars the night before the election in support of FDR. The program included a 94-year-old Republican who had shaken the hand of Abraham Lincoln. According to radio archivist J. David Golden, the broadcast was "well calculated to make the blood of any Republican boil."[15] Virginia familiarized herself with both sides of the political arena, and took Ginger Rogers up on an invitation for afternoon tea with the Republican Candidate for President, Thomas E. Dewey.[16] Dewey was part of a less conservative faction of the Republican Party. His reputation as Governor of New York was impressive. He doubled state aid to education, increased salaries for state employees, and enacted the first state law in the country to prohibit racial discrimination. Still, Virginia kept her loyalties with FDR, and Gahagan-Douglas, who was running at FDR's request.

When considering Virginia's decision to bow out of the legislature race, one must assume that she was aware that the FBI was on the tail of *anyone* who leaned to the left in politics. An informant for the bureau advised them in March 1944, that "Virginia

Bruce is a liberal and not a Communist, despite her activities in the Hollywood Anti-Nazi League." (FBI LA 105-3043) Virginia had spoken on behalf of the HANL at the Roosevelt Hotel in 1939, and was on the executive council for the pro-Roosevelt, pro-New Deal, Motion Picture Democratic Committee (along with many other stars: Bogart, Cagney, Garland, Hayworth, Sinatra, to mention a few). The FBI's constant surveillance of these groups, may have discouraged Virginia from tossing her hat any further into political arena.

After she was elected, Gahagan-Douglas' work on Capital Hill received a great deal of attention from the press. She remained outraged at the accusations that plagued filmdom's political "left." By 1947, celebrities referred to as "friendly witnesses" stepped forward to name names for the HUAC. Robert Taylor claimed he was forced by government agent Lowell Mellett to play the lead in MGM's *Song of Russia.* (At that time, Russia was a U.S. ally. Mellett, remember, was involved with the controversy surrounding *Tennessee Johnson.*) Another "friendly" witness, Richard Arlen, testified, "The real Reds are among the writers. Many are very clever at weaving in propaganda, and we actors have to read it."[17] Ginger Rogers' mother told the Committee that in Dalton Trumbo's screenplay for *Tender Comrade* (1943) Ginger had refused to say the line, "Share and share alike – that's democracy." "I think that's definitely Communist propaganda," huffed Mrs. Rogers.[18] (The phrase, "share and share like," first appeared in print in 1566, in Richard Edward's comedy, *Damon and Pithias.*) *Tender Comrade's* director, Edward Dmytryk (who would later cooperate with the HUAC) and Trumbo were two more names on the "Hollywood Ten" list.

During the anti-Communist purge, Gahagan-Douglas presented her feelings on the subject as sanely as one possibly could to her fellow Congressmen:

... I have seen shanty towns ... I have seen
children with sore eyes and swollen bellies ...
I have seen minorities humiliated and denied
full citizenship. And I tell you that we betray
the basic principle upon which this government
of free people was founded unless this people's
government finds a way by which all the people
can live out their lives in dignity and decency ...
the battle should not rage around the bogus
issue of communism but around the real issue of
monopoly, and the exploitation of people and their
resources. Democracy cannot long survive when
the people permit their lives to be dominated—
economically or politically—by a powerful few.[19]

Virginia's own statement about supporting legislation to "help
the little fellow" echoed Gahagan-Douglas' sentiments. Aside
from her work with domestic programs, and keeping atomic
power out of the hands of the military, Gahagan-Douglas was
influential in desegregating the dining rooms and staff cafeteria
at the nation's House of Representatives in 1946 (100 years *after*
the Civil War!) . Her biggest battle would be with her opponent
in the 1950 California Senate race: Richard Nixon. He sponsored
the Mundt-Nixon Bill (1948), which would have jailed all Communist sympathizers. Nixon felt Gahagan-Douglas to be among
them, calling her "the Pink Lady" and saying she was "pink right
down to her underwear." Using a prototypical smear campaign,
the Hearst news empire, backing Nixon, indicated that Gahagan-
Douglas was plotting to "overthrow the American way of life."[20]

Virginia went where most stars feared to tread, and again
stepped up to the plate for Gahagan-Douglas in 1950. The United

Press announced that Hollywood stars "were scared of politics." "This ballot season the luminaries pulled the covers over their convictions and went into hiding," claimed the report, adding that, "since the congressional investigations of Hollywood, the studios frown on their stars being politically active."[21] Virginia, who was freelancing, appeared on a statewide network on Sunday, May 14, to speak on behalf of Gahagan-Douglas. She was joined by Lucy Ward Stebbins, emeritus professor at the University of California at Berkeley. However, the fear tactics of Nixon's campaign usurped the more honest efforts of Gahagan-Douglas. Bolstered by big business and oil interests, Nixon's strategy was to plant an abundance of hecklers at each of Gahagan-Douglas' appearances. His campaign workers telephoned thousands of homes the night before the election saying Gahagan was a Communist.[22] Nixon won by a large margin. In return for his "gallantry," Gahagan-Douglas coined his famous moniker: "Tricky Dick." It stuck – all the way to Nixon's downfall with Watergate and his resignation from the American Presidency in 1974.

By September 1947, Virginia felt she had gained enough experience in the political arena to run for President of the United States. That is, on the radio show *Cavalcade of America*. She had played such powerhouse women as founder of modern nursing, Florence Nightingale, on *Encore Theatre's* presentation of *The White Angel* (1946), and noted researcher and President of the Society of Bacteriology, Alice Evans, on *Cavalcade's* biographical work *Woman Alone* (1947). Virginia's toughest acting challenge was tackling the role of Belva Lockwood, the only woman nominated not once, but twice, for the U.S. Presidency. She aged from young woman to grandmother during the half-hour presentation. The dexterity of her voice was exceptional in conveying her

October 1944, the newly elected Honary Mayor with her son Christopher

characterization. As Lockwood reaches middle age, her voice is virtually unrecognizable as being that of Virginia Bruce.

The program was curiously titled *The Girl Who Ran for President*, even though Lockwood was 54 years old at the time of her nomination. The story introduces Lockwood as a young teacher being told the reason behind her $8-a-week salary versus a man's $20-a-week salary was simply "It's a man's world, and that's the way of it." Lockwood set out to change "the way of it." She received her law degree from the National University Law School in Washington, D.C. in 1873, and was nominated by the Equal Rights Party as a candidate for president in 1884, running against Grover Cleveland. Lockwood drew up a platform promising "equality and justice for all regardless of color, sex, or nationality, equal voting and property rights for women."[23] Virginia, as Lockwood, generates conviction with her words, "As a nation, we love to parade our Democratic virtues before the world. Yet, a majority of our citizens have absolutely no political rights." At a time when women had no vote, Lockwood pulled in over 4,000 votes, plus the entire electoral vote of Indiana. Aside from her push for women's suffrage, Lockwood was a delegate to the International Peace Conference of 1889 in Paris. Virginia gave a worthy portrayal of Lockwood, and her story was as relevant in 1947 as it had been in 1884. Although Virginia herself never would pursue a political career, she was elected as the first Honorary Mayor of Pacific Palisades in 1944. The appointment pleased Virginia, and compensated for her withdrawal as a legislature candidate. At a press conference sponsored by the community's Civic League, Virginia told Pacific Palisadians, "From now on, you can bring all your troubles to me instead of to Mayor Bowron of Los Angeles."[24]

In December 1943, RKO planned to give Virginia the lead in Nancy Hale's novel *The Prodigal Women*. Hale's representation of a strong feminine character was perhaps ahead of its time. The project was shelved. Instead, Virginia signed with Republic for "safer territory" in *Brazil*. America's "Good Neighbor Policy" was in full swing during WWII, and *Brazil*, endowed with South American music and Brazilian dances, features Virginia playing an author whose "un-neighborly" bestseller, "Why Marry a Latin?," has offended many a Brazilian *hombre*. Her book is considered the worst import to come into Brazil since the coffee worm. Men swarm around the attractive Virginia upon her ar-

Brazil (1944) with Tito Guizar (Republic)

rival at Rio's airport, but back off when they learn she is the offensive author. "Don't tell me these big, strong Brazilians don't have a sense of humor!" she remarks with a smirk to American diplomat Robert Livingston. Confident and opinionated, Virginia is convinced she can write the "definitive" book on Brazil during her two-week stay, but laments she won't have time to complete her unfinished symphony. Not to worry. After humming a few bars of it to her tour guide, Tito Guizar, he finishes it for her. The few bars escalate into the unending ballad, "Rio de Janeiro," which provides *Brazil's* musical climax at Rio's famous Carnival. By this time, Virginia has changed her tune regarding Latin men to an enthusiastic whistle and aims it directly at Guizar.

Like many musicals of the era, *Brazil* relieved audiences from the reality of war. A film critic in Austin, Texas, put it aptly. "The charming Mexican singer, Tito Guizar, and Virginia Bruce romp through this light cinematic [fare] in such a way to make you wish the war were over so you could go yourself."[25] Since Carmen Miranda already had hit Hollywood in 1940, the film's concept wasn't exactly new. *The New York Times* pointed out, "This film excursion to the home of the coffee bean and the Samba is pleasant if not novel diversion . . . The songs and dances are tuneful and sprightly, but its plot is as exciting as a siesta. . . . As the romantic lead [Guizar] leaves in his performance something to be desired. . . . Miss Bruce is beautiful as his partner in romance."[26] Although Guizar's fan base in Mexico exceeded that of Frank Sinatra, his performance in *Brazil* fails to explain his popularity. Guizar does offer smooth renditions of Ary Barroso's music. Barroso, who had shaped Brazilian popular music, entered the 1945 Oscar race for his ballad from *Brazil*, "Rio de Janeiro." It lost to Bing Crosby's hit "Swinging on a Star" from *Going My Way*. *Brazil* also received nominations for Best Score and Best Sound Recording. The dance numbers were diverting and, to add some spice, Carmen Miranda's sister Aurora provided a specialty act. What the film really needed, besides a more charismatic leading man, was Technicolor. To make amends for the film's shortcomings, Republic's "King of the Cowboys," Roy Rogers, makes a surprise appearance at Carnival to sing "Hands Across the Border."

In his weekly review of current films, columnist Jimmy Fidler's comment on *Brazil* simply stated, "Good music; good laughs; 'Good Neighbor' propaganda." Fidler closed his column, as usual, noting the "Best Performance of the Week." This time the honor went to: "Virginia Bruce in *Brazil*. A girl who's too often overlooked makes you wonder why."[27] The problem was that Virginia wasn't seeking out opportunities at major studios that would make full use of her range and talent. Her next assignment at Republic was another so-so comedy with another less-than-exciting actor.

Love, Honor, and Goodbye, released in 1945, reunited Virginia with "B" director Albert Rogell (*Butch Minds the Baby*). Behind the camera was John Alton, who would go on to Oscar fame as the cinematographer for *An American in Paris* (1951). For a leading man, Virginia faced Englishman Edward Ashley, who had been wandering around MGM since 1940, and getting nowhere. The giddy comedy has Virginia as a stage-struck gal with no talent. Husband Ashley finances her play, in the hopes of getting the theatre out of her system. The play flops. She blames *him*, and runs home to mother. She returns repentant, only to find Ashley has invited a tattoo artist (Victor McLaglen), a carnival floozy (Veda Ann Borg) and a toddler to co-habit with him! To defy all logic, Virginia disguises herself as a French nurse in order to investigate what is *really* going on. While incognito, she decides to name her "nurse-self" as correspondent in her *own* divorce suit from Ashley! Bosley Crowther of *The New York Times* did the math on this concoction saying, "A third-rate husband-wife comedy played by a third-rate company adds up to a sixth-rate picture. . . . The big climax of the monotony comes when Miss Bruce dons spectacles and a wig and tries to compromise her husband by posing as an oo-la-la French nurse. 'A great performance,' he calls it. But, if you'd like to know what we think, he should loudly complain to the management and demand his money back."[28] In Canada, critic Frank Morriss kindly called *Love, Honor, and Goodbye* "frothy, lightweight summer fare, and if you are willing to place your trust in the long arm of coincidence you might enjoy it. Miss Bruce does nicely in the role of the flighty wife."[29]

Weslyan University film historian Jeanine Basinger wrote the film's epitaph in 1993, saying, "No movie depicts marriage more dismally than a depressing little minor comedy like *Love,*

Publicity still for Republic –
1945

Honor, and Goodbye . . . its basic plot structure reveals tension, conflict, distrust, doubt, the double standard, and a condescending attitude toward women. . . . Because he loves her, [Ashley] decides secretly to back her in a show so that she can fail."[30] "If it's a flop," Ashley enthuses, "she'll be back home where she belongs!" His remark, as expected, leads up to Virginia wailing, "They laughed in all the wrong places! Your wife's a big flop."

A smug and satisfied Ashley takes her back home "where she belongs." Basinger observed, "Here one sees the depressing truth about common attitudes toward women (they're dumb, keep 'em home, and kids will tie them down) – toward marriage (never tell each other the truth but work subtle scams on each other to get what you want). How could women in the audience fail to grasp the truth about such a movie?"[31] Perhaps it was because audiences were used to it. For eleven years Hollywood's Production Code had preached that marriage and career for women were *not* a viable mix. Organized religion had been saying the same thing for centuries.

In spite of Virginia and Ashley's scheming, the early portion of *Love, Honor, and Goodbye* is brisk, and nicely photographed. Virginia looks every inch the star her character is *attempting* to be. After Virginia and Ashley return home from the "opening-closing" of her fizzled debut, there is a lovely scene reminiscent of *Born to Dance*, wherein Virginia walks out onto her terrace singing "These Foolish Things (Remind Me of You)." The song is intermittently woven with dialogue and dancing between her and Ashley. After that, the film's charms are fast fading. It fails to register the right key as other madcap classics of the same mold, such as *My Favorite Wife*.

After completing *Love, Honor, and Goodbye*, Virginia gave her first house party since Ruben's death. With some 150 guests, Louella was on hand to report, "[Virginia] gave a party at her home the other night that will long be remembered . . . She seemed to have the knack of being everywhere at once and to see each guest personally. Her mother was on hand to help her. Reggie Gardiner, just back from London, gave a toast to Virginia,

Academy Award Theatre – July 17, 1946 – Virginia costarred
with Douglas Fairbanks Jr. in *The Prisoner of Zenda*

which was responded to by the Danny Kayes, Cesar Romero, Mrs. Walter Lang, Lady Mendl, Harry Crocker [publicist], Felix Ferry [producer], and Otto Preminger."[32]

As always, Virginia's main focuses were her children and her home. "Virginia Bruce is doing everything to make her little son Christopher's Christmas a very happy one, because he goes into the hospital January 3rd [1945] for an operation," was a typical news update.[33] Virginia confirmed her personal perspective saying, "I do not believe that 'The show must go on' regardless of circumstances. I think your children, your home, and your health come first. These are considerations that rank above professional life."[34] However, being sole provider didn't allow Virginia to keep her professional life completely at bay. When Susan suggested they buy a new swimming pool with her mother's salary from *Action in Arabia*, Virginia hesitated. "But don't you know that there is a war on, Darling?" she said, somewhat apologetically. "Swimming pools can't be had just now, but maybe *after* the war." "Do you think there will be some of the money left?" Susan inquired. Virginia smiled guiltily, "No, I don't think so."[35] In an attempt to keep expenses at a minimum, Virginia did much of her own housekeeping. When reporter Robbin Coons arrived for an interview, he caught her amid the whirring of a vacuum cleaner. She called to him from an upstairs window saying she would be right down. He commented in his column on the contrast between pre-war Virginia and the current version. On his last visit, while Ruben was still alive, the household was staffed with five servants, and Virginia, "had discoursed on the joys of laziness." But now, Virginia explained, "All the gals are in the same boat, as far as help is concerned. I'm lucky – I've a grand nurse... and Leo, who looks after the horses and cars and grounds and things generally. I never cooked in my life, but I'm learning. I've also done a lot of housecleaning, and laundry, and bed-making. [Life's] been good for us. Of course I still love to relax – but when?"[36]

By the end of their rumored affair, Clark Gable had definitely rekindled Virginia's interest in romance. Aside from paling around with Cesar Romero, Virginia was seen out and about with Gilbert Roland, Ricardo Cortez, producer Anthony Owen, and MGM contract player Fred Brady, who was showering her with flowers (until his wife found out). By the fall of 1945, it appeared Virginia had found a suitable match in literary agent-man-about-town Thomas Cornwell Jackson (known to his pals as "Corney"). The 43-year-old, quiet, be-speckled, dependable, vice-president of the J. Walter Thompson Advertising Agency, managed to keep his name out of the papers. He was a familiar face in Hollywood and had dated Kay Francis, although he failed to make mention in Kay's personal diaries. By January 1946, things were pretty "serious" between Jackson and Virginia. She had signed to make a murder-mystery in Mexico City titled *Accusation*, and was taking her mother and Christopher along with her. Because of Susan's schooling, Virginia invited "Corney" to stay at the house and look after her. Louella Parsons was thrilled about the arrangement, and predicted an engagement announcement the moment Virginia returned from Mexico.[37] There was. But, Corney was not part of the deal.

Virginia was intrigued with the storyline of *Accusation* and impressed with the rich, young Turk in charge of production, Ali M. Ipar. Richard Arlen, her co-star from *Let 'Em Have It*, had signed on to play opposite her. She left for Mexico on January 16, 1946, leaving Corney in charge of things at home. Corney had his plane reservation to go to Mexico and see Virginia a month later. He admitted to Louella, "My purpose in going to Mexico now – [is] to ask her to become my wife."[38] But his trip was postponed, as Virginia and Arlen were still waiting for filming on *Accusation* to begin. One report said that the film's financers had not been forthcoming with the "necessary pesos."[39] A union battle (cameramen) was also targeted as being responsible for the delay. Reporter Dan Walker claimed that Virginia, Richard Arlen, and Warren William, "marooned in Mexico City five weeks at their own expense, waiting for cameramen, threaten to sue their studios."[40] The delay in filming *Accusation*, however, didn't keep Virginia from having a good time and it would appear that she wasn't exactly pining away for Corney Jackson.

Walter Winchell reported, "Virginia Bruce, the cinemadonna, and Ali Ipar of Turkey have Mexico City gossiping like mad."[41] Louella Parsons suspected that the romance between Virginia and Corney had gone cold. "[Jackson] was at the Reagans [Ronald and wife, Jane Wyman] with Gail Patrick," Parsons confirmed.[42] When *Accusation* failed to roll at all, it was reported that Virginia and the good-looking, dark-haired Ali Ipar boarded a plane for Hollywood. However, Virginia arrived by train with Christopher, 4½, who "refused to pose for pictures because he said the flash hurts his eyes."[43] Neither Corney, nor Ali, met her at Union Station. Brother Stanley, now working for RKO, showed up instead. Newshounds were baffled. All Virginia had to say was that both men were "mighty swell boys. It doesn't look too romantic when neither of them show up to meet me."[44] When located, Ipar stated that he and Virginia were "just good friends," and Corney stated, "I'm a perennial bachelor."[45] (As it would turn out, Corney married Gail Patrick and together they co-produced the popular 1960s TV series *Perry Mason*.)

Ipar still intended to make *Accusation*, and told reporters, "My brother, Necip Ipar, is still in Mexico City . . . I am hoping to reassemble my players and return . . . If I do not receive sufficient encouragement for this idea I will produce the film in Hollywood."[46] Virginia had already "spilled the *frijoles*" on the *real* reason *Accusation* hadn't been filmed. Ipar's "sufficient encouragement" meant money from home. "It is tough to get money from Turkey right now," she told the press. She admitted that none of *Accusation's* cast had received salary, but enthused, "We got our expenses, though, and Mexico City is just wonderful right now. I've had a wonderful vacation and the Ipar boys are mighty swell."[47] Ali Ipar had been in the United States since 1940. He was a young man of 25 when he and Virginia met. *Stars and Stripes*, a military newspaper, described him as "a short, slight young man with a black moustache, Hollywood haircut, and a Boyer-brand accent."[48] Ipar was born in Istanbul in 1921 and came from a wealthy family. His father, Hayri Ipar, was a Turkish munitions and sugar magnate. Ali had a fascination for the world of entertainment and Hollywood in particular. The first mention of Ipar in the American press had him dating Linda Darnell (1942). The following year, he produced a modern version of Oscar Straus' *The Chocolate Soldier* (with references to WWII). It featured baritone Charles Purcell and a New York cast. Ipar had purchased complete ownership and control of the Straus operetta. While it was playing on tour in San Francisco, critic Wood Soanes noted that the production's settings gave "evidence of a generous budget allowed by producer Ali M. Ipar."[49] After the tour, Louella Parsons mentioned in her column that Ipar and Venita Oakie (newly separated from husband Jack) had the Beverly Tropics diners "agog." But courting beautiful women was only part of Ipar's vision. He was Turkish correspondent for the *Los Angeles Times* and had partnered with Bing Crosby's brother Everett to form Continental Films Company. Continental had announced a wartime-themed story Ipar had written, *Dateline*

–*Istanbul*.[50] But, for the most part, as one report stated, Ipar remained "a man of mystery in cinema circles."[51]

Other members of the Ipar family had also ventured to California. Ali's brother, Necip Ipar, a student at UCLA, made the news after biting his actress-wife Elane Epar [sic]. She filed for divorce.[52] Ipar's sister, Fatima, was having love troubles around the time Ali and Virginia met. Fatima was attending a Hollywood party with a coast guard officer, when Swedish actor Kurt Kreuger introduced himself to her. Krueger was famous for portraying Nazi officers. An argument ensued between Krueger and Fatima's date. The officer threw a punch at Krueger, and according to one eyewitness, "all hands present lent a hand in throwing [the officer] out."[53] Evidently the Ipars were an exciting family to have around.

On July 8, 1946, Ali Ipar was drafted into the U.S. Army. The following month, it was announced that he and Virginia would have a private wedding at her Pacific Palisades residence. The day before the ceremony, Virginia was hosting a party at her home for Christopher's fifth birthday. Guests had arrived and things were humming along. Suddenly two male intruders showed up at Virginia's doorstep. They identified themselves as agents of the Army's Criminal Investigation Division and were accompanied by two sheriff's deputies. They wanted Ipar. Virginia explained that Ali was out shopping for a wedding ring. The authorities told her they would stick around until he returned. They wanted to question Ipar (who was on leave from Ft. Lewis in Washington) about a little matter of *three* three-day passes he wangled from Camp Beale – something they said "the Army doesn't issue."[54] Virginia, appearing quite ruffled, invited them in. News reporters had sniffed out a good story and eagerly waited outside Virginia's house for an "explanation." The United Press stated,

"The officers played gin rummy for three hours in the library and Miss Bruce went on serving ice cream and cake and party favors to her guests. And when Ipar showed up the policemen bundled him away to Fort MacArthur."[55] Before hauling Ipar away, Virginia excused herself as hostess, to join Ali for a private conference with the authorities. Pvt. Ali M. Ipar's excuses and explanations got him nowhere. As they attempted to handcuff him outside, he loudly protested, "But I'm not AWOL! It's legitimate, I tell you! I got a nine-day pass to get married!"[56] Looking agitated, Ipar turned to reporters, pleading, "I'm in the clear. If someone else has made a mistake, why make me pay for it?"[57] He then calmed down long enough to say he would go quietly if the officers would put the handcuffs away. They agreed. According to the press, Virginia "wept stormily." Ipar was locked up in Fort MacArthur's stockade. Virginia was not allowed to see him. Curiously, she was quoted as saying, "They did this once before last month. I guess the Army just liked him so much they can't bear to let him go."[58]

After an uncomfortable five-hour stretch behind bars, Ipar was released, with apologies. The Army admitted the night before was "all a mistake."[59] Ali's papers were in order. Capt. William Beckerman, provost marshal at Ft. MacArthur, said, "We have nothing on this man and have no reason to hold him." Ali, his arm around Virginia, told the press, "I guess there are different ways to do things: the right way, the wrong way, and the Army way. Well, they did

Fate, sealed with a kiss: Virginia and Ali Ipar August 27, 1946

this the Army way."[60] He forgot to mention "the Ipar way," which would again put him at odds with the law within 24 hours!

Virginia and Ipar decided to go ahead with the August 27th wedding as planned. Only it would take place at 9:00 p.m. instead of 5:00 p.m. Virginia opted for a quiet ceremony at the home of her friends, photographer Shirley Burden and his wife. A four-day honeymoon in Las Vegas would follow. Ipar was due back at Camp Beale, California on September 2nd. The guest list included the Gary Coopers, Gene Tierney and husband Oleg Cassini, and radio producer Hugh (Bud) Ernest and wife Betty Furness (who had co-starred in *Dangerous Corner*). Virginia selected a long-sleeved beige gown, set off with white orchids. Ipar had a tailored Army summer uniform ready for the occasion. Necip Ipar was best man, with Mrs. Burden matron of honor. Stanley Briggs was about to give the bride away, when another disturbance suddenly sprang up.[61] As the bride-to-be, dashing fiancé, and guests waited for the strains of the wedding march, two Beverly Hills police officers appeared with a warrant for Ali's arrest. Everything came to a halt. The warrant charged that Ipar had ignored a citation accusing him of running through a red light on June 25th. He nervously posted a $25 bond and agreed to a court hearing the next Tuesday. He was not to leave town. Guests remained to witness the far-from-dull ceremony and wedding vows. Afterwards, perturbed by the humiliating disturbance, Ipar exclaimed, "What next?"[62]

Indeed, "*What next?*," Virginia should have asked herself. An aborted film production, low on cash, an Army investigation, a warrant for his arrest from the Beverly Hills police, a court subpoena — if she wasn't seeing multiple red flags by now, perhaps she was choosing to turn a blind eye. The honeymoon was cut short – military orders. Major General Paul W. Kendall summoned Ipar back to Fort Lewis, immediately, for further investigation. On August 30th, Ipar anxiously booked air passage for Seattle. "I can't understand it," he told the press, "I asked for a week's leave to be married . . . there was no finagling about it." When asked why she wasn't joining him on board the plane, Virginia simply stated, "I'd love to go with him, but I can't leave the children."[63] The misadventures continued when Ipar's plane was grounded by the weather. He found himself marooned in Portland with 150 other passengers. He hopped the first northbound bus for Ft. Lewis where he would be, according to the general, "dealt with accordingly."[64]

As it turned out, Ipar's acquisition of army passes had been the responsibility of a non-commissioned officer who, according to General Kendall, was charged "guilty of a gross error or gross negligence." A sergeant had signed the passes not realizing all three were for the same man.[65] But the *real* mystery that no one could explain was why Ipar, a Turkish national, was drafted into the army in the first place. Not even the Army could produce an answer to that question. Outsmarting everyone, Ipar applied for discharge as a father. On September 11th, Pvt. Ipar became Private Citizen Ipar – "as a bridegroom with family responsibilities."[66] Ali was released under the father classification on grounds that Susan Ann and Christopher were now his legal responsibility. He arrived at Lockheed air terminal at 10:05 p.m. that same evening. In the middle of a bustling crowd, Ipar stood, clutching a dozen red roses, and waited for Virginia. Witnesses said he looked "gloomy and furtive." Perhaps he believed an early edition of the news which stated that Virginia was preparing a royal welcome home for her new husband. When she didn't show up at all, he took a taxi. *The Los Angeles Times* later reported that Virginia had been "closeted in her palatial Pacific Palisades home" selecting wallpapers and deciding on draperies with her interior decorator. When asked about Ali's arrival, Virginia told the press she was "too tired" to meet him at the airport.[68] Desiring some semblance of normalcy after her dramatic two-week marriage, Virginia's attitude was understandable.

Apparently, Ali's red roses and a night of lovemaking made the nighttime long enough and the dawn bright enough for a new beginning. The following day, Virginia and Ali began what the press referred to as the "second installment of their honeymoon." Ali stood before reporters to say that after a brief rest, he would start writing a book. Before photographers started shooting, Virginia smiled happily, kicked off her shoes (so she would appear a bit shorter next to Ipar) and said, "Now we can have a *real* honeymoon. I just hope there's nothing else left to go wrong."[69] There would be. Plenty.

Endnotes

1   Jack G. Shaheen, *Real Bad Arabs – How Hollywood Vilifies a People*, Olive Brand Pr. N.Y., 2001 pg 43

2   News item, "Casting About," *Port Arthur News(TX)*, 12/12/43

3   Bosley Crowther, review of *Action in Arabia*, New York Times, 2/19/44

4   Wood Soanes, review of *Action in Arabia*, Oakland Tribune, 3/31/45

5   News article, "Will Rogers' son Beats Ford for Seat in Congress," *Fresno Bee*, 11/4/42

6   News article, "Virginia Bruce Is Candidate For Legislature," *Fargo Forum*, 2/28/44

7   News article, "Movie Stars Visit Camp of Migrants to Cheer Children," *Oakland Tribune*, 12/24/38

8   Erskine Johnson, "In Hollywood," 2/8/44

9   Hedda Hopper, "Looking at Hollywood," *LA Times*, 2/19/44

10   Louella Parsons column, *Modesto Bee*, 3/1/44

11   Helen Gahagan Douglas, *A Full Life*, Doubleday & Co. (NY), c 1982, pg 136-137

12   INS news article, "Virginia Bruce Declines Politics," *Long Beach Ind.*, 2/14/44

13   Ibid

14   Karen Foerstel, *Biographical Dictionary of Congressional Women*, pg 64

15   J. David Golden, www.radiogoldindex.com, c. 2006

16   Frederick C. Othman, "Dewey Looks to Square Meal After Hungry Day on Coast," *Ogden Standard Examiner(UT)*, 9/23/44

17   Patricia Clary (UP), "Film Stars Tell committee About Hollywood Reds," *Yuma Weekly*, 5/16/47

18   Ibid

19   Helen Gahagan Douglas, *A Full Life*, Doubleday & Co. (NY), c 1982, pg 233

20   Mary V. Hughes, review of *Tricky Dick and the Pink Lady*, *San Francisco Chronicle*, 1/25/1998

21   News article, "Fear of Bosses Keeps Stars Clear of Politics," *Long Beach Ind. (CA)*, 11/2/50

22   Gahagan Douglas, *A Full Life*, pg 332

23   Estella Hillegas, "Syracuse Alum Only woman to Run for U.S. Presidency," *Syracuse Herald*, 1/18/57

24   "Palisadians Name 'Mayor," *LA Times*, 3/29/44

25   March Townsley, review of *Brazil*, *Austin American*, 2/28/45

26   A.W. review of *Brazil*, *New York Times*, 11/20/44

27   Jimmy Fidler, review of *Brazil*, *Nevada State Journal*, 11/4/44

28   Bosley Crowther review of *Love, Honor, and Goodbye*, *New York Times*, 9/8/45

29   Frank Morriss review of *Love, Honor, and Goodbye*, *Winnipeg Free Press*, 6/27/46

30   Jeanine Basinger, *A Woman's View*, Knopf, N.Y., 1993, pp 346-347

31   Ibid

32   Louella Parsons column, *Charleston Gazette*, 8/28/45

33   Louella Parsons column, *Modesto Bee*, 12/25/44

34   news item, author's collection, "Virginia Bruce says . . . " c. 1945

35   Inga Arvad, "Virginia Bruce's Daughter Desires Swimming Pool," *Kingsport News (TN)*, 10/7/43

36   Robbin Coons, "Hollywood," *The Capital, (MD)*, 11/1/43

37   Louella Parsons column, *Lowell Sun (MA)*, 1/21/46

38   Louella Parsons column, *Charleston Gazette*, 2/25/46

39   Louella Parsons column, *Charleston Gazette*, 3/13/46

40   Dan Walker, news column, "Along Broadway," 3/16/46

41   Walter Winchell column, *Port Arthur News (TX)*, 3/14/46

42   Louella Parsons column, *Modesto Bee*, 3/27/46

43   Ibid

44   "Virginia Bruce Home, but No Suitors at Depot," *LA Times*, 3/24/46

45   Mystery Concerning Virginia Bruce Cleared," *LA Times*, 3/22/46

46   Ibid

47   "Virginia Bruce Home, but No . . . "

48   *Stars and Stripes*, 9/4/46

49   Wood Soanes review of *Chocolate Soldier*, *Oakland Tribune*, 4/3/43

50 Mustapha Bedouin, "Turkey Freed Her Women – Now They Make Nation Independent," *Olean Times-Herald (NY)*, 3/19/43

51 "Private Heads for Honeymoon," *Lima News*, 9/14/46

52 "Bitten by Turkish Hubby; Gets Divorce," *Long Beach Ind.*, 12/1/44

53 "Friends Tell How Actor Was Hit On Jaw by Coast Guard Officer," *Modesto Bee*, 3/18/46

54 "Way Cleared for Marriage of Star," *Middletown Times (NY)*, 8/27/46

55 "Army's Face Red; Ali Freed to Wed Star," *Syracuse Herald*, 8/27/46

56 Ibid

57 "Wedding Plans of Actress Hit Snag," *Frederick Post (MD)*, 8/27/46

58 Ibid

59 "Way Cleared for Marriage of Star," *Middletown Times (NY)*, 8/27/46

60 Ibid

61 "Virginia Bruce Weds Private Despite Guardhouse Delays," *Stars and Stripes*, 8/30/46

62 "Turk Weds Virginia Bruce After Two Tussles With Law," *Coschoctun Tribune*, 8/28/46

63 "General Beckons Honeymooning G.I.," *Joplin Globe*, 8/31/46

64 "Weather Adds Bump To 'Pass' Hubby's Bumpy Honeymoon," *Fresno Bee*, 8/31/46

65 "Army Cuts Star's Honeymoon," *Oakland Tribune*, 8/30/46

66 "Pvt. Ali Ipar Getting His Release From Army," *Walla Walla Union*, 9/11/46

67 "Film Star Plans to Greet Spouse," *Nevada State Journal*, 9/12/46

68 "Ipar Back With Bride, Out of Army," *Los Angeles Times*, 9/12/46

69 "Virginia Bruce and Her Turkish Bridegroom Begin Second Installment of Army-Halted Honeymoon," *Oakland Tribune*, 9/12/46

CHAPTER 15:

"Living In A Dream World"

Although the army released Ali Ipar due to his responsibilities as husband and father, it wouldn't be long before he was making plans to leave the U.S. But first, Virginia had to nurse him through a long bout with pneumonia, which meant her backing out of Republic's *Wyoming*. Described as a strong emotional role in which she would also sing, the part was given to Virginia Grey, Clark Gable's current flame. In mid-November Louella told the sad news, "With her husband in the hospital and both of her children ill, Virginia Bruce has decided that she is more needed at home than on a movie set."[1] Virginia then contracted with Warner Brothers for her Technicolor debut as the turn-of-the-century sensation Lillian Russell in *My Wild Irish Rose*. The film musical planned to reunite her with tenor Dennis Morgan, and would give her the opportunity to sing Russell's trademark hit, "Come Down Ma Evenin' Star." Ali's recovery took longer than expected. Andrea King was summoned as a last-minute replacement for Virginia, and King (who was dubbed) received excellent reviews in the third-billed part.

In a difficult decision, Virginia parted with the Colonial home that she and Ruben had built. She explained to Louella

Parsons, "I sold [my home] to Deanna Durbin. I felt I wanted to start my married life with Ali in my new house on Amalfi Drive."[2] Virginia soon learned that Ipar was stressed financially. For all the press Ipar received substantiating his family's wealth, apparently he was out of cash. In January 1947, it was reported, "Virginia Bruce and her husband Ali Ipar will leave town in a few weeks en route to Turkey where they will try to latch onto some of the money Ali has there."[3] When the time came, Ipar went alone. Before his departure, Virginia reached into her own pocketbook as provider, while Ali fulfilled his ambition as a Hollywood writer. He was among no less than *five* males who hacked away on the Nazi-*noir* exploiter *Women in the Night*. The film's prologue establishes its 'authenticity' by exposing files inside the United Nations with document headings such as "Women Torn to Pieces by Dogs." On screen we are spared *that* degradation. The actual story takes place in Shanghai after Germany's defeat, and involves a cosmic death ray developed by Nazis who operate a classy officer's club. They plan to deploy the death-ray and triumph in World War III! When Japanese Colonel Richard Loo and his underlings arrive in Shanghai to horn in, the Nazis distract them with enslaved call-girls, who have their own secret operation assisting the Allies. Amidst these intrigues, a lesbian liaison in *Women in the Night* got past the censors. A female Nazi guard, Frau Thaler, coos to an attractive brunette, "I haven't seen you all evening. I've missed you." The brunette says nothing, but gives Thaler a smoldering once over, thus offering the most sexually-charged exchange in the film. "That's a very *strange* pair!" comments a bystander. Visually, the film is little more than a lopsided male sexual fantasy. Director William Rowland (who was to have directed Virginia in Ipar's ill-fated *Accusation*) positions his camera as he would a voyeur for scenes of abuse and seduction.

Fortunately, the blonde lead was *not* Virginia Bruce, but Virginia Christine (TV's future Folgers coffee icon, Mrs. Olsen). Christine was used as "white" bait to lure a prominent Japanese professor (Philip Ahn) into his hotel room for a convenient back-stabbing. Tala Birell, "Garbo of the B's," is the sacrificial lamb who saves the day and "blows up the joint." *Women in the Night* was shot at Playa Ensenada Hotel in Mexico *after* Ipar had left for Turkey. With minimal release, Ipar's Hollywood legacy created less than a ripple. After observing "a thoroughly uneasy cast," *The New York Times* called *Women in the Night,* "A sorry little melodrama . . . feeble fiction . . . shoddy and familiar stuff."[4] Surprisingly, the film resurfaced in the 1960s as *Curse of a Teenage Nazi.*

Virginia fraternizes with Jennifer Jones at party, 1947

If Ipar was indeed out of funds, Virginia's radio work more than compensated. When film offers weren't forthcoming, she did numerous broadcasts. One standout performance for Virginia was on the popular radio series *Suspense.* The long-running (1942-62) show was most famous for Agnes Moorehead's riveting performance in *Sorry, Wrong Number.* In *Knight Comes Riding,* Virginia convincingly struck a similar dramatic chord as a love-starved, middle-aged housewife stuck in an unhappy marriage. When her favorite nephew is found dead in her garage, she suspects her husband of the crime. Instead of reporting her suspicions to the police, she becomes sidetracked by a handsome stranger (Howard Duff). Duff charms her into hiring him as a handyman. Before long, Virginia confides to the radio-listener, "I was in love! Falling in love with a boy *years* younger than myself – a stranger that I'd only known a few short weeks. I knew I was living in a dream world and that I'd have to wake up some day. But, I didn't care!" In keeping with *Suspense* radio's tradition, we find out in the last few seconds that Duff is not the shining knight he appears to be. To what extent the dire aspects of Virginia's role in *Knight Comes Riding* would carry over into her personal life with Ipar only time would tell. Newspapers had mentioned that Ali was eleven years younger than Virginia, but, unlike her radio character, no one suspected her of living in a dream world from which she would never wake up.

Radio kept Virginia busy until her next film assignment in the fall of 1947. Her previous success in broadcasts of *Talk of the Town* with Ronald Colman, *The Prisoner of Zenda* with Douglas Fairbanks, Jr., *The Moon is Our Home* with Fred MacMurray, and *Stagecoach* with John Hodiak had radio producers begging for more. She was paged nine times (1937-47) for the popular *Lux Radio Theater — My Favorite Blonde* with Bob Hope and *Pride of the Yankees* with Gary Cooper being two of the most popular of her entries. Producer Mark Hellinger selected Virginia and Humphrey Bogart for the Lux presentation of John O'Hara's *noir*-ish thriller *Moontide*. Virginia, as a suicidal young woman, and Bogart, as the boozing dock-worker who saves her life, cre-ated a memorable program. After pulling her unconscious body out of the Pacific, Bogie gives Virginia a few slugs of whiskey ("Okay, sister! Come on take it!"). By the next morning she's fixing him breakfast and listening to his advice. "If you smiled once and awhile," Bogie tells her, "you wouldn't be a bad lookin' tomato!" Bogart's gruff exterior breaks through Virginia's pessimism to reveal a vulnerable tenderness in them both. *Devotion*, Virginia's final Lux appearance, was broadcast in February 1947. She played *Jane Eyre* author Charlotte Bronte. It is one of the few instances of an actress having played both the author and the title role of the author's most famous work. *Devotion* also starred Jane Wyman (replacing Ida Lupino) as Emily Bronte. Entertaining, if not historically accurate, *Devotion* relates how the Bronte sisters quarrel, cry, and love in their Yorkshire moor-surroundings. Vincent Price, playing the curate Nichols, shows up to pull the sisters' heartstrings. Price seems more interested in the sisters' hapless, alcoholic and artistic brother Branwell, who hastens Price to the attic to show him his "paintings." Price pays the price for these "masterpieces," thus allowing the sisters to leave for Belgium where they pursue writing careers. After heralded success, Virginia returns home to ask Price why he is avoiding her. "I want to protect myself from liking you too much!" he explains. Brother Branwell continues to hold more interest for the curate. "I find Branwell's attempts to shock me *most* diverting," Price confesses. In truth, Nichols and Charlotte married (she died during childbirth). Virginia's best line in *Devotion* was her confession, "I know nothing! I understand nothing! Yet I have dared to write 200,000 words about life!"

It was tradition for Lux performers to have a chat with host Cecil B. DeMille after the 2-3-act presentation. After both *Moontide* and *Devotion* broadcasts, Virginia mentioned her penchant for raising and riding horses. At the time, horseracing was rated "King of Sports," second in popularity to American League Baseball. Virginia still maintained her stables on the acreage she

Virginia was a popular 'voice' on radio. Seen here during a CBS broadcast of Edna Ferber's *So Big* for *Hallmark Playhouse*, co-starring Jeff Chandler. (February 24, 1949) (Courtesy of CBS/Photofest)

had purchased with Ruben, called "Wildtree." She joked with DeMille that her filly's fastest time "was from the barn door to the feedbox." Virginia's collection of iron horseshoes worn by famous racers (which had become her favorite hobby) was steadily growing and bringing her luck. She was adding horseshoes worn by her own racehorses. Lady Morvich, who paid $49.40 to place

334

and $16.90 to show, during a fall 1946 race, was a celebrity in her own right. Another winning filly was Lady Bruce. Virginia co-owned this horse with director John Huston. The three-year-old filly won several races at Bay Meadows in San Mateo. At the $25,000 Hollywood Oaks race in June 1948, Lady Bruce rated as the pace maker for the one-mile event. "Lady Bruce," stated one report, "owned by Virginia Bruce and John Huston . . . has beaten Speculation, winner of last week's Will Rogers Handicap."[5] In his autobiography, *An Open Book*, Huston gave the inside dope on just how good Virginia's expertise was when it came to horses:

> Virginia had been married to John Gilbert and
> after his death she inherited a number of horses
> – about which she knew nothing. She said to me,
> 'John, will you take them? We'll go partners.' . . .
> when we put [Lady Bruce] into training as a
> yearling, we saw pretty soon that [she] was very
> fast. We sent her to be schooled under a trainer I
> didn't know, someone Virginia had recommended.
> The horse developed into a grand-looking mare.
> There was no doubt she was going to win races[6]

Virginia and Huston entered Lady Bruce into an important race at Santa Anita. At the time, Huston was directing the Bogart-Bacall classic *Key Largo*. He was heavily in debt and desperately in need of cash. He was so sure of Lady Bruce that he had *Largo's* cast and crew place bets on her. As Huston was shooting at Warners the day of the race, he gave his wife, actress Evelyn Keyes, all he could scrape up to place on his prize-winning horse. (This included every penny he had in the bank, a loan of $2,000 from Anatole Litvak, and $2,000 more from William Wyler.) Lady Bruce pulled through! "I could scarcely contain myself," remembered Huston. "This was perhaps the greatest news I'd ever received. One minute I'd been scraping the bottom of the barrel, and the next minute – thanks to this marvelous animal – I was rolling in dough. . . . I could now shed the nagging debts that interfered with my life style."[7] Huston prepared to celebrate at the popular Hollywood restaurant Chasen's. Much to Huston's dismay, he learned through the grapevine that Keyes had *not* followed his instructions. She put the money on a loser named Dry instead! Lady Bruce had paid $26.80 for $2.00. Keyes was terrified to face her husband. Stunned, but ever the gentleman, he sent a message for her not to worry and meet the party at Chasen's. She called him at the restaurant first and attempted to explain her actions. Initially, Huston told her "it was only money." She persisted in offering a variety of lame excuses, when Huston suddenly blurted out, "You bitch! You dismal, wretched, silly bitch!" and hung up. "Evelyn did come to Chasen's," Huston recalled, "but, by the time she got there I was so drunk I didn't even recognize her."[8]

Huston's memoir was mistaken on how Virginia "inherited" her horses. Horse fancier Mel Heimer set the record straight in his syndicated column "My New York," stating:

> Miss Bruce's connection with the turf is [as] breeder and owner. A few years ago she was married to Jack Ruben . . . He had a string of polo ponies, and he and Virginia got interested in racing and they set out to breed racehorses. Then, there was a filly named Eternal Lady, beautifully bred, with bloodlines and nicks and Lord knows what all the way back to the great sprinter Eternal, but she was one of those unhappy creatures who darken

the world of the two-buck player by collapsing at
the top of the stretch. . . . Virginia retired her from
racing and bred her to the Kentucky Derby winner
of 1922 Morvich. The result was a filly about the
size of a small hummingbird, called Lady Morvich.
[This was the filly that Virginia assisted in birth
during the middle of the night – she told Heimer
flatly, "It was the most beautiful thing I ever
have seen in my life."] It wasn't long before Lady
Morvich came home at the Del Mar at $214 – the
highest odds [on a $2 pari-mutual bet] ever paid at
that track.

"And how much did Miss Bruce clean up?" asked Heimer. "Oh, I
never bet on horses away from the track," said Virginia. Heimer
gasped, "You mean?" Virginia nodded. "Not a thin dime. Darn
it!" "I think she could be a little more emphatic than that," the
exasperated Heimer wrote in his column. "Where's our profanity
expert? Miss Jones, get me the White House!"[9]

Ali Ipar's visit to Turkey in early 1947 was brief. New York passenger lists indicate that he returned to the U.S. on April 14,
three days after Virginia's mother had passed away. Margaret
Morris Briggs was 63, and died of cardiac arrest. She had battled
heart disease for over ten years.[11] She was cremated and placed
to rest at Forest Lawn. Virginia inherited her parents' home
on Fordyce Road, and Stanley received $10,000. News reports
stated that no provision was made for Earll Briggs, as he would
be "adequately provided for by Miss Bruce."[12] Long before her

mother's unexpected death, Virginia had promised to host the wedding of MGM writer Frederick Stephani at her home. (She had befriended Stephani while on the set of 1937's *Between Two Women*.) Helping her through a difficult time and with her commitment to host Stephani's wedding, Ali assisted with the preparations. Virginia and Ali stood in as matron of honor and best man for the ceremony.

Susan Ann, approaching fifteen, was allowed her first "grown-up" date. Before this momentous event took place, Virginia insisted on riding along for a test drive with Susan's escort — "to make *sure* he was a safe driver."[13] Shortly before Susan's birthday, Ali got word that he would have to return to Turkey. His father was suffering with a serious illness. Virginia had just contracted with Paramount to play opposite Edward G. Robinson in *Night Has a Thousand Eyes*. Having excused herself from *Wyoming* and *My Wild Irish Rose*, she dared not back out of another film production. "[Ali's] father is 65 and right now he needs help," Virginia explained. "I plan to visit him as soon as I finish this picture and I'll probably stay over there three months. I wouldn't mind living in Turkey permanently if it wasn't for the children."[14] Louella Parsons mentioned the couple's farewell dinner at the popular Seacomber's restaurant. A month later, the columnist stated, "I doubt very much Virginia will join [Ipar] as she first planned. Too many things involved."[15] She was right.

As it turned out, Virginia was unable to get into Turkey and Ali was unable to return to the United States. She had been informed that it would be at least three years before Ali could be readmitted.[16] Ipar's previous visa had been for five years. Turkish officials, dismissive of Ipar's responsibilities as husband and father, stated there were "no grounds on which to grant Ipar a visa."[17] They saw him as only a potential immigrant. By November, Virginia was "threatening" Turkish generals who were visiting the United States, saying she would go to Turkey and live with Ipar if he was not allowed back into the U.S. under the quota.

Besides visa problems, Virginia admitted that business affairs were also keeping Ali abroad. She told Harrison Carroll that "love will outweigh career" if Ipar stayed abroad indefinitely.[18] As far as her immediate plans, Virginia told reporters, "If I do hear from him that he can't come over, I'll go over there in time for me to be back by Christmas with my two children."[19] Virginia also formulated a plan to take her children to Istanbul, where her father-in-law (who apparently was on the mend) owned an apartment building that provided an entire floor for each of his children. After several attempted meetings with government officials in Washington, D.C., to no avail, Virginia sailed to Europe. "Ali met me at the boat at Southampton, England," she wistfully reminisced afterwards. "We went to Paris for a week. We moved on to the chateau of my husband's family in Nice. We spent idyllic weeks there, then we went to St. Moritz for New Year's, and, for awhile, to Lausanne, Switzerland. Finally I had to come back because of my children."[20] On a subsequent trip to rendezvous with Ipar, Virginia was not as fortunate. The odds were against a second meeting. While staying in St. Moritz, she ran into Jennifer Jones and recounted her dilemma. The trip was a huge disappointment. She returned to New York on February 9 feeling dejected and defeated. "Virginia Bruce has just returned from Switzerland and France," reported Louella Parsons, "but was not permitted to go into Turkey to see [Ipar] and he could not get permission to visit her in Europe. The Turkish immigration quota is filled for the next 20 years and unless some exception is made in Ipar's case there is small hope of Virginia ever seeing her husband – which is tragic."[21] Hedda Hopper apparently had no sympathy for Virginia's situation, and snapped, "Virginia Bruce is working harder to get her husband, Ali Ipar, back into this country than she ever did at acting."[22]

At the end of April, Ali mysteriously arrived in London where he was reportedly meeting with American Ambassador Douglas in order to "get back to his bride."[23] In the meantime, Virginia persisted in sending attorneys to Washington to press her case for Ali's return. For all her hard work, some of Virginia's intimates began to wonder if Ipar was on the up and up. Jimmy Fidler was one to second guess the situation and stated, "Look for divorce proceedings to be filed by Virginia Bruce against her Turkish spouse Ali, who, rumor has it, could have had a passport to return to the USA anytime he wanted one."[24] What eventually resolved the Ipar-Bruce dilemma plays out like the unlikely conclusion of a Hollywood movie. Syndicated columnist Leonard Lyons reported that the young daughter of an influential Californian was concerned about the predicament of Virginia Bruce, one of her favorite stars. The girl requested that her father help the actress remedy Ipar's involuntary exile. The "influential Californian" (who remained anonymous) met with Virginia, and promised, "I'll get it done." Virginia reportedly shrugged, "Oh, sure." "I'll get in touch with George and Alben," he assured her. "Oh sure," Virginia repeated. Two weeks later Ali Ipar had his visa and was back in California.[25] It turned out that "George" was George Marshall, 5-Star General, *Time* magazine's "Man of the Year" in 1944, and the current U.S. Secretary of State. "Alben" was Alben Barkley, the U.S. Senate majority leader, and about to become the next vice-president of the United States.

Virginia met Ali on the east coast for their third "happy reunion" since marriage. They arrived in Hollywood on July 18th, where they were greeted by Susan Ann and Christopher at the train depot. News items indicated that Virginia "finally obtained [Ipar's] entry as a non-quota immigrant, which means that he may remain in the country permanently."[26] "Permanently" is not what Ali had in mind. He simply stated that he was back "for as long as I want to stay."[27] The next evening Virginia and Ali celebrated with the children at Seacombers. The couple planned for a third honeymoon at the Del Mar Turf and Surf Hotel. Nearby, they could attend the races. News reporter Edith Gwynn ran into Virginia in the corridors at NBC radio and commented, "A happier gal we've never seen beaming. [Virginia] was saying, 'I've got him back for keeps – no visa, no quota number – no nothing'!"[28]

In the spring of 1948, producer Bob Roberts arranged a deal with Virginia to co-star with John Garfield. Filming was to start in mid-May. Virginia's dilemma with Ipar culminated with her being left out of one of the best *film noirs*, *Force of Evil*. Containing one of Garfield's trademark performances, *Force of Evil*, adapted from Ira Wolfert's novel *Tucker's People*, was a dark, despairing, portrait of America that equated the illegal numbers game with capitalism. Virginia was slated to play the seductive Mrs. Tucker whose charms fail to intrigue Garfield. Marie Windsor took over the brief, but memorable role.

Virginia found radio not as grueling a commitment as film, and stuck to it. Aside from co-hosting the NBC talk show *Let's Talk Hollywood* with Pat O'Brien, Virginia co-starred with O'Brien in the 1948 summer series *The Dan Carson Story* (also known as *Rexall Theatre*). She was a replacement for Lynn Bari.

Oakland Tribune critic John Crosby wasn't impressed with the storyline. "This program is particularly distressing," commented Crosby, who then detailed why:

> Dan Carson . . . is one of those relentless do-gooders, sort of a Big Sister in pants, who helps the daylights out of people whether they like it or not. He is played by Pat O'Brien who . . . rather specializes in altruism. Helping him help, is Virginia Bruce, whose heart is also swollen with selflessness. I must admit Miss Bruce on one glorious occasion made a sensible remark. In a fit of exasperation which unfortunately proved temporary, she exclaimed: 'Oh, Danny. I sometimes get very angry at you for mixing in other people's lives.' Out of a sense of duty, I append the briefest possible synopsis of a single episode. A bunch of young city toughs come to O'Brien's lovable little town, are reclaimed from utter damnation by winning a footrace with the local kids, and leave town fine and upstanding young citizens, potential Presidents every one of them. Come along Tiny Tim. I'll match you for the drinks."[29]

In an interview for *Radio Life*, Virginia admitted, "Radio I love best of all. I've wanted to do a regular program for so long." Of all her radio appearances, she was partial to the *Suspense* episode *The Night Man* (1944). The chilling tale had Virginia trapped in an elevator with an escaped convict. "Hysterical scary," Virginia described it, "got to work behind a screen and on filter . . . very exciting."[30] When asked about her all-time favorite film role, she

The Dan Carson Story (1948) rehearsing with co-star Pat O'Brien

selected the part of Audrey Dane in *The Great Ziegfeld*. "It was a small part," Virginia said, "but different from anything I had ever done – and I was always rather proud that I did it in one take." During the interview, which took place at her home, Virginia said that Christopher and Susan "listened attentively" to her radio work. Christopher, 6, would ask, "Did you really cry?" to which Virginia answered, "Sometimes I really did." Virginia mentioned Susan's "excellent singing voice" at school presentations, and her own desire for more time to play golf (admitting that she had inherited her mother's aptitude). *Radio Life's* reporter was intermittently interrupted by the sound of an electric train coming from upstairs. Virginia, giving a glance upwards, laughingly confided, "It's really Chris who makes things hectic around here. We both had a fine time this morning just screaming at each other!"[31]

For a Mother's Day special in 1948, Mutual Broadcasting's *Family Theatre* co-starred Virginia with child star Dean Stockwell in *Mother's Halo Was Tight*. Virginia's character reflects on modern motherhood, feeling that, since 1913, when Mother's Day became an official holiday, many women had let their "halos" go to their head. "Let's admit," Virginia tells a progressive women's group, "that many times it's the families that raise us!" She recalls the time an annoying neighbor telephoned with an "emergency" asking Virginia to baby sit. She didn't want to, but her son (Stockwell) had answered the phone and knew full well the situation. His big blue eyes stared at her while she grappled with whether to make up a phony excuse. After a deliberating pause, she replied, "I'll be right over!" Virginia concluded saying, "Modern mothers don't want reverence, but we've got to wear a halo even if it fits too tight." Halo in tact, Virginia made a decision that must have pleased her own children. She volunteered to join 209 celebrities in the Ringling Brothers parade for St. John's Hospital in Santa Monica. She decorated a float along with Betty Grable, Elizabeth

September 1948 – Virginia in Hollywood's Ringling Brothers parade

Taylor, and Lizabeth Scott. News coverage of the event stated, "Greer Garson topped them all by riding atop an elephant. Ronald Colman, Frank Sinatra, Bing Crosby, and Van Johnson dressed as clowns, but couldn't compete with Carmen Miranda, with a two-foot pile of artificial fruit on her head prancing along with a clown dressed just like her."[32]

In September 1948, Virginia made her final appearance on *Suspense* playing the wife of Robert Young. *Celebration* told the story of husband Young coping with his wife's mental illness from a brain injury. During his weekly visit to the sanatorium where she resides, Young takes her for a scenic drive. Virginia holds the listeners' attention as she displays symptoms of acute hypnomania (paranoia, memory loss, highs and lows) which have lessened the quality of her life, and diminished her relationships. In a painfully realistic moment, she realizes that Young intends to take both their lives with a revolver he has in the car. "I love you more than *living*," Young explains. "It's the only way we can be together. Now, rest against me, sweetheart. Close your eyes." Virginia recognizes and trusts "something" in his voice. Closing her eyes, she asks him, "Will it hurt much, Todd? The gun is so cold on my temple." Suddenly she panics — the gun goes off! The next thing she's aware of is the smell of a hospital, and Young's voice, saying, "When the time came, I couldn't do it!" Virginia had been hit, but the surgery which dislodged the bullet relieved the pressure from her previous injury, thus resolving her problem. (The story ignores the obvious complications arising from what would have appeared to be a husband attempting to murder his mentally ill wife.) A good script by Phyllis Parker kept the tension taut while providing human insight into Virginia and Young's supposedly doomed relationship. *Celebration* was one of the series acclaimed presentations, and received an encore in 1957 with a different cast. By strange coincidence, shortly before the broadcast, Virginia's uncle, Ben Morris, a night watchman at Universal-International in Hollywood, killed himself with a revolver. Morris, Margaret's brother, had been in ill health for several years. He and his wife Hilda were living in North Hollywood.[33]

In October 1948, Paramount released director John Farrow's *Night Has a Thousand Eyes*. It had been a year since the film's completion and three years since Virginia had been on screen. She had a striking new look with her hair pulled back in a stylish bun. Fourth-billed, she managed to impress in a flashback

Night Has a Thousand Eyes (1948) with Edward G. Robinson (Paramount)

sequence as the assistant (and fiancée) to a vaudeville mental-ist (Edward G. Robinson). To his dismay, Robinson's character discovers his clairvoyant gift is genuine. One evening during his act, Robinson turns to Virginia and stops cold. Visually upset, he demands they bring down the curtain. Later, Virginia confronts him. "It was something you *saw*, wasn't it?" she asks him. "Something you saw about *me*." "Don't be silly," says Robinson, wanting to change the subject. "I don't mind if you don't want to tell me," Virginia persists. "Just so it doesn't make any difference about our loving each other."

What Robinson had "seen" compelled him to disappear from Virginia's life. He hoped it would save her. He was wrong. Virginia eventually marries someone else, and as Robinson had foreseen, dies during childbirth. The story jumps into the present where the reclusive Robinson contacts Virginia's daughter, Gail Russell. (Originally, Virginia look-alike Joan Caulfield was assigned to play the part, which explains Robinson's remark about the mother-daughter resemblance. According to Caulfield, director John Farrow's amorous attentions made her back out of the film.)[34] When Robinson reveals "visions" of disaster for *Russell*, John Lund, her sweetheart, thinks Robinson is a fake and involved in a confidence game. Lund notifies the police. The story intrigues up to this point, but the finish is unsatisfying. Still, Robinson shines as a true *noir* figure doomed by his knowledge, and unable to save his own skin.

Robinson's performance was unhampered by the fact that he was targeted in the fall of 1947 by fellow actor Adolphe Menjou's "Hollywood is crawling with communists" speech for the HUAC.[35] The week following Menjou's diatribe, Robinson, a long-time liberal activist, asked permission to testify before the committee. His defense fell on deaf ears. The HUAC only wanted to hear Robinson confess that he had been "duped" by Communist-front organizations. He refused. He watched as his career became a shambles. "I became an absolute pariah," said Robinson.[36] The critics were mixed on *Night Has a Thousand Eyes*. *Newsweek* stated that "Robinson's brooding, doomful performance does a lot to establish the story's plausibility . . . John Farrow . . . stages it with a fair amount of suspense."[37] *The New Republic* said, "Robinson makes a credible warlock, but it's a foolish way for him to waste his talent."[38] Film critic Wood Soanes thought the film "eerie," mentioning the "forthright subordinate performance by Virginia Bruce."[39] The *LA Times* felt, "there is too little of Virginia Bruce."[40] Robinson would later refer to the film as "unadulterated hokum that I did for the money."[41] Although Virginia gave a strong showing in a small role, the outcome echoed her early days at Paramount – a film career that was going nowhere. And for that, she signed with Sigmund Neufeld Productions (Film Classics) for a poverty-row exploiter that vied *Women in the Night* for incredulity.

The faux-documentary *State Department – File 649* fits snugly into the undiplomatic genre of "whites menaced by 'yellow peril'" – something that should have been put out to pasture long before. The film's prologue provides picturesque views of the nation's capitol, while the narrator cheerily announces, "Washington is no longer the capitol of the United States – it is the capitol of the world!" It is *State Department – File 649*'s first task to explain why. It does this by providing a romantic interlude for Virginia and William Lundigan while they are parked in his convertible at the foot of the Lincoln Memorial, and facing the phallic obelisk known as the Washington Monument. All passion is focused on their hopes and dreams for keeping the long arms of America "reaching into every corner of the globe." And, *that* was not an easy job. Americans were having their tongues cut out and arms lopped off in nasty, out-of-the-way places.

In *State Department*, Richard Loo (resurrected from being blown to smithereens in *Women in the Night*) is now Marshal Yun Usu, implementing his reign of terror in Mongolia. He does this, we are led to believe, while driving his luxury mobile home around the remote Mongolian countryside. Loo has a particular distaste for nosey American diplomats such as Virginia and Lundigan. Lundigan is the new vice-consul for Mingoo, described as a "listening post" in Usu's territory. Virginia arrives in Mingoo soon afterwards. Her assignment? Well, as she says, "it just isn't easy to explain." After conferring with the Marshal in his luxury mobile home, Virginia emerges to announce, "The Marshal hates American women. He claims they don't know how to make love!" Hearing this, Lundigan is triggered to install a few sticks of dynamite under the Marshal's mobile home. What he didn't plan on is being blown up along with Usu before the final credits roll. At the finis, back in Washington, we find Virginia, swathed in mink, tears rolling down her face. She watches as Lundigan's name is etched onto a plaque for those who have lost lives keeping the long arms of America forever reaching . . . where they are not welcome. The *New York Times* surmised, "Film Classics hasn't broken new ground. Nor can we believe that its 'documentary' tribute is based on actual fact. . . . Nor can we report that William Lundigan is exactly credible, nor that anyone else in this drab thriller is either interesting or charming to behold."[42]

More interesting than the on-screen antics of *State Department* was the behind-the-scene news of the film's technical advisor, John E. Peurifoy. Harrison Carroll headlined a story in his column, which read:

> Everybody seems to have missed the irony of the
> fact that John E. Peurifoy, Assistant Secretary of
> State, is giving technical advice on Virginia Bruce's
> picture, *State Department – File 649*. For months
> Virginia tried to enlist the aid of Peurifoy and
> his aides in accruing permission for her Turkish
> husband, Ali Ipar, to return to this country.
> Virginia made a special trip to Washington to see
> Peurifoy but couldn't get to him.[43]

It seemed odd that Peurifoy would allocate time from his government position, and waste tax payers' dollars, to offer support for something as dismal and pointless as *State Department – File*

649. His avoidance of a citizen in crisis, such as Virginia, shows Peurifoy was little more than an opportunist. His career in politics is one of the most despicable on record. The year following the release of *State Department,* Peurifoy, as Undersecretary of State, coined the phrase "pervert peril" and began firing gays in government positions. As Ambassador to Guatemala (1953), Peurifoy recommended bombing Guatemala City to put an end to the country's infant democracy. Guatemala's established oligarchy, the Catholic Church and the United Fruit Company (an U.S.-based "Chiquita Banana" merchant, and Guatemala's largest landowner) didn't like the idea of tax legislation, educating Indians, providing health care, and creating a modern capitalist state. U.S. bombs would indeed burst the small nation's democratic 'bubble.'[44] So much for Peurifoy's talent as a diplomat, and the long arms of America "reaching out."

In the spring of 1949, Ali's mother, Mrs. Terhide Ipar (Terhide her maiden name), paid a visit to Amalfi Drive. She also spent time with Ali's brother, Mehmet, a student at Stanford University. On her return to Istanbul, she emphasized to reporter Frank Nye that Ali, "is better known in America as the husband of Virginia Bruce the movie actress."[45] This appeared to be an impossible legacy for Ali to overcome. His career as a Hollywood writer was going nowhere.

On August 24, 1949, Earll Briggs died in Pacific Palisades at the age of 65. News reports claimed he died of a heart ailment. By that time, a series of mini-strokes (or perhaps Alzheimer's) had lessened the quality of his life. When this author contacted Virginia's nephew, Vincent Briggs (Stanley's son), he remem-

State Department-File 649 (1949) with William Lundigan

bered being 10 years old when his grandfather died. "I have one memory of him," Vincent told me. "I was staying at Wildtree, Virginia's place, and I remember him chasing me. He was out of his mind at that time. That's the only memory I have of him."[46] Vincent's recollection may explain why Earll Briggs, the initial impetus behind Virginia's career, had been out of the news loop for several years.

Vincent's parents, Stanley and Mary Lawrence Briggs, divorced when he was five (1944). "When I was young, I didn't see much of my father," recalled Vincent. "I lived with my mother in New York. Stanley was an inventor. He invented all kinds of gadgets. He got them marketed. He did a lot through Bing Crosby Enterprises. There were a number of things he had on the market – a machine that painted golf balls – he did pretty well with that. After playing 18 holes, the ball would be painted to look brand new. He had a stainless-steel device used in conjunction with a toaster to create a melted cheese sandwich. That marketed pretty well."[47] In May 1948, Stanley "the inventor" married Buddy Ebsen's sister, Velma "the dancer." The couple had a son, Michael Magill Briggs (born in 1949), and lived close to Virginia in Pacific Palisades. Velma offered dancing classes at the Ebsen School of Dancing (which operated into the 1990s.)

In the fall of 1949, producer Mike Stokey persuaded Virginia to make her television debut on "the most successful program produced on the West Coast" – the Emmy-winning *Pantomime Quiz*. Based on the old parlor game, Virginia joined Stu Erwin and Howard Da Silva to help stump the regular guests during the shows second season. Television had become a virtual tidal wave in popularity. In 1949, the industry sold 950,000 sets; in 1950, over 2,000,000. Telephone callers, when interrupting a favorite television program, were learning to be as courteous as they would be interrupting dinner.

Virginia contracted with Columbia Pictures for the 1950 film release *Beauty on Parade*. The Wallace MacDonald story cast her as an aging beauty queen who tries to relive her past glories by promoting her daughter (Lola Albright) on the beauty-contest circuit. Due to contract disagreements, yet another role for Virginia bit the dust. Ruth Warrick stepped in as her replacement. Soon afterwards, Susan Ann Gilbert decided to make her own foray into the world of film. Along with Gloria Swanson's daughter, Micheline, and Mary Astor's daughter, Marilyn, Susan tested for the lead in director Ida Lupino's *Nobody's Safe*. As impressed as Lupino was with Susan, Mala Powers, who had acting experience as a child, got the part. Lupino's film, a courageous discourse on the subject of rape victims, was retitled *Outrage*.

Soon after Susan's screen test, Virginia was selected by one of America's top businesswomen to portray her life on *Cavalcade of America*. Rose Markward Knox, President of Knox Gelatin, insisted upon Virginia for the April 1950 presentation, *Lady of Jonestown*, broadcast from New York's Belasco Theatre.[48] Knox's choice was a testament to Virginia's strong showing in previous standout performances such as *The Girl Who Ran for President*. An innovative business woman, Rose Knox turned a strictly male profession on its ear. She instigated many employee benefits that today are taken for granted. She was the first employer (1913) to create a five-day work week and two weeks paid vacation (something unheard of). Knox guided her company safely through the Depression, not laying off a single employee. Virginia pulled the listener into Knox's tale with a voice tempered with age. "I want to tell you about a birthday party," she began. "It was mine – on that day I was 90 years old." During a flashback, widow Knox relates how she took over her husband's firm in 1908, with the idea of turning it over to her son James. She did -- when she was 90, and James was 55! Virginia's vocal dexterity, as young Rose/old Rose, was realistic, and her portrayal heartfelt. The program was a tribute to the strength and humanity of a woman who would be honored as New York State's "2007 Woman of Distinction" in their annual Women's History Month.

Virginia and Ali dining at Restaurant LaRue August 1948

In the spring of 1950, Virginia and Ipar thought seriously of relocating to Turkey. It was a decision that surely strained the marriage. In a previous interview Virginia had explained, "I could take my little boy, he's seven, but my daughter is fifteen and an American girl. Things would be very strange for her in Turkey."[49] Hedda Hopper hinted at the relationship's rough edges in her weekly gossip column. "If you hear Virginia Bruce and her mate Ali Ipar having an argument," Hopper blabbed, "pay no attention. It's just love."[50] Nothing had come of Ipar's film project *My Heart at Large*, which was to star Virginia and Glenn Ford. While the couple grappled with their next step, Virginia made TV commercials for Oldsmobile (at $1,000 per). She also made her television dramatic debut on a half-hour episode of *Silver Theater*, titled *Wedding Anniversary*. Her co-star from *Kongo*, Conrad Nagel, hosted the program which told of a confused woman who prepares to celebrate the anniversary of her second marriage on the date of her *first* wedding. The story was a precursor for the more serious complexities that faced Virginia Ipar.

Surprising no one, by summer, Ali and Virginia were celebrating their departure for Turkey with nights out on the town. One evening they sat ringside, along with Zsa Zsa Gabor and George Sanders, at "Negro song-thrush" Pearl Bailey's debut at the Macombo. The bawdy Bailey, fresh from punching out a lady heckler at New York's Greenwich Village Inn, broke house records wherever she played. In mid-June, Christopher, Virginia and Ali were aboard the *Queen Mary*, headed for Istanbul. (Susan would arrive later.) Virginia was the focus for ship photographers. A passenger from Fargo, Charlotte Treat, was studying a close-up of Virginia on the ship's bulletin board, when who should appear but Virginia herself! Virginia introduced husband Ali to Miss Treat and, the *Fargo Forum* reported, "they all had a nice chat."[51] Istanbul, a city rich in antiquity, was a far cry from Los Angeles, let alone Fargo. It was like taking a step into the ancient past. In its long history, Istanbul, the cultural and economic center of Turkey, had served as capital of the Roman Empire. Virginia's "dream world" with Ali was magically enveloped with palatial surroundings, a rich cultural heritage, and the warmth of Ipar's friends and family. But it was more than she had bargained for. Incredibly, Virginia was to find out that this "new life" in Turkey would make it necessary for her and Ali to divorce.

Endnotes

1 Louella Parsons column, *Syracuse Herald*, 11/15/46

2 Louella Parsons column, *Charleston Gazette*, 8/30/46

3 Dorothy Kilgallen, "Voice of Broadway," *Pottstown Mercury*, 1/1/47

4 Review of *Women in the Night*, New York Times, 1/12/48

5 "Fillies Will Seek Hollypark Victory," *Fresno Bee*, 6/4/48

6 John Huston, *An Open Book*, Da Capo Press, c 2001, pgs 156-157

7 Ibid

8 Huston, *An Open Book*, pg 159

9 Mel Heimer, "My New York," *Monessen Daily Independent (PA)*, 4/8/49

10 Dave Lewis, "Once Over Lightly," *Long Beach Independent*, 7/18/48

11 Margaret Morris Brigs, Certificate of Death, County of Los Angeles, 4/11/47 issued 4/12/47

12 "Virginia Bruce Shares in Her Mother's Estate," *LA Times*, 5/7/47

13 Hedda Hopper, "Looking at Hollywood," *Portland Press*, 5/10/47

14 John Todd, "Around Hollywood," *New Castle News(PA)*, 8/9/47

15 Louella Parsons column, *Middletown Times*, 9/23/47

16 Louella Parsons column, *Modesto Bee*, 11/19/47

17 "Virginia Bruce Will Visit Mate in Europe," *Modesto Bee*, 9/20/47

18 Harrison Carroll, "Behind the Scenes in Hollywood," *Bradford Era (PA)*, 9/2/47

19 "Ali Ipar, in Turkey, Faces Denial of Visa," *Walla Walla Union*, 9/21/47

20 Harrison Carroll, "Virginia Bruce's Interrupted Romance," *The American Weekly*, 5/30/48

21 Louella Parsons column, *Fresno Bee*, 2/16/48

22 Hedda Hopper, "Looking at Hollywood," *LA Times*, 4/2/48

23 Louella Parsons column, *Middletown Times (NY)*, 4/22/48

24 Jimmy Fidler, "In Hollywood," *Joplin Globe*, 6/6/48

25 Leonard Lyons, "Broadway Medley," *San Mateo Times*, 8/10/48

26 "U.S. Relents; Lets Groom In," *Long Beach Independent*, 7/19/48

27 "Virginia Bruce, Hubby Reunited," *Evening Gazette,(IN)*, 7/19/48

28 Edith Gwynn, "Hollywood," *Pottstown Mercury (PA)*, 7/23/48

29 John Crosby, "Do Good Program," *Oakland Tribune*, 7/9/48

30 Joan Buchanan, "Lovely to Look At – And Listen To," *Radio Life*, 7/4/48

31 ibid

32 "Movieland in Circus Romps for Charity," *Waterloo Daily Courier (IA)*, 9/6/48

33 News article, "Film Actress' Uncle Kills Self With Pistol," *Modesto Bee*, 8/19/48

34 Correspondence with archivist Howard Mandelbaum, 1/9/2008

35 "Movie Land Full of Reds Says Menjou," *Vidette-Messenger(IN)*, 10/21/47

36   Edward G. Robinson, "All My Yesterdays," Hawthorne Books, N.Y., 1973, pg 257

37   Review of *Night Has a Thousand Eyes*, *Newsweek*, 10/25/48

38   Review of *Night Has a Thousand Eyes*, *New Republic*, 11/1/48

39   Review of *Night Has a Thousand Eyes*, *Oakland Tribune*, 12/3/48

40   Philip K. Scheuer, review of *Night Has a Thousand Eyes*, *LA Times*, 10/21/48

41   Robinson, "All My Yesterdays," pg 254

42   Review of *State Department-File 649*, *New York Times*, 2/21/49

43   Harrison Carroll, "Behind the Scenes in Hollywood," *Bradford Era (PA)*, 10/14/48

44   Carlos Fuentes, "US Sponsored Terror and Genocide in Guatemala – The Glorious Victory," *El Pais Internacional*, 4/24/1995

45   Frank Nye, "Foto Facts," 4/15/49

46   Vincent Lawrence Briggs, phone conversation with author, 1/16/2007

47   Ibid

48   "Inside Radio," *Zanesville Signal(OH)*, 4/16/50

49   Carroll, "Virginia Bruce's Interrupted . . . "

50   Hedda Hopper column, *Portland Press*, 1/25/49

51   News article, *Fargo Forum*, 10/15/50

c. 1951 Press photo going to, or coming from
Istanbul – with Christopher and Ali

CHAPTER 16:

Istanbul

After Turkey was declared a nation in 1923, the country's first President, Mustafa Kemal Ataturk, led sweeping reforms for westernization. He dissolved the world of sultans, harems and Islamic law. As the "Father of Modern Turkey," Ataturk was determined to create a modern, democratic and secular society. He made remarkable progress. Compulsory education for girls and boys, voting rights, a new Turkish alphabet (less cumbersome than Arabic script), dramatic changes in women's roles, the abolishing of veils, encouraging Turkish men to wear European attire — these and other reforms were willingly adopted by most of the population. Totalitarian, communist, fascist, and Muslim extremist influences were kept at bay. Ataturk's "enlightened authoritarianism" abolished the centuries-old Islamic spiritual head-of-state, known as the Caliph. "There is no need to look at them as something extraordinary," Ataturk, an agnostic, stated. However, after Ataturk's death in 1938, the moderation of Islamic influences aroused political tension. Political leaders often drew upon dormant religious forces to gain power. And, whenever that happened the military stepped in as guardian of the country's secularism. Such was the case of Adnan Menderes, who was Prime Minister during Virginia and Ali's stay in Istanbul. Menderes, and surprisingly Ipar himself, would be targeted in a political upheaval: a *coup d' etat*. And that wasn't the half of it. Even after Ataturk's reforms, women's rights in Turkey were minimal. Virginia became a victim of Turkish law, with devastating consequences.

By 1950 the enchanting metropolis of Istanbul was more isolated and forgotten than ever in its 2,000-year-old history. Formerly known as Constantinople, capital of the Roman, Byzantine, and Ottoman Empires, Istanbul was now overlooked in favor of the new capital in Ankara. Holding on to the memory of a lost empire, Istanbul's affluent had lived off of dwindling family fortunes for decades. Ipar was fortunate being born wealthy in a city at its lowest ebb. Most of the population lived in poverty. Beggars, street peddlers, old men selling prayer books and pilgrimage oils, teahouses filled with unemployed men, pimps on the lookout for one more tipsy tourist – were quite a contrast from Virginia's posh neighborhood on Amalfi Drive. Nobel Prize-winning author Orhan Pamuk describes, in *Istanbul – Memories and the City*, the complex anatomy of Istanbul in the 1950s. The beauty of the city's landscape "resides in its melancholy," states Pamuk. Situated on both sides of the Bosporus strait, Istanbul's metropolis is built on two continents, Asia and Europe. In contrast to the city's ancient domed mosques and "crumbling fountains that haven't worked for centuries," Pamuk recognizes the significance of the Bosporus for *Istanbullus* (residents). "The Bosporus sings of life, pleasure and happiness," Pamuk tells us. "Istanbul draws strength from the . . . deep, dark waters, strong currents . . . the sea air."[1] For *Istanbullus* "to be able to see the Bosporus is a matter of spiritual import . . . windows looking out onto the sea are like the mihrabs in mosques, the altars in Christian churches . . .

all the chairs, sofas, and dining tables in our Bosphorus-facing sitting rooms are arranged to face the view. . . . If you are a ship sailing in from the Marmara, you are met with Istanbul's millions of greedy windows mercilessly crowding one another out to get a better look at your ship and the waters through which it is moving."[2] It was here, on the Bosporus shore by the Sea of Marmara, that Virginia and Ali, gazing through such windows, resided in palatial surroundings.

When this author contacted Ali Ipar in the spring of 2007, Ali recalled, "Our house in Istanbul was on my father's estate, on the waterfront. It was the most beautiful house in Istanbul." Ali described the enormity of his father's mansion. "30,000 square meters and 200 meters on the Sea of Marmara," he said with pride. In his next breath, Ipar assured me the mansion was, "absolutely the most beautiful house in Turkey." "We had two homes," he stated. "The other was in Nice, France – a *chateau*. My father was an industrialist — a very important man. He was a very wealthy man. And," Ali paused thoughtfully, "my father was a very *modest* man." Hayri Ipar's "modesty" was exemplified, according to his son, by the fact that Hayri refused to be called "King of Sugar." Ali explained, "My father preferred to be called 'Father of Sugar.'"[3] No mention was made of Hayri's benevolence in connection to his profits from munitions. According to Ali, Virginia was well received in her new home. "Virginia was very happy in Istanbul," he recalled, "and my family liked her. I was married to her a long time, you know."[4] Ipar talked about his early life, which paralleled Orhan Pamuk's observation that among the wealthy the typical dream is to study in America and settle in the States. Ipar stated, "Both my mother and father were born in Turkey. I was born in Istanbul, on September 27, 1921. And I really had a wonderful childhood. I went to Heidelberg, a famous university city, you know. Then I came to the States in 1940. I had my 19th birthday in the United States. I went to the University of Southern California for a Masters Degree in Political Science. I don't want to brag, but I'm an intelligent man. I was a successful man. I speak fluently, six languages."[5]

After their blissful first year in Istanbul, Ali informed Virginia that he wanted a divorce. The unexpected news was the result of another complex and unusual circumstance that seemed to be a main ingredient in the Virginia-Ali relationship. As usual, it involved news headlines.

"Ex-Film Star Divorced So Her Husband Can Be Turkish Officer," read a typical press release in the last week of July 1951.[6] *Time* magazine reported the paradoxical situation. "In Istanbul, blonde ex-Cinema-actress Virginia Bruce and her wealthy Turkish husband Ali Ipar announced that they were very much in love after five years of marriage – and, that they were going to get a divorce."[7] *The Fargo Forum*, still keeping track of their hometown star, explained,

> Virginia Bruce and her Turkish husband Ali Ipar
> have been divorced in a legal move to permit
> him to become an officer in Turkey's army. . . .
> the action was agreed upon between them after
> Ipar discovered that a four-year-old Turkish law
> forbids any man married to a foreigner to be
> commissioned an officer in the military forces. . . .
> They went to a court near their palatial home on
> the Asiatic coast and each pleaded 'incompatibility'

and were immediately divorced. 'We are still very much in love,' Ipar told newsman, 'this is just one of those awful things that could keep us apart for several years.'[8]

Unexpectedly, Ipar had been called up to do his compulsory military service. Had he opted for the standard induction as a soldier, no divorce would have been necessary. Apparently, Ipar was unaware of the attention their divorce received in the American press. In a letter to this author in 2007, Ali wrote, "Now I will give you a very different incident, in fact, *two* nobody, nowhere, knows about. My marriage to Virginia (1946) got me out of the U.S. Army. My fake, but legal divorce (1951) gave me the chance to be accepted into the Turkish army as a commissioned officer, and not as a plain soldier. World of difference in Turkey from plain soldier to rank of officer. There, at the time, was the stupid and very backward law that no man married to a foreigner could get an officer's commission. Ridiculous. A shame, but true."[9] Ipar insisted that to serve as a plain soldier would have been "terrible and risky."[10] Virginia's reaction to all of this? "It seems incredible," Virginia told reporters, "that the Turkish army, loaded with American officers and enlisted men, refuses to permit an officer to be married to an American."[11] She agreed with Ipar on the non-commissioned soldiers status, and stated, "Enlisted personnel live in unbelievable squalor, so we decided to get divorced."[12]

Newspapers had a field day with these turn of events. It was reported that Ali had moved into Hayri Ipar's townhouse apartments, while Virginia, Susan, and Christopher stayed with Ipar's family. The townhouse, which Virginia had previously mentioned in interviews, was not an uncommon family complex among the wealthy. With a separate floor for each adult offspring, these modern, but un-picturesque edifices were simply a replacement for the extended family mansion of old. Author Orhan Pamuk portrays his own family on their private floor, gathered in their western-styled sitting room, and not knowing quite what to do in it. According to Virginia, Ali wasn't faced with such a quandary, as he never resided in the Ipar apartments at all. A few years afterwards, she told reporter Bob Thomas, "We went on living together [in the Ipar mansion] for the year he was in the army. Everything was the same, except that Ali had to hide on the balcony whenever the doorbell rang."[13]

During Virginia and Ali's "fake" divorce, director Joe Mankiewicz was doing location shooting in Turkey for the James Mason thriller *Five Fingers*. Upon his return to the U.S., Mankiewicz commented to the press that Istanbul was the greatest city of contrasts he had ever seen – ancient gems mixed right in with American flour sacks and broken cola bottles at the local bazaars. He visited Virginia, and stated, "It's amazing how Virginia Bruce, the little girl from Fargo, North Dakota, fits into the life there. She's married into one of the richest families in Turkey." Mankiewicz also stated that Virginia, Ali, and his parents were all in mourning over the suicide of Ali's brother. Mankiewicz remembered, "Half the bells of the town were in mourning."[14] In the spring of 1952, Virginia's buddy Cesar Romero also paid her a visit after completing a film assignment in India. "I wouldn't think of flying over Istanbul without stopping off to see Virginia Bruce," he told the press. "Friends, after all, are perhaps our most valuable possessions." He observed that Virginia's surroundings were "quite luxurious." "Virginia has a very happy and comfortable life though she misses her friends who reside in Hollywood," Romero explained.[15] He reported to Louella Parsons that: Virginia and Ali would certainly remarry; beautiful Susan Ann was

1951 Virginia with her brother-in-law Mehmet Ipar (a
student at Stanford) (courtesy of Vincent Briggs)

the "belle of the place;" and young Christopher spoke Turkish
"like a native." Romero noticed that the Ipar family was devoted
to Virginia.[16] He stated to columnist Harrison Carroll that Virginia would finally return to the U.S. that November and that Ali
would follow.[17] After dutifully explaining Virginia's "mysterious
divorce," gossip columnists reported that Romero was performing "sensational rumbas" at the Mocambo with another good
pal, Joan Crawford.

Before Ali was released from the army, it was announced that Virginia would resume her film career – in Turkey. *The Fargo Forum* reported, "Now comes the news that [Virginia] is going to resume her movie activities. . . . Virginia has had quite a turbulent time of it, as we piece together the story of her life, and these past two years have been no exception . . . Now, it appears, the army stint is over. And so is the divorce!"[18] Ali made the announcement of their remarriage a few minutes after he received his honorable discharge in late October and stated, "I never felt divorced. I hope I've seen the army for the last time."[19] Ali's hiding-on-the-balcony days were over. As a lieutenant, he had served as aide to General Resit Erkhan, commandant of Istanbul. On November 13, 1952, Virginia wed for the fourth time. The simple ceremony took place at the Ipar mansion. A "good-bye" cocktail party followed, and the couple sailed on the Italian ship *Barletta* for Naples. On the 17th, Virginia was joined by Susan Ann and Christopher for a voyage on the *Independence* to New York and home. Indeed, Virginia *had* resumed her film career. Ali was not joining them on the *Independence*, but was instead headed for London to process a color film, starring Virginia, that he had written, directed, and produced.[20] Ali had somehow managed to conquer this feat during his last two months as a commissioned officer!

When I asked Ali how Virginia spent her time during her two-and-a-half-year stay in Istanbul – was she charmed by the city's colorful Grand Bazaar? Did she marvel at the marble ruins, the courtyards of mosques, streets filled with vendors selling fried mussels, pilaf, chestnuts, fish bread, yogurt drinks, and sherbets? – Ali answered simply, "I made a *picture* with her, *Salgin*. She was still in her good days when I wanted to produce the picture. I wrote, produced, and directed. I made the picture with Virginia in double-version. I shot it silently and dubbed it later."[21] Ali's enthusiasm for the project is understandable. Western influences, so prominent after Ataturk's rule, had opened up creative possibilities and dreams for *Istanbullus*. Earlier in the century, depictions of the human form in sculpture, painting, or film were considered idolatry and were forbidden. By the 1950s the visual arts in particular were flourishing. Happily, the burgeoning film industry provided Ali with an opportunity to finally direct. When Virginia did venture out into the city, heads were always turned in her direction. "As a blonde American movie star, Virginia was something of a celebrity in the streets," stated one report. "There was much gazing and some pinching, a habit indulged in with even ordinary travelers."[22]

Virginia and the children arrived in New York on November 26, 1952. The port was tied up while Longshoremen protested a state check on waterfront crime. Eight piers were closed down, which affected four large Trans-Atlantic liners. The American export liner, *Independence*, with Virginia, Susan, Christopher and 930 other passengers on board, was among them. Mob violence and corruption among longshoreman was a major problem in New York. The tense situation was well documented in the film classic *On the Waterfront* (1954). During the "Wildcat Walkout" of 1952, Virginia's trunks and other heavy pieces remained aboard until the demonstration ended.[23] Amid all the fuss, Virginia and the kids propped their chins up cheerfully for photographers, while resting their elbows on their luggage.

Upon their return to Hollywood, Hedda Hopper reported that Virginia looked younger than when she left town, and that

Susan Ann "didn't want to leave Turkey."[24] Susan's half-sister, Leatrice Gilbert Fountain, concurred with Hopper's report, telling this author, "All the time Ali was serving in the Turkish Army, Virginia and her children lived with Ali's mother in a lovely house on the Bosporus. I spoke to Susan about her life there and she said it was beautiful. They were very happy."[25] On December 18th, Ali arrived in New York from London. He worked steadily over the next few months dubbing his silent film into what he called "double-version" (Turkish and English).

Susan Ann summer of 1953

After several months, Ali began receiving queries as to *Salgin's* release. "I'm still working on my picture," he told reporters. "But more important, won't you say I am in no trouble with my country, nor with my marriage. My only trouble is my golf game."[26] There *were* problems with distributing the film. *Salgin* (translated as "The Plague") never really made it to theatres, but was released on TV in 1954 . . . as in, *early morning* TV. Shot in Istanbul with a local cast, the film told of an epidemic striking the city and how it was conquered with Virginia's help. Virginia starred as a Turkish Red Crescent (Red Cross) nurse. Reviews for the film (renamed *Istanbul* for release in the U.S.) are practically nil. *Lowell Sun* columnist Charles G. Sampas, a friend of beat generation writer Jack Kerouac, was

c1951-52 (l-r) Virginia, unknown (probably Fatma Ipar's husband), Sally Sands, Ali, Fatma Ipar Bir (Ali's sister) (courtesy of Vincent Briggs)

one of the few who caught it. "I'm a perennial after-midnight TV explorer," wrote Sampas. "The other 'ayem' I was nearly floored by a Turkish movie. Yep, I said Turkish. It starred Virginia Bruce, who stayed in Turkey several years while her husband, a Turkish subject, served in the army there. The film had English voices dubbed in, and it was set in Istanbul, and its suburbs. Anyway, it was different scenery, but the same boy meets girl, boy loses girl, boy regains girl plot. Love has its problems, geography not-withstanding . . . "[27] In truth, the storyline avoided the usual boy-meets-girl curve. While Virginia helped conquer "the plague," she also fell in love with a doctor, who happened to be married to her sister. The film's only asset, aside from its American star, was the cinematography of Ilhan Arakon, who, in 1954, received an award for *Salgin's* photography at Istanbul's second annual Association of the Friends of the Turkish Film. *Salgin* was noted for being the first color film in Turkish cinema. Arakon would have a respected career culminating in a Lifetime Achievement award at the 2000 Ankara International film Festival.

While *Salgin/Istanbul* fizzled on American TV, Virginia turned her attention toward television. Ipar kept mostly out of sight commuting between Hollywood and Istanbul. "*Some commuting!*" wagged Louella Parsons.[28] Dorothy Kilgallen offered more details on Ali's "commutes," saying, "The Ali Ipars (Virginia Bruce) are having more troubles. He can't take out American citizenship papers without having his property and bank accounts confiscated in his native Turkey."[29] In July 1953, Ipar headed once again to Istanbul. "Virginia Bruce will be lonesome," reported Harrison Carroll. "Husband Ali Ipar left for Turkey on motion picture business."[30] In August, Virginia signed on for *Lux Video Theatre's* teleplay *Something to Live For.* The episode began a revolution in the television industry. *Something to Live For* was the first of Lux's programs to be *filmed* as opposed to being performed "live." Most networks balked at paying the $8,000 required to lens a 30-minute show, regardless of the repeated airplay such a venture would profit them.[31] As it turned out, the procedure was considered a success and set a precedent. Virginia's co-stars were Otto Kruger and Amanda Blake (future Miss Kitty on *Gunsmoke*). The script called upon Virginia to play a retired actress who gives her "greatest performance" to save her twenty-year marriage to husband Kruger, from an "unprincipled and ambitious young actress starring in her husband's new play (Blake)."[32] Erskine Johnson noted in his column, "Virginia is dazzlingly beautiful as ever in the Gross-Krasna telefilm for Lux Theatre 'Something to Live For.'"[33] No one was more dazzled by Virginia than the young co-star who played her daughter, Karen Sharpe, who would later become the wife of the legendary director Stanley Kramer. I contacted Karen in January 2007, and she couldn't have been more enthusiastic about my Virginia Bruce project.

> You know, she was the very first movie star I ever met, when I was about ten years old – I didn't live here. I came out from Texas with my parents. My uncle lived in Pacific Palisades. The very first movie star I was introduced to by my uncle, who was not in show business at all, was Virginia Bruce. She was very lovely. She was very gracious to me. And, interestingly enough, she ended up playing my mother some years later. Not enough has been done on her. And, she was a major star of her day. She was so lovely, and had a certain dignity and way of conducting herself, which no longer exists. She was like you thought and wanted a star to be like. Virginia Bruce was a great example of a gracious star. She was so sweet. I must have been twenty-one when we did the Lux show, and she remembered meeting me when I was ten. She loved her kids. When I married Stanley, I couldn't worship my career, make a successful marriage, and be a mother. And, I raised his two children. I never looked back. And, I think Virginia was the same kind of person. Family was more important. So, I admire her for that. So many people could never let go.[34]

When asked for specifics about Lux's *Something to Live For*, Karen remembered,

Virginia played my mother. It was a period
piece. I remember I was in a doorway in a long,
beautiful, velveteen dress. Amanda Blake was the
other woman who attempted to take my father
(Otto Kruger) away. I think, I got my parents
back together. I remember a scene pleading with
him not to have the other woman in our life. Otto
Kruger was just great. He had a very distinctive
style of speaking, and phrasing. I had some special
scene with him. I remember he coached me on
that. I was very green at the time. Virginia Bruce
was underrated in my opinion. She had a woman's
weight as an actress on the screen. She had depth
of weight when she was working. There are some
women who display a "female" presence and some
who display a woman's presence, and Virginia had
a woman's presence and that is a great compliment.
I don't know how else to express it. That's what I
would like to say about her. For me, it was really
so unique to be able to meet her at 10 or 11, and
then work with her much later. I worked again with
Amanda many years later on *Gunsmoke*. I did two
Gunsmokes. But, she was not gracious like Virginia
Bruce. Amanda was nice, she was okay. There was
a certain air about Virginia. She listened to you,
and there was a sweetness about her. A genuine
sweetness. I really, really, liked her.[35]

One of Virginia's last radio performances was broadcast that fall.
Stars Over Hollywood featured Virginia in *The Lady and the Law*.
Act I, teeters on the edge of suspense as Virginia tells the lis-

Summer 1953. Virginia starred in *Something to Live For* on *Lux Video Theatre*.
Shown here with Otto Kruger.

tener, "I realized I was falling in love with this man . . . and, I
was afraid, very much afraid." Who was the man? A prisoner on
parole, for whom Virginia, as public defender was attempting to
get an acquittal. The well-written, and directed piece was based
on a story by Edward Verdier. In October, Virginia starred in
Woman's World for the half-hour anthology series *General Electric Theater*. Otto Kruger was again on board.

On the home front, Virginia was lonesome for Ali. Columnist
Erskine Johnson reported the now familiar tune that, "Virginia
Bruce is all smiles. Hubby Ali Ipar, in Turkey, cabled her that he
will be coming to Hollywood to join her in a month."[36] "I adored
Turkey," Virginia told writer Zelda Cini, who was interviewing
a series of stars living in Pacific Palisades. "It was so beautiful

and I can scarcely wait for Ali to get home. Saturday. Sunday's his birthday and Tuesday's mine. We're going to have a party." Cini noted that Virginia exuberated "all the animated sparkle of a child."[37] The interview was sidetracked several times while Virginia let her drooling Great Dane, Rufus, "Out!" – told a wailing Chris, "Quiet! . . . Susan's trying to sleep" – and went outside to tell Leo Marquez to turn off the nerve-shattering putt-putt of a powered lawnmower. Breathless, Virginia came back inside to emphasize, "Leo's been with me for years. He's a wonderful gardener." Then the phone rang – for Susan. "She's 20," said Virginia. "John Gilbert's daughter and my first born." When asked about Gilbert, Cini commented on the "haunting nostalgic note in Virginia's husky voice." Virginia recalled softly, "He was awfully cute. And Brilliant. And difficult, terribly, terribly difficult." After glancing at her watch, Virginia exclaimed, "Heavens!" and turned toward the staircase, "Chris, it's five o'clock, are you ready to go?" After a moment's dead silence, twelve-year-old Chris' boy-into-man voice indignantly called down, "Yes, but I'm going to change again. Everything. Every single thing. Shoes and pants and everything." Virginia looked at Cini and admitted, "I'm embarrassed." She got up and walked to the staircase. "Why are you going to change now, Chris?" she asked woefully. "Everything's too long," he answered. "The pants are too long, everything's too long and I look awful." Virginia made excuses, explaining that Chris was going to the Lads and Lassies dance at the Riviera. When Chris emerged, handsome and sophisticated, wearing "a symphony of brown and beige," he gravely shook Cini's hand. "Sorry I was such a stinker," he stated. "Guess I'm just a spoiled brat." Cini noted he smiled exactly like his mother, and hurried out the door. Virginia politely excused herself in order to drive Chris to his event. Cini didn't seem to mind, as it offered her the opportunity to enjoy the lanai, with its picture window and spectacular view of the garden, canyon and hills. Cini then browsed through the numerous books that enhanced the comfortable, colorful, family room. Among the crowded shelves was a two-volume biography of Shelley, politician Sumner Welles' *Time for Decision* (Welles was influential in establishing the "Good Neighbor Policy" and the United Nations), Tallulah Bankhead's autobiography, and *Red Cross Home Nursing*. When Virginia returned, she enjoyed relating stories to Cini about Ziegfeld, living in a tiny room at the Barbizon-Plaza in New York, the people she had known and the films she had made. When asked about

A *Lux* TV presentation of *Meet Jo Cathcart (1954)*
with Bruce Bennett (Courtesy of CBS/Photofest)

her family, Virginia stated, "Only Stan and I are left. He's a tennis pro, and an inventor on the side." She then offered a sales talk on Stan's latest invention, a coffee pourer. Cini emphasized that Virginia had a quality about her that "under-emphasized the tragedies which had also beset her." [38]

Upon Ali's return to the U.S., Virginia, once again, put her career on hold. It would be a year before she took on another acting assignment.

When Virginia returned to the small screen a year later, she opted for another *Lux Theater* episode, written by Emmy-nominated John McGreevey. Van Heflin introduced the story, *Meet Jo Cathart,* in which Virginia, as a crippled woman, lived "theatrically" to compensate for being denied an acting career. Her false world threatens the happiness of her marriage to husband Bruce Bennett. After the September broadcast, the Ipars returned to Istanbul. It had been announced that Cesar Romero persuaded Virginia to appear on his popular TV series, *Passport to Danger.* But Ali had other plans for her and Cesar. He wanted to produce a film, in London, and co-star the two devoted friends. While Ali worked out the film's details, he and Virginia gave her former MGM co-star, Walter Pidgeon, an insider's look at Istanbul during his visit to Turkey.[39] Pidgeon, still under contract at the studio, liked to quip, "I was like a kept woman during my twenty-one years at MGM."

Mankiewicz, Romero, and Pidgeon, paying homage to the Ipars in Istanbul, certainly attested their friendship for Virginia. Their visits also exemplified Hollywood's fascination with foreign wealth and nobility. Among the *noblesse* the feeling was mutual. Courting the Hollywood celebrity dated back to the days of silent film. Gloria Swanson acquired the title of Marquise de la Falaise del a Coudraye, until she gave it up after consummating her affair with a prominent American, Joseph P. Kennedy. Her dashing ex-husband, Henri de la Falaise, would simply acquire another Hollywood trophy-wife in Constance Bennett. While residing in Ankara during her first marriage (1937), Zsa Zsa Gabor claims to have been lovers with Ataturk himself![40] The fixation with Hollywood and royalty would climax in 1956 with Grace Kelly's "wedding of the century" to the Prince of Monaco. In the summer of 1954, Columnist Harrison Carroll spoofed tinsel town's obsession with "crowned heads" by stating, "Virginia Bruce and 'royal' husband Ali Ipar were at the Mocambo to see Eartha Kitt."[41] Louella Parsons mentioned being treated "royally" by the Ipar family while in Europe. Of course, the Ipars had no royal ancestry whatsoever. Ali himself never made any such claim, and was quick to point out the absurdity of royal wannabes mixing in the Hollywood scene. "Ali Kahn, my namesake – the prince married to Rita Hayworth, I should say *fake* prince from India," emphasized Ipar, "was the son of the richest man of the world – the old Aga Kahn." Ipar proudly added, "Rita and I had a big, big affair."[42] (Ironically, the wealthy Kahn would empty Rita's bank account. Adding insult to injury, the Catholic Church declared Hayworth's marriage "illicit." Poor Rita was condemned by the Pope.)[43] Apparently, Ali's sister Fatma ('Sazi') Behr married into royalty. In 1954, Virginia and Ali were star witnesses during prosecution for "Princess Sazi's" claim against Bank of America. The prosecution involved the $300,000 estate of her late husband.[44]

To bring in the New Year, 1955, Virginia and Ali attended oil millionaire Arthur Cameron's party for the Shah and Empress of

Iran. The heavily guarded affair required the use of Secret Service men, private detectives, and the Beverly Hills police department – thirty officers in all.[45] Ex-skating star Sonja Henie also attended. The fun-loving Cameron, generous to his ex-wives in three previous divorce settlements, would refuse the request of 4th wife Ann Miller for a $7 million annulment, giving her instead a paltry million. One thing Cameron had in common with Virginia was generosity. Virginia had coughed up big bucks to finance *Salgin*, and would reach deep into her pocketbook once more for Ali's next project, a British release, titled *Reluctant Bride*. One wonders about Ali's accessibility to the princely sums of cash in the Ipar family coffers. Still, it is understandable that Virginia would want to see Ali reach success in the medium he so much admired. But, that wasn't meant to be.

Ali stated in a letter to this author, "*Salgin* was produced, written, and directed by me . . . the other, *The Reluctant Bride*, was co-financed by me and made in London."[46] Ipar takes all the credit. He also takes great pride in his Hollywood connections, business and otherwise. Ali's romantic conquests were unprecedented, according to him. "Listen," he told me in a phone conversation, "I had a big romance with practically all the most beautiful girls in Hollywood, before I married Virginia. Linda Darnell, Hedy Lamarr . . . many others. I had a long life in Hollywood for many years."[47] His nostalgia and enthusiasm for the past are genuine. Ali's grand ambitions were not so very different from many other males among the wealthy *Istanbullus*. Big dreams and bankruptcies were common for the city's rich elite living off family fortunes to pursue the western lifestyle. Orhan Pamuk saw his own family fall apart as a result of his father's pipedreams, financial losses, infidelities, and absences. Pamuk points out a significant factor in understanding the "Ali Ipars" of old Istanbul. He emphasizes over and again the power of Istanbul's *huzun* (a shared, hazy state of melancholy), which clouds the success and failures of the city's sons. During her stay in Istanbul, Virginia could have easily learned to recognize and understand what Ali was up against. This author must acknowledge the dignity and honor that emerged from Ali Ipar during our conversations. Although *huzun* is not necessarily rooted in the romantic, Pamuk suggests that it ordains that no love will end peacefully. "Just as in the old black and white films," Pamuk writes, "if the setting is Istanbul, it is clear from the start that the *huzun* the boy has carried with him since birth will lead the story into melodrama."[48] And, so it was, and would continue to be for Ali Ipar and Virginia Bruce.

Endnotes

1   Orhan Pamuk, *Istanbul – Memories and the City*, Vintage Books, N.Y., c. 2003, pgs 50-51

2   Pamuk, *Istanbul* . . . pg 204

3   Phone conversation with Ali Ipar, 5/8/2007

4   Ibid

5   Ibid

6   "Ex-Film Star Divorced So Her Husband Can Be Turkish Officer," *Greely Daily Tribune (CO)*, 7/30/51

7   *Time Magazine*, 8/6/51

8   "Ali Ipar Divorces Virginia to Get His Army Commission," *Fargo Forum*, 6/29/51

9   Letter from Ali Ipar dated 5/3/2007

10   Phone conversation with Ali Ipar, 5/8/2007

11   "Ali Ipar Divorces Virginia . . . "

12   Bob Thomas, "Virginia Bruce Is Back – Playing Mother of Kim," *Fargo Forum*, 12/6/59

13   Ibid

14   Hedda Hopper column, "Looking at Hollywood," *Syracuse Post Standard*, 8/6/51

15   Edwin Schallert, "Bachelor Romero, Social Asset in Films, Astute in Business," *Los Angeles Times*, 7/13/52

16   Louella Parsons column, *Albuquerque Journal*, 5/7/52

17   Harrison Carroll, "Mysterious Divorce Cleared; May Rewed," *Lethbridge*

Herald(Alberta), 5/21/52

18 news column, *Fargo Forum*, 7/27/52

19 "Virginia Bruce to Remarry Her wealthy Turkish Husband Soon," *Lowell Sun*, 11/2/52

20 "Virginia Bruce Remarries Turk," *Charleston Daily Mail*, 11/13/52

21 Phone conversation with Ali Ipar, 4/29/2007

22 Steve Scheuer, "Virginia Bruce Works Little Now," *Charleston Gazette*, 7/25/57

23 "Wildcat Walkout Ties Up N.Y. Port," *The Daily Review, (Hayward ,CA)*, 11/26/52

24 Hedda Hopper column, *Valley Morning Star (TX)*, 1-12-53

25 Email from Leatrice Gilbert Fountain, 1/20/2007

26 Louella Parsons column, *Albuquerque Journal*, 4/10/53

27 Charles G. Sampas, review for *Istanbul, Lowell Sun*, 11/11/54

28 Louella Parsons column, *Albuquerque Journal*, 4/10/53

29 Dorothy Kilgallen column, *Charleston Gazette*, 3/28/53

30 Harrison Carroll column, *Lethbridge Herald(Alberta)*, 7/7/53

31 Hal Humphrey, "Lux Theater Switches to Hollywood Film," *Oakland Tribune*, 8/21/53

32 Terry Vernon, "Tele-Vues," *Long Beach Independent*, 8/13/53

33 Erskine Johnson, "Johnson in Hollywood," *Long Beach Independent*, 9/2/53

34 Phone conversation with Karen Sharpe Kramer, 1/14/2007

35 ibid

36 Erskine Johnson . . . 9/2/53

37 Zelda Cini, "Glamorous Virginia Bruce is Captivating Mrs. Ali Ipar," September 1953 interview republished in *Hollywood Studio Magazine* April 1977

38 ibid

39 Louella Parson's column, *Daily Oklahoman*, 11/23/54

40 Zsa Zsa Gabor, "One Lifetime is Not Enough," Simon and Schuster (NY), 1991, audiocassette 1

41 Harrison Carroll column, "In Hollywood," 8/17/54

42 Conversation with Ali Ipar, 5/8/2007

43 James Robert Parish, *Hollywood Divas*, Contemporary Books, Chicago, 2003, pg 130

44 "Virginia Bruce in $303,475 Estate Case," *LA Times*, 8/17/54

45 Harrison Carroll, "In Hollywood," *Lethbridge Herald*, 1/20/55

46 Letter from Ali Ipar to author, 5/3/2007

47 Conversation with Ali Ipar, 5/3/2007

48 Pamuk, *Istanbul* . . . pgs 106-107

CHAPTER 17:

Prison Widow

As the 1950s progressed, the government of Turkish Prime Minister Adnan Menderes created surmounting problems for itself. Favoring Islam, and going against Ataturk's secular ideal, Menderes built a thousand mosques during his tenure. In 1955, while he strengthened ties with Muslim states, the Turkish press began a state-supported campaign to galvanize public opinion against the city's Greek minority. This culminated in a mass attack upon Greek citizens. The Menderes-sponsored riot became known as the "Istanbul Pogrom." Over 4,000 Greek-owned businesses were vandalized, or destroyed. Greek Orthodox churches and schools were burned. Women were raped, men were forcibly circumcised, and lives were lost. Despite strong evidence that Menderes orchestrated the pogrom, he and his officials blamed Turkish Communists. Greece pressed for human rights violations through the United Nations, and found little sympathy. As expected, the United States and Britain absolved Menderes, who continued to suppress political opposition, enforce censorship, and seek control over the nation's Universities. Intolerant of any criticism, Menderes had many journalists arrested. His popularity among intellectuals and the military reached a low ebb. Despite his dictatorial methods, Menderes *had* allowed more private enterprise. Seizing what he saw as opportunity, Ali Ipar invested in a Turkish shipping business. Unfortunately, the resulting increase in import goods had Turkey teetering on the verge of insolvency. Ipar's suspected ties to Menderes would place his life in jeopardy. His eventual arrest dealt Virginia more anguish than she could have ever anticipated.

In early 1955, Virginia made her British film debut in *Reluctant Bride*. The comedy was originally slated for Olivia de Havilland and Alan Ladd. When de Havilland's interest in the project dimmed, the lead role was offered to Maureen O'Sullivan. Scheduled for an RKO release, the producer hoped that O'Sullivan's husband, John Farrow, would direct. In a matter of weeks, O'Sullivan turned down the role. Another "reluctant" star (Donna Reed) was announced, before the project was shelved. Things got rolling again when Virginia and Cesar Romero were set to co-star. Unfortunately, Cesar Romero's TV schedule for *Passport to Danger* forced him to forgo the opportunity. John Carroll, who appeared with Virginia in MGM's *Hired Wife*, took on the assignment, and the investment of co-financing the feature with Ali Ipar. Although Virginia played the title role of the "reluctant bride," Carroll got top billing.

After completion, Virginia and Ali had a short stay in Istanbul before returning home via Frankfurt and London. The stopover in Frankfurt afforded the couple a quick visit with Stewart Granger, who had just completed George Cukor's *Bhowani Junction* in Pakistan. While Granger's film was a stateside box-office hit, the romantic comedy *Reluctant Bride* played mostly

Reluctant Bride (1955) with John Carroll (Courtesy of Photofest)

to drive-in theaters. *Reluctant Bride's* director, Henry Cass, had guided Alec Guinness, Margaret Rutherford, and Audrey Hepburn through some modestly-budgeted British films in the early 1950s. Oscar-winning scenarist Frederick Stephani (Virginia hosted his wedding in 1947) concocted the story of orphaned siblings who are suddenly custody of a properly-minded maternal aunt (Virginia) and a playboy paternal uncle. Aunt Virginia, an entomologist, and Uncle John Carroll, a Texas oilman, are told that whoever marries first will get full custody. Naturally, the two dislike each other. Throw in a gold-digging girlfriend for Carroll, a pompous professor fiancé for Virginia, a soccer game that goes amuck, a little brandy to remedy the situation — and before long, Virginia's flirtatious side shows up to save the day. Amid the mayhem, cupid's arrow keeps it "all in the family" — Virginia and Carroll tie the knot.

Upon her return to the U.S., Virginia discovered that her daughter, employed as a secretary at J. Walter Thompson Advertising Agency in Hollywood, was getting serious about matrimony herself. Susan had met John Gehring Waldron, an advertising executive, on a blind date shortly after her return from Istanbul in 1952. In 1955, Waldron proposed. Virginia gave her approval of young Waldron as a suitable match. The wedding took place at Virginia's residence on Amalfi Drive the following year, on March 10, 1956.[1] Reverend Kenneth Carey of the Episcopal Church, who had baptized Susan, officiated. Strangely, Virginia was not present at the wedding. Most likely, she was traveling with Ipar. Susan Ann's Uncle Stanley and his wife were the only attendants. Like the tagline from *Reluctant Bride*, Susan Ann "Should Have Said 'No' When She Said 'Yes.'" The marriage didn't last long.

Ali's visits to Turkey remained frequent. In August 1956, he returned to Istanbul, where, according to Louella Parsons, he was "taking care of his father's lucrative business."[2] Ali came back to the States just before Christmas. Parsons noted that, "Virginia feels she has had enough of the long separations from [Ali], so she says she will go back to Turkey with her husband and put her 15-year-old son in boarding school in northern California. When Ali returns to Istanbul he will release *The Reluctant Bride*, the independent picture he made last year in England with Vir-

Reluctant Bride (1955) Virginia as a hockey-playing entomologist

ginia and John Carroll."[3] Two years after its British release, Ipar-Carroll Productions finally made the deal with 20th Century-Fox for *Reluctant Bride's* U.S. release in June 1957. 20th Century-Fox paid Ipar and Carroll $50,000 for the U.S. distribution rights, and used the title *Two Grooms for a Bride*. The film went nowhere. In the meantime, as the family's main breadwinner, Virginia busied herself with a number of television assignments.

Televised programs such as *The Loretta Young Show* provided ample opportunity for the stars of Hollywood's Golden Age to maintain their careers. Instead of Loretta's trademark swirling through doors to greet her TV audience on September 4, 1955, guest hostess Rosalind Russell appeared to introduce *Weekend in Winnetka* starring Virginia, Gene Raymond, Elinor Donahue and Natalie Schafer. The broadcast was a popular one and received repeated showings for several years. Virginia played an attractive widow who buys into the rumors that her daughter (Donahue) is on the verge of becoming a juvenile delinquent. Gene Raymond played Bruce's fiancé.

Virginia appeared twice on the two-season anthology *Science Fiction Theatre*. Minus the genre's usual bug-eyed monsters, each episode of the series was based on plausible scientific theory. Hal Erickson's book on syndicated television states that Virginia's appearance on the episode titled *Dead Storage*, written by the series' creator Ivan Tors, typified *Science Fiction Theatre's* more "cerebral" approach. "The theory of 'freezing' the dead in hopes of bringing them back to life in the future," states Erickson, "resulted in a story about a scientist (Virginia Bruce) who revived an ancient mastodon found frozen in an iceberg, then suffered the anguish of a 'biological mother' when the beast withered and died."[4] In each of *Science Fiction Theatre's* introductions, host Truman Bradley gave credibility to the subject at hand. Two of the series best-known directors were William Castle and Jack Arnold (remembered for several '50s film classics such as *The Incredible Shrinking Man*). For her second appearance in December 1955, Virginia was directed by Tom Gries, who would later receive acclaim for the TV movie on Charles Manson, *Helter Skelter* (1976). In *Friend of the Raven*, Virginia works for the State Clinic for the Deaf and Mute. She is called upon to deal with a boy, absent from school, who communicates with animals using a sixth sense. The boy (Richard Eyer) intuits impending danger in the wildlife community that has surrounded him since birth. During one of her visits, Virginia is walking in the countryside when she is confronted by a rattlesnake. Out of nowhere the boy suddenly appears, calms the snake, and thus establishes a connection with Virginia. She tries to convince an unsympathetic co-worker that the boy has a "gift." "He saved my life!" she explains. "He sensed I was in danger." Instead of signing a court order to remove the boy from his home, she rips it up. Eventually, Virginia and the boy's father stand by as a University doctor performs brain surgery on the boy. Eyer gains the ability to talk at the cost of losing his ability to communicate with animals. The question for the viewer is raised: who really has the problem? Was the boy so bad off before? *Science Fiction Theater's* episodes were shot in color and are easily accessible for collectors. The series ventured into territory that later would become controversial, such as the Macdonald Carey episode in which he experiments with LSD.

Studio 57 provided two television opportunities for Virginia. In *Out of Sight*, Virginia, as manager of a New York hotel for women, helps a young woman dealing with her fiancé's blindness. The second episode teamed Virginia with Pat O'Brien in *Who's Calling*. They play a couple faced with a series of strange phone calls. Events unravel to reveal that O'Brien, a successful realtor, had once killed a man for money. TV columnist John Crosby panned the mystery-drama and found the formula all too familiar. "The other day," commented Crosby, "I heard Virginia Bruce, playing a wife, tell Pat O'Brien, playing her husband, not to worry: 'We'll talk about it in the morning.' Now, I'm reasonably sure I never laid eyes on this little stinker of a picture before, but I seem to recall Virginia Bruce saying, 'We'll talk about it in the morning' to her husband before, conceivably in some prior life."[5] In April 1956, NBC's daytime *Matinee Theater*, a live color TV drama series, starred Virginia in *People in Glass*. Like Bette Davis' character in *Now, Voyager*, Virginia played the daughter of a snobbish matriarch. Her mother discourages Virginia's attempt to change her own circumstances, and disapproves of her involvement with a "common" man who owns a greenhouse. *Matinee Theatre*, although very popular, was cancelled after three years, because RCA (which owned NBC) felt people weren't buying color TV sets fast enough.

During the week of television's 1956 Fall Preview, Virginia made a much ballyhooed "live" appearance as Mildred Pierce on *Lux Video Theatre*. (For some reason, the series was no longer filmed before airplay.) In 1945, *Mildred Pierce* had helped redefine Joan Crawford's career – she received an Oscar. In the years that followed, the story was presented twice on *Lux Radio*. Rosalind Russell took the lead role in 1949, and Claire Trevor in a 1954 repeat. Zachary Scott reprised his role as Monte, the dissipated opportunist and playboy, in both radio versions, as well as the September 20, 1956, presentation opposite Virginia. The show premiered Lux's seventh television season. Substantial ads, with photos of the cast, appeared in major newspapers. "Host Gordon MacRae welcomes you to the first in the new, all-live, all-color Fall series," the ads promised. "Virginia Bruce, Zachary Scott, and Patric Knowles star in *Mildred Pierce* one of the most talked-about Hollywood successes of all time . . . the story of the mother who sacrificed her own happiness for the most selfish daughter in the world!" (Colleen Miller played Virginia's spoiled-brat daughter, Veda.) Virginia and Scott had rehearsed daily from September 12 until the show's airdate. The result? *Time Magazine's* verdict was blunt. "Blonde Virginia Bruce was dragged mercilessly through a bleak, attenuated version of *Mil-*

Stars of TV's *Lux Video Theatre* – (l-r) Sarah Churchill, Ann Blyth, Otto Kruger, Virginia, Ruth Hussey, and Marilyn Erskine (June 1956)

dred Pierce on NBC's *Lux Video Theater*." Another critic observed, "*Lux Theatre* skidded on its own soap in the sensational premier last eve. *Mildred Pierce* was purest trash, but Virginia Bruce was just as beautiful as her John Gilbert era."[6] Not long after the season's premier, columnist Eve Starr commented that Virginia's old beau, Corney Jackson, was credited for being "largely responsible for *Lux Video Theatre* being what it is today."[7] Perhaps Lux's lackluster attempt for Virginia's *Mildred Pierce* was her payback for dumping Corney for Ali in 1946.

Many sources state that Virginia made her *Ford Television Theatre* debut in 1952. But, upon viewing the episode *So Many Things Happen*, one discovers that the Virginia in question was Virginia Field. Bruce's debut on the program was in February 1957. She co-starred with Paul Henried in a story written by J. Walter Ruben's old pal Wells Root. *The Connoisseur* involved an artistic American couple (Bruce and Henried) living a bohemian life in Europe. Their more practical daughter, Kathryn Grant (soon to be Bing Crosby's wife), chooses the more conservative life with a realtor, much to her parents' dismay. It would be Virginia's last dramatic television role. TV critic Steve Scheuer interviewed Virginia on the Columbia lot. She stated that she was living "quietly in Pacific Palisades with her two children." No mention was made of Susan's marriage, or of Virginia's new grandson. "I'm a stay-at-home," stated Virginia. "I've lost my drive. When my husband Ali goes to Turkey on business, then I go to work for something to do. That's why I'm doing this. I'm in a rut."[8] Virginia mentioned her travels and thought it would be a good idea if the government sponsored programs to allow citizens "to see cultures much older than ours, to see the differences in traditions, custom, thinking." "It's a shame people can't see the rest of the world," she remarked. "We would have much greater understanding if we all traveled. But you have to see for yourself to really appreciate it." As the Cold War dominated international relations, Scheuer asked Virginia where Turkey stood. "Turkey is solidly on our side," she said. "They hate the Russians with a passion . . . the Army is strong and fairly well trained, and, strangely enough, has many blonde, blue-eyed soldiers."[9] Virginia got out of her "rut" the following year and dabbled once again in politics. As "Mrs. Ali Ipar," she hosted a cocktail party for Harvard graduate Mel Lennard, the Democratic candidate for the House of Representatives 16th Congressional District, on Sunday, July 27, 1958.[10] Lennard, an attorney-at-law and labor mediator, was also a Pacific Palisades resident. Despite California governor Pat Brown's support, Lennard's campaign garnered only 42% of the vote.

Virginia's remark that the Turks "hate the Russians with a passion," (a news item released in July 1957) came soon after an unexpected visit by the FBI to her home on Amalfi Drive. On a directive from New York's FBI office, a Secret Agent showed up at her door-step on June 27, 1957. The interview focused on Virginia's association with suspected Soviet spies. Millionaire "leftist" Alfred K. Stern and his wife Martha Dodd Stern (daughter of FDR's Ambassador to Germany, William E. Dodd) were in the news at the time. A Federal indictment charged the couple, now residing in Mexico, with conspiracy. President Eisenhower was pushing Mexico to deport the couple so they could appear before a New York Federal Grand Jury. Little did Virginia know that agents had been trailing her since 1944 in regards to the Sterns. (A 1954 FBI report on Stern, also had brother Stanley Briggs under surveillance.)

Virginia was straightforward with information, and stated that while in Fargo her parents were acquainted with uncles of Howard K. Stern (a native of Fargo). She had dated him briefly when he arrived in Los Angeles in 1937, and mixed with him socially thereafter. The report specified:

> Mrs. Ipar stated that in all probability Stern
> fancied himself in love with her. She said she
> was extremely pleased when she learned that
> he had married Martha Dodd, the daughter of
> Ambassador William Dodd. Mrs. Ipar stated that
> Alfred Stern in 1955 was in contact with her at
> infrequent intervals and each contact was social in
> nature. [FBI files on Virginia include all the details
> involved with her assistance in helping Stern obtain
> a fur coat for Martha, wholesale.]
>
> Mrs. Ipar stated that during the time she has
> known Alfred Stern he has never asked her for

any money or donations, nor has he asked her
to engage in any business enterprises with him.
Further, he never gave her any reason to believe
that he was working for the Soviet Union, nor did
she ever get the impression that he was sympathetic
to the Soviet Union. She stated it would never
occur to her that he would do anything hostile
to the United States. (FBI LA 105-30-34 –filed
6/28/57)

The report concluded that "she may be withholding information"
as to her involvement in business enterprises associated with
Stern, which were supposed covers for espionage. More interesting than Virginia's "subversive" activities, was documentation of
a conversation between Alfred and Martha Stern. "[Stern] asked
Martha if she thought Ali and Virginia would make a good marriage. Martha said that she can see what he sees in her, but she
cannot see what she sees in him." (FBI LA-105-3043 -7/24/55)
(Although the Justice Department dismissed the indictment
against the Sterns in 1979, the couple remained in exile, both
dying in Prague).

Soon after *Two Grooms for a Bride* was released in the U.S., Virginia and Ali attended John Carroll's August 1957 opening at the
Mocambo. Conrad and Nicky Hilton hosted a party afterwards, at
which the Ipars were present. Carroll had a pleasant baritone voice
and engaged the Mocambo stint for the fun of it. His investments
in real estate and the shrimp industry had left him a wealthy man.
Ipar, on the other hand, was still trying to make his mark. His and

Virginia's money soon found its way into the Turkish shipping industry. Ali purchased four ships in 1958-59, thus creating the Ipar Transport Company of Istanbul. The ships had been seized by the Turkish Commerce Bank in 1958, due to the financial problems of previous owners. One of the vessels, a 7,030-ton 431-foot cargo liner, had the honor of becoming Virginia's namesake. The *S.S. Virginia Ipar* was built in 1941 (Dundee, Scotland) as part of England's WWII Ministry of War Transport. Her voyage destinations for Ipar Transport were the Mediterranean, Continental Europe, England, and the U.S. East Coast. Another ship was christened after Ali's beloved brother, the *S.S. Necip Ipar*.

Virginia's own sojourns to Istanbul had come to an end. She explained her dilemma, in early 1959, to Harrison Carroll. "Ali will be leaving in a few days for Turkey," she informed Carroll. "I don't know when we will see each other again. I tried living in Istanbul, but I got lonesome for my children. We had other sadnesses. Ali's [brother] Necip, with whom we were very close, died. Ali himself had diphtheria. He barely survived it. He was allergic to the serum."[11] Ali may have survived, but it was only to encounter the worst nightmare of his life. Ipar Transport was a doomed and misguided venture that wouldn't last long.

In the aftermath of Istanbul's Pogrom of 1955, the Greek community continued to flounder amid the devastation. Their only hope was compensation from the Turkish state, which didn't have the financial means or interest to do anything to help. Orhan Pamuk notes that wealthy Jews were also seen as a threat to the state. A Wealth Tax imposed on them during WWII paved the way to seize their lands and factories. "It was impossible to become seriously wealthy without entering into deals with politicians," writes Pamuk, "everyone assumed that even the well-meaning rich had tainted pasts."[12] The wealthy who escaped the scrutiny of the government were prominently featured in the society columns. Pamuk recalled his mother feasting on the news gossip of the Ipar family. "Muazzez Ipar is off to Rome!" read one column. "We've never seen this Istanbul socialite looking quite this happy. What's cheered her up we wonder? Could it be the dashing man at her side?"[13]

In 1959, society glamour disintegrated into turmoil when the conflict between Menderes' ruling party and the Republican Peoples Party leader Ismet Inonu (who had been a close friend of Ataturk) intensified. As major opposition included the Turkish army, things didn't look promising for Menderes. He was met head-on with a military coup on May 27, 1960. The coup, which came as no surprise, was accomplished with little violence and was accepted quickly throughout the country. It brought the end of the "Menderes Decade." Menderes, other party members, and "friends" were arrested to be put on trial on the Bosporus island of Yassiada. A total of 592 defendants were relocated to Yassiada. Among them was Ali Ipar.

United Press documented Ali and Virginia's plight the following spring in a feature news item titled "Prison Widow Virginia Bruce Can Only Wait." Joe Finnigan, reporting from Hollywood, described the dramatic scenario.

> Virginia Bruce, once a leading Hollywood
> star, is now spending lonely days in a Pacific
> Palisades house near here awaiting her husband's
> release from a Turkish jail. . . . Miss Bruce has
> been inactive partly because of her husband's
> imprisonment. . . . Ali Ipar is being held on an
> island by Turkish authorities. He was placed there
> last year with members of the Turkish Government
> after a political upheaval.[14]

For the remainder of the article, Virginia did all the talking. She was filled with doubts and very discouraged.

> I don't have any plans. I don't know if I can work or not. I'm just very nervous. My husband is in prison. He's started writing letters, although they are censored. He hasn't been sentenced yet. He's been convicted for something involving freighters. They claimed he bought the freighters fraudulently. It's not true. He didn't purchase them. He more or less ran them for somebody else. They took my husband's mother and went through her safe deposit box, taking money and jewels. Maybe they'll give them back someday. I haven't thought of going over to Turkey. I'm a citizen of Turkey because of my marriage to him. Who knows, they might put me in jail too.[15]

Strangers When We Meet (1960)
Virginia cheerfully encourages Kirk Douglas and daughter Kim Novak's extra-marital affair (Courtesy of Columbia Pictures/Photofest)

Taking into consideration the military coup, Ali's arrest, and his impending trial, it was good fortune that Virginia hadn't returned to Istanbul. Shortly before this turn of events, Virginia occupied herself with a screen "comeback" playing Kim Novak's mother. Louella Parsons wondered why Virginia was willing to make such a career move. "Why not?" Virginia responded. "I am a grandmother. My daughter Susan has a little boy."[16] Filming for *Strangers When We Meet*, a high-powered glamour-epic about adultery, began in the early summer of 1959. Bob Thomas, who had been covering Hollywood for the Associated Press since 1944, was a trusted source in the film industry. Access to the movie moguls, interviews with film legends, and breaking news of "comebacks" were his specialty. "Virginia Bruce — Beautiful at 49 — Returns to Films," was a prominent Bob Thomas coast-to-coast news feature. "She has the same peaches-and-cream skin, the lovely blonde hair," penned Thomas.

> A pound or two has been added, but at 49 Virginia Bruce is still strikingly beautiful. She's back in movies after a 10-year [sic] absence, playing Kim Novak's mother in *Strangers When We Meet*. When you point out that this is hardly credible, she readily admits her age and remarks that she has a daughter . . . the same age as Kim, 26. Miss Bruce has had a life with many triumphs and a sizable share of tragedies. She talked candidly about them as she prepared for her film return.[17]

Virginia gave her view to Thomas on the demise of John Gilbert's career saying, "Everyone says that his voice killed his career when sound came in. That wasn't true. He had a wonderful, romantic voice. But the love scenes he did in silents weren't the same in sound. He said to Catherine Dale Owen 'I love you. I love you. I love you.'

And they threw tomatoes at the screen." Virginia elaborated on the reason she wasn't with Ali in Istanbul. "My son, Chris Ruben, hated living in Turkey. He had been back here with relatives, but I decided to return and give him some kind of home." When asked about Ali, Virginia didn't mince words. "It's pure hell," she admitted. "I haven't seen him since July, because he is so involved in his shipping business in Turkey. But he is trying to arrange things so he can gradually retire and settle down here."[18] (At the time, little did Virginia suspect that Ali would be "settling down" . . . in prison.)

Strangers When We Meet, based on Evan Hunter's 1958 bestseller, focused on illicit love in suburbia. The tryst in question involved housewife Kim Novak and a successful architect played by Kirk Douglas. Novak's husband shows no interest in lovemaking. In Hunter's novel he wears a locket around his neck bearing a portrait of his mother. The more attuned viewer would certainly suspect he was gay. (Such territory was *verboten* for mainstream American publishers, and still a Hollywood Production Code no-no.) Douglas wants to explore his architectural "dreams," but his wife (Barbara Rush) wants him to focus on more lucrative, commercial offers. Kirk (whose trademark dramatics are kept at an appealing low simmer) turns to an acquaintance (Novak) for emotional support. She turns to Douglas for the passion lacking in her own marriage. Any guilt Novak experiences is heightened by the fact that her own mother (Virginia) had also strayed off the beaten path during marriage.

Virginia works well under Richard Quine's direction, establishes her character immediately, and locks it in. She holds the screen whenever she appears and encourages the viewer to want to know more about her. Virginia sees right through what Novak is experiencing – sexual frustration and temptation for Douglas. It's almost as if she looks straight into her daughter's future. She wants Novak to rip loose and find passionate love. Novak, however, still holds a grudge against her mother and has no interest in motherly advice. "I'm not a tramp," Virginia tries to explain to her daughter. Novak avoids any sort of empathy Bruce has to offer. It's Novak's loss, as well as the audience's. What exactly had happened to Virginia? The details of her past remain a mystery. As in Evan Hunter's novel, the dynamic between mother and daughter is sacrificed for the antics of a pulp-fiction author (Ernie Kovaks) – who hires Douglas to design his house. Kovaks' *carte blanche* offer, financially and architecturally, is exactly the opportunity Douglas has dreamed about. (Granted, Kovaks was a remarkable talent and innovator for 1950s television. On screen, as the storyline of *Strangers When We Meet* progresses, he comes across as an annoyance.)

Virginia watches as Novak remains in denial of what's happening. Finally, when Douglas pays a visit to Novak's home while she is feeling under-the-weather, Virginia witnesses what she has suspected all along. She brings tea into the room where Douglas and Novak are visiting. Glances that consume pages of dialogue between mother and daughter are consolidated into brief sentences after Douglas leaves. "So . . . it happened to you!" Virginia says sagely. The benumbed Novak responds, "Yes, Mother. It's happened to me." Virginia hopes Novak will *understand* and forgive. But their perfunctory exchange is as close as she comes to getting her wish.

Considering the horrific consequences stars of the '30s and '40s paid on screen for infidelity, Novak and Douglas (who did *not* get along during filming) offered a fresh take. It was rare to see a non-judgmental treatment for such popular, albeit touchy cinematic fare. However, *The New York Times* critic felt the film, "a desperate attempt to be adult and modern about things that turn out to be terribly familiar and dull."[19] Film critic Ken Winters countered the *Times*, praised author Hunter's dialogue as being "far from stupid," and stated that Quine's direction "touched the pulse" of the subject. (Quine and Novak were romantically involved.) Winters praised Novak and Douglas, saying "both do their work with care, sincerity and more skill than is sometimes attributed them. Virginia Bruce, one-time screen glamour girl, turns in a modest, tasteful performance as the mother in whose wayward footsteps Miss Novak follows."[20] "Virginia Bruce, as Miss Novak's mother is excellent in support," noted Copley film critic Charles Hull.[21] Despite the brevity of her role, *Strangers When We Meet* was a respectable screen swansong for Virginia Bruce. Her egging Novak to have a *real* affair of the heart was an uncanny reflection of Virginia herself. "I wish you fall in love someday," Virginia tells Novak. "I wish to God you *really* fall in love." The film title would prove prophetic. It would be more than four years before she and Ali Ipar met face-to-face again. By that time, they had indeed become strangers.

When I first contacted Ali Ipar in the spring of 2007, and told him of my project for a Virginia Bruce biography, he wrote to me a few days later, saying the idea was, "a very agreeable and welcome surprise. Any mention of my departed, sweet, and much loved wife Virginia makes me happy. Virginia deserves the best of everything. I can see her now in the Paradise she deserved."[22]

Endnotes

1   Hedda Hopper, "John Gilbert's Daughter to Be Married Saturday," *Los Angeles Times*, 3/6/56

2   Louella Parsons column, *Albuquerque Journal*, 12/1/56

3   ibid

4   Hal Erikson, *Syndicated Television*, McFarland, London, 1989, pg 70

5   John Crosby, "Have You Second Sight This Summer?" *Oakland Tribune*, 7/15/56

6   "Radio-TV Notebook," *Kingsport News (TN)*, 9/22/56

7   Eve Starr, "Inside TV," *Star-News Pasadena (CA)*, 1/3/57

8   Steve Scheuer, "Virginia Bruce Works Little Now," *Charleston Gazette*, 7/25/57

9   ibid

10   "Community Calendar," *Los Angeles Times*, 6/27/58

11   Harrison Carroll, "In Hollywood," *Lancaster Eagle Gazette (OH)*, 1/13/59

12   Pamuck, *Istanbul . . .* pg 190

13   Pamuck, *Istanbul . . .* pg 189

14   Joe Finnigan, "Prison Widow Virginia Bruce Can Only Wait," *Fresno Bee (CA)*, 4/11/61

15   ibid

16   Louella Parsons, "Virginia Bruce In 'Strangers,'" *Cedar Rapids Gazette*, 10/20/59

17   Bob Thomas, "Virginia Bruce, Beautiful at 49, Returns to Films," *Indiana Evening Gazette (PA)*, 12/4/59

18   ibid

19   A.H. Weiler, review for *Strangers When We Meet*, *New York Times*, 6/30/60

20   Ken Winters, review of *Strangers When We Meet*, *Winnipeg Free Press*, 11/12/60

21   Charles Hull review of *Strangers When We Meet*, *Press-Courier (CA)*, 10/6/60

22   Letter to author from Ali Ipar, 5/3/2007

CHAPTER 18:

"... In The Paradise
She Deserved"

The coastal vicinity of Pacific Palisades has views of the lush green Santa Monica Mountains to the north, and to the south a shimmering blue Pacific Ocean. Over the years, Palisades (which is within the vicinity of Los Angeles) saw cabins replaced by bungalows, and bungalows demolished to make way for multimillion-dollar homes with expensive views. *Twilight Zone* creator Rod Serling, a displaced New Yorker (who at one time rented from Virginia), had mixed feelings about LA in general and referred to the area as "The Land of Mink Swimming Pools." Originally, Palisades consisted of a 6600-acre land grant given in 1839 to Francisco Marquez (a descendant of whom was Virginia's groundskeeper). In 1911, the scenery provided an ideal location for the "Western" film factory known as Inceville. By 1922, the area had been christened "Pacific Palisades." It was Will Rogers, owning a large ranch adjacent to Palisades, who encouraged film stars to make Palisades their home. Clean air and ocean breezes attracted many to the family-oriented, yet affluent subdivisions. More specifically, Virginia's home on Amalfi Drive was in Palisades Riviera, which had streets named after Mediterranean coastal towns. Amalfi is among the most beautiful resorts in Italy.

1960 -Ayds Diet Candy
Campaign photo

Virginia obviously loved her surroundings, as her home with J. Walter Ruben on Maroney Lane was only a few minutes west of 1329 Amalfi Drive, the home of Virginia and Ali. Aside from time spent in Istanbul, Virginia had resided comfortably in her home since 1946. In 1949, the Pacific Palisades Chamber of Commerce was officially organized. One of the time-honored events of the Chamber was the selection of the town's honorary mayor. Virginia had held the appointment since 1944 through the Civic League. The new Chamber reinstated her position through 1953 (giving her the longest tenure to date). She proved a wonderful ambassador for the community. Virginia was succeeded by comedian Jerry Lewis, and by 1960 voice-master Mel Blanc (Bugs Bunny, Porky Pig, Daffy Duck, et al) held the position. As the early 1960s progressed, Virginia withdrew from her career and her community. When asked, she told reporters her life had become a succession of sedatives and long-distance phone calls in her endeavor to return Ali to the United States. Her dedication to ensure Ali's return would ultimately bring an end to the life and beautiful surroundings she had earned, paid for, and enjoyed.

Looking fit and trim, Virginia became a spokesperson for the low-calorie Ayds diet candy in 1959, soon after she had signed on for Columbia's *Strangers When We Meet*. Paulette Goddard, Joan Bennett, Hedy Lamarr, and other former movie queens had also promoted the popular reducing treat, whose secret ingredient was phenylpropanolamine. The manufactures claimed the drug reduced the sense of taste. Ironically, Virginia was quoted as saying, "Ayds candy … curbs your appetite without drugs!"[1] Eventually, the FDA issued a warning that Ayds "candy" increased the risk of stroke. (By the 1980s, awareness of the disease AIDS eventually curbed consumer appetite for the candy. Promotions such as, "Why take diet pills when you can enjoy Ayds?" provoked unintentional humor – the product was withdrawn from the market.) Virginia's promo for Ayds appeared in magazines and newspapers through the fall of 1960. Ads like "Virginia Bruce Says 'I Lost 9 lbs. on Ayds Plan'" and "Virginia Bruce tells Hollywood's Secret of Staying Slim After 30," explained how, taken before meals, Ayds curbed her appetite.[2] Two years later, Virginia confessed that her diet also included a steady intake of tranquilizers.

A completely unexpected turn of events in 1961 made the 51-year-old, youthful-looking Virginia a grandmother for the second time. Susan Ann's marriage to Santa Monica realtor Jack Waldron had folded, and in the interim she began dating the son of Virginia's groundskeeper, Leo Marquez. Leo had been in Virginia's employ since she and J. Walter Ruben moved to Pacific Palisades in 1938. Ruben had hired the young Spanish gardener at the recommendation of building contractor Joseph Zukin. Not long after Marquez began working for the Rubens, Virginia learned from their talks that Marquez's family had once owned all the land occupied by movie stars in the Santa Monica Mountains, including where her own home stood.[3] She was touched by his story – fate's fleeting hand of ownership and possessions. It would have its irony. In the summer of 1960, Susan and Marquez's son, Steve, renewed their childhood friendship. The two had grown up together on Ruben and Virginia's horse ranch at Wildtree. According to Virginia's nephew, Vincent Briggs, the blossoming romance (and eventual marriage) caused a "huge scandal."[4] In this author's conversation with Steve Marquez in the summer of 2007, he felt his and Susan's relationship was nothing out of the ordinary, and had only good things to say about Virginia and Ruben. "My dad [Leo] thought very highly of Virginia," said Marquez. "He was Virginia's gardener and horse trainer. She and Ruben had thoroughbreds. I was often helping my father up there at Virginia's. She was a fine woman, plus she was my mother-in-law. When Ruben died, my dad looked after Virginia pretty much. I liked Ruben. He got streptococcus of the throat. That's before they had all this new medicine. I guess he couldn't breath. He shouldn't have died. He was a hell of a man. He always treated my dad alright, and my family."[5] In the spring of 1961, Susan and Steve's daughter Francesca was born, and according to Steve, the marriage was over by the time their daughter was a year old. He made a point of saying, "Virginia enjoyed being a grandmother. Francesca spent quite a bit of time with her."[6] Virginia pointed out during a 1962 interview that her duties as a grandmother kept her busy in Pacific Palisades.[7] Susan would eventually head north to start a new life, and Steve, with the help of his sister, raised Francesca. When asked about Ali Ipar, Steve's tone changed. "Ali Ipar wasn't around very much," he offered. "I wasn't very fond of him."[8]

The Turkish High Court of Justice began trials on the island of Yassiada on October 14, 1960. Before the trials began, Virginia became concerned about any exaggerations to the press, on her part, as to the severity or "unfairness" of Ali's case. She notified Louella Parsons to release the following statement: "Virginia Bruce telephoned to say that she had been misinformed about her husband Ali Ipar's plight. She has received word directly from him that he's merely undergoing routine investigation in Turkey, feels he has been justly treated, and he has a sincere belief in the present Turkish government."[9] Her statement was a cover for something far more serious. The trials, which consisted of 18 cases (the Ali Ipar Case among them), lasted for eleven months and concluded on September 6, 1961. Out of the 592 defendants, 228 were designated as capital punishment cases. On September 17th, ex-prime minister Menderes was executed (hanging), after being charged with violating the constitution. Reference was made during the trials to the pogrom of 1955, for which he was blamed. Fifteen other defendants were sentenced to death.[10] Ali Ipar was convicted on January 20, 1961 "of violating Turkish currency regulations and fraudulently purchasing three merchant ships abroad."[11] Ipar's connection to Menderes and vice-premier Bork was also established. The Turkish military tribunal stated that both leaders misused their authority to "aid and abet Ipar."[12] An Associated Press report noted, "Ipar is liable to a prison term of from one to five years."[13] Shortly after his trial, Ipar was sentenced to a two-year prison term (from the time of his arrest). He was also fined the equivalent of $2,976,000.[14] Unadvisedly, Louella Parsons amplified the evidence against Ipar, and ran a column emphasizing Ali's connection to Menderes!

> The black clouds that have hung over Turkish
> patriot Ali Ipar, husband of pioneer American

Actress Virginia Bruce, are heartbreaking. Virginia says she has frantically tried to contact him or someone who can help. She hasn't heard from Ali directly for two years. Since his political leader and very close friend Menderes was hanged for his so-called crimes a few days ago, final sentence of the army, which has recently taken over, has been passed on Ali. It calls for two more years in prison and a fine of $3,000,000! As wealthy as the Ipar family is, this is practically impossible to meet. The Ipar family was very close to both the prime minister Menderes and President Bayar, who is waiting for his sentence. Poor Virginia has had a tragic life.[15]

Louella then tooted her own horn for something as inconsequential as a luncheon.

I met President and Mrs. Bayar and prime minister Menderes when I was in Istanbul at the opening of the Hilton Hotel—and the Bayars were so hospitable to the Americans and gave a luncheon for us.[16]

The toll Ali's trial took on Virginia wasn't nearly as astonishing as the aftermath. In February 1962, six months prior to the completion of his two-year sentence, Ali was released. Reports stated that Ipar's hefty fine had not been paid, and that government officials "may take court action to attach his property to collect it."[17] By July, the United Press informed Virginia's fans that her life had become "a succession of tranquilizers and long distance telephone calls."[18] The cause? Her arduous, drawn-out task of ensuring Ali's return to the United States. One would think Virginia was accustomed to dealing with Ali's problems by now, but their long separation underscored the situation. Virginia reiterated her plight to the press from what one reporter called "the den of her magnificent hilltop home." News articles commented that Virginia looked a great deal younger than her 52 years. "It was all very complicated," Virginia began. "Some ships Ali owned were involved and he never did get a chance to clear his name. So he served 19 months in prison and was released last February. But he still owes the government $3 million." Virginia stated that Ali had left Turkey and was staying in Paris. "Ali was a permanent resident of the United States until he went back to Istanbul . . . but, while he was imprisoned that expired. As I understand it, you have to have a permanent resident visa renewed every year. Now he's waiting for our state department to take some action."[19] Virginia's phone calls abroad were taking a different kind of toll. "Ali and I start talking and forget about the time," she smiled. "Sometimes the bill runs to $85 a call. Lately I've been trying to hold the long-distance calls to one a week. I'm just going along day to day trying not to become too emotionally involved with the situation. I take a lot of tranquilizers and hope that the end of our separation is in sight. It's not easy, but there really isn't much else to do."[20]

Ali obviously wasn't stewing or pining away to return to the United States. Not long after his release from the Yassiada prison, he celebrated his new freedom by attending the 1962 Cannes Film Festival. Table-hopping Broadway columnist Leonard Lyons caught up with Ali at the May event. Lyons noted that spring rain at Cannes had dampened the hopes of starlets who brought scant bikinis to attract cameramen. Silent film comedian Harold Lloyd was in attendance to exhibit a compilation of his best screen comedies. Charles Boyer, Katharine Hepburn, and Gene Tierney all participated in the 16-day event. After bumping into Ipar, who readily agreed to answer questions (getting one's name in Lyon's New York column was considered an "in"), Lyons mentioned that although Ali's fleet of ships, his lands, his banks and properties had been confiscated, "Ipar shrugged to the prosecutors: 'You haven't really taken anything. You haven't taken away my six languages, my 20 years of education, my experience.'"[21] Ali proclaimed to Lyons, "With all this I'll make my fortune again – and more!"[22]

During Ali's "confinement" in Cannes and Paris, Virginia finally made headway for his return to the States. Gossip monger Dorothy Manners, who would soon take over the column of an ailing Louella Parsons, reported in August 1962 that the red tape which "bound up" Ipar in France had been "snipped." He was onboard the S.S. *United States* and "on his way to Hollywood to be reunited with the wife he has not seen in four years."[23] One would think that Virginia's ordeal had finally come to an end. It must have come as a shock when Ali never showed up. He decided to have an extended layover in New York. It lasted well over a year. In September, Walter Winchell announced, "The Virginia Bruce-Ali Ipar idyll is over. Intimates blame their long Apartacho [sic] plus his political prison term in Turkey . . . ."[24] Ali wasted no time to get back in action. By November 1962, Winchell snooped around to report, "Linda Darnell's attentive escort about town is Turkey's Ali Ipar, recently unlatched from Hollywood-darling Virginia Bruce."[25] Darnell, back east touring in a play, learned her husband had fathered an illegitimate child with a Yugoslavian actress. Darnell filed for separation. It appeared that Ali was doing more than consoling her. Ali's reunion with Darnell, whom he dated in 1942, came as a complete surprise. It was a reality that Virginia could not deal with. She began to substitute alcohol for the tranquilizers she had been taking. She needed *something* to assuage her disappointment and hurt. In the summer of 1963, New York columnist Louis Sobol reported that Ali was "whipping out his autobiography" with the assistance of Valerie Douglas, a one-time Hollywood Press agent.[26] Louella Parsons expressed her puzzlement over Virginia and Ali's "separa-

tion," saying, "When I think of the anguish Virginia Bruce went through when her husband Ali Ipar was imprisoned in Turkey, I am surprised that she is divorcing him. Virginia says they still love each other, but his interests are entirely in Europe . . . She will divorce him under Turkish law – by proxy."[27] Virginia, however, instead of filing for divorce, remained hopeful and Ali finally showed up at her doorstep.

c. 1964 Ali Ipar
(Courtesy of
Ali Ipar)

In January 1964, Virginia's nephew Vincent Briggs completed his 2-year stint in the service. He had been drafted out of UCLA in 1962. She welcomed him to stay with her in Pacific Palisades while he adjusted to civilian life. Vincent's most haunting memory of the occasion was the return of Ali Ipar. It had been two years since Ipar's release from prison. As an eyewitness to the event, Vincent recalled, "I was staying with Virginia when I got out of the army – on Amalfi Drive – I drove her car around a lot – a Thunderbird. I was with her the day Ali Ipar walked in the door. I'll never forget it. Virginia was in the den bar. They had a beautiful bar there, a beautiful house – a big house. She was sitting by the bar. She had been drinking all day long. She looked terrible. So, Ali walks in. He looks at her for the first time in *years*, and says, 'Oh my God! What happened to you?'"[28] Virginia was devastated. Although they had talked of divorce, the longed-for reunion with husband Ali was not what she had expected. Vincent admitted, "Oh, she was on alcohol. I don't know about tranquilizers. She was overweight. She was such a beautiful woman at one time. Ali's time in prison was a killer for her. I'm not inside her brain or anything, but she loved the guy. She really loved him. And, she spent a fortune on him. My father [Stanley] was very upset with Ali because of all the money he extracted from her. His various film projects – she financed them. Didn't work."

In the aftermath of Ali's return, Vincent recalled, "Virginia and I had a good relationship. We communicated. Christopher was in the Air Force at the time. He wasn't there. Anyway, Ipar sent Virginia somewhere to get dried out. It didn't help. She still had a problem"[29] Ali's attempt to "help" included filing for divorce. According to news reports on January 17, 1964, they both filed suits against each other. The divorce was granted to Virginia by an Istanbul court. Neither was present for the judgment.[30] Turkish law regulating matrimonial property was in complete favor of the husband. A separate property regulation (from 1926) deemed the supremacy of men in marriage – meaning that all properties acquired during a marriage went to the husband. Women were essentially left with nothing. Religious conservatives argued that a move toward equality would "destroy love and affection in the family" and "increase the rate of divorce and consequently ruin Turkish society."[31] The law would not be challenged until the year 2000, when Turkish women's groups introduced a Civil Code which stated that matrimonial property be split 50/50. Fortunately, the Turkish Parliament approved the new Civil Code, which came into effect on January 1, 2002. Their landmark decision was several decades too late to be of any help to Virginia Bruce. The whole dilemma that faced Virginia was reiterated to me by Leatrice Gilbert Fountain.

A few years after Virginia and Ali divorced for the second time, John Gilbert's daughter Leatrice was researching her father's life, and she made a point to visit Virginia. It was a poignant reunion. Leatrice remembered:

> The last time I saw Virginia was in 1973. I was in Los Angeles doing research for my book. I stayed with Suzanne Vidor (director King's daughter and an old friend), and she introduced me to everyone I needed to know and managed to get me an appointment with Virginia, who was living in Pacific Palisades, or near there. Her house was small and crowded with furniture left over from better times.

> I would not have recognized her. All the fine bones in her face were gone under layers of fat. She looked haggard and old. Even her voice was hoarse and cracked. I had never seen such a transformation, and I was so shocked that I almost forgot what I came to talk with her about. Once we started, however, her memory was sharp and clear. She said, "It's ironic, all the money I am living on today is from the two annuities your father gave me in our divorce agreement. Everything else is gone." Virginia stated that during their brief marriage [Gilbert's] drinking wiped out any chance they might have had for a happy marriage.

She explained, "Jack was so depressed, he was destroyed, really by Mayer, and what the studio had done to him, and he felt helpless to go against them . . . There was no one left to defend him, except for the designer Cedric Gibbons, but there wasn't much Cedric could do. Jack still had his looks. He was young, highly intelligent and bent on self destruction. It was living a tragedy to be with him."[32]

Leatrice offered this author, "I don't know how much you know about her marriage to Ali Ipar, and I don't want to burden you with unnecessary verbiage, but if you need information about it, I can tell you what happened." I asked, and this is what she had to say:

Virginia fell madly in love with Ipar. (He looked a little like Jack.) He was probably the great love of her life. She used every connection she had to further his career, which never got very far. At one point, under Turkish law, Ipar had to return to Turkey and serve his time in the armed forces. Also, under Turkish law, an officer could not be married to a foreign national, so he and Virginia obtained a divorce (in name only). Again, under Turkish law, if a man divorced his wife, he automatically retained all her property, so that Virginia's money inherited from my father and from Ruben, all went into Ali Ipar's hands. She trusted him completely and they returned to the States. Afterwards, Ipar took off for South America where he married again and lived happily on Virginia's lost fortunes."[33]

Leatrice concluded her recollections with what she referred to as "another sad note." "After our last painful interview," said Leatrice, "Virginia wrote to me occasionally. She told me that Ali had returned to California and they were seeing each other. That same Christmas I received a romantic Christmas card from her inscribed from 'Mrs. Ali Ipar.' [Virginia's legal name was Virginia Ipar] I never heard from her again . . . Virginia deserves to be remembered, and I am glad you are taking on the job."[34]

Aside from an appearance on television's popular *Today Show* in early 1965, Virginia's career came to a close. That same year, Mike Connolly, whom *Newsweek* claimed to be filmland's "most influential" columnist, announced that Virginia was slated to play Sister Mary Demetrios in producer Bill Frye's *Life with Mother Superior*. Columbia pictures had already signed Rosalind Russell for the title role (which had initially been offered Greta Garbo for $1 million).[35] With the added box-office appeal of teen star Hayley Mills, the movie would prove to be a hit. Sadly, Bruce was not up on screen when the film, retitled *The Trouble with Angels*, was released. 1930s second-lead Binnie Barnes ended up wearing Bruce's wimple.

Connolly was also keeping tabs on Ali Ipar. In an October 1964 column, he noted that Ali had registered into a Sunset Strip high-rise. Ipar's latest commercial venture was packaging frozen Turkish food. Connolly jibbed, "Between deep freeze sessions [Ipar] is dating Rita Hayworth and Lana Turner."[36] The romance with Hayworth turned serious. By New Year's, Walter Winchell reported that "Turkish socialite" Ipar and Hayworth were "making the same romantic shadow."[37] Journalist Dorothy Kilgallen summed up the inevitable end of their affair in February, stating, "Rita Hayworth's romance with Ali Ipar, once married to Virginia Bruce, who was once married to someone else – appears to be finished. Rita's chums think the reason was geographical; Ali likes to stay in Europe."[38] Kilgallen's geography was a bit off. According to Ipar, he retreated to South America. Ipar's own comment to this author regarding his and Virginia's second divorce was, "We just separated amicably, and then I went to Brazil. I wanted to get away from Turkey as far as I could. So, stupidly, I went to Brazil, you know. And, then I got married there three years later. So, that's my story. I have one daughter by my Brazilian wife. Unfortunately, I am the last Ipar. My brother died. So, no one else will continue with the name."[39] Ipar turned enthusiastic recalling his affair with Hayworth. He repeated his claim to romancing a number of Hollywood beauties, "and especially Rita Hayworth," he stressed. "This was after my divorce. I mean I was separated – but, ahhh, that was after Virginia – Virginia died, I do not know what year. [Virginia died in 1982.] But, Rita and I had an affair. She wanted to take her little girls — she had one girl by Orson Welles, Rebecca, and one girl named Jasmine." (Ipar lost his train of thought here. Hayworth's "little girls" were ages 15 and 20 at the time of her affair with Ipar.) Ipar did not elaborate on what ended his tryst with Hayworth, but he did state that Virginia was accepting of his Brazilian wife, Maria. "Virginia and I remained very good friends," he stated. "She even invited my Brazilian wife and my little daughter to her home when we came back to visit."[40]

One of Ipar's visits to Virginia, before his Brazilian marriage, made news. In the fall of 1968 Virginia was reported seriously ill in the Motion Picture Country Hospital in Woodland Hills. Reports stated that Ipar, living in Rio de Janeiro, was "flying to her bedside."[41] His appearance, at a crucial moment, had its effect. A week later, United Press International gave an update on the condition of her health stating, "Actress Virginia Bruce, 58, was reported 'feeling much better' . . . The hospital has refused to disclose the nature of her illness."[42]

c.1967 candid shot

The marriage of Ipar and his Brazilian wife Maria held. In 2007, when I contacted him in Palm Springs, his wife was in France, which I gathered was their main residence. During a conversation I had with Virginia's nephew Vincent, he was surprised to learn Ipar was still around. "Ali? He's still alive? Jesus! He had a condo up there in Palm Springs. I've met his wife. She can't speak English, I know that. I met her in my father's apartment. Beautiful! She also had money! They *had* to have money. Last time I saw Ali, he was huge. He looked great from the neck up. I didn't know him well. My father [Stanley] never forgave him. Ipar took all Virginia's money – invested it unwisely – wanted to be a big producer. He had a big-name star as a wife."[43]

Ipar, who was cordial and pleasant during our phone conversations, insisted I call him "Ali." He saw himself as Virginia's benefactor after all her losses. Ipar epitomized the male prerogative of his culture. "I helped her a lot toward the end," he explained. "In other words, she needed help. She needed financial help."[44] Ipar seemed to be a proud man who feels his life has been a great success. His family, his education, his connection to Hollywood – have given him a sense of accomplishment. "I'm almost 86 years old. I'm hard of hearing," Ali admitted. "My father died when he was 82-83 years old. My mother died very late, she was 94. She survived many of her children, and I'm the only living child of them. And, I'm pretty much on my way to go too!" he laughs. Apparently, Ali had initially resisted when he and Virginia discussed marriage in 1946. "When I married Virginia, I was eleven years younger," recalled Ali. "And I told her, 'Are you sure, Virginia?' She said, 'What's the difference?' She looked much younger, she was born in 1910."[45] As confirmed by author Orhan Pamuk, Ipar's privileged upbringing in Istanbul resulted in a world view and behavior that was typical among his peers. The impact of Ipar's life decisions, of course, was not a "bed of roses" for Virginia Bruce. Still, she must have been aware of what made him tick and was willing to overlook what others saw as pretension and opportunism. As her nephew Vincent observed, "She loved the guy. She really loved him!"

Ipar's relationship with Susan and Christopher became estranged. "I haven't seen them," Ipar stated, "they sort of — Susan disappeared. I don't even know whether she is alive. She was a funny sort of child. Christopher returned with us to Turkey and then he went back. He's married. He hasn't been close to me. So, I didn't call him this time. I should have really, but, you know." Ipar's relationship with his homeland remained troublesome, to say the least. When I asked if he ever returned to Istanbul, he simply stated, "I go back once and awhile. But . . . there was the military overthrow . . . *prison* . . . they accused me unfairly. I'm sort of heartbroken, you know. So, that's about it." Ipar had returned to the U.S. in 2007, to face an appearance in court. "I have a lawsuit with this house [Palm Springs], because I bought it from a very dear friend of mine," explained Ipar. "He wanted the payments in cash . . . twenty years later, a promissory note came up. So, I have a lawsuit."[46] Ipar also battled Merrill-Lynch International Inc., from 1997-2001. The particulars involved a 1991 London investment of $1,200,000. A court in Geneva, Switzerland finally resolved the issue.[47] For Ipar, life has continued to prove . . . interesting.

One unexpected turn of events in Virginia's life, after retirement, involved the adventures of Susan Ann. Susan relocated to Oregon, where she met up with a Klamath Native American named Al Smith (a.k.a., Alfred Leo Smith, Jr.). Smith was a fifty-year-old recovering alcoholic who had rebuilt his life and was determined to help others do the same. As a boy, Smith was placed in a Catholic boarding school and forbidden to speak his native tongue. After his "education" he headed in a downward spiral. When he wasn't drinking, he was begging. By 1957, he resolved to change his life and join Alcoholics Anonymous. Smith began to integrate the aspects of his Native-American culture that had been denied him. He took a job as counselor at a Roseburg, Oregon facility, during which time Susan Ann entered his life. He wasn't exactly husband/father material. In spite of this, Susan and Al started a family. Their son David was born in 1969. David explained to this author that his father's relationship with Susan was "in-between his two marriages."[48] Susan gave birth to a daughter Marisha in 1971. Smith eventually left to pursue his life's work on behalf of Native Americans. He is recognized as the main force behind one of the most significant Supreme Court decisions in recent years: the Religious Freedom Restoration Act of 1993. The legislation reestablished the right for Native-American use of peyote as a spiritual sacrament. (Ironically, Smith noted that his clients overcame substance abuse more easily after participating in the centuries-old peyote religion.) Both David and Marisha attended a 1999 celebration in honor of their father's achievements held at the University of Oregon on his 80th birthday.[49]

With Smith out of the picture, single motherhood was a struggle for Susan. She married Robert Lee Miller of Portland, Oregon, in 1972. David remembers his mother calling Ali Ipar at one point, who wired her some money. "My mom talked good about Ali," said David. "She said good things about him. They had a halfway decent relationship. It was good enough where she was able to call him and ask for help."[50] Virginia helped Susan out as best she could. David expressed the importance of Grandma Virginia in his life. "My Grandma called all the time. I loved talking to her," recalled David. "I talked to her almost a couple times a week at least. I only got to see her once, though. My mom couldn't afford to fly down to Los Angeles. Grandma came up here. I remember the details. Our house was too small, so she went and got a hotel. I remember that. When I was a little boy, she sent me a subscription to *National Geographic*, because I loved that kind of stuff. I used to get the magazine every month. Coming from her, it meant a lot. She would send things up to us. I couldn't wait to talk to her every time she called. Oh, I loved her, always."[51] When Virginia passed away, it came as a crushing blow to Susan and her children. "When she died," recalled David, "it was horrible for me. My mother, too. I loved talking to my grandma, and I missed her. She died of cirrhosis, I believe. It was just hard. Because my mom didn't have anybody. And, I didn't either."[52] (Susan remained married to Robert until her death on December 3, 2004 at age 71.)

The most telling aspect of Susan's new life in Oregon was her complete detachment from her Hollywood roots. She said nothing to David and Marisha about their grandmother's connection to Hollywood. They had no clue as to who their grandfather John Gilbert was. After Susan passed away, it came as a complete shock to her children to discover Virginia's photographs and memorabilia from her film career. "My mother kept us away from the Hollywood scene," said David. "I didn't even know . . . I just realized all this stuff since my mother passed away. I inherited a lot of Hollywood scrapbooks and photos of my grandmother. I got a hold of a lady who is the president of the John Gilbert Appreciation Society. I am trying to break into acting myself. Acting is in my blood. I look a lot like my grandfather John Gilbert . . . but my grandmother, also. I am half Native-American Modoc, and then my mother's side which is English, Irish, French and Welch – it gives me an exotic look."[53] David indicated, with much enthusiasm, his intention to keep the name of John Gilbert and Virginia Bruce alive.

Virginia's son Christopher also maintained distance from his connection to Hollywood. His life has focused on his career. After Christopher's stint with the Air Force, he continued his passion for flying. Virginia's nephew, Vincent Briggs, commented, "Virginia's two kids were miles apart. Susan was always a little immature – mentally, but very attractive. Chris flies corporate jets. He's never home. He married Carole and they had three daughters — he adopted Carole's son, Clint. After he divorced Carole, he married Nellie and they had one daughter. So, he has four kids of his own, and Clint."[54] (This would add up to the eight natural grandchildren Virginia mentioned during a photo-shoot taken shortly before her death.)

Vintage Hollywood stars enjoyed a wave of nostalgia that emerged during the 1970s and '80s. The release of MGM's inaugural *That's Entertainment!* (1974) broke all-time summer movie attendance records. The studio's musical archives yielded an amazing two-hour extravaganza. Highlights included Virginia in MGM's most elaborate production number, Irving Berlin's "A Pretty Girl is Like a Melody," from *The Great Ziegfeld*. MGM publicity for the film featured a photo of Virginia as "Spirit of the Follies," gracing the apex of a 175-step spiral staircase. On film, Frank Sinatra narrated, "In 1936, *The Great Ziegfeld* won an Oscar for the best picture of that year, and it's no wonder. Virginia Bruce and a gang of lovely ladies flooded up Hollywood's biggest staircase." The number was one of many musical numbers toasted. Sorely missing, however, was Bruce's rendition of Cole Porter's "I've Got You Under My Skin," from *Born to Dance*. Surprisingly, the number failed to be included in either of the *That's Entertainment!* sequels. Producer Jack Haley, Jr. (then-married to Liza Minnelli) focused heavily on the films of Liza's mother, Judy Garland, and his father-in-law, director Vincente Minnelli. Song-and-dance numbers of Sinatra, Astaire, and Gene Kelly were also given preferential treatment.

Nostalgia publications, such as Richard Lamparski's *Whatever Became of . . .* series, paid tribute to Virginia. The second edition detailed her career and personal life. Lamparski simply stated that after playing Kim Novak's mother in *Strangers When We Meet*, Virginia "lived quietly in her beautiful home in Pacific Palisades."[55] Aside from being mentioned in film biographical collections, Virginia stayed out of the news. In May 1977, Hearst columnist Jack O'Brian, who mixed celebrity gossip with right-wing politics, paid tribute to Virginia when he ended his column by stating, "Virginia Bruce, maybe the most beautiful screen star ever, is recovering from major surgery."[56] Virginia's hometown paper, *The Fargo Forum*, occasionally updated readers on her activities. When the Class of 1928 celebrated their 50th anniversary in 1978, they were surprised not to hear from her. Eighty classmates registered for the two-day event. *Forum's* columnist, Doris Eastman, wrote, "One graduate they had figured they would hear from, even though they were sure she wouldn't be able to come, is Virginia Briggs Bruce."[57] Eastman stated that no one could understand Virginia's silence, as she had always shown interest in any news about her former classmates. A week after the column appeared, Virginia telephoned former classmate Charles Callahan, who was responsible for tracking down alumni. "Virginia apologized for not answering the letters," wrote Eastman, "she would have liked to be at the reunion, but couldn't make it."[58]

Australian author Colin Briggs (no relation) made contact with Virginia in 1981 for two interviews at her much smaller Pacific Palisades residence. He paid tribute to her in a couple of magazine articles, stating that after Jean Harlow died, Bruce was MGM's "only blonde contract player with star appeal." Briggs commented, "Though illness handicapped the last decade of her life, on the occasions I met her she was always chirpy, witty and very optimistic. The year before her death she visited Norma Shearer at the Motion Picture Country Home and remarked how Shearer still had her beautiful profile, but sadly, was unable to communicate anymore."[59] Briggs noted that Virginia had been at the Country Home's hospital as a result of a broken hip [1973]. "There were rumors of a drinking problem," said Briggs, "but the woman I met was stone cold sober, not to mention intelligent and funny. She was enjoying reading the latest novels and biographies . . . Her brother Stan and his wife Betty remained close . . . Stan was an inventor of note, she proudly mentioned. . . . On my second visit she opened up considerably about the great love of her life Ali Ipar."[60] "He was eleven years my junior," commented Virginia. "We met in 1945. My time with him, although often we were much separated was the happiest of all my life. We divorced in 1964 and he remained in Turkey [sic], where he remarried and had a family. Just last year he visited me and again we voiced our lasting love for each other."[61] The 1980 visit Virginia referred to would have been the last time she and Ipar saw each other. How she managed to find consolation in Ali's voicing his "lasting love" would seem to be a stretch, but apparently it is what she wanted to hear more than anything else.

Briggs paid tribute to Virginia as an actress, calling her:

> An extremely adroit comedienne ... [Virginia]
> had the same brittle, worldly wise style that
> Lauren Bacall developed so well ... Her dramatic
> "thesping" was also assured, and she was equally at
> home playing a sensitive, emotional heroine or an
> icy sophisticated man trap. While her beauty and
> natural unspoiled personality brought her fame,
> fortune, popularity and success, it did not bring her
> lasting love. In her particular case the saying "lucky
> in cards, unlucky in love" would be prophetic.[62]

Author James Watters, along with Hollywood photographer Horst (who had photographed Garbo, Dietrich and Bergman, et al.), began a project in 1979 to locate and photograph, as Watters put it, "actresses who have illumined our lives, affected our styles, haunted our dreams – then and now."[63] Their publication, *Return Engagement,* featured 74 vintage stars. Mary Astor, Virginia's costar from *Woman Against Woman,* greeted Watters and Horst at the Motion Picture Country Home. Astor seemed content in the one-room cottage she shared with a pet canary. Horst photographed Astor riding her bike, and posed smiling in a chair. Astor jested, "If you run into Alan Alda, tell him he can put his shoes under my bed anytime."[64] Luise Rainer, who was star-billed above Virginia in *Escapade* and *The Great Ziegfeld,*

1981 Looking classy in spite of ill-health

posed with what Watters referred to as a "relentless smile." He compared her to a traffic cop, as he observed Rainer, "Swinging her arms, grasping her breast-bone, eyes popping . . . over dramatizing her tale of the innocent in Hollywood . . . more mannered than modest." "Sometimes life does imitate the movies," Watters cagily remarked after their visit.[65] More genuinely in tune with reality were Myrna Loy and Maureen O'Sullivan. Both the ex-MGM co-stars of Virginia were living in Manhattan. Loy was working on her excellent autobiography, *Being and Becoming.* The youthful-looking O'Sullivan enthused she was "ready for anything." John Gilbert's third wife, Ina Claire, greeted Watters and Horst atop Nob Hill (San Francisco's exclusive residential area). One of the "grande dames" of San Francisco society, Claire looked down on the city below and spoke of "Paris, Rome and Salzburg." Gilbert's first wife, Leatrice Joy, was in fine form at age 87 and living in Connecticut. Her daughter (Leatrice Fountain) had recently thrown away Joy's roller skates. Watters commented, "Even with two later marriages, Leatrice's love for Gilbert remains inviolate. She swears he was the only man 'I truly, truly loved, and I'm just grateful to be the mother of his daughter.'"[66]

By the time Watters and Horst were received by Virginia in the winter of 1981-82, she had reentered the Country Home Hospital. Stanley's wife, Betty, called Watters, to tell him that Virginia "changed her mind, she wants to be photographed, even in the hospital. She's going to wear her good pearls."[67] Betty explained to Watters how much their visit might mean to Virginia. When they arrived at her small and spare room, a bouquet of flowers sat on a side table. A note was attached that said, "It was wonderful seeing one of my all-time loves. Bob Hope." Virginia was propped up in a metal chair. "Her voice, smoky and seductive, alone defies the years," commented Watters. "I can't smile for the camera, really I can't," said Virginia. "I'll look serious for you. I'm *so* dramatic anyway." She whispered, with a touch of heartbreak. "Do you know Norma Shearer is just down the hall? She was the biggest of them all, and here she is blind and dying, after all that, all that fame and riches and now this. Maybe I haven't had it so tough. Two of my husbands died on me and my daughter's been on welfare, but I've got eight grandchildren and well. . . ." Watters noted that Virginia tried to smile, but opted to light up a Chesterfield instead. "People do remember me," Virginia added. "I just signed 15 old stills for somebody, things I never had ever seen before. I've been in and out of this place so much people just know where to find me." Watters mentioned that Virginia's involvement with Ipar "more or less ended her career, but not the headlines . . . her husband was in one controversy after another . . . ." [68]

Virginia's pose for Horst, by the flowers that Bob Hope had sent, was indeed a heartbreaker. Wearing no make-up and a floral print frock which sadly clashed with the long double-strand of pearls, her suggested "serious" expression spoke for itself. Horst's camera was honest. Virginia's photograph captured her wistful melancholy. One would have to look hard to recognize the woman who had been Hollywood's "Most Beautiful Blonde." In the late afternoon just before Watters and Horst departed, Virginia managed a faint smile, which Watters found "touching." "Do you think when I'm gone," Virginia wondered aloud, "anyone will remember that I had awfully dreamy eyes?"[69]

Several weeks after Watters and Horst visited Virginia, she took a turn for the worse. Virginia's nephew, Vincent Briggs, was the executor for her will. "I was seeing Virginia on a regular basis," recalled Vincent. "I had dinner with her once a week, at her place, for years at a time. I'd drop by for dinner and we'd chat. I was at her bedside when she passed on. In fact, I taped something from her, two weeks before she succumbed – what she wanted to leave for whom and so forth. My father was the original executor, but they had a big argument. So, she crossed him off. She had cancer. This wasn't lung cancer – it was other than lung. She was in the bed. . . . We were all there, my father, my stepmother. They kept Virginia alive until she was just skin and bones. She was in a coma."[70] Vincent reminisced that he thought of Virginia as a "modern woman" and "headstrong." "She was the boss," Vincent emphasized. "She loved Ali and the whole scenario with him. She started drinking and kept on drinking until she died. I call love a form of temporary insanity."[71]

Virginia Bruce passed away on February 24, 1982. She was 71. *The New York Times* noted that she "portrayed the quintessential Ziegfeld showgirl in the lavish 1936 musical film *The Great Zieg-*

feld, and was the last wife of John Gilbert, the silent-screen lover. Noted for her fragile beauty, Miss Bruce was a popular leading lady of the 1930's and 40's."[72] Most obituaries simply stated that she had died "after a long illness." A private funeral followed.

I asked Vincent Briggs what he had liked about his aunt, Virginia Bruce. He responded: "She was different. She was very independent. She was in charge . . . like Hillary Clinton . . . a woman in charge. She wasn't subservient. Maybe she was subservient to her husbands, but she was headstrong, especially for women in those days. That would be what I liked about her."[73]

When Virginia's grandson David Smith was going through the memorabilia that she had saved, he came across a project she had been working on. "You know what I've got here?" David said to me. "It's a hardback book that my grandma was trying to put together of her home in Pacific Palisades. It's called, 'My Heart Was Set on Colonial.' It's a scrapbook of each room – but, it wasn't finished."[74] The photos that David mentioned were from a 1940 *House and Garden* feature which toured the home and surrounding acreage at Wildtree where she and Ruben had resided. Although Virginia was compelled to accept the consequences of her marriage to Ali Ipar, she had allowed herself to look back to a happier time with Ruben and a marriage that held together. In fact, she had specified that after cremation, her ashes would return home to Wildtree. Her nephew Vincent recalled with a chuckle, "Chris Ruben, and my father Stan, took Virginia's ashes and got into a small one-engine plane. She wanted her ashes distributed over Wildtree. Well, when they opened the plane window and let the ashes go, they flew right back into the plane!"

When I talked to Ipar, I was surprised when he asked, "When did Virginia die? Do you have her . . . " He hesitated a moment. I stated, "1982." "Ah, in 1982," he replied. "I didn't remember when she died. I was already in Brazil, you see. I couldn't go to her funeral." After a thoughtful pause, he remarked, "I appreciate that you are writing about Virginia."[75]

Before venturing to California in 1928, Virginia had an uncanny encounter with a psychic that she felt marked her as "fated." Virginia told confident Gladys Hall in 1936,

> A curious thing happened to me before I came to
> Hollywood. A long time before, when I was just a
> schoolgirl back home in North Dakota, I went to
> a clairvoyant one day and she told me that I was
> destined for tragedy. . . . Perhaps part of my tragedy
> will be that I do spoil men. I seem to be the type
> to attract men who are much stronger and more
> forceful than I am. I think that it is not irrelevant to
> what we are talking about for me to speak of Jack
> [Gilbert]. Because, after all, my belief that women
> should spoil men and most of my theories about
> the relationships between men and women spring,
> naturally, from my marriage to Jack."[76]

Understandably, by the end of her traumatic marriage to John Gilbert, Virginia came to a conclusion regarding what she called "a dangerous topic for me to talk about." "When I get to thinking about being a wife to a man," Virginia stated, "I feel equal to any woman from the standpoint of love, or sacrifice and devotion. We women take a lot. Perhaps we like it . . . I think every woman is masochistic at heart."[77]

One could suppose that the dream 18-year-old Virginia Briggs mentioned in one of her first Hollywood interviews had come true with Ali Ipar . . . at a great cost. "My chief purpose in life is to fall in love," she had declared. "I don't know why I want to, but I do."[78] Fifty years later, she felt her dream had been fulfilled. In truth, Virginia avoided the reality of her situation with Ipar. Instead of letting go and moving on into something deeper than a dream, she mirrored the very bridge of the Cole Porter song she had introduced:[79]

> I'd sacrifice anything, come what might, for the
>   sake of having you near,
> In spite of a warning voice that comes in the night
>   and repeats and repeats in my ear,
> Don't you know, little fool, you never can win,
> Use your mentality, wake up to reality
> But each time I do, just the thought of you makes
>   me stop, before I begin
> Cause I've got you . . . under my skin

Endnotes

1   Virginia Bruce, "I Lost 9 lbs on Ayds Plan," *Tucson Daily Citizen*, 1/18/60
2   "Virginia Bruce Tells Hollywood's Secret of Staying Slim After 30," *New York News*, 9/11/60
3   News column, *Charleston Daily Mail*, 3/26/39
4   Conversation with Vincent Briggs, 5/29/2007
5   Conversation with Steve Marquez, 6/29/2007
6   ibid
7   "Virginia Bruce Trying to Get Husband Back in U.S.," *San Mateo Times*, 7/21/62
8   Conversation with Steve Marquez, 6/29/2007

Chapter Eighteen

9   Louella Parsons column, *San Antonio Light*, 8/26/60

10   Ali Ulurasba, *An Illustrated History of Turkish Democracy*, 2004, pg 79 www.byegm.gov.tr

11   "Ex-Hollywood Star's Husband Is Convicted," *Lethbridge Herald*, 1/20/61

12   ibid

13   ibid

14   "Virginia Bruce's Mate is Freed From Prison," *Fresno Bee*, 2/8/62

15   Louella Parsons, "Actress Virginia Bruce Can't Contact Her Turkish Husband," *Albuquerque Journal*, 9/25/61

16   ibid

17   "Virginia Bruce's Mate . . . "

18   "Virginia Bruce Trying to Get Husband Back into U.S.," *San Mateo Times*, 7/21/62

19   ibid

20   ibid

21   Leonard Lyons, "Lyon's Den," *San Mateo Times*, 5/22/62

22   ibid

23   Dorothy Manners column, *Cedar Rapids Gazette*, 8/10/62

24   Walter Winchell column, 9/12/62

25   Walter Winchell column, *Cedar Rapids Gazette*, 11/7/62

26   Louis Sobol, "New York Cavalcade," *Cedar Rapids Gazette*, 9/5/63

27   Louella Parsons column, "Louella's Movie-Go-Round," *Albuquerque Journal*, 10/16/62

28   Telephone conversation with Vincent Briggs, 5/29/2007

29   ibid

30   "Virginia Bruce Winds Divorce in Istanbul," *Fresno Bee*, 1/17/64

31   "Successful Law Reform," *The Star Online*, 3/27/2006

32   Email from Leatrice Gilbert Fountain, 1/19/2007

33   Email from Leatrice Gilbert Fountain, 1/20/2007

34   ibid

35   Mike Connolly, "Notes From Hollywood," *Star News (CA)*, 2/19/65

36   Mike Connolly, "Notes From Hollywood," *Star News (CA)*, 10/20/64

37   Walter Winchell column, *Humboldt Standard*, 1/7/65

38   Dorothy Kilgallen, "On Broadway," *News Journal (OH)*, 2/25/65

39   Conversation with Ali Ipar, 4/29/2007

40   Ibid.

41   "Actress Virginia Bruce Seriously Ill," *Press-Telegram (CA)*, 10/31/68

42   "Ailing Actress Shows Improvement," *Nevada State Journal*, 11/8/68

43   Conversations with Vincent Briggs, 1/16/2007 and 5/29/2007

44   Conversation with Ali Ipar, 4/29/2007

45   ibid

46 ibid
47 Ie Cour Civile, www.polyreg.ch/d/informationen/bgeunpubliziert/Jahr_2000/ Entscheide_4C_2000/4C.209__2000.html
48 Conversation with David Smith, 1/17/2007
49 Garrett Epps, *To an Unknown God*, St Martins, N.Y. pp15-16, 43, 108, 233, 254
50 ibid
51 ibid
52 ibid
53 Conversation with David Smith, 1/17/2007
54 Conversation with Vincent Briggs, 5/29/2007
55 Richard Lamparski, *Whatever Became of . . . ?* Crown Publishes, N.Y., 1968, pp 202-203
56 Jack O'Brian, "On Broadway," *News Journal (OH)*, 5/7/77
57 Doris Eastman, "80 Members of Class of 1928 Came for First Reunion," *Fargo Forum*, 6/11/78
58 Doris Eastman, "Virginia Called," *Fargo Forum*, 6/18/78
59 Colin Briggs, "The History of the Beautiful MGM Blonds," *Hollywood Studio Magazine*, 3/89
60 Colin Briggs, "Virginia Bruce – Incandescent Beauty," *Films of the Golden Age*," Summer 2003 pp 38-49
61 ibid
62 ibid
63 James Watters, "Return Engagement," Crown Publishers, N.Y. 1984, pg 6
64 Watters, "Return . . . " pg 8
65 Watters, "Return . . . " pg 39
66 Watters, "Return . . . " pg 77-79
67 Watters, "Return . . . " pg 91
68 ibid
69 ibid
70 Conversation with Vincent Briggs, 5/29/2007
71 ibid
72 "Virginia Bruce, 72, Actress Portrayed Ziegfeld Showgirl," *New York Times*, 2/26/82
73 Conversation with Vincent Briggs, 10/15/2007
74 Conversation wit David Smith, 1/17/2007
75 Conversations with Ali Ipar, 4/29/2007, 5/8/2007
76 Gladys Hall, "Do Women Spoil Men?" *Modern Screen*, 6/36
77 W.E. Oliver, "Virginia Bruce's Hero," *Los Angeles Evening Herald Express*, 11/2/35
78 "Fargo Star Tells Story," *Fargo Forum*, 6/26/29
79 Cole Porter, "I've Got You Under My Skin," Chappell & Co. (London) c. 1936

Virginia Bruce & The Mystery of Madame Wang's

American Pop Artist Andy Warhol surrounded himself with an eclectic mix of people. Old screen stars, such a Paulette Goddard, were among them. It would not have been a stretch of the imagination for him to approach Virginia Bruce for a part in one of his underground productions. Most every online filmography, including the Internet Movie Database and Turner Classic Movies, list *Andy Warhol Presents - Madame Wang's*, a 1981 entry, as Virginia Bruce's final film appearance. For some reason, those who witnessed her performance could not decide whether or not it was *really* her on the screen. After being absent from films for 21 years, what exactly did Virginia Bruce look like? Playing the title character, many were surprised at how tall Virginia appeared. Wearing an obvious ash-blonde wig, make-up applied with a trowel, and adorned in either mink, or Chinese robes – she was not a pretty sight. Whatever possessed her to come out of retirement? Was it the money? Was she attracted to the storyline? On screen we see an East German (Patrick Shoene) jumping ship in Los Angeles in hopes of finding Jane Fonda and starting a Communist revolution. He is convinced Americans are cowards until he gets sidetracked by the punk crowd. He meets Virginia's character (Madame Wang) at a garage sale. Madame Wang runs a trendy nightclub that provides opportunity for new punk bands. It was a rather odd vehicle for Virginia to choose as a "comeback."

During my research I learned that Andy Warhol had nothing at all to do with *Madame Wang's*. The film's director, Paul Morrissey, was connected to Warhol's Factory in the '60s and early '70s and created some of the best works associated with Warhol: *Lonesome Cowboys, Trash, Women in Revolt,* and *Heat.* Morrissey wrote, produced, and directed these films. Warhol only contributed his name above the title. In 1975, Morrissey became an independent filmmaker completely in charge of his own projects. The promotional title, *Andy Warhol Presents - Madame Wang's,* was simply a tribute to Morrissey's connection to Warhol. Classic Hollywood director George Cukor thought Morrissey created "a marvelous kind of world, and a marvelous kind of mischief, holding nothing back and just watching it happen." "Nobody has any kind of guilt in these pictures," remarked Cukor. "None of the attitudes are conventional – you never see a tear – that's extremely refreshing! . . . These pictures I luxuriate in. They're so bold and undiluted and really new. I applaud him for doing that most difficult thing."[1]

In *Madame Wang's,* Morrissey does an impressive job of juxtaposing the "lowest rung" of the American ladder (an odd mix of street people who live in an abandoned Masonic Building) and the "highest rung" ultra-wealthy who appear to be tottering precariously from their own games and eccentricities. We watch lead character Shoene attempting to fit as an American, ultimately being unsuccessful as a pimp, a thief and a prostitute. Shoene is left in a complete daze after a wealthy socialite uses him as a boy-toy in order to make her own husband "punish" her. The final blow is his discovery of one of the numerous *un*-revolutionary Jane Fonda Workout Salons so popular at the time. Shoene decides to abandon his plan for revolution, and auditions for Madame Wang. While a guitarist grinds away, the extremely good-looking, semi-nude, Shoene, properly adorned in punk make-up and leather, takes out his knife and begins slicing his own flesh. Virginia's Madame Wang eyes him hungrily. The nightclub audience is riveted. Madame Wang is impressed. She has struck gold. "This kid's got something! See if we can get him!" she breathlessly advises an assistant. Despite his success at Madame Wang's, Schoene decides to return to Europe. America, filled with scenes of futility, somehow connects Shoene to the courage inherent in *all* humanity. During Schoene's farewell to a young streetwalker he has befriended, he asks her, "By the way, whatever happened to all your cowards?"

When this author contacted director Paul Morrissey in 2007, he cleared up, once and for all, the mystery of Virginia Bruce and Madame Wang. "I'm afraid I have disappointing news," Morrissey told me in a phone conversation. "It was a *man* who played the part of Madame Wang. Very masculine. He was a big fan of Virginia Bruce and simply used her name. He was in his 60's, had been married and had five children. He was in real estate. I don't even know his real name. He was a cross-dresser, not very good-looking. Someone suggested he play the part of Madame Wang. I said, 'But he's a man!' They said, 'What does it matter?' Apparently, it didn't."[4] The film itself had other gender-bending/ drag characters. It made sense somehow for Madame Wang to be the product of a classic Hollywood actress and a cross-dressing heterosexual male.

Morrissey told me of an incident at a *Madame Wang's* premier. "At a showing in Europe," recalled Morrissey, "a critic came up to me and said, 'That isn't *the* Virginia Bruce, is it?'" Morrissey was dumbfounded that *anyone* would mistake this male cross-dresser as Virginia Bruce. "He looked more like Lionel Barrymore!" remarked Morrissey. Perhaps the most surprising remark Morrissey made to me was his belief that the 1934 Production Code was the best thing to ever happen to Hollywood. His point being that all the great women's roles came *after* the Code (his favorite being Norma Shearer's *Marie Antoinette*). Ironically, there isn't a single credit within Morrissey's body of work that would have *ever* been released under the Code's self-righteous, invasive jurisdiction.

Madame Wang's – played by cross-dresser "Virginia Bruce," also known as Virginia Prince. Prince (born 1912) played a principle (and controversial) role in the development of the transgender community (1950-80)

Endnotes

1 Gavin Lambert, *On Cukor*, Putnam, pp 153-154
2 Gary Morris, "Slapstick Realist – The Cinema of Paul Morrissey," *Bright Lights Film Journal*, 9/96
3 Maurice Yacowar, *The Films of Paul Morrissey*, Cambridge University Press, 1993 (Introduction)
4 Conversation with Paul Morrissey, 1/22/2007

Photo Credits

Every effort has been made to trace the copyright holders of the photographs included in this book; if any have been inadvertently overlooked, the author and publisher will be pleased to make the necessary changes.

All photos, unless otherwise noted, are from the author's collection. The author would like to express his thanks to the following individuals for the lending of photos: Howard Mandelbaum (of Photofest), Vincent Briggs, Laura Wagner, John Drennon, and Ali Ipar.

Virginia Bruce 1936 (MGM)

Virginia Bruce Film Credits

1) *Fugitives (1929) – Fox –* (silent with synchronized music score) William Beaudine (d) Cast: Madge Bellamy, Don Terry, Arthur Stone, Earle Fox, *Virginia Bruce (bit)*, Jean Harlow

2) *Hard to Get (1929) – Fox –* (Edna Ferber story *Classified*) William Beaudine (d) Cast: Dorothy Mackaill, Charles Delaney, James Finlayson, Louise Fazenda, Jack Oakie, *Virginia Bruce (model)* 80m

3) *Blue Skies (1929) – Fox –* Alfred L. Werker (d) Cast: Helen Twelvetrees, Frank Albertson, Rosa Gore, *Virginia Bruce (party guest)* 60m

4) *River of Romance (1929) – Paramount –* (play by Booth Tarkington *Magnolia*) Richard Wallace (d) George Cukor (dialogue director) Cast: Charles "Buddy" Rogers, Mary Brian, June Collyer, Henry B. Walthall, Wallace Beery, Anderson Lawler, *Virginia Bruce (uncredited)* 78m - remade *Mississippi (1935)*

5) *Fashions of Love (1929) – Paramount –* Victor Schertzinger (d) Cast: Adolphe Menjou, Fay Compton, Miriam Seegar, John Miljan, *Virginia Bruce (uncredited)* 73m – remake of *The Concert (1921)*

6) *Illusion (1929) – Paramount* – Lothar Mendes (d) Cast: Charles "Buddy" Rogers, Nancy Carroll, June Collyer, Kay Francis, Regis Toomey, Knute Erikson, William Austin, Paul Lukas, Lillian Roth, *Virginia Bruce (party guest)* 84m

7) *Woman Trap (1929) – Paramount* – (play by Edwin J. Burke *Brothers*) William A. Wellman (d) Cast: Hal Skelly, Chester Morris, Evelyn Brent, William B. Davidson, Joseph L. Mankiewicz, *Virginia Bruce (nurse)* 82m

8) *Why Bring That Up? (1929) – Paramount* – George Abbott (d) Cast: Charles Mack, George Moran, Evelyn Brent, Harry Green, *Virginia Bruce (bit)* 82m

9) *The Love Parade (1929) – Paramount* – (based on *The Prince Consort* by Leon Xanrof and Jules Chancel) Ernst Lubitsch (d) Cast: Maurice Chevalier, Jeanette MacDonald, Lupino Lane, Lillian Roth, Edgar Norton, Eugene Pallette, Margaret Fealy, *Virginia Bruce (Second Lady in Waiting),* Jean Harlow 150m

10) *Lilies of the Field (1930) – First National* – Alexander Korda (d) Cast: Corinne Griffith, Ralph Forbes, John Loder, Eve Sothern, *Virginia Bruce (Doris)* 60m

11) *Slightly Scarlet (1930) – Paramount* – Louis J. Gasnier, Edwin H. Knopf (d) Cast: Evelyn Brent, Clive Brook, Paul Lukas, Eugene Pallette, Helen Ware, *Virginia Bruce (Enid Corbett)* 70m

12) *Only the Brave (1930) – Paramount* – Frank Tuttle (d) Cast: Gary Cooper, Mary Brian, Phillip Holmes, James Nell, Morgan Farley, *Virginia Bruce (Elizabeth),* William Bakewell 66m

13) *Young Eagles (1930) – Paramount*- William A. Wellman (d) Cast: Charles "Buddy" Rogers, Jean Arthur, Paul Lukas, Stuart Erwin, *Virginia Bruce (Florence Welford)* 70m

14) *Paramount on Parade (1930) – Paramount –* Dorothy
Arzner, Otto Brower, Edmund Goulding, Victor Heerman,
Edwin H. Knopf, Rowland V. Lee, Ernst Lubitsch, Lothar
Mendes, Victor Schertzinger, Edward Sutherland, Frank
Tuttle (d) Cast: Iris Adrian, Richard Arlen, Jean Arthur,
Mischa Auer, William Austin, George Bancroft, Clara Bow,
Evelyn Brent, Mary Brian, Clive Brook, *Virginia Bruce*,
Nancy Carroll, Ruth Chatterton, Maurice Chevalier, Gary
Cooper, Cecil Cunningham, Leon Errol, Stuart Erwin,
Kay Francis, Skeets Gallagher, Harry Green, Mitzi Green,
James Hall, Phillips Holmes, Helen Kane, Dennis King,
Abe Lyman and his band, Fredric March, Nino Martini,
David Newell, Jack Oakie, Warner Oland, Eugene Pallette,
William Powell, Charles "Buddy" Rogers, Lillian Roth, Fay
Wray 101m – (Virginia was also in the Spanish language
version, *Galas de la Paramount*)

15) *Safety in Numbers (1930) – Paramount –* Victor Schertzinger (d) Cast: Charles "Buddy" Rogers, Kathryn Crawford, Josephine Dunn, Carole Lombard, Roscoe Karnes,
Virginia Bruce (Alma McGregor), Louise Beavers 80m

16) *The Social Lion (1930) – Paramount –* (Story by Octavus
Roy Cohen *Marco Himself*) Edward Sutherland (d) Cast:
Jack Oakie, Mary Brian, Skeets Gallagher, Olive Borden,
Charles Sellon, *Virginia Bruce (bit)* 72m

17) *Raffles (1930) – United Artists –* (novel: *The Amateur
Cracksman* by E. W. Hornung) Samuel Goldwyn (p) Harry
D'Arrast, George Fitzmaurice (d) Cast: Ronald Colman,
Kay Francis, Bramwell Fletcher, Frances Dade, David Tor-
rence, Alison Skipworth, *Virginia Bruce* 72m - previously
filmed in 1917, 1925; remade in 1939

18) *Let's Go Native (1930) – Paramount –* (screenplay by

George Marion, Jr. and Percy Heath) Leo McCarey (d)
Cast: Jeanette MacDonald, Jack Oakie, James Hall, Skeets
Gallagher, Kay Francis, William Austin, David Newell,
Eugene Pallette, *Virginia Bruce (secretary)* 75m

19) *Whoopee! (1930) – United Artists –* (play by Owen Davis
The Nervous Wreck) Sam Goldwyn, Florenz Ziegfeld Jr. (p)
Thornton Freeland (d) Busby Berkeley (choreographer)
Cast: Eddie Cantor, Ethel Shuta, Paul Gregory, Eleanor
Hunt, Jack Rutherford, Spencer Charters, Albert Hackett,
Chief Caupolican, *Virginia Bruce (Goldwyn Girl)*, Claire
Dodd, Betty Grable, Ann Sothern, Marian Marsh, Jeanne
Morgan 94m - two-strip Technicolor; Oscar-nominated
for Best Art Direction; remade *Up in Arms (1944)*

20) *Follow Thru (1930) – Paramount –* Lloyd Corrigan, Lau-
rence Schwab (d) Cast: Charles "Buddy" Rogers, Nancy
Carroll, Zelma O'Neal, Jack Haley, Eugene Pallette, Thelma
Todd, Claude King, *Virginia Bruce (bit in locker room)*,
Frances Dee 92m – two-strip Technicolor

21) *Hell Divers (1931) – MGM -* George W. Hill (d) Cast: Wal-
lace Beery, Clark Gable, Conrad Nagel, Dorothy Jordan,
Marjorie Rambeau, Marie Prevost, Cliff Edwards, John
Miljan, Robert Young, *Virginia Bruce (scene deleted)* 109m

22) *Are You Listening? (1932) – MGM –* Harry Beaumont (d)
Cast: William Haines, Madge Evans, Anita Page, Karen
Morley, Neil Hamilton, Wallace Ford, Jean Hersholt, Joan
Marsh, John Miljan, Hattie McDaniel, *Virginia Bruce (bit)*
73m

23) *The Wet Parade (1932) – MGM –* (based on the Upton
Sinclair novel) Victor Fleming (d) Cast: Walter Huston,
Dorothy Jordan, Robert Young, Neil Hamilton, Wallace
Ford, Lewis Stone, Emma Dunn, Jimmy Durante, Joan

Marsh, Clara Blandick, *Virginia Bruce (billed 8th in the ads, but scenes may have been deleted)* 118m

24) *The Miracle Man (1932) – Paramount –* (based on the Robert Hobard Davis novel & George M. Cohan play) Norman Z. McLeod (d) Cast: Sylvia Sidney, Chester Morris, Robert Coogan, Ned Sparks, Hobart Bosworth, Lloyd Hughes, *Virginia Bruce (Margaret Thornton)*, Boris Karloff, Irving Pichel, Florine McKinney, Jackie Searle 85m – (Tyrone Power Sr. was originally set to play the "Patriarch," but succumbed before production began)

25) *Sky Bride (1932) – Paramount –* (based on the novel by Bogart Rogers) Stephen R. Roberts (d) Cast: Richard Arlen, Jack Oakie, Robert Coogan, *Virginia Bruce (Ruth Dunning)*, Louise Closser Hale, Charles Starrett, Randolph Scott 78m

26) *Winner Take All (1932) – Warners –* Roy del Ruth (d) Cast: James Cagney, Marian Nixon, Guy Kibbee, Dickie Moore, *Virginia Bruce (Joan Gibson)*, Alan Mowbray 66m

27) *Downstairs (1932) – MGM –* (based on story by John Gilbert) Monta Bell (d) Cast: John Gilbert, Paul Lukas, Virginia Bruce, Hedda Hopper, Reginald Owen, Olga Baclanova, Karen Morley 77m

28) *A Scarlet Weekend (1932) – Maxim –* (based on the Willis Kent novel *A Woman in Purple Pajamas*) George Melford (d) Cast: Dorothy Revier, Charles K. French, *Virginia Bruce (Alma McGregor)* 63m - (considered a lost film)

29) *Kongo (1932) – MGM –* (based on play by Chester de Vonde and Kilbourn Gordon) William J. Cowan (d) Cast: Walter Huston, Lupe Velez, Conrad Nagel, *Virginia Bruce (Ann Whitehall)*, C. Henry Gordon 86m – remake of *West of Zanzibar (1928)*

30) *Jane Eyre (1934) – Monogram –* (based on the Charlotte Bronte novel) Christy Cabanne (d) Cast: *Virginia Bruce (Jane Eyre)*, Colin Clive, Beryl Mercer, David Torrence, Aileen Pringle, Edith Fellows 62m – (There have been 5 silent film versions of the Bronte novel. The second sound version starred Joan Fontaine in a 1944 release. A 1970 TV Film starring Susannah York is also highly regarded) - DVD Alpha Video (2004)

31) *Dangerous Corner (1934) – RKO –* (based on play by J.B. Priestley) Phil Rosen (d) Cast: *Virginia Bruce (Ann)*, Conrad Nagel, Melvyn Douglas, Erin O'Brien-Moore, Ian Keith, Betty Furness, Henry Wadsworth, Doris Lloyd 66m

32) *The Mighty Barnum (1934) – United Artists –* Walter Lang (d) Cast: Wallace Beery, Adolphe Menjou, *Virginia Bruce (Jenny Lind)*, Rochelle Hudson, Janet Beecher, Herman Bing 85m

33) *Society Doctor (1935) – MGM –* (based on play by Theodore Reeves *The Harbor*) George B. Seitz (d) Cast: Chester Morris, Robert Taylor, *Virginia Bruce (Madge Wilson)*, Billie Burke, Raymond Walburn, Henry Kolker, Dorothy Peterson, William Henry 67m

34) *Shadow of Doubt (1935) – MGM –* George B. Seitz (d) Cast: Ricardo Cortez, *Virginia Bruce (Trenna Plaice)*, Constance Collier, Isabel Jewell, Arthur Byron, Betty Furness, Regis Toomey 74m

35) *Times Square Lady (1935) – MGM –* George B. Seitz (d) Cast: Robert Taylor, *Virginia Bruce (Toni Bradley)*, Pinky Tomlin, Helen Twelvetrees, Isabel Jewell, Nat Pendleton, Jack LaRue 68m

36) *Let 'Em Have It (1935) – United Artists –* Sam Wood (d) Cast: Richard Arlen, *Virginia Bruce (Eleanor Spencer)*,

Alice Brady, Bruce Cabot, Harvey Stephens, Eric Linden, Joyce Compton, Gordon Jones 96m – DVD Sony (2005)

37) *Escapade (1935)* – *MGM* – Robert Z. Leonard (d) Cast: William Powell, Luise Rainer, Frank Morgan, *Virginia Bruce (Gerta)*, Reginald Owen, Mady Christians, Laura Hope Crews 92m – remake of a German film *Maskerade (1934)*

38) *The Murder Man (1935)* – *MGM* – Tim Whelan (d) Cast: Spencer Tracy, *Virginia Bruce (Mary Shannon)*, Lionel Atwill, Harvey Stephens, Robert Barrat, James Stewart 69m

39) *Here Comes the Band (1935)* – *MGM* – Paul Sloane (d) Cast: Ted Lewis, *Virginia Bruce (Margaret)*, Harry Stockwell, Ted Healy, Nat Pendleton, Donald Cook, Spanky McFarland 86m

40) *Metropolitan (1935)* – *20th Century-Fox* – Richard Boleslawski (d) Cast: Lawrence Tibbett, *Virginia Bruce (Anne Merrill Beaconhill)*, Alice Brady, Cesar Romero, Thurston Hall, Luis Alberni, George Marion, Sr. 74m

41) *The Garden Murder Case (1936)* – *MGM* – (based on the S. S. Van Dine novel) Edwin L. Marin (d) Cast: Edmund Lowe, *Virginia Bruce (Zalia Graem)*, Benita Hume, Nat Pendleton, Gene Lockhart, H.B. Warner, Frieda Inescort, Jessie Ralph, Kent Smith 61m.

42) *The Great Ziegfeld (1936)* – *MGM* – Robert Z. Leonard (d) Cast: William Powell, Myrna Loy, Luise Rainer, Frank Morgan, *Virginia Bruce (Audrey Dane)*, Fanny Brice, Reginald Owen, Ray Bolger, Nat Pendleton, Raymond Walburn 176m – Nominated for 6 Oscars (won for Best Picture, Best Actress – Luise Rainer, and Best Dance Direction) – DVD Warner Home Video (2004)

43) *Born to Dance (1936)* – *MGM* – Roy del Ruth (d) Cast: Eleanor Powell, James Stewart, *Virginia Bruce (Lucy James)*,

Una Merkle, Sid Silvers, Frances Langford, Raymond Walburn, Alan Dinehart, Buddy Ebsen, Juanita Quigley 106m – Nominated for 2 Oscars (Best Song nomination "I've Got You Under My Skin" lost to "The Way You Look Tonight" from *Swingtime*)

44) *Women of Glamour (1937) – Columbia –* (based on play by David Belasco *Ladies of the Evening*) Gordon Wiles (d) Cast: *Virginia Bruce (Gloria Hudson)*, Melvyn Douglas, Reginald Denny, Pert Kelton, Leona Maricle, Thurston Hall, Mary Forbes 68m – remake of *Ladies of Leisure (1926) (1930)*

45) *When Love is Young (1937) – Universal –* (based on the McCall's Magazine story *Class Prophecy* by Eleanore Griffin) Hal Mohr (d) Cast: *Virginia Bruce (Wanda Werner)*, Kent Taylor, Walter Brennan, Greta Meyer, Christian Rub, William Tannen, Jean Rogers 76m

46) *Between Two Women (1937) – MGM –* (story by Erich von Stroheim) George B. Seitz (d) Cast: Franchot Tone, Maureen O'Sullivan, *Virginia Bruce (Patricia Sloan)*, Cliff Edwards, Janet Beecher, Charles Grapewin 88m

47) *Wife, Doctor, and Nurse (1937) – 20ᵗʰ Century-Fox –* Walter Lang (d) Cast: Loretta Young, Warner Baxter, *Virginia Bruce (Miss Stephens - 'Steve')*, Jane Darwell, Sidney Blackmer, Paul Hurst, Charles Judels, Minna Gombell 85m

48) *Bad Man of Brimstone (1937) – MGM –* J. Walter Ruben (d) Cast: Wallace Beery, *Virginia Bruce (Loretta Douglas)*, Dennis O'Keefe, Lewis Stone, Joseph Calleia, Bruce Cabot, Guy Kibbee, Cliff Edwards, Guinn Williams, Noah Beery 89m

49) *Arsene Lupin Returns (1938) – MGM –* George Fitzmaurice (d) Cast: Melvyn Douglas, *Virginia Bruce (Lorraine de Grissac)*, Warren William, John Halliday, Nat Pendleton, E. E.

Clive, Monty Wooley, George Zucco 82m – (Virginia was
originally cast in the 1932 version *Arsene Lupin* with John
and Lionel Barrymore. Her role went to Karen Morley)

50) *The First Hundred Years (1938)* – *MGM* – (based on Norman Krasna story) Richard Thorpe (d) Cast: Robert Montgomery, *Virginia Bruce (Lynn Conway)*, Warren William,
Lee Bowman, Binnie Barnes, Alan Dinehart, Nydia Westman, E. E. Clive, Harry Davenport 73m

51) *Yellow Jack (1938)* – *MGM* – (based on Sidney Howard-
Paul de Kruif play) George B. Seitz (d) Cast: Robert Mont-
gomery, *Virginia Bruce (Frances Blake)*, Lewis Stone, Andy
Devine, Henry Hull, Charles Coburn, Buddy Ebsen, Henry
O'Neill, Janet Beecher 83m

52) *Woman Against Woman (1938)* – *MGM* – (from the novel
Enemy Territory by Margaret Culkin Banning) Robert
Sinclair (d) Cast: *Virginia Bruce (Maris Kent)*, Herbert
Marshall, Mary Astor, Marjorie Rambeau, Zeffie Tilbury,
Juanita Quigley, Janet Beecher, Sarah Padden 61m

53) *There Goes My Heart (1938)* – *United Artists* – (story by Ed
Sullivan) Norman Z. McLeod (d) Cast: Melvyn Douglas,
Virginia Bruce (Joan Butterfield), Patsy Kelly, Alan Mow-
bray, Nancy Carroll, Eugene Pallette, Claude Gillingwater,
Arthur Lake, Harry Langdon 83m

54) *There's That Woman Again (1939)* – *Columbia* – Alexander
Hall (d) Cast: Melvyn Douglas, *Virginia Bruce (Sally Rear-
don)*, Margaret Lindsay, Stanley Ridges, Gordon Oliver 72m

55) *Let Freedom Ring (1939)* – *MGM* – (original story by Ben
Hecht) Jack Conway (d) Cast: Nelson Eddy, *Virginia Bruce
(Maggie Adams)*, Victor McLaglen, Lionel Barrymore,
Edward Arnold, Guy Kibbee, Charles Butterworth, H.B.
Warner, Raymond Walburn 87m

56) *Society Lawyer (1939)* – MGM – (from the Arthur Somers Roche novel *Penthouse*) Edwin L. Marin (d) Cast: Walter Pidgeon, *Virginia Bruce (Pat Abbott)*, Leo Carillo, Eduardo Ciannelli, Lee Bowman, Herbert Mundin, Ed Brophy 77m – remake of *Penthouse (1933)*

57) *Land of Liberty (1939)* – MGM – Cecil B. DeMille (editor) Cast: Don Ameche, George Arliss, John Barrymore, Lionel Barrymore, Warner Baxter, Wallace Beery, *Virginia Bruce (in archive footage from Yellow Jack)*, Claudette Colbert, Bette Davis, Irene Dunne, Henry Fonda, Clark Gable, Walter Huston, Jeanette MacDonald, Joel McCrea, Dickie Moore, Claude Rains, James Stewart, Spencer Tracy, Loretta Young 138m – 125 feature films and newsreel footage were used in this patriotic effort to document the history of the United States. *Land of Liberty* was shown extensively at the New York World's Fair and the San Francisco Exposition (1939-40) – proceeds from the theatrical release were donated for emergency war relief.

58) *Stronger Than Desire (1939)* – MGM – (adapted from W. E. Woodward novel *Evelyn Prentice*) Leslie Fenton (d) Cast: *Virginia Bruce (Elizabeth Flagg)*, Walter Pidgeon, Lee Bowman, Ann Dvorak, Ilka Chase, Rita Johnson, Ann Todd 78m – remake of *Evelyn Prentice (1934)*

59) *Flight Angels (1940)* – Warners – (original story *Flight 8* by Jerry Wald and Richard Macaulay) Lewis Seller (d) Cast: *Virginia Bruce (Mary Norvell)*, Dennis Morgan, Ralph Bellamy, Wayne Morris, Jane Wyman, Jane Clayton 74m

60) *The Man Who Talked Too Much (1940)* – Warners – (based on play *The Mouthpiece* by Frank J. Collins) Vincent Sherman (d) Cast: George Brent, *Virginia Bruce (Joan Reed)*, Brenda Marshall, Richard Barthelmess, William Lundigan,

George Tobias, John Litel 76m – remake of *The Mouthpiece (1932)*; remade as *Illegal (1955)*

61) *Hired Wife (1940)* – *Universal* – (Story by George Beck) William A. Seiter (d) Cast: Rosalind Russell, Brian Aherne, *Virginia Bruce (Phyllis Waldon)*, Robert Benchley, John Carroll 95m

62) *The Invisible Woman (1940)* – *Universal* – (Story by Kurt Siodmak and Joe May) Edward Sutherland (d) Cast: *Virginia Bruce (Kitty Carroll)*, John Barrymore, John Howard, Charles Ruggles, Oscar Homolka, Charles Lane, Margaret Hamilton 72m – Oscar nominated for "Best Special Effects" – DVD Universal (2004) Invisible Man Legacy Collection

63) *Adventure in Washington (1941)* – *Columbia* – Alfred E. Green (d) Cast: Herbert Marshall, *Virginia Bruce (Jane Scott)*, Gene Reynolds, Samuel S. Hinds, Ralph Morgan, Vaughn Glaser, Charles Smith, Dickie Jones 84m

64) *Butch Minds the Baby (1942)* – *Universal* – (Based on Damon Runyon story) Albert S. Rogell (d) Cast: *Virginia Bruce (Susie O'Neill)*, Broderick Crawford, Dick Foran, Shemp Howard, Porter Hall, Grant Withers 75m

65) *Pardon My Sarong (1942)* – *Universal* – Erle C. Kenton (d) Cast: Bud Abbott, Lou Costello, *Virginia Bruce (Joan Marshall)*, Robert Paige, Lionel Atwill, Leif Erickson, William Demarest, The Ink Spots 84m – DVD Universal (2004) Best of Abbott and Costello V. 1

66) *Careful, Soft Shoulders (1942)* – *20th Century-Fox* – Oliver H. P. Garrett (d and original screenplay) Cast: *Virginia Bruce (Connie Mather)*, James Ellison, Aubrey Mather, Sheila Ryan, Ralph Byrd, William B. Davidson 69m

67) *Action in Arabia (1944)* – *RKO* – (Based on the novel *The*

Fanatic of Fez by M. V. Heberden) Leonide Moguy (d)
Cast: George Sanders, *Virginia Bruce (Yvonne Danesco)*,
Lenore Aubert, Gene Lockhart, Robert Armstrong, Alan
Napier, H. B. Warner 75m

68) *Brazil (1945) – Republic* – Joseph Santley (d) Cast: Tito
Guizar, *Virginia Bruce (Nicki Henderson)*, Edward Ever-
ett Horton, Robert Livingstone, Richard Lane, Veloz and
Yolanda, Fortunio Bonanova, Roy Rogers 91m – Oscar
nominated for: Best Original Song "Rio de Janeiro," Best
Music Scoring, Best Sound

69) *Love, Honor and Goodbye (1945) – Republic* – Albert S.
Rogell (d) Cast: *Virginia Bruce (Roberta Baxter)*, Edward
Ashley, Victor McLaglen, Nils Asther, Helen Broderick,
Veda Ann Berg 87m

70) *The Night Has a Thousand Eyes (1948) – Paramount* -
(Based on the novel by Cornell Woolrich) John Farrow (d)
Cast: Edward G. Robinson, Gail Russell, John Lund, *Vir-
ginia Bruce (Jenny Courtland)*, William Demarest, Richard
Webb, Jerome Cowan 81m

71) *State Dept. – File 649 (1949) – Sigmund Neufeld Produc-
tions* – Sam Newfield (a.k.a., Peter Stewart) (d) Cast:
William Lundigan, *Virginia Bruce (Marge Weldon)*, Ray-
mond Bond, Nana Bryant, Richard Loo, Philip Ahn, John
Holland, Frank Ferguson 87m – Cinecolor – DVD Alpha
Video (2004)

72) *Salgin (Istanbul - USA) (1954) – Ipar International* – Ali
Ipar (d) Cast: *Virginia Bruce (nurse)*, Kenan Artun, Metin
Birer, Gloria Doman, Edward Yeretz 67m – Turkey's first
color feature

73) *Reluctant Bride (Two Grooms for a Bride - USA) (1955)
– 20ᵗʰ Century-Fox* – Henry Cass (d) Cast: John Carroll,

Virginia Bruce (Laura Weeks), Brian Oulton, Kay Callard, Michael Caridia 75m

74) *Strangers When We Meet (1960)* – *Columbia* – (Based on Evan Hunter novel) Richard Quine (d) Cast: Kirk Douglas, Kim Novak, Ernie Kovaks, Barbara Rush, Walter Matthau, *Virginia Bruce (Mrs. Wagner)*, Kent Smith, Helen Gallagher, John Bryant, Roberta Shore 117m – Color – DVD Sony (2005)

75) *That's Entertainment (1974)* – *MGM* – Compilation of archive footage from MGM musicals. Produced and directed by Jack Haley Jr. Co-hosts: Fred Astaire, Bing Crosby, Gene Kelly, Peter Lawford, Liza Minnelli, Donald O'Connor, Debbie Reynolds, Mickey Rooney, Frank Sinatra, James Stewart, Elizabeth Taylor 154m (Virginia Bruce in scene from *The Great Ziegfeld*) – DVD Warner Home Video (2004)

Film Shorts

1) *A Dream Comes True (1935)* – *Warners* – Cast: Max Reinhardt, Dick Powell, James Cagney, Joe E. Brown, Frank McHugh, Jean Muir, Olivia de Havilland, Mickey Rooney, Victory Jory, Hugh Herbert, Verree Teasdale, *Virginia Bruce (seen at a Hollywood premier with Cesar Romero)*, Errol Flynn, Sybil Jason, Marion Davies, George Brent 8m – a behind-the-scenes promotional short for the film *A Midsummer's Night's Dream* – DVD Warner Home Video (2007) *A Midsummer's Nights Dream*

2) *Pirate Party on Catalina Isle (1935)* – *MGM* – Gene Burdette (d) Cast: Charles "Buddy" Rogers, Chester Morris, *Virginia Bruce (Herself)*, Cary Grant, Randolph Scott, Mickey Rooney, Errol Flynn, Johnny Downs, Leon Errol, Marion

Davies, Robert Armstrong, Lili Damita 19m – Technicolor
DVD Warner Home Video (2006) *David Copperfield*

3) *Screen Snapshots (Series 16, No. 1) (1936)* – Columbia
– Ralph Staub (d) Cast: *Virginia Bruce (Herself)*, James
Cagney, Bette Davis, Madge Evans, Errol Flynn, Betty
Furness, Ann Harding, Elissa Landi, Frank McHugh,
Cesar Romero, Rosalind Russell, Ann Sothern, Johnny
Weissmuller 10m – Hodgepodge of happenings in Hol-
lywood: Ken Maynard's private circus, and a visit to The
Westside Tennis Club

4) *Behind the Movie Lens (1938)* – MGM – Cast: *Virginia
Bruce (Herself)*, Wallace Beery, Guy Kibbee, Dennis
O'Keefe 4m – promotional short for *Bad Man of Brimstone*
filmed at Zion National Park. Includes theatrical trailer

5) *Hollywood Goes to Town (1938)* – MGM – Herman Hoffman
(d) Cast: Norma Shearer, Tyrone Power, John Barrymore,
Louis B. Mayer, Adrian, *Virginia Bruce (Herself arriving at
premier)*, J. Walter Ruben, Barbara Stanwyck, Robert Taylor,
Judy Garland, Jeanette MacDonald, Hedy Lamarr, Clark
Gable, Doug Fairbanks Jr. 9m – documentary on the pre-
mier of *Marie Antoinette* at Cathay Circle Theatre – DVD
Warner Home Video (2006) *Marie Antoinette*

6) *Hollywood Hobbies (1938)* – MGM- George Sidney (d)
Cast: Joyce Compton, Sally Payne, Clark Gable, Robert
Young, Allan Jones, Joan Davis, *Virginia Bruce (Herself)*,
Spencer Tracy, James Cagney, Mary Pickford, James Stewart, Dick Powell, Tyrone Power, Ritz Brothers 10m – Two
star-struck girls take a tour of Hollywood and run into
many of their favorite stars. Virginia is seen at a baseball
game taking photos with her camera – DVD Warners
Home Video (2006) *Boomtown*

7) *Screen Snapshots (Series 18, No. 9 Stars on Horseback)
    (1939) – Columbia* - Ralph Staub (d) Cast: William Boyd,
    Joe E. Brown, *Virginia Bruce (Herself)*, Bing Crosby, Clark
    Gable, Allan Jones, Carole Lombard, Jean Parker, Barbara
    Stanwyck, Robert Taylor, Charles Starrett 10m – Holly-
    wood stars attend a horseshow

8) *Screen Snapshots (Vacation at Del Mar) (1949) – Colum-
    bia* – Ralph Staub (d) Cast: George Raft, J. Carroll Naish,
    Virginia Bruce (herself), Dinah Shore, Phil Harris, Virginia
    Grey, Harry von Zell

9) *Hollywood Without Make-up (1963)- Filmaster Inc* – Rudy
    Behlmer (d) Cast: Ken Murray, Mary Astor, Lucille Ball,
    Humphrey Bogart, Clara Bow, *Virginia Bruce (Herself)*,
    Rory Calhoun, Charles Chaplin, Gary Cooper; Jackie
    Cooper, Linda Darnell, Marion Davies, Joan Davis, Ol-
    ivia de Havilland, Dolores del Rio, Irene Dunne, Douglas
    Fairbanks Jr., Charles Farrell, Errol Flynn, Clark Gable,
    Greta Garbo, John Gilbert, Cary Grant, Oliver Hardy, Wil-
    liam Randolph Hearst, William Holden, Bob Hope, Walter
    Huston, Van Johnson, Charles Laughton, Stan Laurel, Fred
    MacMurray, Herbert Marshall, Marx Bros., Joel McCrea,
    Louella Parsons, Dick Powell, Tyrone Power, Debbie Reyn-
    olds, Charles "Buddy" Rogers, Albert Schweitzer, Robert
    Taylor, Mae West 50m – Ken Murray's fun-loving home-
    movies of Hollywood's elite (Some sources say original
    release was in 1950)

10) *Invisible Woman (1966) - Universal* – Edward Sutherland
    (d) Cast: *Virginia Bruce (Kitty Carroll)*, John Barrymore,
    Margaret Hamilton, Charles Lane, Mary Hudson 9m –
    This was a nine minute abridgement of the 1940 release,
    sold for the 16mm home movie market

(September 10, 1945) *Lux Radio* presentation of suspense drama *Experiment Perilous* with George Brent (Courtesy of CBS/Photofest)

Virginia Bruce on Radio

Abbott and Costello (NBC)
> 1940 (8/21/40) *Virginia Bruce*, Robert Cummings, Allan Jones

Academy Award Theatre (CBS)
> 1946 (7/17/46) *The Prisoner of Zenda* – Douglas Fairbanks Jr., *Virginia Bruce*, (Princess Flavia)

Betty Crocker Magazine of the Air (ABC)
> 1950 (5/5/50) *Virginia Bruce*

Bing Crosby Show – Kraft Music Hall (NBC)
    1936 (3/26/36) Jean Hersholt, *Virginia Bruce*
    (6/18/36) *Virginia Bruce*, Pat O'Brien

    1940 (4/4/40) Virginia *Bruce*, Bob Burns
    (7/11/40) Eddie Albert, *Virginia Bruce* sings "Button Up
    Your Overcoat" with Bing
    (11/7/40) Bob Burns (host) *Virginia Bruce*, Enzio Pinza,
    Dorothy Lamour, Nat Pendleton
    1941 (1/30/41) *Virginia Bruce*, Ogden Nash, Bob Burns,
    Connie Boswell
    (4/24/41) *Virginia Bruce*, Don Ameche, Bob Burns,
    Connie Boswell

Bob Hope Show (NBC)
    1943 (4/13/43) Bob Hope, *Virginia Bruce*
    1944 (1/11/44) Bob Hope, *Virginia Bruce*, Frances Langford,
    Stan Kenton and is orchestra - In a skit, Virginia is
    treated by "Dr. Hope"

Breakfast Club (KFWB) Two-hour broadcast dedicated to the
LA metropolitan press
    1930 (1/9/30) Gary Cooper, Joe E. Brown, *Virginia Bruce*,
    Max Fischer & orch.

Care Salute (CBS) – Special
    1949 (12/24/49) Gala CBS Yuletide program. Ricardo
    Montalban (Master of Ceremonies), *Virginia Bruce*,
    Charles Boyer, Danny Kaye, Francis Lederer, Alida Valli,
    Mexican Boys Choir. In cooperation with the Children's
    fund of CARE of Los Angeles

Cavalcade of America (NBC)

> 1947 (6/16/47) *Woman Alone – Virginia Bruce (Alice Evans)*
> (9/22/47) *Girl Who Ran For President – Virginia Bruce
> (Belva Lockwood)*
> 1949 (3/28/49) *Boy Wanted – Virginia Bruce (Miss Ran-
> some)* – As head of an adoption agency, Virginia handles the
> complexities and challenges involved.
> 1950 (4/18/50) *Lady of Johnstown – Virginia Bruce (Rose
> Knox)*

CBS Playhouse

> 1949 (2/24/49) *Virginia Bruce*

Chase and Sanborn Hour – Charlie McCarthy (NBC)

> 1938 (8/21/38) *Fishing – Virginia Bruce* in skit with **Edward**
> Arnold
> 1939 (3/5/39) *Balcony Scene* – Don Ameche in skit with
> *Virginia Bruce*
> (5/7/39) *Dictation – Virginia Bruce*
> (7/9/39) Don Ameche, Stu Erwin, Dorothy Lamour,
> *Virginia Bruce* in skit with Ameche *If At First You Don't
> Succeed* (by Diana Carlson)
> 1940 (9/29/40) *Virginia Bruce* interview

Chateau (KFI)

> 1936 (5/9/36) *The Mouthpiece* – Warren William, Genevieve
> Tobin – *Virginia Bruce* sings "You" from *The Great
> Ziegfeld*

Comedy Caravan (CBS)

> 1943 (5/14/43) Jack Carson, *Virginia Bruce*

Command Performance (AFRS)

> 1949 (11/29/49) *Virginia Bruce (MC)*, Groucho Marx, The
> Moon Mists

Democratic National Committee Program (CBS) –Night before the election

> 1944 (11/6/44) *The Roosevelt Special* (political program)
> Joan Bennett, Humphrey Bogart, *Virginia Bruce*, Claudette Colbert, James Cagney, Linda Darnell, Paulette Goddard, Judy Garland, Groucho Marx, John Garfield, Tallulah Bankhead, Susan Hayward, others

Encore Theatre (CBS)

> 1946 (7/9/46) *The White Angel – Virginia Bruce (Florence Nightingale)*, Earle Ross, Eleanor Audley, Eric Snowden, Ben Wright – this program duplicated the scenario of the 1936 Kay Francis film. Upon the production's 'Curtain Call' Virginia encouraged young women to consider the nursing profession.

Family Theatre (Mutual Network)

> 1948 (5/6/48) *Mother's Halo Was Tight* – David Young (d) Gene Kelly (host) *Virginia Bruce*, Dean Stockwell, John Beal

Good News of … (NBC)

> 1938 (2/10/38) Robert Taylor (host), James Stewart, John Carradine, Frank Morgan, Fanny Brice, Allan Jones, *Virginia Bruce* and Robert Taylor in the skit *Where There's Smoke*
> (3/10/38) Robert Taylor (host), Robert Montgomery, Frank Morgan, Fanny Brice, Rita Johnson, Connie Boswell, *Virginia Bruce* and Robert Montgomery plug *First Hundred Years*
> (5/26/38) Robert Taylor (host), Robert Montgomery, Robert Young, Una Merkle, Frank Morgan, Fanny Brice, *Virginia Bruce* and Robert Montgomery do a scene from

Yellow Jack
1939 (1/5/39) Melvyn Douglas (host), Frank Morgan,
Fanny Brice, *Virginia Bruce* and Melvyn Douglas in *A
Rose by Any Name*
(3/30/39) Robert Young, Walter Pidgeon, Frank
Morgan, Fanny Brice, Miliza Korjus, *Virginia Bruce* and
Walter Pidgeon in *Moral Victory*
(4/6/39) Robert Young, Melvyn Douglas, *Virginia
Bruce*
(4/13/39) Robert Young (host), Melvyn Douglas, Frank
Morgan, Fanny Brice, *Virginia Bruce* and Melvyn
Douglas in *I'll Be Suing You*
1940 (2/15/40) Edward Arnold (host), William Gargan,
Fanny Brice, Connie Boswell, *Virginia Bruce* appears in
Purple and Fine Linen

Hallmark Playhouse (CBS)
1949 (2/24/49) *So Big* (By Edna Ferber) – *Virginia Bruce*,
Jeff Chandler

Hedda Hopper Show (This is Hollywood) (NBC)
1947 (5/3/47) *Centennial Summer* – *Virginia Bruce*, Mark
Stevens, Vanessa Brown – Virginia's role as Edith has
her competing with her sister Julia (Vanessa Brown) for
the same man. "Love is a game," says Virginia, "you
have to trap a man!" Virginia's "Edith" was reminiscent
of her take on Audrey Dane in *The Great Ziegfeld*.

Host Hedda Hopper confronted Virginia after the
presentation, saying, "Virginia Bruce! You were a hateful
hussy! Why after tonight's performance Virginia Bruce
could be vice-president in charge of conniving females."

Virginia laughed, "Wasn't Edith a nasty gal, Hedda?"
"She certainly was," Hopper replied. "You certainly
played the part right up to the hilt! Virginia, I'm
surprised at you, and such a nice girl too!"

Herbert Marshall Show
   1941 (11/3/41) *Virginia Bruce* is guest on premier show
   1942 (1/26/42) *Virginia Bruce*

Hollywood Hotel (CBS)
   1935 (4/12/35) *Let 'Em Have It* – Richard Arlen, *Virginia
   Bruce*, Bruce Cabot
   1937 (7/2/37) *Between Two Women* – Franchot Tone,
   Maureen O'Sullivan, *Virginia Bruce*

Hollywood Playhouse (NBC)
   1938 (2/20/38) *Lloyds of London* – Tyrone Power, *Virginia
   Bruce*
   1939 (2/12/39) *Peter Ibbetson* – Charles Boyer, *Virginia
   Bruce*

Hollywood Star Time (CBS)
   1944 (6/?/44) Talk Show
   1946 (11/30/46) *Stagecoach* – *Virginia Bruce*, John Hodiak

Hollywood Story (Mutual)
   1949 (1/13/49) Erskine Johnson (host), *Virginia Bruce*
   interview

Intrigue (CBS)
   1946 (8/28/46) Charles Vanda (d) Joseph Schildkraut
   (narrator) *Smiler With the Knife* – *Virginia Bruce*

Jack Benny (NBC)
   1943 (1/31/43) Jack Benny, Dennis Day, Eddie "Rochester"

Anderson, Gregory Ratoff, *Virginia Bruce* (Originating from Quantico, Virginia Marine Base) – Virginia did two more service shows with Benny

(non-broadcasts) in Newport News and Norfolk, Va.

Let's Talk Hollywood (NBC)
  1948 (7/11/48) *Virginia Bruce* and Pat O'Brien (hosts)
    (8/8/48) *Virginia Bruce* and Pat O'Brien (hosts)
    (8/22/48) *Virginia Bruce* and Pat O'Brien (hosts)

Lux Radio Theatre (CBS) (Hosted by Cecil B. DeMille)
  1937 (1/4/37) *Men in White* – Spencer Tracy, *Virginia Bruce (Laura)*, Frances Farmer
    (9/27/37) *Cimarron* – Clark Gable, *Virginia Bruce*
  1940 (2/26/40) *Swing High, Swing Low* – *Virginia Bruce*, Rudy Vallee
  1941 (12/8/41) *The Doctor Takes a Wife* – Melvyn Douglas, *Virginia Bruce*, Lynne Carver (John Daly interrupted with a bulletin on the U.S. 5-hour-old involvement in WWII)
  1942 (10/19/42) *My Favorite Blonde* – Bob Hope, *Virginia Bruce*
  1943 (10/4/43) *The Pride of the Yankees* – Gary Cooper, *Virginia Bruce* – after the presentation, it was mentioned that Cooper was going to bathe on screen in DeMille's new production *The Story of Dr. Wassel*.

Virginia piped up, "Gary Cooper in a DeMille bathtub scene! There's just one thing I want to know (she pauses) . . . What kind of soap did he use?" – Thus providing a segue into a Lux Soap commercial.

1945 (4/30/45) *Moontide* – Humphrey Bogart, *Virginia Bruce*

(9/10/45) *Experiment Perilous* – George Brent, *Virginia Bruce*

1947 (2/17/47) *Devotion* – *Virginia Bruce*, Jane Wyman, Vincent Price

Make Believe Town (CBS)

1949 (8/8/48) *Virginia Bruce* (host), Lurene Tuttle in *A Very Important* Appointment

(8/16/48) *Virginia Bruce* (host) *Hollywood Romance* This 30 minute series aired Monday through Friday. Virginia was the hostess and the original deal was to have her take the lead in each episode, which dramatized life in Hollywood

MGM Musical Comedy Theatre (Mutual)

1952 (2/17/52) *Honolulu* – *Virginia Bruce*, Robert Alda – Although Virginia resided in Turkey at the time, this program was listed in both the Tucson (AZ) and San Mateo (CA) news media.

Movietown Radio Theatre (Hollywood Theater) (ZIV)

1947 (10/31/47) *To Love Again* – *Virginia Bruce*

New National Guard Show

(date unknown) Program 26 – *An Old Debt* – *Virginia Bruce*

Old Gold (Harold Lloyd) Comedy Theatre (Blue Network)

1945 (1/28/45) Harold Lloyd (host) *Appointment for Love* – *Virginia Bruce*, Paul Henreid, Bob Williams

Phillip Morris Playhouse (CBS)

1/8/43 *Fifth Avenue Girl* – *Virginia Bruce*

1/22/43 *Mr. and Mrs. Smith* – *Virginia Bruce*, Chester Morris

Political Broadcast (CBS)
> 1944 (9/18/44) From the California State Democratic
> Convention – *Virginia Bruce* is guest of Mrs. Edward G.
> Robinson

Post Toasties Time (NBC)
> 1942 (8/20/42) *Virginia Bruce* joins Frank Morgan for the
> sketch *It's Fun to be Fooled* (by Mark Hellinger) -
> Meredith Wilson and orchestra

Proudly We Hail (Army Syndication)
> (Date unknown) *Take One, Miss Palmer* – *Virginia Bruce*,
> Marjorie Reynolds

Radio's Reader Digest (CBS)
> 1946 (1/13/46) *A Story That Haunted Me* – *Virginia Bruce* –
> A story by Anthony Abbott (a.k.a. Charles Fulton
> Ousler) inspired by FDR's telling him of the true
> adventures of a girl on a trip to wartime Europe

Rexall Theatre – The Dan Carson Show (NBC)
> 1948 (Sunday evenings premiering 6/30/48) Pat O'Brien,
> *Virginia Bruce* – Virginia signed for the series in April
> 1948, replacing Lynn Bari

Rudy Vallee (NBC)
> 1941 (4/10/41) Gold-mining camp skit wherein *Virginia
> Bruce* plays a dance-hall girl who is prayed upon by
> John Barrymore. Rudy Vallee comes to her rescue.

Screen Guild Theatre (CBS)
> Guest stars donated their salaries to the Motion Picture
> relief fund
> 1943 (3/1/43) *This Above All* – Herbert Marshall, *Virginia*

Bruce, Alan Mowbray

(10/11/43) *Love Affair* – Herbert Marshall, *Virginia Bruce*, Luis Alberni

1945 (1/22/45) *Love Before Breakfast* – *Virginia Bruce*, Brian Donlevy

(3/26/45) *Princess and the Pirate* – Bob Hope, *Virginia Bruce*

(10/1/45) *Those Endearing Young Charms* – Robert Young, *Virginia Bruce*

1946 (1/14/46) *History is Made at Night* – *Virginia Bruce*, Paul Lukas

(5/13/46) *Talk of the Town* – Ronald Colman, *Virginia Bruce*, Allyn Joslyn

1947 (3/24/47) *The Moon is Our Home* – Fred MacMurray, *Virginia Bruce*, Robert Young (Faith Baldwin story)

Silver Theatre (CBS)

1940 (11/3/40) *For All Good Men* – *Virginia Bruce*

1943 (12/5/43) *Help Wanted* – Herbert Marshall, *Virginia Bruce*

1946 (6/23/46) *Romance Inc.* – Conrad Nagel (host) *Virginia Bruce*

Soldiers With Wings

1943 (3/13/43) From West Coast Air Force Training Center in Santa Ana – *Virginia Bruce* is guest

Stage Door Canteen (CBS)

1943 (1/14/43) Bob Hope, *Virginia Bruce*, Monty Wooley – Opening of Stage Door Canteen in Cleveland

Star and the Story (CBS)

1944 (4/23/44) *The Moon's Our Home* – Walter Pidgeon, *Virginia Bruce*

Stars in the Afternoon (CBS)

    1946 (9/22/46) Preview of CBS Fall line-up. Garry Moore (host) *Virginia Bruce*, Ann Sothern, Frank Sinatra, Dinah Shore, Vaughn Monroe, Ralph Morgan, Patrice Munsel, Jimmy Durante

Stars Over Hollywood (CBS)

    1947 (10/24/47) *Virginia Bruce*

    1949 (8/5/49) *That Time in Boston* – *Virginia Bruce*

    1950 (7/1/50) *Light on the Widow's Walk* – *Virginia Bruce*

    1953 (9/19/53) *The Bridge* – Lionel Barrymore – *Virginia Bruce* promotes next week's program

    (9/26/53) *The Lady and the Law* – *Virginia Bruce*

Suspense (CBS)

    1943 (9/16/43) *The Cross-Eyed Bear* – *Virginia Bruce*, John Loder

    1944 (1/27/44) *The Locked Room* – *Virginia Bruce*, Allyn Joslyn, George Zucco

    (10/26/44) *The Night Man* – *Virginia Bruce*, Richard Whorf

    1947 (5/22/47) *Her Knight Comes Riding* – *Virginia Bruce*, Howard Duff

    1948 (9/23/48) *Celebration* – Robert Young, *Virginia Bruce*

This is My Best (CBS)

    1945 (1/16/45) *Let There Be Honor* – *Virginia Bruce*, John Hodiak

(12/25/45) *22 Years to Christmas – Virginia Bruce*

Tower of Times
1936 (4/12/36) Edwin Schallert (host) *Virginia Bruce* (interview)

You Were There (Red Cross Program)
1946 (8/11/46) *Virginia Bruce* plays the lead in a drama about disaster aboard the S.S. Yukon, and the heroic efforts of the Red Cross

(Unknown Program)
1947 (10/25/47) *Crime Can Be Beautiful – Virginia Bruce*

Virginia and Otto Kruger in the comedy
Woman's World for *GE Theater.* (October 1953)

Virginia Bruce on Television

Ford Television Theatre (ABC)

>   1957 (2/6/57) *The Connoisseur* – Oscar Rudolph (d) *Virginia
>   Bruce (Ruth Crest)*, Paul Henreid, Kathryn Grant,
>   William Leslie, Nestor Paiva – (Written by Wells Root)
>   (Produced by Irving Starr)

General Electric Theatre (CBS)

>   1953 (10/25/53) *Woman's World* – *Virginia Bruce (Adele)*,
>   Otto Kruger, Peter Lawford, Ann Rutherford, Tom
>   Keene, Marilyn Erskine

Lux Video Theatre (NBC)

>1953 (8/6/53) *Something to Live For* – James Mason (host) *Virginia Bruce*, Otto Kruger, Karen Sharpe, Amanda Blake, Lewis Martin

>1954 (5/20/54) *Blind Fury* – James Mason (host) *Virginia Bruce (Intermission Guest)*, Dean Jagger, Sarah Selby, Paul Picerni, Moria Turner

>(9/30/54) *Meet Jo Cathart* – Van Heflin (host) *Virginia Bruce (Jo Cathart Archer)*, Bruce Bennett, Craig Hill, Beverly Garland, June Evans, Joan Freeman, Duncan Richardson

>1956 (9/20/56) *Mildred Pierce* – Gordon MacRae (host) *Virginia Bruce (Mildred Pierce)*, Zachary Scott, Patric Knowles, Colleen Miller, Michael Whalen, Lydia Reed, Shirley Mitchell, Betty Blythe

Loretta Young Show (Letter to Loretta) (NBC)

>1955 (9/4/55) *Week-End in Winnetka* – Rosalind Russell (guest host) *Virginia Bruce (Dee Norman)*, Elinor Donahue, Ann Doran, John Eldredge, Gene Raymond, Natalie Schafer

Matinee Theatre (NBC) -Color

>1956 (4/11/56) *People in Glass* – John Conte (host) Lawrence Menkin (d) *Virginia Bruce (Margaret Ames)* – (Written by Robert H. Lindsay and Kathleen Lindsay) (Produced by Albert McCleery)

Pantomime Quiz (CBS)

>1949 (11/15/49) Mike Stoker (host) – *Virginia Bruce*, Stu Erwin, Howard da Silva

Science Fiction Theater (ZIV)

    1955 (10/7/55) *Dead Storage* – Truman Bradley (host) *Virginia Bruce (Dr. Myrna Griffin)*, Booth Colman, Walter Coy, Robert H. Harris, Douglas Henderson (Ivan Tors story)

    (12/2/55) *Fried of a Raven* – Truman Bradley (host) Tom Gries (d) *Virginia Bruce (Jean Gordon)*, Richard Eyer, Charles Cane, William Ching, Barney Phillips

Silver Theatre (CBS)

    1950 (5/22/50) *The Wedding Anniversary* – Conrad Nagel (host) *Virginia Bruce*, Louis Jean Heydt, Rita LaRoy, Ann Doran, Robert Rice, Alphonse Martell – (Re-aired in 1955 as "Broadway Playhouse") 30m

Studio 57 (Syndicated)

    1956 (2/12/56) *Who's Calling* – *Virginia Bruce (Beth Breen)*, Pat O'Brien, Clancy Cooper, Tim Graham, Harlan Warde – (Re-aired as "Undercurrent" in the summer of 1956)

    (6/11/56) *Out of Sight* – *Virginia Bruce (Maggie)*, Douglas Dick, Rachel Ames, Robert Fortier, Wilfred Knapp, Joseph Mell – (Re-aired as "Encore Theatre" in August 1956)

Today Show (NBC)

    1965 (?/?/65) Morning news and talk show. Hugh Downs, Barbara Walters (anchors), *Virginia Bruce (guest)*

Virginia Bruce on Stage

Smiles (1930-31) – Ziegfeld Theatre (11/18/1930 – 1/10/1931)
    63 performances

Musical-Comedy in two acts
Florenz Ziegfeld Jr. (p) William A. McGuire (d) Ned Wayburn (choreographer) Joseph Urban (scenic design) Jack Harkrider (costume design) Vincent Youmans (music) Clifford Grey, Harold Adamson, Ring Lardner (lyrics) Cast: Marilyn Miller, Jean Ackerman, Larry Adler, Adele Astaire, Fred Astaire, Bob Hope, Claire Dodd, Eddie Foy Jr., Paul Gregory, Harriet Lake (Ann Sothern), *Virginia Bruce (ensemble)*

America's Sweetheart (1931) – Broadhurst Theatre (2/10/1931-6/6/1931) 135
Performances – Musical Comedy in two acts
Laurence Schwab, Frank Mandel (p) Monte Wooley (d) Bobby Connolly (choreographer) Donald Oenslager (scenic design) Charles Le Maire (costume design) Richard Rodgers (music) Lorenz Hart (lyrics) Cast: Harriett Lake (Ann Sothern), Jeanne Aubert, Dorothy Dare, Jack Whiting, *Virginia Bruce (Miss Mulligan)*, Bud Clark, Inez Courtney – Virginia was understudy to Jeanne Aubert, who introduced the Rodgers and Hart songs "A Lady Must Live" and "I Want a Man"

In May 1936, Virginia was elected president of the Hollywood Branch of the "Glorified Ziegfeld Girl's Club."

Virginia Bruce Recordings

I've Got You Under My Skin – *(1936)* – Regal Zonophone Recordings (Brunswick 7765)

Easy to Love – *(1936)* – Regal Zonophone Recordings (Brunswick 7765) With Eddie Ward's MGM Orchestra (recorded

October 5, 1936) (Both recordings are available on the CD
"The Ultimate Cole Porter" – Volume 2 – Pearl – Gem 0115
- Pavilion Records Ltd., Sussex, England;
www.pavilionrecords.com)

December 18, 1937 – *Virginia, surrounded by well-wishers and a bright future.*
(l-r) Mrs. Bert Taylor, Countess di Frasso, devoted husband Jack Ruben, actress Kay
Francis, Jack Warner and his wife Ann, and Countess di Frasso's brother, Bert Taylor.

Index

Index

Index

About the Author

Scott O'Brien lives in Sonoma County, California, and is the author of *Kay Francis – I Can't Wait to be Forgotten* which was selected as one of the "Best Books of 2006" by *Classic Images*. Scott has written articles for such publications as *Films of the Golden Age*, *Filmfax*, *The Seeing Eye*, and *Classic Images*. He has been guest author on the web's *Silver Screen Oasis*, KRCB radio's *A Novel Idea*, *San Francisco Silent Film Festival*, *Silver Screen Audio*, and San Francisco's KRON-TV morning news with movie maven Jan Wahl. He can reached through his websites at: www.virginiabrucebiography.com and www.kayfrancisbiography.com

Printed in the United States
205065BV00009B/203/P